Can Personality Change?

Can Personality Change?

Todd F. Heatherton
& Joel L. Weinberger,
Editors

American Psychological Association, Washington, DC

First printing January 1994
Second printing January 1997

Published by
American Psychological Association
750 First Street, NE
Washington, DC 20002

Copies may be ordered from
APA Order Department
P.O. Box 92984
Washington, DC 20090-2984

In the UK and Europe, copies may be ordered from
American Psychological Association
3 Henrietta Street
Covent Garden, London
WC2E 8LU England

Typeset in Goudy by Techna Type, Inc., York, PA

Printer: Quinn Woodbine, Inc., Woodbine, NJ
Cover and Jacket Designer: Anne Masters, Washington, DC
Technical/Production Editor: Paula R. Bronstein

Library of Congress Cataloging-in-Publication Data
Can personality change? / edited by Todd F. Heatherton and Joel Lee Weinberger.
    p.   cm.
    Includes bibliographical references and index.
    ISBN 1-55798-425-5 (acid-free paper)
    1. Personality change.   2. Change (Psychology)   I. Heatherton,
Todd F.   II. Weinberger, Joel Lee.
BF698.2.C36   1993
155.2'5—dc20   93-26477
                                                                          CIP

British Library Cataloguing-in-Publication Data
A CIP record is available from the British Library.

Printed in the United States of America

To our parents,
Marlene and Fred Sandercock
Morris and Edith Weinberger

CONTENTS

CONTRIBUTORS

A. George Alder, Department of Psychology, University College of the Cariboo

Roy F. Baumeister, Department of Psychology, Case Western Reserve University

Steven M. Boker, Department of Psychology, University of Virginia

Nathan Brody, Department of Psychology, Wesleyan University

David M. Buss, Department of Psychology, University of Michigan

Janet C'deBaca, Department of Psychology, University of New Mexico

Paul T. Costa, Jr., Gerontology Research Center, National Institute on Aging, National Institutes of Health

Roger D. Davis, Department of Psychology, University of Miami

Carlo C. DiClemente, Department of Psychology, University of Houston

Carol E. Franz, Department of Psychology, Williams College

Todd F. Heatherton, Department of Psychology, Harvard University

Ravenna Helson, Institute of Personality and Social Research, University of California at Berkeley

Dan P. McAdams, Program in Human Development and Social Policy, Northwestern University

Robert R. McCrae, Gerontology Research Center, National Institute on Aging, National Institutes of Health

William R. Miller, Department of Psychology, University of New Mexico

Theodore Millon, Department of Psychology, University of Miami

John R. Nesselroade, Department of Psychology, University of Virginia

Patricia A. Nichols, Department of Psychology, Harvard University

Lawrence A. Pervin, Department of Psychology, Rutgers—The State University of New Jersey

Steven J. Scher, Department of Psychology, University College of the Cariboo

Abigail Stewart, Department of Psychology, University of Michigan

Joel L. Weinberger, The Derner Institute, Adelphi University

PREFACE

The Jesuit maxim, "Give me a child until he is seven, and I will show you the man," is the thesis of Michael Apted's well-known documentary *35 Up*. This documentary follows the development of British schoolchildren through interviews at ages 7, 14, 21, 28, and 35. A striking aspect of this film is the apparent stability in personality from childhood through adulthood. The child interested in the stars and science becomes a university professor of physics; the boy who finds his childhood troubling and confusing develops an apparent schizotypal personality; the reserved upper-class girl at age 7 wears a crested sweater in her pastoral retreat at age 35; a 7-year-old successfully predicts not only his future career, but the schools that he will eventually attend. Are people really so stable? Is our personality at age 80 preordained at age 8?

As psychologists, we both have been interested in the issue of personality change for some time. One of us (Weinberger) is a clinical psychologist who over the years has watched clients struggle to achieve genuine change. During lunch one day, a colleague brought up the question of whether personality can change. The issue was hotly debated, but unresolved, in the ensuing discussion, and Weinberger began to query a number of colleagues for their perspectives on whether personality changes. Interestingly, there appeared to be little consensus as to whether personality was stable or malleable. The other of us (Heatherton) is a social–personality psychologist who studies dieting behavior. A fascinating aspect of dieting is the intensity with which people diet, in spite of the evidence that fewer than one or two percent of individuals manage to achieve or maintain permanent weight loss. This has led to an examination of whether people are able to effect change in any aspect of their lives. Our joint interest in the topic of whether personality can change surfaced in a meeting of the planning committee for Science Weekend, a three-day conference sponsored by the American Psychological Association (APA) and held in conjunction with APA's Annual Convention. Our task was to identify the most important issues facing contemporary psychology. We quickly identified the question of the true extent of the stability of personality as one of the most interesting and important unanswered questions in the field of psychology.

In discussing this topic with our colleagues, we have been amazed at the variety of opinions and theories about personality stability. Indeed, our own readings of this literature convinced us that there was evidence both supporting and challenging the view that personality can change. We were impressed with recent work on behavioral genetics that suggests many personality traits are inborn and deeply ingrained. We were also intrigued by Costa and McCrae's[1] work demonstrating that personality traits appeared to be quite stable over adult development. Conversely, we have both been influenced by several perspectives that emphasize the malleability of personality. A variety of longitudinal studies provided compelling evidence that people go through substantial changes in attitudes, behaviors, and important aspects of personality. For instance, Ravenna Helson's[2] research has demonstrated that women go through striking changes during midlife transitions. Similarly, George Vaillant's[3] well-known study of maturational changes in adulthood uncovered dramatic changes in personality following childhood and adolescence.

This volume presents a diversity of perspectives on the question of whether personality can change, mainly focusing on changes in personality across adulthood. There seems to be a consensus that personality goes through many changes and transitions during childhood and adolescence, and therefore few of the chapters consider the early development of personality. Our focus is also on what can be described as normal personality processes rather than on changes in psychopathology or maladaptive behaviors. Although clinical issues are discussed in a number of chapters (see especially Pervin's and Weinberger's), the issue of whether psychotherapy affects personality is beyond the scope of this volume. Similarly, there is a growing consensus that major trauma can bring about major psychological changes, including personality changes. These changes currently are not well understood and are better conceptualized as an aspect of trauma rather

[1]Costa, P. T., Jr., & McCrae, R. R. (1980). Still stable after all these years: Personality as a key to some issues in aging. In P. B. Baltes & O. G. Brim, Jr. (Eds.), *Life-span development and behavior* (Vol. 3, pp. 65–102). San Diego, CA: Academic Press.
Costa, P. T., Jr., & McCrae, R. R. (1989). Personality continuity and the changes of adult life. In M. Storandt & G. R. VandenBos (Eds.), *The adult years: Continuity and change* (pp. 45–77). Washington, DC: American Psychological Association.
McCrae, R. R., & Costa, P. T. (1990). *Personality in adulthood.* New York: Guilford Press.
[2]Helson, R., & Moane, G. (1987). Personality change in women from college to midlife. *Journal of Personality and Social Psychology, 53,* 176–186.
[3]Vaillant, G. E. (1977). *Adaptation to life.* Boston, MA: Little, Brown.

than as an aspect of personality. The chapter by Miller and C'deBaca discusses sudden transformational experiences that might be produced by traumatic events, but their focus is on the change experience rather than on the properties of the traumatic events.

One of the most important aspects of understanding whether personality can change is understanding how change is measured. A number of impressive new statistical procedures have been developed for measuring change, and the interested reader is advised to consult the 1991 APA publication, *Best Methods for the Analysis of Change: Recent Advances, Unanswered Questions, Future Directions,*[4] for a complete treatment of this topic. The issue of personality measurement is implicit in a number of the current chapters, and is explicitly addressed in three chapters (Alder & Scher; Costa & McCrae; Nesselroade & Boker). These chapters demonstrate that a growing sophistication has developed in the understanding of the best ways to measure personality change, and they make specific recommendations for the best ways to conduct and analyze longitudinal studies of personality.

The volume is divided into four major sections. In the first section, Costa and McCrae, Brody, and Buss consider various agents of stability. This section includes both theory and data that emphasize the relatively enduring quality of personality traits. Also included is a discussion of sociobiological and behavioral genetic aspects of personality. In the next section, Davis and Millon, Nesselroade and Boker, Alder and Scher, and DiClemente consider theoretical issues relevant to the measurement and conceptualization of personality change. They point out that new models of personality change need to be considered, and a variety of analogies and conceptual frameworks are presented. The third section reviews evidence of maturational changes across the life span. Franz, and Helson and Stewart present evidence demonstrating that aspects of personality are altered by contextual and situational challenges. In the final section, Miller and C'deBaca, Baumeister, McAdams, and Pervin consider various theoretical models of personality change. This section includes perspectives on defining personality, understanding transformational experiences, and elucidating the motivational processes underlying personality change.

As described earlier, the original impetus for this volume occurred during a meeting of the Science Weekend planning committee for the 100th Annual Convention of the APA in Washington, DC. The planning committee for Science Weekend 1992 selected three topical themes to be highlighted at the convention, one of which was the question, Can personality change? Under the guidance of Track Chair Joel Weinberger, committee members Robert McCrae, Todd Heatherton, and Melba Vasquez invited

---

[4]Collins, L. M., & Horn, J. L. (1991). *Best methods for the analysis of change: Recent advances, unanswered questions, future directions.* Washington, DC: American Psychological Association.

leading theorists and researchers from clinical, social, and personality psychology to address this important issue. We are extremely pleased that that event served as a springboard for the present focused volume, which is designed to present a comprehensive look at the diversity of viewpoints surrounding this issue.

We are grateful to the entire planning committee for the APA Science Weekend, and especially to Virginia Holt and Cheri Lane from the APA Science Directorate. We are also grateful to our reviewers who agreed to read one or more of the chapter submissions. They are Nalini Ambady, Holy Cross College; George Alder, University College of the Cariboo; Patricia Nichols, Harvard University; Richard Koestner, McGill University; Richard McNally, Harvard University; Robert Bornstein, Gettysburg College; Nancy Snidman, Harvard University; Jonathan Shedler, Derner Institute, Adelphi University; and George Stricker, Derner Institute, Adelphi University. We are also indebted to Julia Frank-McNeil and Gary VandenBos for their unwavering support of this project and to Mary Lynn Skutley, Peggy Schlegel, and Paula Bronstein for their editorial expertise and guidance. Most of all we are indebted to the Science Weekend presenters and the contributors to this volume.

TODD F. HEATHERTON
JOEL L. WEINBERGER

INTRODUCTION

1

CONCEPTUAL ISSUES IN ASSESSING WHETHER PERSONALITY CAN CHANGE

TODD F. HEATHERTON and PATRICIA A. NICHOLS

Can personality change? This question has absorbed psychologists since William James first proposed that personality was set "in plaster" by early adulthood (James, 1890; see also McCrae & Costa, 1990). Not all psychologists have agreed with James's assertion of stability. For instance, Erikson (1950) cogently argued that adults, just like children, mature and change as they go through life's stages (see also Vaillant, 1977). Likewise, one of the basic assumptions of clinical psychology is that individuals are able to make important changes in many aspects of their lives. At the extreme, some have even proposed that personality may be so malleable that it changes from situation to situation (Mischel, 1968). More recently, personality psychologists have argued both that basic personality traits tend to be relatively stable over the life course (Caspi & Herbener, 1990; Costa & McCrae, 1980) and that personality goes through maturational changes and adaptations (Helson & Moane, 1987; Ozer & Gjerde, 1989). This volume explores multiple perspectives on the issue of whether personality can change.

Whether personality can change is arguably one of the most important and interesting questions facing contemporary personality psychologists. An examination of the issue reveals a wide array of intriguing questions, such as those related to the definition and measurement of personality, the normal developmental course of personality through the life span, the nature of psychological change, and the question of volitional control over the self. In this chapter we introduce some of the complex issues that need to be addressed in understanding the stability or malleability of personality.

WHY SHOULD PERSONALITY BE STABLE OR MALLEABLE?

From a functional perspective, why should personality be either stable or malleable? Cogent arguments can be provided both for why individuals should remain stable and why they should be able to change. To say that we understand someone's personality, that we understand them as a person, is to say that there is some degree of stability in their actions and mannerisms. Indeed, most definitions of personality invoke some notion of enduring characteristics and temperamental styles. In our interactions with others, we want them to be stable across time and across situations. We want to be able to predict their behavior, and we want to be able to rely on them to usually behave according to our expectations. When we choose partners for long-term relationships, we are essentially hoping that the person we choose to be with today will be the same person in the future (or at least that he or she will change in predictable and logical ways). We also wish to have some sense of coherence in our own self-understanding. To feel as if we are the same person today as we were yesterday helps us cope with the vagaries of a changing world, assists us in self-regulatory tasks, and helps us foster a positive sense of identity.

Most developmental forces appear likely to have a stabilizing influence on personality. For instance, to the extent that personality is established in part by genetic and biological influences, personality should be generally stable (see chapters by Buss and Brody, this volume). Adaptations and traits that have developed over the course of human evolution should be relatively ingrained and unchanging. Moreover, many of the developmental forces that shape our personality occur during early childhood, and much of our personal sense of self is developed before we reach adolescence. Thus, there are many reasons to assume that a certain degree of stability in personality is not only inevitable, but perhaps quite desirable.

On the other hand, there are reasons that we might want some malleability in personality. The spouse considering taking back an unfaithful spouse will want to believe that he or she has truly changed. Parole boards release prisoners back into society with the belief that they have changed their criminal ways. Individuals entering rehabilitation programs or beginning psychotherapy hope that they will be able to make dramatic changes in important aspects of their lives. Hence, we want personality to change when it has an adverse effect on interpersonal relationships, mental or physical health, or on functioning in society.

Moreover, during our lives we encounter many different social contexts and developmental challenges that might affect our personalities (see chapters by Helson & Stewart and Franz, this volume). Thus, the inability to change and to adapt to situational and cultural demands may lead to poor psychological functioning.

It can be argued that simply being involved in a social world is likely to promote personality change. After all, significant others provide feedback and positive reinforcement for relationship-enhancing attitudes and behaviors, and they provide negative feedback regarding attitudes and behaviors that are relationship-damaging. Thus, interpersonal relationships might shape or modify our personalities. A variety of evidence indicates that social support is an important component of life change (Clifford, Tan, & Gorsuch, 1991). Family, friends, co-workers, and health care professionals can provide emotional and esteem support, feedback, information, reinforcement, and direct assistance that a person involved in trying to change frequently needs (Clifford et al., 1991; Marlatt, 1985).

However, some studies have shown that social support is not always predictive of motivation or behavioral change (Kelly, Zyzanski, & Alemagno, 1991). This may be because people tend to associate with others who have similar ideas, personalities, and backgrounds (Caspi & Herbener, 1990) and choose as their confidants people who will back their decisions and behaviors (Baumeister, 1991). It is possible that these others will hinder change, partially because they may feel threatened by the implications of potential changes. A spouse who likes you "just the way you are" is unlikely to encourage your attempts at personal growth or other personality changes. Indeed, such changes might be viewed as a threat to the social relationship. Thus, it appears that significant others often actively support or hinder change depending on their own vested interests in the outcome.

WHAT IS PERSONALITY?

Personality psychology is an incredibly diverse and diffuse field. As many authors in this volume point out, personality can be defined to encompass almost all aspects of human life and experience. How personality is defined obviously plays a large role in whether it is viewed as stable or malleable. For instance, if personality is defined as standing on basic traits, then perhaps we should not expect to see much change. After all, the measurement instruments commonly used to assess personality traits are assumed to be reliable and stable over time. However, if the definition of personality is expanded to include motives, life goals, and overall psychological functioning, then there may be room for change. Costa and McCrae (this volume) argue that we need to differentiate basic tendencies from the characteristic adaptations that result from the interactions between basic tendencies and the social environment. In contrast, Helson and Stewart (this volume) suggest that key motives, attitudes, and adaptations are an important component of personality. It is not the attempt of this chapter to define the scope of personality, but readers should be aware that the answer to the question of whether personality can change is affected by the definition of personality (cf. Pervin, this volume).

The chapter by McAdams in this volume specifically addresses the critical issue of defining personality. McAdams sets out three levels of personality functioning: dispositional traits (e.g., the Big Five traits), personal concerns (e.g., goals and tasks), and the whole person (assessed through life narratives). As McAdams demonstrates, the issue of whether personality can change depends on which level researchers use to define personality.

HOW DO WE MEASURE PERSONALITY?

Some methods of measuring personality would seem to foster the finding that personality is very stable. For instance, self-reports on global traits, in which respondents are limited to choosing one response among five or seven possible responses, seem unlikely to reveal a great deal of personality change. Consider an item on a personality scale that has response options of 1 through 5. Individuals who score 4 or 5 are unlikely to later select responses 1 or 2, even if they believe that they have changed. Rather, individuals who originally scored 4 may believe they have changed, but select the response of 3 because they have not changed that much. Thus, the available response categories may be too gross for the amount of change that occurs. Alternatively, the meaning of selecting a 4 may itself change from Time 1 to Time 2, perhaps depending on the social and cultural context. How extraverted a person reports being may differ from the liberal 1960s to the conservative 1980s. Similarly, if all members of a cohort change in a systematic direction, the relative referent group changes and people might acknowledge that they have changed, but still select a 4 because compared with others they are still a 4. Of course, it is also possible that changes in scores will be due to error in measurement rather than to genuine changes in true scores (McCrae, in press). These issues are discussed at length in the ensuing chapters, especially the chapters by Costa and McCrae and by Helson and Stewart.

Another way to assess personality is through life narratives (McAdams, this volume) or personal interview (Miller & C'deBaca, this volume). With these methods, researchers examine change in a person's life from the person's own perspective. In these cases, personality is more broadly defined than by simple traits, and therefore change is often readily apparent. This method is not without its limitations, however. McFarland, Ross, and Giltrow (1992) showed that older adults tend to be biased in their recollections of past experiences, including their views of their personality in the past. They tended to bias their recollections in terms of implicit theories of aging. That is, they reported changing on dimensions on which they believed most older adults change (e.g., they believed older people show an increase in understanding and satisfaction with life and a decrease in activity and the ability to remember things). Similarly, a change in health status may be interpreted as a change in personality. At issue is the accuracy of recollections. As George Vaillant noted "It is all too common for caterpillars to become butterflies and then to maintain that in their youth they had been little butterflies. Maturity makes liars of us all" (1977, p. 197). Indeed, when Costa and McCrae (1989) separated one of their samples into groups based on whether subjects believed they had changed or not, the group who believed that they had "changed a good deal" did not differ from the group who "stayed pretty much the same" in terms of test–retest correlations on basic traits. This suggests that researchers should use caution when using retrospective accounts of change.

As most of the contributors to this volume argue, what is needed are more longitudinal studies that use multiple methods of assessing personality. Nesselroade and Boker (this volume) argue that data need to be collected at irregular intervals over long periods of time in order to control for systematic biases. We are now witnessing the culmination of many long-term studies of personality stability and change (see chapters by Helson & Stewart, Costa & McCrae, and Franz), and we can be optimistic that these various methodologies and techniques will continue to inform us about the aspects of personality that remain stable and those that appear to be more malleable. In addition, data archives (e.g., the Henry Murray Center of Radcliffe College) provide researchers with ready access to data from multiple longitudinal studies so that they can test their theories across different cohorts and contexts.

HOW DO WE ANALYZE CHANGE?

The statistical methods used to measure change have a profound influence on whether personality is seen as stable or malleable. For instance, some researchers have questioned whether difference scores or test–retest correlations are able to capture the phenomenon of personality change (Alder & Scher, this volume). Chapters by Nesselroade and Boker, and by Alder and Scher, address some relatively new statistical techniques to measure change. For instance, one way to examine personality change is to use individual growth curves (Alder & Scher, this volume; Francis, Fletcher, Stuebing, Davidson, & Thompson, 1991), which may allow for a more precise estimate of individual change.

Other researchers contend that we need to look at individual lives to understand change (McAdams, 1993; Murray, 1938). Even if the norm is stability (and therefore group means show little change and test–retest correlations are very high), there might still be a substantial number of individuals who experience profound changes in personality. This suggests that we might wish to look at the outliers in longitudinal studies to see if there are systematic patterns among those who do show indications of personality change.

WHAT ARE THE TYPES OF CHANGES THAT PEOPLE MAKE?

Just as we need to be cognizant of the need to define personality, we also need to develop a better understanding of what exactly is meant by the term *change*. If people do change, do they change gradually over long periods of time, over brief periods of adjustment, or suddenly and dramatically, or do all three types of personality change occur? How much change does there need to be before we say that a person has changed? Are maturational developments that occur over decades evidence of genuine change or do maturational changes lead to a different state of the same construct? In therapy, people often try to make relatively sudden and dramatic changes in some aspect of their lives. Although the person who changes from shy to outgoing has changed, has the person who feels a little bit better about themselves changed? Is personality change better represented by the analogy of hot water becoming tepid, or by cold water turning into ice? The latter implies a very different state of being, whereas the former implies continuity and gradual settling (Miller & C'deBaca, this volume).

A variety of past research suggests that personality change is best described as gradual and subtle. For example, evidence of gradual change can be found in King's (1973) *Five Lives at Harvard*, in which researchers examined the effect of the college experience on personality. King wrote, "The personality change in our five cases, with the possible exception of Hugh Post, was quiet, subtle, and not very exciting. It was evolutionary change, more difficult to describe than change that is dramatic, abrupt, and revolutionary" (p. 189). The changes "reflected an unfolding or gradual development rather than a sudden emergence of a new behavior or other striking change" (p. 218).

In contrast to these gradual changes, there are also what Miller and C'deBaca (this volume) refer to as quantum changes—sudden and dramatic changes that appear to alter individuals to the core. Individuals who go through religious or spiritual transformations, individuals who make abrupt changes in career aspirations or in occupation, and individuals recovering from traumatic events all seem to go through major and dramatic change. Vaillant's (1977) 35-year follow-up of participants in the Grant Study led him to conclude that

> if we follow adults for years, we can uncover startling changes and evolutions. We can discover developmental discontinuities in adults that are as great as the difference in personality between a nine-year-old and what he becomes at fifteen. (p. 372)

We are far from understanding the causes of such change, but part of the reason for our lack of understanding is that researchers have not been looking for such changes. As Davis and Millon (this volume) note, our conceptual models of change do not often include these radical shifts in personality (see also Block, 1971, and Helson & Stewart, this volume).

Perhaps, as noted by many of the contributors to this volume, we need to consider new and different models of personality change. Current psychological theories view change as linear, wherein change follows predictable progressions and maturations. One novel approach to understanding change might be to consider chaos theory, in which small initial perturbations produce enormous nonlinear change. The application of new and diverse perspectives on models of change may provide us with fresh insights into the issue of stability of personality (see chapters by Davis & Millon, Miller & C'deBaca, and Nesselroade & Boker).

A final issue that needs to be addressed is our bias to look for only positive instances of change. Do people experience both positive and negative changes in personality? Most researchers in this area have tended to concern themselves with positive change and personal growth. However, it also seems possible that people might experience personality change that interferes with successful adaptation. Models of change may be less powerful, and less accurate, when we consider only one end of the distribution of possible changes.

CAN PEOPLE CHOOSE TO CHANGE?

Even if we accept that some people seem to go through fundamental changes in personality, the question still remains whether people can choose to change, or whether change is always thrust on them. Many of the changes described in this volume represent maturational changes that are pretty much inevitable. Thus, change occurs due to increased age, change in social or cultural context, or change in living circumstances. Yet, many people are interested in self-directed change. Many individuals devote considerable energies to trying to change; they attend self-help groups, read self-help books, enter therapy, and initiate efforts to change. The fundamental question is whether people can choose to change their personalities.

The large literature on self-motivated behavioral change may provide interesting insights for personality researchers trying to understand whether individuals can choose to change aspects of their personalities. Good analogies to volitional personality change are the changes that occur when individuals try to give up problematic substances or when they try to achieve and maintain a thinner body size. Research on this topic has benefited from excellent conceptual models, such as the one described by DiClemente in this volume. Personality researchers might find it very fruitful to consider whether these models of behavioral change can be applied to personality.

HOW DO PEOPLE DESCRIBE ATTEMPTS AT CHANGE?

One way to examine volitional attempts at personality change is to interview people who have tried to change and succeeded and compare their accounts with those of people who have tried to change and failed. We recently conducted a study that sought to address the attributions people make for successful and unsuccessful life change experiences (Heatherton & Nichols, 1993). A total of 119 students from the Harvard Extension School served as volunteers in our study. We asked them to describe instances in which they were either able or not able to make major life changes. The self-reported successful change stories differed in substantial and predictable ways from the stories of unsuccessful change. Although not all subjects in this study were trying to change their personalities, the attributions that individuals made for being able to change or not being able to change were quite similar across the domains in which the attempts were being made (e.g., some people tried to change their personalities, some tried to quit drug habits, others tried to change troubled relationships). Previous research has shown that the attributions people make about the change process are important for maintaining change (Sonne & Janoff, 1982; Weiner, 1985). For instance, attributing change to internal factors is associated with greater maintenance of change than is attributing change to external factors (Schoeneman & Curry, 1990; Sonne & Janoff, 1979).

Our study used the micronarrative technique (Baumeister, Stillwell, & Wotman, 1990; Gergen & Gergen, 1988) to analyze how and why people changed or did not change. One group of subjects was asked to describe in detail a sudden and dramatic change that had occurred in any aspect of their lives. The other subjects were asked to describe an aspect of their lives they would like to suddenly and dramatically change and to tell why they believed they had been unable to make the change. The stories were then coded and compared to determine which factors were most closely related to successful change and which factors were most likely to be mentioned as hindrances to change.

Micronarratives are autobiographical stories that focus on specific events. They represent the person's subjective evaluation of the event. These stories may not be totally accurate, in that people selectively construct, retrieve, and distort the narratives to fit their own self-concepts, but they do represent what the person believes is important (Baumeister et al., 1990). Micronarratives have become increasingly useful in studying motivation in topics that are difficult to test using conventional laboratory methods, for example, anger (Baumeister et al., 1990), guilt (Baumeister, Stillwell, & Heatherton, in press), the termination of intimate relationships (Harvey, Flanary, & Morgan, 1988; Harvey, Weber, Galvin, Huszti, & Garnick, 1986; Vaughan, 1986), and criminal and antisocial activity (Katz, 1988).

The micronarrative technique is useful for studying personality change attempts, a difficult topic to examine for a variety of reasons. Change is a complex process involving many motivational, cognitive, and situational factors, all of which may be simultaneously important to effecting change. In many cases it will be impossible to establish which of these factors is most important. Similarly, it may be impossible for people to ever really know how they changed. It is likely that most individuals do not have access to the cognitive processes that create change (Freud, 1937/1964; Nisbett & Wilson, 1977). That is, although individuals may be motivated to provide an explanation for change, it seems likely that their inferences about change processes will be based on their idiosyncratic beliefs about processes of change (McFarland et al., 1992).

Although individuals may be unable to specify the precise factors responsible for change, they are able to recount the events leading to change, the methods they used in an attempt to effect change, the difficulties they had with these attempts, and the strategies they used to maintain change (Prochaska, Velicer, Guadagnoli, Rossi, & DiClemente, 1991). By considering all the factors simultaneously, individuals may develop personal theories to account for the success or failure of their attempts at change. Such accounts may provide a wealth of information about personal beliefs and attributions regarding change, as well as indicate precipitating and ongoing events that may be related to successful change.

Emotional Aspects of Change

Both change and nonchange subjects in our study reported substantial amounts of negative affect, including hassles, frustrations, and emotional distress. People were motivated to leave unhappy relationships, to change unfulfilling careers, to change their attitudes toward themselves and their lives, to achieve more healthful life-styles, and to change undesirable personality traits. For example, one woman who had been unable to change an oppressive family relationship wrote,

> I know that I'm scared of being too successful because I am afraid of having people depend on me and take more from me than I'm already giving them (which is already too much). I don't want to spend all my energy on other people. Maybe rather than have any success myself that I would have to share, I would like to have all my failure and disappointment to myself.

However, we found that individuals who reported making major changes described much stronger negative affect, including major suffering. For instance, a woman who was finally able to leave an abusive relationship wrote, "My whole life was one of helplessness. I was never believed. I became extremely upset and frightened." After fleeing from the situation, her life changed from "a life of hell to one filled with happiness and many loving friends." She now finds it "hard to believe that [her life] actually existed the way that [she] lived it."

The Importance of Focal Events

A common theme in the successful change stories was the occurrence of some sort of focal incident that triggered the change attempt. Fifty-nine percent of the change stories compared with only nine percent of the nonchange stories contained descriptions of focal events. Miller and Rollnick (1991) noted that such focal events change the balance sheet of costs and benefits associated with the target behavior, such that they can represent the proverbial "straw that breaks the camel's back." These events lead people to reevaluate how their behavior fits in with their overall self-perception. One woman in our study who was living a type of hippie existence experienced such a focal event when she discovered that she was pregnant. She wrote, "I became disgusted with my life and decided I had had enough." This pregnancy led her to move back to her hometown and assume a more traditional life-style. Her story indicates that many aspects of her personality changed during this transition. In contrast, the non-changers were more likely to describe themselves as feeling confused and unfocused following focal events.

Often the behavior that individuals wish to change is dissonant with how they would like to view themselves. Baumeister (this volume) notes that people, motivated to see themselves and their behaviors in the best possible light, frequently hold positive illusions. When focal events lead to a reevaluation, behaviors that are not consistent with one's identity create unpleasant dissonance and motivate the person to try to alter the behavior. Thus, the focal event creates a crystallization of discontent that people cannot ignore. One woman described how taking a course on the psychology of women led to such a crystallization of discontent and subsequent life change:

> It opened up a Pandora's box. . . . I realized my relationship with my husband was not satisfying to me. . . . I could not tolerate the status quo any longer. . . . I had changed in my core. I was ready to go it alone—whatever it meant, in search of my own true independence and inner validity.

Change in Identity

Our findings indicated that people who reported successfully changing believed that the establishment of a new identity was critical for long-term change. This new identity formed after the reevaluation of life goals and meanings (Baumeister, this volume). Successful changers frequently reported a flash of insight into their problematic attitudes and behaviors, and their stories indicated that they had developed a sense of wisdom about the factors that had previously prevented them from changing. Those who had not successfully changed were less committed to the change process, were more ambivalent about the desirability of change, and were more likely to be clinging to their current role and identity. Stall and Biernacki (1986) proposed that the development of a new identity was one of the most important steps for maintaining change. The change in identity incorporates the changed behavior so that the previous behavior is no longer part of the self. One man in our study who had not been able to change said, "When I do make the effort to overcome my shyness, I feel that it is not really me acting, that it is someone else." In contrast, successful changers made comments like "I have changed in my core" and "I could see a total change in my personality."

Attributions for Change

Individuals who reported successful change were more likely to claim that they had control in general, and they were less likely to refer to external obstacles to change. This supports the hypothesis that attributions of personal agency and internal control are important for maintaining behavioral change (Schoeneman & Curry, 1990; Sonne & Janoff, 1979; Weiner, 1985). However, it is quite possible that such attributions resulted from, rather than caused, attitudinal and behavioral change. Micronarrative accounts are by nature correlational and no cause–effect determinations can be made. Nonetheless, the factors that individuals currently regard as important for maintaining change may be genuinely important in doing so. People who believe that they have conquered their cigarette addiction through willpower or who have forced themselves to be more outgoing may have created a self-fulfilling prophecy that helps maintain their behavioral change. Independent of the factors truly responsible for change, people's beliefs about which factors are important may be the critical foundations underlying their ability to remain changed.

These narratives not only provided considerable support for various theories of change, but, even more important, they also provided a glimpse at the phenomenology of the change experience. Our analysis indicated that there were important emotional, motivational, cognitive, and interpersonal processes that facilitated or inhibited change. Moreover, we found that these processes acted in confluence, so that individuals reported all of them as being important for effecting change.

Of course, we have no direct evidence that people actually managed to make fundamental changes in their attitudes or behavior. In fact, in terms of the goals of the current volume, many of the changes represented behaviors rather than aspects of personality. Nonetheless, many of the stories described explicit attempts to change identity and personality traits. Individuals who reported making such personality changes expressed feelings that they had changed to the core, that they had become different people. Thus, many people believe that they are able to effect major changes in personality. Obviously future research, such as natural history studies, is necessary to examine whether individuals are able to make such profound changes in personality.

NEED FOR THIS VOLUME

Personality change has been an important topic in psychology for many years. It is an issue that cuts across subdisciplines and is of special interest to developmental, social, personality, and clinical researchers. Recent theoretical and empirical advances indicate that now is the perfect time to gather multiple perspectives on personality change into one comprehensive volume. For instance, the perspectives of behavioral genetics and sociobiology have provided details about which aspects of personality appear to be most stable. Similarly, many fine longitudinal studies of personality development have provided important data for the examination of basic issues of stability and change, and an understanding of normal life course transitions. Moreover, we now have sophisticated statistical techniques and powerful computer resources to analyze large longitudinal data sets. As a result, this seemed to us to be the ideal time to publish a comprehensive volume on aspects of personality change.

OVERVIEW OF THE BOOK

This volume is divided into four sections. In the first section various agents of stability are considered. Costa and McCrae present evidence indicating that basic traits (i.e., the Big Five) do not change significantly and tend to have strong test–retest correlations, even after many decades. Brody, using the analogy of intelligence, argues that genetic endowment produces relative stability of personality. Buss argues that evolutionary forces lead individuals to seek out contexts and situations that reinforce dispositional traits.

In the next section, various perspectives on theory and methodology are presented. Davis and Millon argue that many of our current paradigmatic conceptions of personality appear to preclude change. They argue that we need to consider new theoretical approaches, possibly those used by related physical sciences. The chapters by Nesselroade and Boker and by Alder and Scher examine measurement issues and models of personality change. Both chapters offer a number of instructive examples of sophisticated mathematical models of change. The chapter by DiClemente focuses on applications of the transtheoretical change model to personality change. This model is an especially influential model in the study of addictive behaviors, and DiClemente raises the intriguing question of whether insights gained from studying behavioral change can be applied to understanding personality change.

In the third section, personality transitions across the life span are considered. Franz examines changes in implicit motives and preoccupations, especially those related to generativity during midlife. Helson and Stewart present a variety of important studies demonstrating that personality does appear to change as a consequence of changing social roles and societal contexts.

In the final section, there are four chapters dealing with various conceptions of change. Miller and C'deBaca present their theory of quantum change, that is, sudden transformations of the entire person. Baumeister describes how the crystallization of discontent motivates attempts at major life change. Such crystallization occurs when individuals gain insight into the pattern of negative factors associated with their current situations. McAdams's chapter helps clarify differences between various definitions of personality by pointing out that there are different levels of analysis or different ways of considering the person. McAdams cogently argues that the issue of stability of personality depends on which level of the person we are examining. Pervin's chapter considers various ways of looking at personality change and discusses the implications of the various models. In the conclusion, Weinberger discusses the common themes and important issues that emerged in this volume. Weinberger also addresses clinical issues in personality change, with a specific emphasis on what is changed by psychotherapy.

REFERENCES

Baumeister, R. F. (1991). *Meanings of life.* New York: Guilford Press.

Baumeister, R. F., Stillwell, A., & Heatherton, T. F. (in press). Guilt as inter-personal phenomenon: Two studies using autobiographical narratives. In J. Tangney & K. Fischer (Eds.), *Self-conscious emotions: Shame, guilt, embarrass-ment, and pride.* New York: Guilford Press.

Baumeister, R. F., Stillwell, A., & Wotman, S. R. (1990). Victim and perpetrator accounts of interpersonal conflict: Autobiographical narratives about anger. *Journal of Personality and Social Psychology, 59,* 994–1005.

Block, J. (1971). *Lives through time.* Berkeley, CA: Bancroft.

Caspi, A. & Herbener, E. S. (1990). Continuity and change: Assortative marriage and the consistency of personality in adulthood. *Journal of Personality and Social Psychology, 58,* 250–258.

Clifford, P. A., Tan, S. Y., & Gorsuch, R. L. (1991). Efficacy of a self-directed behavioral health change program: Weight, body composition, cardiovascular fitness, blood pressure, health risk, and psychosocial mediating variables. *Journal of Behavioral Medicine, 14,* 303–323.

Costa, P. T., Jr., & McCrae, R. R. (1980). Still stable after all these years: Personality as a key to some issues in aging. In P. B. Baltes & O. G. Brim, Jr. (Eds.), *Life-span development and behavior* (Vol. 3, pp. 65–102). San Diego, CA: Academic Press.

Costa, P. T., Jr., & McCrae, R. R. (1989). Personality continuity and the changes of adult life. In M. Storandt & G. R. VandenBos (Eds.), *The adult years: Continuity and change* (pp. 45–77). Washington, DC: American Psychological Association.

Erikson, E. (1950). *Childhood and society.* New York: Norton.

Francis, D. J., Fletcher, J. M., Stuebing, K. K., Davidson, K. C., & Thompson, N. M. (1991). Analysis of change: Modeling individual growth. *Journal of Clinical and Consulting Psychology, 59,* 27–37.

Freud, S. (1964). An outline of psychoanalysis. In Jo Strachey (Ed. and Trans.), *The standard edition of the complete psychological works of Sigmund Freud* (Vol. 23, pp. 141–208). London: Hogarth Press. (Original work published 1937).

Gergen, K. J., & Gergen, M. M. (1988). Narrative and the self as relationship. In L. Berkowitz (Ed.), *Advances in experimental social psychology* (Vol. 21, pp. 17–56). San Diego, CA: Academic Press.

Harvey, J. H., Flanary, R., & Morgan, M. (1988). Vivid memories of vivid loves gone by. *Journal of Social and Personal Relationships, 3,* 359–373.

Harvey, J. H., Weber, A. L., Galvin, K. S., Huszti, H. C., & Garnick, N. N. (1986). Attribution in the termination of close relationships: A special focus on the account. In R. Gilmour & S. Duck (Eds.), *The emerging field of personal relationships* (pp. 189–201). Hillsdale, NJ: Erlbaum.

Heatherton, T. F., & Nichols, P. A. (1993). *Micronarrative accounts of successful and unsuccessful life change experiences.* Manuscript submitted for publication.

Helson, R., & Moane, G. (1987). Personality change in women from college to midlife. *Journal of Personality and Social Psychology, 53,* 176–186.

James, W. (1890). *Principles of psychology.* New York: Holt.

Katz, I. (1988). *Seductions of crime: The moral and sensual attractions of doing evil.* New York: Basic Books.

Kelly, R. B., Zyzanski, S. J., & Alemagno, S. A. (1991). Prediction of motivation and behavior change following health promotion: Role of health beliefs, social support, and self-efficacy. *Social Science and Medicine, 32,* 311–320.

King, S. H. (1973). *Five lives at Harvard.* Cambridge, MA: Harvard University Press.

Marlatt, G. A. (1985). Cognitive factors in the relapse process. In G. A. Marlatt & J. R. Gordon (Eds.), *Relapse prevention* (pp. 128–200). New York: Guilford Press.

McAdams, D. (1993). *The stories we live by: Personal myths and the making of the self.* New York: William Morrow.

McCrae, R. R. (in press). Moderated analyses of longitudinal personality stability. *Journal of Personality and Social Psychology.*

McCrae, R. R., & Costa, P. T. (1990). *Personality in adulthood.* New York: Guilford Press.

McFarland, C., Ross, M., & Giltrow, M. (1992). Biased recollections in older adults: The role of implicit theories of aging. *Journal of Personality and Social Psychology, 62,* 837–850.

Miller, W. R., & Rollnick, S. (1991). *Motivational interviewing: Preparing people to change addictive behavior.* New York: Guilford Press.

Mischel, W. (1968). *Personality and assessment.* New York: Wiley.

Murray, H. A. (1938). *Explorations in personality.* New York: Oxford University Press.

Nisbett, R. E., & Wilson, T. D. (1977). Telling more than we can know: Verbal reports on mental processes. *Psychological Review, 84,* 231–259.

Ozer, D. J., & Gjerde, P. F. (1989). Patterns of personality consistency and change from childhood through adolescence. *Journal of Personality, 57,* 483–507.

Prochaska, J. O., Velicer, W. F., Guadagnoli, E., Rossi, J. S., & DiClemente, C. C. (1991). Patterns of change: Dynamic typology applied to smoking cessation. *Multivariate Behavioral Research, 26,* 83–107.

Schoeneman, T. J., & Curry, S. (1990). Attributions for successful and unsuccessful health behavior change. *Basic and Applied Social Psychology, 11,* 421–431.

Sonne, J. L., & Janoff, D. S. (1979). The effect of treatment attributions on the maintenance of weight reduction: A replication and extension. *Cognitive Therapy and Research, 3,* 389–397.

Sonne, J. L., & Janoff, D. S. (1982). Attributions and the maintenance of behavior change. In C. Anataki & C. Brewin (Eds.), *Attribution and psychological change* (pp. 83–96). San Diego, CA: Academic Press.

Stall, R., & Biernacki, P. (1986). Spontaneous remission from the problematic use of substances: An inductive model derived from a comparative analysis of the alcohol, opiate, tobacco, and food/obesity literatures. *International Journal of the Addictions, 21,* 1–23.

Vaillant, G. E. (1977). *Adaptation to life.* Boston: Little, Brown.

Vaughan, D. (1986). *Uncoupling.* New York: Basic Books.

Weiner, B. (1985). An attributional model of achievement theory and emotion. *Psychological Review, 92,* 548–573.

I

AGENTS OF STABILITY

2

SET LIKE PLASTER? EVIDENCE FOR THE STABILITY OF ADULT PERSONALITY

PAUL T. COSTA, JR., and ROBERT R. McCRAE

Near the end of his chapter on "Habit" in the *Principles of Psychology*, William James (1890/1981) made one of modern psychology's first pronouncements on the course of adult development:

> Already at the age of twenty-five you see the professional mannerism settling down on the young commercial traveller, on the young doctor, on the young minister, on the young counsellor-at-law. You see the little lines of cleavage running through the character, the tricks of thought, the prejudices, the ways of the "shop," in a word, from which the man can by-and-by no more escape than his coat sleeve can suddenly fall into a new set of folds . . . . In most of us, by the age of thirty, the character has set like plaster, and will never soften again. (pp. 125–126)

This passage raises three issues that are likely to be addressed in various ways in the chapters of this book. The most obvious is the claim that personality in adulthood is fixed: unchanging and perhaps unchangeable. We review evidence suggesting that, in most cases, personality traits are indeed unchanging; we leave to other authors the question of whether they are unchangeable.

A second issue concerns the age at which personality can be considered fully developed. Most people in our culture assume that adulthood begins at age 21, with the end of adolescence. Recent theories of a midlife crisis or transition (e.g., Levinson, Darrow, Klein, Levinson, & McKee, 1978) predict continued change well after age 30. We present some data on this question that tend to support James's contention that personality development ends somewhere between 25 and 30.

DEFINING PERSONALITY

But before turning to either of these empirical questions we must deal with a third, more basic issue: What do we mean by *personality?* James did not use that term; instead, he spoke of *character,* and did so in the context of a chapter on habit. By *habit* he meant a routinized, learned behavior, of which he gave such examples as biting one's nails, playing a scale on the piano, and getting dressed. *Character* was for him the complex concatenation of all these habits that fixed us in our social roles and determined our moral behavior. Of modern personality theorists, only Skinner (1974) viewed personality as a repertoire of learned behaviors.

Other personality psychologists have given a remarkably diverse set of answers to the question, What is personality?, in part because people themselves are so complex. Personality has been construed in terms of the self (Lecky, 1945), patterns of learned expectations (Bandura, 1977), the structure of mind (Warren & Marmichael, 1930), a profile of traits (Guilford, 1959), and the life of the individual as a whole (Murray, 1938). Whether personality can or cannot change depends on which of these definitions one adopts. When Murray and Kluckhohn (1953, p. 8) wrote that "from one point of view, the history of the personality *is* the personality," they appear to have offered a definition in which continuous change is not only possible but inevitable. Conversely, if one were to define personality as the genes that underlie temperament, change—barring genetic engineering—would be precluded.

The simplest solution to this problem would be to offer our own definition of personality in terms of five dimensions of personality traits, and then to proceed to the empirical evidence. But many of the authors in this book do not share our definition, and might consider the data we offer irrelevant. As a basis for communication, what is needed is a framework in which different approaches to the definition of personality can be integrated and compared, and that can allow us to say that personality in this respect can change, but in that respect—perhaps—cannot. For this purpose we will offer a very general metatheoretical model of the person

22   COSTA AND McCRAE

that includes the elements in many definitions of personality and that seems to be particularly useful in approaching issues of stability and change. We take as a starting point the definition of personality given by Allport in 1961: "the dynamic organization within the individual of those psychophysical systems that determine his characteristic behavior and thought" (p. 28).

There seem to be three elements of this definition: (a) a "dynamic organization," or set of processes that integrate the flow of experience and behavior; (b) "psychophysical systems" that represent basic tendencies and capacities of the individual; and (c) "characteristic behavior and thought," such as habits, attitudes, and relationships, that we call *characteristic adaptations*. To these three elements we wish to add three more: (d) external influences or the environment, broadly construed to include both the immediate situation and the broader social, cultural, and historical context; (e) objective biography, "every significant thing that a [person] felt and thought and said and did from the start to the finish of his life" (Murray & Kluckhohn, 1953, p. 30); and (f) the self-concept, the individual's sense of who he or she is.

These elements make up the raw material of most personality theories, that is, what they are trying to explain and how they attempt to explain it. Theories differ in the elements they emphasize and in the causal and developmental relations they postulate among the elements. For example, Bandura's (1977) *self-efficacy* can be seen as an aspect of the self-concept, and its development from repeated interactions with the environment suggests that Bandura might draw a causal arrow from external influences to self-concept. (In fact, Bandura's 1978 model suggested reciprocal influences.)

The six elements might be configured in many different ways; Figure 1 illustrates our version. It is a complicated figure because people are complex. We assume that the meanings of external influences and objective biography are clear, but comment on the other parts of the figure.

By *basic tendencies* we mean certain very general potentials—dispositions, limitations, and capacities—that the individual has. They may be inherited or acquired and may or may not be malleable in adulthood. Their chief characteristic is that they are abstract tendencies that could be manifest in many different ways. We would include here basic personality or temperament traits such as extraversion and conscientiousness, but also many other attributes of the individual that affect his or her adaptation to life, including physical health and attractiveness, gender and sexual orientation, and intelligence and artistic abilities.

Over the course of human development, these basic tendencies interact with external influences to produce *characteristic adaptations*. A child with musical abilities who is given piano lessons will develop the skills required to play piano, and may also develop a love of music. Extraverts

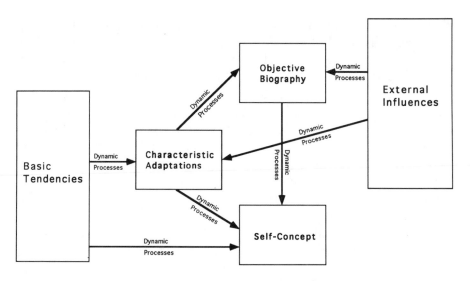

Figure 1: A model of the person, containing elements used in various definitions of personality. This particular configuration of elements represents one specific theory of personality.

who reached adolescence in the 1960s learned to dance the twist; contemporary adolescent extraverts learn hip-hop. Skills, habits, beliefs, attitudes, interests, and personal projects are all characteristic adaptations; we would also include here social roles and relationships, which are interpersonal adaptations. All these are concrete realizations of basic tendencies.

The *self-concept* is the individual's view of what he or she is like. Core aspects of the self-concept, aspects that define the individual, can be called the person's *identity*. Studies of the spontaneous self-concept (McCrae & Costa, 1988) show that personality traits and abilities, habits and activities, roles and relationships, and facts of personal history are all mentioned when respondents are asked to answer the question, "Who am I?" Thus, the self-concept in our model is essentially an epiphenomenon that passively mirrors basic tendencies, characteristic adaptations, and objective biography (and thus indirectly external influences). Of course, other theorists (e.g., Markus & Nurius, 1986) see the self as an active guide to behavior.

Dynamic processes are the mechanisms that relate the various elements in the model; in the figure, it is represented not as a separate box but as the collection of causal arrows that connect other elements. Learning, for example, is a process that allows external influences to shape characteristic adaptations. Defense mechanisms may be involved in selectively forming the self-concept from aspects of the objective biography. Dynamic processes are perhaps less easily conceptualized than the other elements in this model, but they have played a central role in many theories of personality. Loevinger's (1966) ego development, Allport's (1955) propriate functioning, and Block and Block's (1980) ego-resiliency and ego-control are examples of conceptualizations of dynamic processes.

In the figure that represents our version of personality theory, the largest boxes are assigned to basic tendencies and external influences, because these two are seen as the ultimate sources of explanation. For us, the fundamental units of personality are located in the domain of basic tendencies, but other theorists would emphasize other elements, and a consideration of some of these alternatives is informative.

THEORIES OF PERSONALITY AND IMPLICATIONS FOR CHANGE

With this model as a framework, it is possible to review a number of different approaches to personality. In recent years there has been a growing movement to define personality psychology as the study of lives (McAdams & Ochberg, 1988; Rabin, Zucker, Emmons, & Frank, 1990), an approach that was articulated as long ago as 1938 by Henry Murray. The basic insight here is that personality cannot be grasped at a single cross section; it is necessary to see how it unfolds over a lifetime. For the purposes of this chapter, the issue is how to view objective biography: Is it, by definition, a part of personality, or is it an outcome, determined in part by personality and in part by other, external influences?

Although they do not explicity label the object of their study "personality," Levinson and his colleagues (1978) might be considered personality theorists who hold the former view. They are interested in the study of adult development, which they regard as the development of the life structure, both internal and external. Whether the life structure develops according to the fixed pattern they hypothesize is a matter of considerable debate (McCrae & Costa, 1990), but there is no question that it changes over time. If personality is biography, there is no doubt that personality changes.

But other psychologists associated with the tradition of studying lives do not necessarily assume that life history is part of personality. Murray and Kluckhohn (1953) were quite explicit on this point:

> The term "personality" has been reserved for the hypothetical structure of the mind, the consistent establishments and processes of which are manifested over and over again (together with some unique or novel elements) in the internal and external proceedings which constitute a person's life. Thus personality is not a series of biographical facts but something more general and enduring that is inferred from the facts. A biographer might describe every significant thing that a man felt and thought and said and did from the start to the finish of his life without conceptualizing a single part of his personality. (p. 30)

From this perspective, whether personality changes or is stable is an empirical question. The personologist would need to infer the personality of the individual from biographical facts during two or more periods of life and determine whether there were any changes. Vaillant (1977) used something like this approach, studying vignettes of behavior collected at different ages to examine the maturation of defenses in early adulthood. Although recollections may be biased (McFarland, Ross, & Giltrow, 1992), gerontologists who have studied retrospective accounts of life from older individuals frequently remark on apparent stability. Reichard, Livson, and Peterson (1962), for example, stated that "the histories of our aging workers suggest that their personality characteristics changed very little throughout their lives" (p. 163). At present, life history researchers are only beginning to develop a consensus on how personality should be inferred from biography and what personality variables should be studied, so it is premature to consider the question of personality stability answered in either direction.

For the same reason, it is difficult to give a definitive answer to the question of whether the dynamic processes of personality change in adulthood. Freud (1923/1962) certainly believed that the interacting structures of id, ego, and superego reached a point of dynamic equilibrium early in life, and could be changed, if at all, only with years of psychoanalysis. But Freud's structures cannot easily be measured, so empirical confirmation of this view is difficult. Loevinger has provided a measure of her conception of the central organizing principle, ego level (Loevinger & Wessler, 1970). Her sentence completion test of ego development shows growth between childhood and the end of high school (Loevinger, 1993), but cross-sectional comparisons show little mean level change thereafter. For example, McCrae and Costa (1980) reported a correlation of .01 between age and total protocol ratings on the Washington University Sentence Completion Test (Loevinger & Wessler, 1970) in a sample of 239 men aged 35 to 80. Haan (1977) defined personality in terms of styles of coping and defense; the use of these coping mechanisms shows little relation to age (Costa, Zonderman, & McCrae, 1991). Of course, these examples do not exhaust the range of variables that can be considered dynamic processes, but—aside from cognitive abilities, which surely are involved in the organization of behavior—we know of no personality process that shows consistent age changes in adulthood.

Like the objective biography that it partially reflects, the self-concept undoubtedly changes with age. Young adults do not think of themselves as grandmothers or senior citizens, or as survivors of a heart attack; in 40 years these may be salient aspects of their self-concept. But there are other aspects of the self-concept that show evidence of considerable stability. Mortimer, Finch, and Kumka (1982) assessed a multidimensional self-concept in college students followed 10 years after graduation; they found retest correlations over that period ranging from .52 to .63. The most commonly measured aspect of the self-concept is self-esteem (Rosenberg, 1979), which shows both short-term fluctuations (Heatherton & Polivy, 1991) and long-term stability. For example, self-esteem as rated from responses to the Twenty Statements Test (Kuhn & McPartland, 1954) is unrelated to age in adults, neither increasing nor decreasing (McCrae & Costa, 1988).

One particularly intriguing aspect of change in the self-concept concerns its accuracy. In Figure 1, the self-concept appears to be a direct reflection of basic tendencies, characteristic adaptations, and life history. But, as Epstein (1973) noted, the self-concept is a theory of the self, and it may be a relatively poor one. Many personality theorists, notably Rogers (1961), have suggested that psychopathology results from incongruence between the self-concept and the underlying tendencies and adaptations of the individual; helping clients understand themselves would be seen by many psychotherapists as a basic change in personality. Rogers assumed that the *self* (one's self-concept) is malleable under the right therapeutic conditions, but the *organism* (one's basic tendencies) may be unchanging.

Many kinds of psychotherapy focus on changing what we call *characteristic adaptations*, perhaps better called *maladaptations* in this case. Phobias and drug dependencies clearly fall into this category, as do pathological (e.g., abusive) relationships. These concrete problems are often the target of successful interventions, so if one equates personality with characteristic adaptations, personality change is clearly possible.

An extreme instance of this view is provided by Skinner (1974). In *About Behaviorism,* he wrote that

> a self or personality is at best a repertoire of behavior imparted by an organized set of contingencies. The behavior a young person acquires in the bosom of his family composes one self; the behavior he acquires in, say, the armed services composes another. (p. 149)

The intent of Skinner's definition is to strip personality of any special status as an explanatory term; it is merely a collection of learned behaviors, given such coherence as it has by the systematic influences of a particular environment.

To some degree, individuals continue to learn new behaviors across the life span, both because technological advances continue to reshape our lives and because there are age-related changes in social roles and in physical capabilities. Retirees who take to the road in their new campers must make radical changes in their day-to-day behavior. If personality is nothing but behavior, then personality manifestly changes throughout life. However, some learned behaviors—nervous habits, speech patterns and accents, skills like typing and riding bicycles—are remarkably constant across periods of decades, and perhaps James was impressed by these features in reaching his conclusion on the stability of character.

Perhaps, however, James's conclusion was based on a deeper insight than his theory of habits allowed him to express. Perhaps he intuited that, in some very basic sense, there is stability in personality. In this sense he may have implicitly defined personality in terms of what we have called basic tendencies. In that category there are a number of dispositions and capacities that characterize the individual's potential adaptation to life. Theorists who see this as the core of personality differ in whether or not they include the full range of basic tendencies within the domain of personality proper. Cattell, for example, included intelligence as one of the 16 basic factors of personality (Cattell, Eber, & Tatsuoka, 1970), and Block (1961) included not only verbal fluency but also physical attractiveness in his Q-sort descriptions of personality.

It is well-known that there are age-related changes in many cognitive abilities, the components of what Horn and Cattell (1972) called "fluid intelligence". It is also clear that there are age-related changes in physical health and appearance, activity level, and sex drive. But these are not considered aspects of personality by many theorists. If we exclude them, we are left with a huge array of tendencies, dispositions, motivations, and styles that most of us would recognize as prototypical personality traits, including nervousness, excitability, originality, altruism, and cautiousness. It is characteristics like these that are most commonly assessed in personality questionnaires, and it is from personality questionnaire data that conclusions about the stability of personality are most commonly derived. The empirical study of this question has made extraordinary strides in the past 20 years.

EMPIRICAL EVIDENCE ON PERSONALITY STABILITY

It is fair to say that as recently as the 1970s, neither laypersons nor gerontologists nor personality psychologists had a clear notion of what happened to personality traits with age. There were certainly age stereotypes, but they were often mutually inconsistent: Old people were depicted as both wise and foolish, as generative and nurturing grandparents, and also as self-centered hypochondriacs. The classic theories of Jung (1933) and Erikson (1950), and the more recent stage theories of adult development (Gould, 1978; Levinson et al., 1978) offered competing visions of what happened with age, but they remained largely untested theories. Hundreds of cross-sectional studies had been conducted comparing older and younger subjects on measures of extraversion and rigidity and ego strength, but they were difficult to integrate and often contradictory (Neugarten, 1977). Even personal experience did little to illuminate the question, because few of us had lived long enough to have a sense of whether, how much, in what ways, and under what conditions people changed.

This remarkable state of ignorance was corrected in the next few years by two major advances in personality research. The first was the recognition that the hundreds of personality traits proposed by theorists and embedded in the natural language of trait adjectives could be organized in terms of the basic dimensions of the five-factor model (Digman, 1990; John, 1990; McCrae, 1992). This model allowed us to integrate results from many studies and to approach the question of stability or change in personality systematically. By sampling traits defining each of the five factors of neuroticism (N), extraversion (E), openness (O), agreeableness (A), and conscientiousness (C), we could make meaningful generalizations about the hundreds of personality scales and thousands of trait adjectives that had not yet been studied.

The second advance, more empirical than theoretical, was the analysis of data from longitudinal studies of personality that had been begun decades earlier, including the Institute of Human Development studies (Eichorn, Clausen, Haan, Honzik, & Mussen, 1981), the Normative Aging Study (Costa & McCrae, 1978), the Kelly Longitudinal Study (Conley, 1985), the Duke Longitudinal Study (Siegler, George, & Okun, 1979), the University of Minnesota's Cardiovascular Disease Project (Finn, 1986), and the Baltimore Longitudinal Study of Aging (Costa & McCrae, 1988, 1992b). These studies differed widely in initial rationale, the sample composition and initial age of the participants, and the instruments used to measure personality. But they were nearly unanimous in their conclusions on the stability of personality in adulthood.

Nesselroade (this volume) has explained in great detail the complex methodology needed to assess stability and change in personality. At the risk of oversimplification, we will limit our comments to the two most obvious types of analyses: those that compare mean levels in groups to estimate normative changes in personality variables with age, and those that examine retest correlations to estimate the stability of individuals' rank ordering.

Stability of Mean Levels

Both cross-sectional and longitudinal methods can be used to study mean level differences, if we assume that cross-sectional differences among age groups are due to aging itself, and not to sampling bias, systematic attrition, or generational differences. Cross-sectional studies are fairly consistent: They tend to show small declines in N, E, and O and small increases in A and C. In a national sample of nearly 10,000 men and women aged 35 to 84, correlations of age with short measures of N, E, and O ranged from $-.12$ to $-.19$. In a more recent study of 1,539 men and women aged 21 to 64 using full-length measures of the five factors from the Revised NEO Personality Inventory (NEO-PI-R; Costa & McCrae, 1992a), correlations of N, E, O, A, and C with age were $-.12$, $-.12$, $-.12$, $+.17$, and +.09, respectively. All these correlations were statistically significant ($p < .001$), although age accounted for less than 3% of the variance in any of the scales.

Very similar values were found for 277 single peer ratings of Baltimore Longitudinal Study of Aging participants aged 29 to 93. Figure 2 shows the regression curves for these peer ratings across the interval from 30 to 80. Note that there was a significant curvilinear effect for O and that neither the linear nor the curvilinear effect was significant for C. With the exception of O in the decade from 30 to 40, predicted mean values at all ages are within the average range of scores. One practical implication is that one set of norms can be used for all adults over age 30.

One might be tempted to conclude from these rather consistent results that there are modest changes across the full life span in the mean levels of personality traits. But it must be recalled that these are cross-sectional results, and many alternative explanations are possible. For example, there is some evidence that very disagreeable individuals are prone to coronary disease (Costa, McCrae, & Dembroski, 1989), so the higher levels of A among older cohorts might be due to the premature death of their antagonistic age peers. In fact, longitudinal studies do not provide much support for the view that these cross-sectional differences reflect maturational changes. A six-year longitudinal study of self-reports and spouse ratings on

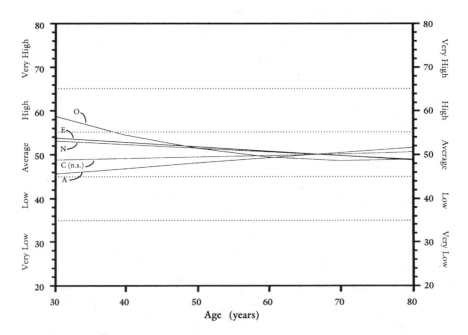

Figure 2: Plotted regression equations predicting domain scores on the Revised NEO Personality Inventory in single peer ratings ($N = 277$) from age. N = Neuroticism, E = Extraversion, O = Openness, A = Agreeableness, C = Conscientiousness.

the NEO-PI (Costa & McCrae, 1988) did show a longitudinal decline in self-reported N, but it also showed a longitudinal increase in spouse-rated N. There were no significant changes in either E or O. Similarly, a seven-year longitudinal study of peer ratings found a significant increase in C for women, but no other significant longitudinal effects for their sex for any of the five factors (Costa & McCrae, 1992b).

Because longitudinal studies are so rare and difficult, and because they seem to provide direct and unambiguous measures of change, it is tempting to interpret significant longitudinal effects as proof of age changes, when, of course, many other explanations are inevitably possible. Replication is as important in longitudinal research as in any other scientific endeavor. The most consistent longitudinal change we have found in adults over age 30 is a decline in activity level, seen in analyses of the NEO-PI (Costa & McCrae, 1988), the Guilford-Zimmerman Temperament Survey, or GZTS (Douglas & Arenberg, 1978), and observer ratings of energy level (Field & Millsap, 1991). Note that this variable is closely tied to the physical condition of the individual, and thus falls on the borderline we draw between personality traits and other basic tendencies of the individual.

Stability of Individual Differences

In contrast to the many null or nearly null findings with regard to mean level changes, the results of studies of stability in individual differences are large and striking. Table 1 summarizes results of a number of studies, with scales from different instruments grouped by the factor they share. The table is incomplete because some instruments do not provide measures for each of the factors, and because some of the studies (notably Helson & Moane, 1987) did not report retest correlations for all scales. Over intervals ranging from 3 to 30 years, these correlations are invariably significant, and most of them are impressive in magnitude. The median correlation for each group of scales is about .65

All of the instruments in Table 1 are self-report questionnaires, but studies of observer ratings of personality yield very similar results. For example, the six-year retest correlations for spouse ratings on N, E, and O were .83, .77, and .80, respectively (Costa & McCrae, 1988). Seven-year retest correlations for the five factors in single peer ratings ranged from .63 to .81 (Costa & McCrae, 1992b). It is, of course, possible that these correlations represent a fixed image of the target in the rater's mind, just as stability in self-reports might be attributed to a crystallized self-concept (McCrae & Costa, 1982). But studies at the Institute for Human Development (Block, 1971; Field & Millsap, 1991; Haan, Millsap, & Hartka, 1986) have also shown stability in rated personality using different sets of raters at different time periods, a design that would be unaffected by such fixed images.

TABLE 1
Stability coefficients for Selected Personality Scales in Adult Samples

Factor/Scale	Source	Interval	r
Neuroticism			
NEO-PI N	Costa & McCrae, 1988[a]	6	.83
16PF Q4: Tense	Costa & McCrae, 1978[b]	10	.67
ACL Adapted Child	Helson & Moane, 1987[c]	16	.66
Neuroticism	Conley, 1985[d]	18	.46
GZTS Emotional Stability (low)	Costa & McCrae, 1992a[e]	24	.62
MMPI Factor	Finn, 1986[f]	30	.56
		Median:	.64
Extraversion			
NEO-PI E	Costa & McCrae, 1988	6	.82
16PF H: Adventurous	Costa & McCrae, 1978	10	.74
ACL Self-Confidence	Helson & Moane, 1987	16	.60
Social Extraversion	Conley, 1985	18	.57
GZTS Sociability	Costa & McCrae, 1992a	24	.68
MMPI Factor	Finn, 1986	30	.56
		Median:	.64
Openness			
NEO-PI O	Costa & McCrae, 1988	6	.83
16PF I: Tender-Minded	Costa & McCrae, 1978	10	.54
GZTS Thoughtfulness	Costa & McCrae, 1992a	24	.66
MMPI Intellectual Interests	Finn, 1986	30	.62
		Median:	.64
Agreeableness			
NEO-PI A	Costa & McCrae, 1988[g]	3	.63
Agreeableness	Conley, 1985	18	.46
GZTS Friendliness	Costa & McCrae, 1992a	24	.65
MMPI Cynicism (low)	Finn, 1986	30	.65
		Median:	.64
Conscientiousness			
NEO-PI C	Costa & McCrae, 1988	3	.79
16PF G: Conscientious	Costa & McCrae, 1978	10	.48
ACL Endurance	Helson & Moane, 1987	16	.67
Impulse Control	Conley, 1985	18	.46
GZTS Restraint	Costa & McCrae, 1992a	24	.64
		Median:	.67

Note: Interval is given in years; all retest correlations are significant at $p < .01$. [a]398 men and women initially aged 25 to 84. [b]424 men initially aged 25 to 82. [c]78 women initially aged 27. [d]189 women initially aged 18 to 35. [e]133 men initially aged 30 to 67. [f]78 women initially aged 43 to 53. [g]360 men and women initially aged 24 to 84. NEO-PI = NEO Personality Inventory, ACL = Adjective Check List, GZTS = Guilford–Zimmerman Temperament Survey, MMPI = Minnesota Multiphasic Personality Inventory.

Some writers have observed that with a median correlation of .65, Time 1 measures typically account for less than half the variance in Time 2 measures, and they have argued that this suggests as much change as stability (Rubin, 1981). Such an argument assumes that personality measurement is error-free, which is certainly not the case. Estimates of the stability of true scores can be obtained by disattenuating correlations for retest unreliability (e.g., Heise, 1969). When this procedure is followed, stability coefficients usually exceed .90 (Costa & McCrae, 1988, 1992b;

Costa, McCrae, & Arenberg, 1980), suggesting almost perfect stability in rank order. It would appear that, in this sense at least, personality really is set like plaster.

But anyone who has lived in an older house knows that plaster is not granite. With time, moisture, and the settling of the house, it begins to crack and crumble. Studies of personality that have followed individuals over long intervals have noted that stability coefficients also decay with time (Conley, 1984). Whether this is due to major changes in a few individuals—the plaster cracking—or to minor changes in many individuals— the plaster crumbling—is not yet clear. But it does seem to be a robust phenomenon. For example, in a small sample of men who were administered the GZTS on five occasions, the median retest correlation for the 10 scales declined from .77 over six-year intervals to .63 over 30 years. Correcting for unreliability and extrapolating over a 50-year interval from 30 to 80, the median projected retest stability for the 10 scales was .60 (Costa & McCrae, 1992b). It appears that about three fifths of the variance in true scores for personality traits is stable over the full adult life span.

PERSONALITY DEVELOPMENT IN THE 20s

Critics of the stability view of adulthood sometimes argue that the questionnaires and rating forms used to assess personality artificially inflate estimates of stability because the instruments are somehow designed to be insensitive to change (Shanan, 1991). These arguments seem to confuse short-term reliability, which is a requirement of personality trait measures, with long-term stability, which most certainly is not. To our knowledge, no one has ever selected items for a personality test on the basis of longterm stability. Items in personality inventories occasionally rely on unchanging facts of personal history—for example, "As a child I rarely enjoyed games of make-believe"—but stability has been amply documented using measures that contain few or no such items. There is no reason why a respondent should not strongly agree with the item "I am easily frightened" on one occasion, and strongly disagree on another.

But the most compelling evidence that personality scales are not insensitive to change is the fact that they can and do show changes under conditions when changes actually occur. Strauss and Pasupathi (1992), for example, showed dramatic changes in rated personality of individuals with progressive neuropsychiatric disorders. And changes in self-reports are also found, if the respondents are young enough.

In a recent cross-sectional analysis, we compared NEO-PI-R scores for three age groups: college students aged 17 to 20 at two different universities; and employees of a large national organization divided into two age groups, 21 to 29 and 30 to 64 (Costa & McCrae, in press). The total sample was nearly 2,000. Analysis of variance within gender groups revealed a large number of significant differences. Both male and female college students scored significantly ($p < .01$) higher than adults on Anxiety, Angry Hostility, Depression, Self-Consciousness, Impulsiveness, Vulnerability, Gregariousness, Excitement Seeking, and Openness to Fantasy. They scored significantly lower on Trust, Straightforwardness, Compliance, Competence,Order, Dutifulness, Achievement Striving, and Self-Discipline. Whengrouped by the factors to which these scales belong, a familiar pattern becomes apparent: Age is negatively associated with measures of N and E, and positively related to measures of A and C. College students thus show, in exaggerated form, the same kind of age differences previously reported for cross-sectional studies of older adults.

In this case, however, the results of longitudinal studies suggest that these are true age changes. Studies by Haan et al. (1986), Mortimer et al. (1982), Jessor (1983), and Helson and Moane (1987) suggest that between college age and middle adulthood there are changes in the direction of better psychological adjustment, decreased sociability, and increased social concern and responsibility. Both cross-sectional and longitudinal studies might be interpreted as showing an increase in maturity in the decade of the 20s.

Equally important is evidence that there are differential changes in this time period, reflected in lower retest correlations. Finn (1986) compared two cohorts—college students aged 17 to 25, and men aged 43 to 53—on 30-year retest stability for Minnesota Multiphasic Personality Inventory (MMPI) factor scales. The median stability coefficient was .53 for the older group, but only .38 for the younger. Helson and Moane (1987) showed higher stability coefficient on the California Psychological Inventory for the interval from age 27 to age 43 than for the much shorter interval from age 21 to age 27. Siegler et al. (1990) estimated that only half the variance in personality traits of college students was stable into middle adulthood.

Somewhere between age 21 and age 30 personality appears to take its final, fully developed form. It would be of great interest to have systematic longitudinal studies of individuals from each year between 17 and 30, but current data suggest that for most people full maturity is reached in the late 20s. Helson and Moane (1987, p. 179) reported that "age 27 seems to have been at or near a watershed" in personality development. James's observation has considerable empirical support.

STABILITY OF PERSONALITY AND CONTINUITY IN ADULT LIFE

All of these conclusions are based on observational studies of normal individuals. They tell us what normally happens to people, not what might happen with effective interventions. Even with this proviso, however, many people find the prospect of stability in personality to be depressing. Some years ago O. G. Brim was quoted as saying "when you focus on stability, you're looking at the dregs, the people who have gotten stuck. You want to look at how a person grows and changes, not at how a person stays the same" (Rubin, 1981, p. 24). An article in the popular press on our work ran under the headline, "Your personality—you're stuck with it" (Hale, 1981).

This pessimistic assessment of the facts stems to a considerable extent from confusion about what we mean by personality. Let us return to the model of the person in Figure 1 and reconsider it in the light of the evidence on stability. Our data speak to the stability of basic tendencies, specifically basic tendencies in personality traits. To the extent that basic tendencies affect other elements in this model, they too will tend to show stability. Thus, we should expect some degree of stability in the self-concept, and this is frequently found (e.g., Mortimer et al., 1982). We have argued (McCrae & Costa, 1990) that basic personality traits also influence the dynamic processes that organize the flow of behavior and experience, so our findings might in part explain the stability of ego level (McCrae & Costa, 1980) and of coping mechanisms (McCrae, 1989).

Stable personality traits affect characteristic adaptations, but so do external influences. The result is that behaviors, attitudes, skills, interests, roles, and relationships change over time, but in ways that are consistent with the individual's underlying personality. It is because they reflect enduring dispositions that these features are characteristic of the individual; it is because they change as new challenges, threats, and opportunities occur across the life span that they are called adaptations. Stability in personality thus gives rise to continuity in life (cf. Shanan, 1991).

To take but a single example, men and women who are open to experience are more likely to make midcareer shifts than those who are closed to experience (McCrae & Costa, 1985); think of such open people as Gauguin and Whitman and William James himself, who gave up psychology after publication of the *Principles* to devote his attention to philosophy (Haynie, 1984). Such a midlife change requires new habits and skills, and may have a profound impact on the individual's life history. But the change itself is characteristic, because the need for variety is part of what it means to be open to experience. And the new adaptations are also likely to be characteristic of the basic tendencies of the individual: James the philosopher was as penetrating a thinker and as graceful a writer as James the psychologist.

Twenty years ago personality psychologists had a very limited understanding of personality in adulthood. The emergence of the five-factor model of personality traits and the results of several longitudinal studies have illuminated this area dramatically. We now know that in many fundamental ways, adults remain the same over periods of many years and that their adaptation to life is profoundly shaped by their personality. People surely grow and change, but they do so on the foundation of enduring dispositions.

REFERENCES

Allport, G. (1955). *Becoming: Basic considerations for a psychology of personality.* New Haven, CT: Yale University Press.

Allport, G. W. (1961). *Pattern and growth in personality.* New York: Holt, Rinehart & Winston.

Bandura, A. (1977). *Social learning theory.* Englewood Cliffs, NJ: Prentice Hall.

Bandura, A. (1978). The self system in reciprocal determinism. *American Psychologist, 33,* 344–358.

Block, J. (1961). *The Q-sort method in personality assessment and psychiatric research.* Springfield, IL: Charles C Thomas.

Block, J. (1971). *Lives through time.* Berkeley, CA: Bancroft Books.

Block, J. H., & Block, J. (1980). The role of ego-control and ego-resiliency in the organization of behavior. In W. A. Collins (Ed.), *Development of cognition, affect, and social relations: The Minnesota symposium on child psychology* (Vol. 13, pp. 39–101). Hillsdale, NJ: Erlbaum.

Cattell, R. B., Eber, H. W., & Tatsuoka, M. M. (1970). *The handbook for the Sixteen Personality Factor Questionnaire.* Champaign, IL: Institute for Personality and Ability Testing.

Conley, J. J. (1984). The hierarchy of consistency: A review and model of longitudinal findings on adult individual differences in intelligence, personality, and self-opinion. *Personality and Individual Differences, 5,* 11–26.

Conley, J. J. (1985). Longitudinal stability of personality traits: A multitrait–multimethod–multioccasion analysis. *Journal of Personality and Social Psychology, 49,* 1266–1282.

Costa, P. T., Jr., & McCrae, R. R. (1978). Objective personality assessment. In M. Storandt, I. C. Siegler, & M. F. Elias (Eds.), *The clinical psychology of aging* (pp. 119–143). New York: Plenum Press.

Costa, P. T., Jr., & McCrae, R. R. (1988). Personality in adulthood: A six-year longitudinal study of self-reports and spouse ratings on the NEO Personality Inventory. *Journal of Personality and Social Psychology, 54,* 853–863.

Costa, P. T., Jr., & McCrae, R. R. (1992a). *Revised NEO Personality Inventory (NEO-PI-R) and NEO Five-Factor Inventory (NEO-FFI) professional manual.* Odessa, FL: Psychological Assessment Resources.

Costa, P. T., Jr., & McCrae, R. R. (1992b). Trait psychology comes of age. In T. B. Sonderegger (Ed.), *Nebraska symposium on motivation: Psychology and aging* (pp. 169–204). Lincoln: University of Nebraska Press.

Costa, P. T., Jr., & McCrae, R. R. (in press). Stability and change in personality from adolescence through adulthood. In C. F. Halverson, G. A. Kohnstamm, & R. P. Martin (Eds.), *The developing structure of temperament and personality from infancy to adulthood.* Hillsdale, NJ: Erlbaum.

Costa, P. T. Jr., McCrae, R. R., & Arenberg, D. (1980). Enduring dispositions in adult males. *Journal of Personality and Social Psychology, 38,* 793–800.

Costa, P. T., Jr., McCrae, R. R., & Dembroski, T. M. (1989). Agreeableness vs. antagonism: Explication of a potential risk factor for CHD. In A. Siegman & T. M. Dembroski (Eds.), *In search of coronary-prone behavior: Beyond Type A* (pp. 41–63). Hillsdale, NJ: Erlbaum.

Costa, P. T., Jr., Zonderman, A. B., & McCrae, R. R. (1991). Personality, defense, coping, and adaptation in older adulthood. In E. M. Cummings, A. L. Greene, & K. H. Karraker (Eds.), *Life-span developmental psychology; Perspectives on stress and coping* (pp. 277–293). Hillsdale, NJ: Erlbaum.

Digman, J. M. (1990). Personality structure: Emergence of the five-factor model. *Annual Review of Psychology, 41,* 417–440.

Douglas, K., & Arenberg, D. (1978). Age changes, cohort differences, and cultural change on the Guilford-Zimmerman Temperament Survey. *Journal of Gerontology, 33,* 737–747.

Eichorn, D. H., Clausen, J. A., Haan, N., Honzik, M. P., & Mussen, P. H. (Eds.). (1981). *Present and past in middle life.* San Diego, CA: Academic Press.

Epstein, S. (1973). The self-concept revisited: Or a theory of a theory. *American Psychologist, 28,* 404–416.

Erikson, E. H. (1950). *Childhood and society.* New York: Norton.

Field, D., & Millsap, R. E. (1991). Personality in advanced old age: Continuity or change? *Journal of Gerontology: Psychological Sciences, 46,* P299–P308.

Finn, S. E. (1986). Stability of personality self-ratings over 30 years: Evidence for an age/cohort interaction. *Journal of Personality and Social Psychology, 50,* 813–818.

Freud, S. (1962). *The ego and the id* (J. Riviere, Trans.). New York: Norton. (Original work published 1923)

Gould, R. L. (1978). *Transformations.* New York: Simon & Schuster.

Guilford, J. P. (1959). *Personality.* New York: McGraw-Hill.

Haan, N. (1977). *Coping and defending.* San Diego, CA: Academic Press.

Haan, N., Millsap, R., & Hartka, E. (1986). As time goes by: Change and stability in personality over fifty years. *Psychology and Aging, 1,* 220–232.

Hale, E. (1981, June 8). Your personality—you're stuck with it. *The Idaho Statesman.*

Haynie, N. A. (1984). James, William (1842–1910). In R. J. Corsini (Ed.), *Encyclopedia of psychology* (Vol. 2, p. 257). New York: Wiley.

Heatherton, T. F., & Polivy, J. (1991). Development and validation of a scale for measuring state self-esteem. *Journal of Personality and Social Psychology, 60,* 895–910.

Heise, D. R. (1969). Separating reliability and stability in test–retest correlation. *American Sociological Review, 34,* 93–101.

Helson, R., & Moane, G. (1987). Personality change in women from college to midlife. *Journal of Personality and Social Psychology, 53,* 176–186.

Horn, J. L., & Cattell, R. B. (1972). Age differences in fluid and crystallized intelligence. *Acta Psychologica, 26,* 103–129.

James, W. (1981). *The principles of psychology* (Vol. 1). Cambridge, MA: Harvard University Press. (Original work published 1890)

Jessor, R. (1983). The stability of change: Psychosocial development from adolescence to young adulthood. In D. Magnusson & V. L. Allen (Eds.), *Human development: An interactional perspective* (pp. 321–341). San Diego, CA: Academic Press.

John, O. P. (1990). The "Big Five" factor taxonomy: Dimensions of personality in the natural language and in questionnaires. In L. A. Pervin (Ed.), *Handbook of personality theory and research* (pp. 66–100). New York: Guilford Press.

Jung, C. G. (1933). *Modern man in search of a soul* (W. S. Dell & C. F. Baynes, Trans.). New York: World Book.

Kuhn, M. H., & McPartland, T. S. (1954). An empirical investigation of self-attitudes. *American Sociological Review, 19,* 68–76.

Lecky, P. (1945). *Self consistency: A theory of personality.* New York: Island Press.

Levinson, D. J., Darrow, C. N., Klein, E. B., Levinson, M. L., & McKee, B. (1978). *The seasons of a man's life.* New York: Knopf.

Loevinger, J. (1966). The meaning and measurement of ego development. *American Psychologist, 21,* 195–206.

Loevinger, J. (1993). Measurement of personality: True or false. *Psychological Inquiry, 4,* 1–16.

Loevinger, J., & Wessler, K. (1970). *Measuring ego development: I. Construction and use of a sentence completion test.* San Francisco: Jossey-Bass.

Markus, H., & Nurius, P. (1986). Possible selves. *American Psychologist, 41,* 945–969.

McAdams, D. P., & Ochberg, R. L. (Eds.). (1988). Psychobiography and life narratives [Special issue]. *Journal of Personality, 56*(1).

McCrae, R. R. (1989). Age differences and changes in the use of coping mechanisms. *Journal of Gerontology: Psychological Sciences, 44,* P161–P169.

McCrae, R. R. (Ed.). (1992). The Five-Factor Model: Issues and applications [Special issue]. *Journal of Personality, 60*(2).

McCrae, R. R., & Costa, P. T., Jr. (1980). Openness to experience and ego level in Loevinger's Sentence Completion Test: Dispositional contributions to developmental models of personality. *Journal of Personality and Social Psychology, 39,* 1179–1190.

McCrae, R. R., & Costa, P. T., Jr. (1982). Self-concept and the stability of personality: Cross-sectional comparisons of self-reports and ratings. *Journal of Personality and Social Psychology, 43,* 1282–1292.

McCrae, R. R., & Costa, P. T., Jr. (1985). Openness to experience. In R. Hogan & W. H. Jones (Eds.), *Perspectives in personality* (Vol. 1, pp. 146–172). Greenwich, CT: JAI Press.

McCrae, R. R., & Costa, P. T., Jr. (1988). Age, personality, and the spontaneous self-concept. *Journal of Gerontology: Social Sciences, 43,* S177–S185.

McCrae, R. R., & Costa, P. T., Jr. (1990). *Personality in adulthood.* New York: Guilford Press.

McFarland, C., Ross, M., & Giltrow, M. (1992). Biased recollections in older adults: The role of implicit theories of aging. *Journal of Personality and Social Psychology, 62,* 837–850.

Mortimer, J. T., Finch, M. D., & Kumka, D. (1982). Persistence and change in development: The multidimensional self-concept. In P. B. Baltes & O. G. Brim, Jr. (Eds.), *Life-span development and behavior* (Vol. 4, pp. 264–315). San Diego, CA: Academic Press.

Murray, H. A. (1938). *Explorations in personality.* New York: Oxford University Press.

Murray, H. A., & Kluckhohn, C. (1953). Outline of a conception of personality. In C. Kluckhohn & H. A. Murray (Eds.), *Personality in nature, society, and culture* (2nd ed., pp. 3–52). New York: Knopf.

Neugarten, B. L. (1977). Personality and aging. In J. E. Birren & K. W. Schaie (Eds.), *Handbook of the psychology of aging* (1st ed., pp. 626–649). New York: Van Nostrand Reinhold.

Rabin, A. I., Zucker, R. A., Emmons, R. A., & Frank, S. (Eds.). (1990). *Studying persons and lives.* New York: Springer-Verlag.

Reichard, S., Livson, F., & Peterson, P. G. (1962). *Aging and personality.* New York: Wiley.

Rogers, C. R. (1961). *On becoming a person: A therapist's view of psychotherapy.* Boston: Houghton Mifflin.

Rosenberg, M. (1979). *Conceiving the self.* New York: Basic Books.

Rubin, Z. (1981). Does personality really change after 20? *Psychology Today, 15,* 18–27.

Shanan, J. (1991). Who and how: Some unanswered questions in adult development. *Journal of Gerontology: Psychological Sciences, 46,* P309–P316.

Siegler, I. C., George, L. K., & Okun, M. A. (1979). Cross-sequential analysis of adult personality. *Developmental Psychology, 15,* 350–351.

Siegler, I. C., Zonderman, A. B., Barefoot, J. C., Williams, R. B., Jr., Costa, P. T., Jr., & McCrae, R. R. (1990). Predicting personality in adulthood from college MMPI scores: Implications for follow-up studies in psychosomatic medicine. *Psychosomatic Medicine, 52,* 644–652.

Skinner, B. F. (1974). *About behaviorism.* New York: Knopf.

Strauss, M. E., & Pasupathi, M. (1992, August). Personality assessment in neuropsychiatric disorders through informant reports. In R. R. McCrae (Chair), *Advances in the assessment of the five-factor model of personality.* Symposium conducted at the 100th Annual Convention of the American Psychological Association, Washington, DC.

Vaillant, G. E. (1977). *Adaptation to life*. Boston: Little, Brown.

Warren, H. C., & Carmichael, L. (1930). *Elements of human psychology* (rev. ed.). Boston: Houghton Mifflin.

3

PERSONALITY EVOKED: THE EVOLUTIONARY PSYCHOLOGY OF STABILITY AND CHANGE

DAVID M. BUSS

A long-standing dogma in this century's social sciences has been that the nature of humans is that they have no nature (except perhaps a few basic drives and a few domain-general learning mechanisms). Evidence has been accumulating over the past decade that this view is untenable empirically (Brown, 1991; Buss, 1991b). Conceptual analyses by scientists in artificial intelligence, psycholinguistics, cognitive psychology, and evolutionary psychology are showing why such a view is untenable theoretically, even in principle (Tooby & Cosmides, 1992). Humans could not possibly perform the numerous, complex, situationally contingent tasks they do routinely without considerable intricate and domain-dedicated psychological mechanisms. These mechanisms, coupled with the adaptive problems they were designed to solve, in the context of the social, cultural, ecological, and internal inputs that reliably activate them, provide a starting point for a description of personality stability and change.

In this chapter, I present an evolutionary psychological model of strategic individual differences that provides a cogent explanation for why some aspects of personality remain stable whereas others change over time. The core of the model contains two essential propositions. First, individuals recurrently confront different adaptive problems over time, determined in part by their own personalities and by the personalities of significant others in their social environment. Second, individuals differ in the behavioral strategies they use to solve species-typical adaptive problems. Personality thus remains stable because the evolved psychological mechanisms endure over time, because the adaptive problems that individuals confront often recur over time, and because people retain successful strategies for recurrent adaptive problems. On the other hand, personality changes when different adaptive problems are encountered over time, when unsuccessful problem-solving strategies are replaced, and when new solutions are added to the strategic repertoire.

I expand this model of strategic differences in the remainder of the chapter by exploring various psychological mechanisms, which in some cases appear to be sex linked, in terms of stability of individual differences. I stress the importance of distinguishing between *mechanisms* and *manifest* behavior in exploring personality stability and change. As an example of how such a model can be applied, I use the adaptive problem of mate retention, focusing specifically on the psychology of jealousy and on the individually different tactics people use to deal with mate retention. As an example of research that supports such a model, I present the results of a longitudinal study of 100 newly married couples and their adaptive problems over a period of four years.

PSYCHOLOGICAL MECHANISMS

Tooby and Cosmides (1990) articulated compelling arguments for why our basic psychological mechanisms are likely to be species-typical, that is, shared by most or all humans. Essentially, all complex mechanisms require dozens, hundreds, or even thousands of genes for their development. Sexual recombination, by shuffling genes with each new generation, makes it exceedingly unlikely that complex mechanisms could be maintained if genes coding for complex adaptations varied substantially among individuals. Natural selection and sexual recombination tend to impose relative uniformity in complex adaptive designs. This is readily apparent at the level of physiology and anatomy; all people have two eyes, a heart, a larynx, and a liver. Individuals can vary quantitatively in the strength of their heart or in the efficiency of their liver, but they do not vary in their possession of basic physiological mechanisms (except by unusual genetic or environmental accident). This suggests that individual differences, including heritable ones, are unlikely to represent differences in the presence or absence of complex adaptive mechanisms. Individual differences cannot be understood apart from human nature mechanisms, any more than differences in the turning radius and stopping ability of cars can be understood apart from the basic automotive mechanisms such as steering wheels and brakes.

Determinations regarding exactly which couplings are part of human nature must be based on empirical study. Possible candidates that have emerged over the past several decades as a result of such research include childhood fears of loud noises, darkness, snakes, spiders, and strangers; characteristic emotions such as anger, envy, passion, and love; characteristic facial expressions such as happiness and disgust; competition for limited resources; competition for desirable mates; specific mate preferences; classification of kin; love of kin; preferential altruism directed toward kin; play; deceit; concepts of property; enduring reciprocal alliances or friendships; enduring mateships; temporary sexual relationships; retaliation and revenge for perceived personal violations; sanctions for crimes against the group or its members; rites of passage; concepts of self; concepts of intentions, beliefs, and desires as part of a theory of mind; status differentiation; status striving; prestige criteria; psychological pain on loss of status or reputation; humor; gender terminology; division of labor by gender; sexual attraction; standards of sexual attractiveness; sexual jealousy; sexual modesty; tool making; tool use; tools for making tools; weapon making; weapon use; coalitions that use weapons for warfare; collective identities; cooking and fire use; and probably hundreds more (see Brown, 1991, for an extended list of possibilities).

Since the cognitive revolution, psychologists have become increasingly aware of the necessity for understanding decision-making rules and other information-processing devices that exist inside people's heads. Although psychologists have largely jettisoned behaviorism's unworkable black box anti-mentalism, many have retained (perhaps inadvertently) the behavioristic assumption of equipotentiality: They assume that cognitive mechanisms are general purpose and free of content-specialized procedures (Tooby & Cosmides, 1992).

Evolutionary psychology, in contrast to most traditional social science positions, views evolved psychological mechanisms as saturated with content, operating differently in response to different contextual inputs signaling adaptive problems. Just as the body contains a large number of specific and dedicated physiological mechanisms (taste buds, sweat glands, lungs, heart, kidneys, larynx, pituitary gland), so, according to evolutionary psychologists, must the mind contain a large number of specialized psychological mechanisms, each designed to solve a different adaptive problem. Because what constitutes a successful solution to adaptive problems differs across domains—criteria for successful food selection, for example, differ from criteria for successful mate selection—the requisite psychological solution mechanisms are likely to be special-purpose and domain-dedicated.

Individuals differ, however, and fundamental differences must be central to any comprehensive psychological theory. To move from the analysis of psychological mechanisms in human nature to the analysis of individual differences, it is useful to go through an intermediate step, and that is the analysis of sex differences, which may be regarded as one class of individual differences. Evolutionary psychology provides a unique metatheory for predicting when we should and should not expect sex differences. Men and women are expected to differ only in the limited domains in which they have faced recurrently different adaptive problems: (a) over human evolutionary history, (b) during their development, or (c) over different environments currently inhabited. In domains in which the sexes have faced, or currently confront, the same adaptive problems, no sex differences are expected.

Throughout history, men and women have faced many highly similar adaptive problems. Both sexes needed to maintain body temperature, so both sexes have sweat glands and shivering mechanisms. Repeated friction to certain areas of the skin was a "hostile force of nature" to both sexes in ancestral environments, so men and women have evolved callous-producing mechanisms. Both sexes needed to solve the adaptive problem of identifying a good cooperator for strategic confluence when seeking a long-term mate, and this may be one reason why both sexes value kindness in a partner so highly across all cultures whose partner preferences have been studied (Buss, 1989).

In several domains, however, the sexes have faced different adaptive problems. For 99% of human evolutionary history men faced the adaptive problem of hunting and women of gathering, possible selective reasons for men's greater upper body strength and spatial rotation ability and for women's greater spatial location memory ability (Silverman & Eals, 1992). Internal female fertilization and gestation created the adaptive problem of uncertainty of parenthood for men, but not for women. Cryptic ovulation created the adaptive problem for men of knowing when women were ovulating (Alexander & Noonan, 1979). The dual male mating strategy of seeking both short-term sexual partners and long-term marriage partners created the adaptive problem for women of having to discern whether particular men saw them as temporary sex partners or as potential spouses (Buss & Schmitt, 1993). Sex differences in mate preferences (Buss, 1989), sexual fantasies (Ellis & Symons, 1990), courting strategies (Buss, 1988a; Tooke & Camire, 1991), jealousy (Buss, Larsen, Westen, & Semmelroth, 1992), derogation of competitors (Buss & Dedden, 1990), and mate retention tactics (Buss, 1988b) correspond remarkably well to these sex-linked adaptive problems. Evolutionary psychology offers the promise of providing a coherent theory of strategic sexual differences as well as strategic sexual similarities.

STABLE INDIVIDUAL DIFFERENCES

The construction workers who are laboring on the building next door have thick callouses on their hands. My academic colleagues down the hall do not. These individual differences in callous thickness are highly stable over time. At one level of analysis, the variance can be traced solely to variance in the reliably recurring experiences of the two groups. At another level of analysis, the existence of the species-typical callous-producing mechanism is a central and necessary element in the causal explanation of observed individual differences. Just as men and women differ in the adaptive problems they confront, different individuals within each sex face different adaptive problems over time. Some manifest differences are the strategic products of species-typical mechanisms responding to recurrently different adaptive problems across individuals.

Recurrent adaptive problems can also be socially imposed. Consider the adaptive problems one confronts by being married to a highly agreeable mate versus one who is highly disagreeable. Disagreeable persons may impose on their spouses the recurrent adaptive problem of verbal and physical abuse (Buss, 1991a), and subject their spouses to the manipulation tactics of coercion (e.g., one mate demanded that the other mate do something) and the silent treatment (e.g., one mate did not respond to the other mate until that mate did it; Buss, 1992). Consider the basic trait of conscientiousness. In a four-year longitudinal study, we found evidence that persons scoring low on Conscientiousness impose on their spouses recurrent acts of infidelity, whereas those scoring higher on Conscientiousness remain more sexually faithful (Buss, 1991a). Thus, the personality characteristics of one's mate can create socially imposed adaptive problems that recur over time. Stable individual differences in manifest behavior such as jealousy may flow from the different recurrent problems to which people are subjected.

In these examples, the individual differences are environmental, at least in the variance sense. If my academic colleagues were to trade places with the construction workers, then the manifest individual differences would reverse. If the person married to the high Conscientious mate were to trade mates with the person married to the low Conscientious mate, then the manifest individual differences in experiencing jealousy presumably would also reverse.

Nonetheless, we cannot rule out the genotype–environmental correlation processes proposed by Plomin, DeFries, and Loehlin (1977) and Scarr and McCartney (1983). Some individuals, because of heritable skills, interests, or proclivities, may preferentially select academic work or construction work as occupations, or high Conscientious or low Conscientious persons as mates. These selections, in turn, may create repeated exposure to friction-free or infidelity-free versus friction-prevalent or infidelity-prevalent environments, which then differentially activate the relevant species-typical mechanisms.

There are five central points in my argument thus far: (a) stable manifest individual differences can be caused by differences in the recurrent adaptive problems to which different individuals are exposed; (b) the personality characteristics of others inhabiting one's social environment play a critical role in determining the adaptive problems to which one is exposed; (c) the complex species-typical mechanisms are necessary and central ingredients in the causal explanation of individual differences because without them the observed individual differences could not occur; (d) the manifest individual differences are strategic outcomes of recurrently different input into species-typical mechanisms; and (e) it is critical to distinguish stability and change at the level of manifest outcomes (e.g., actual callouses) from stability and change at the level of underlying mechanisms (e.g., callous-producing mechanisms).

There are undoubtedly many recurrent environmental individual differences of precisely this sort. Firstborn children probably face recurrently different adaptive problems compared with laterborn children. These problems apparently trigger in the firstborn a greater tendency toward identification with the status quo, the parents, and the established scientific theories, and in the later born a greater tendency toward rebellion and identification with revolutionary scientific theories (Sulloway, in press). Laterborn children apparently have less to gain by identifying with a niche that is already occupied by an older sibling. This suggests a species-typical mechanism that bifurcates conformist versus rebellious strategies depending on a nonheritable environmental feature, birth order, that signals or reliably predicts differential success of alternative strategies.

Individuals who grow up in environments in which resources are unpredictable, such as inner city ghettos, may adopt a more impulsive personality style because it would seem adaptively foolish to delay gratification. In contrast, those growing up in middle class suburbs in which resources and future prospects are more predictable may adopt a personality strategy involving greater delay of gratification. The resulting individual differences represent strategic solutions to the different adaptive problems encountered.

A third example involves having a long-term mate who recurrently imposes an adaptive problem on his or her spouse. Some mates, for example, may recurrently show signs of sexual infidelity. These signs may trigger or activate sexual jealousy mechanisms that in turn may lead to recurrent use of tactics of mate retention. The central point of all these examples is that recurrently different social or environmental input into species-typical mechanisms can produce stable, strategically patterned, individual differences.

Recurrently different input into species-typical psychological mechanisms, of course, may come from heritable individual differences, whatever their ultimate origin (i.e., whether they originated from selection for alternative genetically based strategies, frequency-dependent selection, genetic noise, pathogen-driven selection for genetic uniqueness, or assortative mating). Individuals with an ectomorphic body type, for example, confront different adaptive problems than those who are mesomorphic. Ectomorphs may risk being at the receiving end of greater aggression than their more muscular peers, an adaptive problem that typically must be solved by means other than physical aggression. Genetic differences, in other words, pose different adaptive problems for different individuals.

Heritable dimensions of individuals—such as differences in body type, keenness of vision, oratory skills, physical attractiveness, and spatial ability—provide important input into species-typical mechanisms. These individually different inputs tell the organism about the adaptive problem it is facing. The resulting product consists of strategic individual differences that are stable over time. The observed strategic differences are correlated with genetic variance, but cannot be understood apart from the central role played by our species-typical psychological mechanisms that were designed to receive input—both environmentally and heritably based—regarding the adaptive problems being confronted.

In addition to facing different adaptive problems, some individuals experience greater success at pursuing certain strategies rather than others:

> Selection operates through the achievement of adaptive goal states, and any feature of the world—either of the environment, *or of one's own individual characteristics* [italics added]—that influences the achievement of the relevant goal state may be assessed by an adaptively designed system. (Tooby & Cosmides, 1990, p. 59)

Individuals who are mesomorphic, for example, typically will experience far greater success at enacting an aggressive strategy than individuals who are ectomorphic. (Tooby & Cosmides, 1990, called this phenomenon "reactive heritability.")

Individual differences in physical attractiveness provide another example. There is evidence that physically attractive men are better able to successfully pursue a short-term mating strategy involving many sexual partners (Gangestad & Simpson, 1990). Physically attractive women are better able to pursue a long-term strategy of seeking and actually obtaining higher status, higher income marriage partners (Taylor & Glenn, 1976). Relative physical attractiveness functions as input into species-typical or sex-typical psychological mechanisms, which then canalize the strategic solutions of different individuals in different directions.

The personality characteristics represented by the Big Five (Surgency, Agreeableness, Conscientiousness, Emotional Stability, and Intellect-Openness) may partially represent individual differences in the resources individuals can draw on to solve adaptive problems. The individual scoring high on Surgency (bold, energetic, extraverted, ascendant) may be able to deploy socially dominant solutions such as condescension (Buss, 1991a). The person scoring high on Agreeableness (trusting, kind) may be successful at eliciting cooperation from others in solving adaptive problems. The person scoring high on Conscientiousness (reliable, orderly, disciplined) may solve adaptive problems through industry and sheer hard work. The person scoring high on Emotional Stability (calm, secure, relaxed) may rely on steadiness of nerves, inner resiliency, and the capacity to rally from setbacks to solve adaptive problems. The person scoring high on Intellect-Openness (perceptive, insightful) may be adept at deploying creative cognitive solutions to adaptive problems.

In sum, this framework proposes a key role for personality in creating and solving adaptive problems: (a) Personality characteristics can play a causal role in determining the adaptive problems to which one is exposed; (b) the personality characteristics of people inhabiting one's social environment can play a causal role in imposing particular problems; (c) personality characteristics influence the strategic solutions that people deploy to solve the adaptive problems that they confront.

I believe that the theoretical and empirical work subsumed by this general framework will have to be explored domain by domain, adaptive problem by adaptive problem (Tooby & Cosmides, 1992). A theory concerning the way that individuals who differ in physical attractiveness encounter different adaptive problems, and have different success with the enactment of some strategies, may tell us little about the strategic consequences of individual variation in body type, oratory skills, or spatial ability. Ultimately, of course, it will be useful to integrate domain-specific theories into a more general theory of strategic individual differences.

In this chapter, I provide one illustration of how this form of analysis might proceed. Focusing on the adaptive problem of mate retention, I specifically examine the psychology of jealousy and the individually different tactics people use to deal with this adaptive problem.

JEALOUSY

Jealousy is a cognitive–emotional–motivational complex that is activated by a threat to a valued relationship. It is considered sexual jealousy if the relevant relationship is a sexual one, but there are types of jealousy that do not involve sexual threat. Jealousy is often activated by cues to the apparent loss of key resources provided by a relationship, cues such as eye contact between one's partner and a rival, decreased sexual interest on the part of one's partner, and an increase in the partner's flirting with one's same-sex competitors. Jealousy channels attention, calls up relevant memories, and activates strategic cognitions. It may motivate actions designed to reduce or eliminate the threat and retain the valued relationship, thus retaining the valued resources the relationship provides.

Jealousy is neither a peripheral nor trivial emotion, for it is experienced in all known cultures (Daly, Wilson, & Weghorst, 1982). It has been implicated as a major mechanism driving the coercive constraint of women, including veiling, harems, clitoridectomy, infibulation, spousal battering, and even homicide (Daly & Wilson, 1988). Empirical studies, using global indexes, that focus on which sex is more jealous (e.g., "To what degree do you consider yourself to be a jealous person?") typically show no sex differences (Salovey, 1991; White & Mullen, 1989). Both men and women experience jealousy under certain conditions, typically those involving a threat to a valued relationship by an intrasexual rival. But are the sexes really the same in their experience of jealousy? Are the events that trigger jealousy given the same weight by men and women? What adaptive problems might this powerful emotion have evolved to solve?

Because both men and women over evolutionary history have been damaged by relationship loss, both sexes have faced adaptive problems to which jealousy may have evolved as one solution. Several evolutionary psychologists have predicted that the sexes will differ in the weight given to events that activate jealousy (Daly et al., 1982; Symons, 1979). Because fertilization and gestation occur internally within women and not men, over evolutionary history men have faced an adaptive problem not shared by women, that is, paternity uncertainty. The reproductive threat to a man comes from the possibility of sexual infidelity by his partner.

In species such as ours, a woman's certainty in genetic parenthood would not have been compromised if her partner had sex with other women. Women, in this situation, however, may be at risk for the loss of their partner's time, attention, commitment, protection, investment, and resources. This would come as a double blow, because the loss would also be an intrasexual competitor's gain if these resources were diverted toward another woman and unrelated children. For all these reasons, evolutionary psychologists have predicted that the inputs that activate jealousy for men will be biased toward cues that relate to the sex act per se, whereas for women the inputs will be more biased toward cues to the loss of commitment and investment from a man.

Consider this question: What would upset or distress you more: (a) imagining your mate having sexual intercourse with someone else, or (b) imagining your mate forming a deep emotional attachment to someone else? In a series of studies, we found that the overwhelming majority (85%) of women to whom this dilemma was posed found emotional infidelity to be more distressing; the majority of men (60%) reported that sexual infidelity would be more distressing (Buss et al., 1992). These sex differences were also observed in physiological arousal in response to imagining the two different scenarios. In measures of heart rate, electrodermal activity, and electromyographically recorded frowning, men showed greater physiological arousal to imagined sexual infidelity than to emotional infidelity. Women, in contrast, tended to become more physiologically aroused by imagined emotional infidelity than to sexual infidelity (Buss et al., 1992). These results support the hypothesis that men's and women's psychological and physiological mechanisms are tailored to differences in adaptive problems.

We also found an important effect of ontogenetic experience. Among another college sample, the majority of men who had never been in a committed sexual relationship reported being more upset by imagining emotional infidelity in a partner. In contrast, the majority of men who had experienced a committed sexual relationship reported being more upset by imagining sexual infidelity in a partner. This experience had no effect on women's responses. If this cross-sectional result replicates using a longitudinal design, then what appears on the surface to be instability in men's responses will instead be more accurately described as the ontogenetic activation of a sex-typical evolved mechanism. This highlights again the crucial importance of distinguishing between mechanisms and manifest behavior in exploring personality stability and change.

ADAPTIVE PROBLEMS IN MARRIED COUPLES

I conducted a longitudinal study of 100 married couples, in part to identify which adaptive problems within a marriage recur and which change over time. Temporal stability coefficients for the adaptive problems reported to be experienced by a spouse, from Year 1 to Year 4 of marriage, ranged from low to high. Women's exposure to the problem of physical and verbal abuse, for example, showed a high degree of stability over time, with a coefficient of $+.73$ ($p < .001$). In contrast, the problem of sexual aggressiveness from the husband showed no stability over time in the individual-differences sense ($+.02$, ns). Most showed moderate stability, with coefficients between $+.30$ and $+.60$ (uncorrected for attenuation due to unreliability of measurement), suggesting some consistency but also some change over time. The consistency implies that individuals in married couples recurrently confront similar adaptive problems over time, problems that differ from those of individuals in different marriages.

Considerable change occurred for some adaptive problems. In particular, the problem of a spouse being neglecting-rejecting (perhaps signaling a withdrawal or diversion of investment) increased over time for the sample as a whole. For example, women reported substantial increases over time from Year 1 to Year 4 of marriage for the behaviors described by these statements: "He ignored my feelings; He did not tell me that he loved me; He failed to pay attention when I spoke to him; He failed to buy me a small gift once in a while; He did not spend enough money on me." This most likely reflects a diminution of effort devoted to the problems of mate attraction and bonding, and a redirection of effort toward alternative adaptive problems such as hierarchy negotiation, child rearing, and extra-pair mating (Buss, in press).

If sex differences in jealousy are strategically patterned, are individual differences within sex also strategically patterned? I restrict my attention to two forms of strategic individual differences: (a) Do some individuals predictably experience the adaptive problem of mate infidelity more than others by virtue of their own personality characteristics and the personality characteristics of their spouses? (b) Do different individuals deploy predictably different mate retention tactics, in part determined by their own personalities?

The Role of Personality in Creating Adaptive Problems

To examine the role of personality in the creation of adaptive problems, I conducted a longitudinal study of 100 married couples. During their newlywed year, I assessed five major factors of personality through parallel instruments from three data sources: self-report, spouse report, and independent interviewer reports. Four years later, subjects completed a battery of instruments that included one called "Sources of Irritation and Upset" that contained 150 previously nominated actions that a member of the opposite sex could do that might irritate, anger, annoy, or upset someone. Previous factor analyses of this instrument yielded 15 major sources of problems, including a cluster labeled "Infidelity." The Infidelity factor contained the following related complaints: "He/she saw someone else intimately; He/she had sex with another person; He/she was unfaithful to me; He/she went out with another person." I then correlated personality characteristics assessed during the newlywed year with reports of infidelity four years later.

Low Conscientious men and women, as predicted, tended to inflict this adaptive problem on their spouses more than men and women scoring higher in Conscientiousness. An unexpected finding was that women who scored high on Intellect-Openness tended to inflict infidelity on their spouses. Perhaps women who are open to experiences in general may be more open to sexual experiences outside of the marital context. These results suggest that the personality characteristics of significant others inhabiting one's social milieu, in this case one's mate or mates, play a key role in creating adaptive problems.

Are some people exposed to the problem of spousal infidelity because of their own personality? To answer this question, we correlated personality characteristics of persons with the degree to which they complained about spousal infidelity. Submissive men and women—those scoring low on Surgency—tended to complain that their spouses were unfaithful more than those scoring higher on Surgency. These findings are correlational, so obviously no firm conclusions can be drawn about causality. But they do suggest that submissive people may be more at risk of encountering the problem of spousal infidelity; and marrying a mate who scores low on Conscientiousness or marrying a woman who scores high on Openness may put one at risk of incurring this adaptive problem.

The Role of Personality in Solving Adaptive Problems

Previous research has identified 19 distinct tactics that people use to retain their mates, tactics ranging from vigilance (e.g., kept a close eye on mate at the party) to violence (e.g., hit a rival who was making moves on mate; Buss, 1988b). I assessed the use of these tactics in the same sample of couples at two time periods (newlywed year and fourth year of marriage) using two data sources (self-report and spouse report).

Men scoring high on Surgency tend to retain their wives by frequent acts of resource display: He spent a lot of money on her; he bought her an expensive gift; he took her out to a nice restaurant. Men scoring low on Surgency tend to use debasement as a mate retention tactic: He told her that he would change in order to please her; he became a "slave" to her; he gave in to her every wish. Men scoring high on Agreeableness tend to display love and care: He told her that he loved her; he went out of his way to be kind, nice, and caring; he was helpful when she really needed it. In contrast, men scoring low on Agreeableness tend to derogate their mate: He told other guys terrible things about her so that they wouldn't like her; he told other guys that she was not a nice person; he told other guys that she was stupid.

Men scoring low on Conscientiousness tend to threaten infidelity: He flirted with another woman in front of her; he went out with other women to make her jealous. Men scoring low on Emotional Stability tend to derogate competitors: He cut down the appearance of other males; he told her the other guy was stupid. Men scoring low on Intellect-Openness tend to threaten violence: He yelled at other guys who looked at her; he stared coldly at the other guy who was looking at her; he threatened to hit the guy who was making moves on her.

These findings are correlational, so I cannot draw conclusions about causality. They do suggest, however, that personality characteristics are linked with the alternative tactics that men use to solve the problem of mate retention. Personality traits, as traditionally assessed, are linked in coherent ways with the tactics people use to accomplish goals and solve adaptive problems. An essential part of personality, in other words, consists of the recurrent strategies people use to solve adaptive problems.

IMPLICATIONS FOR STABILITY AND CHANGE

This framework provides a coherent theoretical rationale for when we will observe personality stability and change (Block, 1981; McCrae & Costa, 1990) and, perhaps even more important, an answer to why some aspects of personality remain stable whereas others change. Stability is expected at several levels. First, many of our evolved species-typical mechanisms will remain stable over time, even if they remain unactivated. All humans, including cloistered academics, retain their callous-producing mechanisms, even if they rarely encounter the repeated skin friction necessary to activate these mechanisms. This is stability in the species-typical sense.

Second, stability in the individual-differences sense (see Block, 1971, for an extended analysis of different forms of stability), that is, stability in manifest individual differences, can be produced by stable environmental recurrences of exposure to adaptive problems. Just as differences in callous thickness between academics and construction workers are stable over time, so differences in experiencing hostility from others may be stable over time (Dodge & Coie, 1987). Differences in expressions of jealousy, to use another example, may be stable over time due to being married to a spouse who displays frequent cues to infidelity. Stable differences in the adaptive problems to which one is exposed, of course, may be created by properties of individual actors, either heritably or environmentally based. The recurrent barrage of sexual "come-ons" experienced by physically attractive women, for example, may be an adaptive problem that stems from heritable differences in physiognomy. The key point is that stability of manifest personality is determined in part by the recurrences in the adaptive problems to which individuals are exposed.

A third source of stability stems from the retention of successful or well-practiced problem solving strategies. Some strategies rely on the exploitation of certain personal qualities. Those with many material resources, for example, can retain their mates with lavish gifts that are inaccessible to those less financially endowed. Those lacking positive inducements of any kind may be forced to resort to self-abasing tactics, such as subordinating oneself to the goals of one's mate, or to cost-imposing tactics, such as threats and violence (Wilson & Daly, 1992). Well practiced strategies are generally more effective than less well practiced ones, and therefore some stability occurs through the retention of well practiced, effective strategies. This account is similar to the fascinating theory recently proposed by Caspi and Moffitt (in press) that suggests that individual differences manifest themselves most strongly in times of transition, in part because individuals deploy strategies to deal with those transitions that have worked for them in the past, can be enacted quickly, and require little energy, presumably because they have been well practiced.

This framework simultaneously provides a metatheoretical account of when and why we will observe change. First, change in underlying mechanisms may occur over ontogeny with species-typical shifts in adaptive problems. The most obvious example is puberty. Women develop enlarged breasts and their reproductive apparatus becomes functional in order to solve adaptive problems that were irrelevant during childhood. Predictable psychological shifts undoubtedly accompany these changes, such as increased interest in the opposite sex, a honing of one's mate preferences, increased attention to one's physical appearance, and the onset of vivid sexual and romantic fantasies.

Second, change can occur as a result of developmental shunting of individuals down one path versus another. Those growing up in households without fathers, for example, may be shunted into a more promiscuous short-term mating strategy, whereas those growing up with investing fathers may be shunted into a more monogamous long-term mating strategy (Belsky, Steinberg, & Draper, 1991). Presumably, individuals have psychological mechanisms that help to determine whether or not securing a long-term mate is likely, or whether or not the individual would do better to extract a variety of resources from different shorter term mates.

Third, change in manifest behavior can occur as result of change in the adaptive problems to which one is exposed. Just as shifting from a friction-prevalent occupation to a friction-free one causes change in one's manifest callouses, so a shift from a low Conscientious to a high Conscientious mate may cause a change in manifest jealousy. More transient shifts in the adaptive problems to which one is exposed may produce more transient shifts in manifest behavior.

The fourth source of change occurs when an old strategy for solving an adaptive problem is eliminated, or a new strategy is acquired or activated. Crying as a tactic for getting one's way becomes less effective as one moves from childhood to adulthood, prompting its diminution with development. Gaining a job promotion may permit the use of resource-bestowal as a strategy for attracting and retaining mates, a strategy that may previously have been inaccessible. New strategies are added and old strategies are jettisoned, in part based on changes in the assets one can exploit and on shifts in effectiveness with changing circumstances.

Thus, personality stability and personality change can both be understood within a single integrative conceptual framework. This framework provides a metatheoretical account of why and under what conditions we expect stability and change. Perhaps through this integrative framework for examining stability and change, we can start bridging the traditions that historically have isolated the study of individual differences from the study of human nature.

REFERENCES

Alexander, R. D., & Noonan, K. (1979). Concealment of ovulation, parental care, and human social evolution. In N. A. Chagnon & W. Irons (Eds.), *Evolutionary biology and human social behavior* (pp. 402–435). North Scituate, MA: Duxbury Press.

Belsky, J., Steinberg, L., & Draper, P. (1991). Childhood experience, interpersonal development, and reproductive strategy: An evolutionary theory of socialization. *Child Development, 62,* 647–670.

Block, J. (1971). *Lives through time.* Berkeley, CA: Bancroft Books.

Block, J. (1981). Some enduring and consequential structures of personality. In A. Rabin, J. Aronoff, A. Barclay, & R. Zucker (Eds.), *Further explorations in personality* (pp. 27–43). New York: Wiley.

Brown, D. E. (1991). *Human universals.* Philadelphia, PA: Temple University Press.

Buss, D. M. (1988a). The evolution of human intrasexual competition: Tactics of mate attraction. *Journal of Personality and Social Psychology, 54,* 616–628.

Buss, D. M. (1988b). From vigilance to violence: Mate retention tactics. *Ethology and Sociobiology, 9,* 291–317.

Buss, D. M. (1989). Sex differences in mate preferences: Evolutionary hypotheses tested in 37 cultures. *Behavioral and Brain Sciences, 12,* 1–49.

Buss, D. M. (1991a). Conflict in married couples: Personality predictors of anger and upset. *Journal of Personality, 59,* 663–688.

Buss, D. M. (1991b). Evolutionary personality psychology. *Annual Review of Psychology, 42,* 459–491.

Buss, D. M. (1992). Manipulation in close relationships: Five personality factors in interactional context. *Journal of Personality, 60,* 477–499.

Buss, D. M. (in press). *The evolution of desire.* New York: Basic Books.

Buss, D. M., & Dedden, L. A. (1990). Derogation of competitors. *Journal of Social and Personal Relationships, 7,* 395–422.

Buss, D. M., Larsen, R., Westen, D., & Semmelroth, J. (1992). Sex differences in jealousy: Evolution, physiology, and psychology. *Psychological Science, 3,* 251–255.

Buss, D. M., & Schmitt, D. (1993). Sexual strategies theory: The evolutionary psychology of human mating. *Psychological Review, 100,* 204–232.

Caspi, A., & Moffitt, T. E. (in press). Continuity amidst change: A paradoxical theory of personality coherence. *Psychological Inquiry.*

Daly, M., & Wilson, M. (1988). *Homicide.* Chicago: Aldine.

Daly, M., Wilson, M., & Weghorst, S. J. (1982). Male sexual jealousy. *Ethology and Sociobiology, 3,* 11–27.

Dodge, K. A., & Coie, J. D. (1987). Social information-processing factors in reactive and proactive aggression in children's peer groups. *Journal of Personality and Social Psychology, 53,* 1146–1158.

Ellis, B. J., & Symons, D. (1990). Sex differences in sexual fantasy: An evolutionary psychological approach. *Journal of Sex Research, 27,* 527–556.

Gangestad, S. W., & Simpson, J. A. (1990). Toward an evolutionary history of female sociosexual variation. *Journal of Personality, 58,* 69–96.

McCrae, R. R., & Costa, P. T., Jr. (1990). *Personality in adulthood.* New York: Guilford Press.

Plomin, R., DeFries, J. C., & Loehlin, J. (1977). Genotype–environment interaction and correlation in the analysis of human behavior. *Psychological Bulletin, 84,* 309–322.

Salovey, P. (Ed.). (1991). *The psychology of jealousy and envy.* New York: Guilford Press.

Scarr, S., & McCartney, K. (1983). How people make their own environment: A theory of genotype → environment effects. *Child Development, 54,* 424–435.

Silverman, I., & Eals, M. (1992). Sex differences in spatial abilities: Evolutionary theory and data. In J. Barkow, L. Cosmides, & J. Tooby (Eds.), *The adapted mind* (pp. 533–544). New York: Oxford University Press.

Sulloway, F. (in press). *Born to rebel.* Cambridge, MA: MIT Press.

Symons, D. (1979). *The Evolution of Human Sexuality.* New York: Oxford University Press.

Taylor, P. A., and Glenn, N. D. (1976). The utility of education and attractiveness for females' status attainment through marriage. *American Sociological Review, 41,* 484–498.

Tooby, J., and Cosmides, L. (1990). On the universality of human nature and the uniqueness of the individual: The role of genetics and adaptation. *Journal of Personality, 58,* 17–68.

Tooby, J., and Cosmides, L. (1992). Psychological foundations of culture. In J. Barkow, L. Cosmides, and J. Tooby (Eds.), *The Adapted Mind* (pp. 19–136). New York: Oxford University Press.

Tooke, W., and Camire, L. (1991). Patterns of deception in intersexual and intrasexual mating strategies. *Ethology and Sociobiology, 12,* 345–364.

White, G. L., & Mullen, P. E. (1989). *Jealousy: Theory, research, and clinical strategies.* New York: Guilford Press.

Wilson, M., & Daly, M. (1992). The man who mistook his wife for a chattel. In J. Barkow, L. Cosmides, & J. Tooby (Eds.), *The adapted mind* (pp. 289–322). New York: Oxford University Press.

4

.5 + or − .5: CONTINUITY AND CHANGE IN PERSONAL DISPOSITIONS

NATHAN BRODY

In this chapter I consider change and continuity in personal dispositions over the life span. The chapter is divided into three parts. In the first part, Levels of Analysis, change and continuity in intelligence and personality are analyzed in terms of changing relationships among three types of constructs: genotypes, phenotypes, and latent traits. I conclude that these constructs are more congruent for intelligence than for personality traits.

In the second part of the chapter, Constancy and Change in Dispositions, I examine changes in personality and intelligence over the life span. I review longitudinal studies as well as twin and adoption studies that indicate that genotypes contribute to stability and change in intelligence. I argue that phenotypes and genotypes for intelligence tend to become congruent over the life span. By contrast, the changing relationship between phenotypes and genotypes for personality traits over the life span are indeterminate.

In the final part of the chapter, Induced Change, I review the results of planned interventions with regard to both intelligence and personality, with an emphasis in the latter on Neuroticism. I argue that planned interventions lead to changes that are small relative to the influence of genotypes and to evidence for the relative stability of personal dispositions.

I do not provide a comprehensive analysis of these several areas of research. I do attempt to present a framework for a comparative analysis of personality traits and intelligence leading to the conclusion that research on intelligence permits greater quantitative precision in the analysis of continuity and change than does research on personality traits. Therefore, I use what is known about research on intelligence as a basis for considering continuity and change in personality traits.

Change in dispositions may occur spontaneously or as a result of planned intervention. The relative importance of unplanned change compared with that of planned change can be assessed by analyses of changes in a common metric (e.g., changes in standard deviation units). These changes, in turn, may be translated into a metric of percent of variance accounted for. Continuities, spontaneous changes, and planned changes in dispositions, as well as the influence of genotypes on dispositions, may all be analyzed in terms of a common metric of percent of variance accounted for.

LEVELS OF ANALYSIS

Personal dispositions may be defined at three different levels of analysis. First, there are phenotypic scores for various personal dispositions. A phenotypic measure is typically a score derived from an operationally defined measurement procedure. IQ scores are phenotypic measures of intelligence, and scores derived from trait ratings or self-reports are operationally defined phenotypes for personality traits. Second, a phenotypic score may be construed as an imperfect index of a hypothetical latent trait. A latent trait is assumed to have a true score value for a personal disposition. Individuals may be assumed to have a true value of intelligence that is imperfectly assessed by an IQ test score. So too, individuals may be assumed to have a true value of Extraversion that is only imperfectly assessed by a trait rating. Heteromethod aggregate scores for different methods of assessing a personal disposition permit a more accurate inference of the hypothetical value of a latent trait than inferences based on a single method of measurement. Latent traits for personal dispositions may be assumed to be influenced by genes. If this is correct, then each person has a biological genotype, defined at the moment of conception, that may be construed as the hypothetical genotypic level of a personal disposition. Because phenotypes and latent traits for personal dispositions are almost certainly not determined solely by genotypes, the hypothetical genotypic trait score is not identical to either the phenotypic score or the latent trait score.

Changes in intelligence may be understood by analyzing relationships among three variables. There is a phenotype for intelligence defined by an individual's score on a test of intelligence. Alternatively, a phenotypic measure of intelligence can be based on the derivation of the first principal component of a more or less representative battery of tests of intellectual ability. A latent trait of intelligence may be defined as a hypothetical construct corresponding to Spearman's theory of *g* (Spearman, 1904). *g* is a hypothetical construct because it refers to the common dimension that is present in all possible measures of intellectual ability, including measures that have not been discovered or examined. I assume that individuals differ in genotypes that influence intelligence. Phenotypic measures of intelligence are highly correlated with *g* (the latent trait for intelligence). Intellectual test items are positively correlated and form a positive manifold. Aggregated scores for performance on items that are similar such as vocabulary test items are positively correlated with items assessing a different intellectual ability such as spatial reasoning items. Because of the positive manifold among scores on intellectual tasks, aggregated performance across a diverse set of intellectual tasks will be highly correlated with aggregated performance scores on an independent set of tasks assessing intellectual abilities. This implies that all possible measures of *g* based on performance on an omnibus set of measures will be positively correlated. Empirical correlations for different omnibus measures usually exceed .8 (Jensen, 1980).

Heritability

Heritability estimates define the relationship between variations in phenotypes and genotypes for intelligence. Current estimates of the heritability of intelligence based on modeling estimates of relationships among various groups of individuals are close to .5 (Chipuer, Rovine, & Plomin, 1990; Loehlin, 1989). Heritability estimates are not characteristics of the trait but are population estimates. Therefore, a heritability of .5 is an estimate of the percentage of variance in phenotypes that is attributable to variations in genotypes in a given population. Heritability estimates may vary for different populations that have different genotypes and that encounter different environments. If the environments to which individuals are exposed change, heritability estimates may change.

Change in Heritability

In order to understand changes in intelligence over the life span, it is necessary to consider age-related changes in the heritability of intelligence. Several independent sources of data indicate that the heritability of intelligence is a monotonically increasing function of age (McGue, 1992). Longitudinal data from adoption and twin studies provide support for this assertion. Consider the results of the Texas Adoption Study. Adopted children were tested when they were between 3 and 14 years old and 10 years later. Correlations between adoptees and biologically unrelated siblings reared in the same family and between adopted children and their adopted parents declined from the initial assessment to a second assessment 10 years later. Correlations between the IQs of adoptees and their biological mother's IQ exhibited a slight and nonsignificant increase from the initial to the second assessment (Loehlin, Horn, & Willerman, 1989). These results are congruent with additional adoption data indicating that correlations between the IQs of postadolescent adoptees and their biologically unrelated siblings are near zero (see Brody, 1992, chap. 5 for a review of these studies). These data imply that the impact of the family environment on the development of IQ declines after early childhood. Quantitative analyses of the influence of genotypes on phenotypes for the Texas Adoption Study also indicate that changes in IQ from the first to the second assessment are influenced by genotypes not initially expressed at the first assessment. The heritability of IQ at the second assessment is higher than the heritability of IQ at the initial assessment.

Twin studies also provide evidence for increases in the heritability of IQ as a function of age. Wilson (1983, 1986) administered intelligence tests to twins in a longitudinal study. Correlations for monozygotic (MZ) twins increased from initial assessments at 3 months of age to the last assessment at age 15. MZ correlations tended to track changes in the reliability of IQ tests. Dizygotic (DZ) correlations were close to MZ correlations at initial assessments and tended to diverge as the twins grew older. The curves representing changes in MZ and DZ correlations as a function of age continue to diverge for data obtained for the first 15 years of life. McGue (1992) analyzed MZ and DZ correlations obtained in various studies as a function of the age of the samples studied. His analyses indicate that the increasing divergences between MZ and DZ correlations for IQ observed by Wilson for the first 15 years of life continue over the adult life span. MZ correlations tend to drift upward or to remain constant close to the reliability of test scores. DZ correlations continue to decline over the life span.

The Swedish Adoption/Twin Study of Aging provides information about the effects of adoption and twin status on intelligence for older adults (Pedersen, Plomin, Nesselroade, & McClearn, 1992). Correlations were obtained for measures of intelligence for a systematically selected sample of twins who were reared together or apart. The subjects had an average age of 59. The correlations were .80 and .78 for MZ twins reared together and apart, respectively. The correlations for DZ twins reared together and apart were .22 and .32, respectively. The degree of resemblance among MZ and DZ twin pairs was not related to estimates of their degree of separation or the differences in the social status of the homes in which they were reared. The heritability estimate for intelligence based on these data was .80. (See also Bouchard, Lykken, McGue, Segal, & Tellegen, 1990, for comparable data derived from the Minnesota Study of Twins Reared Apart.)

This brief review of data on the heritability of intelligence indicates that the genotype of intelligence is relatively congruent with the phenotype of intelligence. Because the phenotype of intelligence is congruent with the latent trait of intelligence, the genotype for intelligence and the latent trait for intelligence are relatively congruent.

Personality

It is possible to conceptually distinguish among phenotypes, latent traits, and genotypes of personality traits. In several respects, however, the empirical and theoretical relationships among these different variables for personality traits are not analogous to the relationships among these variables for intelligence. Phenotypes for personality traits are not based on aggregates of behavorial measures. Typically, they are obtained from self-report and peer ratings. If intelligence were assessed in the same manner as personality traits, we would ask individuals to rate their vocabulary. It is possible to factor analyze a set of behavioral measures in different situations in order to obtain a phenotypic measure of a personality trait that is analogous to a phenotypic measure of intelligence. Jackson and Paunonen (1985) reported the results of a factor analysis of measures of Conscientiousness that exemplifies this approach to the development of phenotypic measures of personality traits. In practice, this approach is not used because of the difficulty of collecting behavioral data in a variety of situations that are relevant to a personality trait. It is easy to construct behavioral measures of diverse intellectual skills that can be administered to individuals without elaborate equipment in a short period of time. It is difficult to obtain comparable personality measures.

It is difficult to ascertain the relationship between the phenotype of a personality trait (typically a self-report or peer rating measure) and the hypothetical latent trait that is being measured. We know that trait ratings do predict aggregate behavioral measures in the small number of studies in which efforts have been made to observe an individual's behavior extensively. For example, Small, Zeldin, and Savin-Williams (1983) obtained correlations between .59 and .83 for counselor ratings of prosocial behavior for children in their groups and aggregated frequency count measures for five different prosocial behaviors obtained from observing children for several weeks in a wilderness camping situation. Although there are isolated studies in the literature indicating that behavioral measures and trait ratings are related, and self-reports and peer ratings of personality traits are related

(r = approximately .5; see McCrae & Costa, 1990), it is not possible to ascertain the degree of relationship between trait ratings and the alleged behavioral manifestations of a trait. Therefore, the relationship between latent traits and phenotypes cannot be precisely determined.

Heritability

The relationship between phenotypes and genotypes appears to be different for personality traits than it is for intelligence. Current heritability estimates for personality traits based on self-report measures for adult samples are lower than those for intelligence. Loehlin (1992) summarized the available data for the Big Five personality traits: Extraversion, Agreeableness, Conscientiousness, Adjustment or Neuroticism, and Culture or Openness to Experience. Trait theorists assume that these five traits constitute an adequate taxonomy for the description of personality (Digman, 1990). Loehlin's analyses indicate that the heritability estimates range between .28 and .49, implying that from one fourth to one half of the variance of self-report measures of personality are attributable to variations in genotypes.

According to Loehlin's (1992) estimates, the heritability of personality phenotypes is lower than the heritability of intelligence for adult samples. It should be noted, however, that heritability estimates for personality traits are based on self-report indexes rather than on behavioral measures or heteromethod aggregates of different personality trait measures. Whether more adequate measures of traits based on aggregates of different kinds of measures of adult personality would yield higher or lower heritability estimates is unknown. Heath, Neale, Kessler, Eaves, and Kendler (1992) recently reported heritability estimates for Extraversion and Neuroticism measures based on aggregates of self-report and co-twin ratings for these traits. They obtained heritability estimates of .73 and .63 for Extraversion and Neuroticism, respectively. The results of this study suggest that the heritability of personality traits would increase if heteromethod aggregates were used as the phenotypic measures of personality.

Change in Heritability

Divergences between heritability estimates for personality and intelligence occur most dramatically in analyses of changes in heritability over the life span. There is evidence for increasing heritability for personality traits in early childhood, but there is little evidence for an increase in the heritability of personality over the adult life span. Both MZ and DZ twin correlations for self-report measures of personality tend to decline with age (McCartney, Harris, & Bernieri, 1990). Heritability estimates for personality traits remain relatively constant because MZ and DZ twin correlations do not exhibit increased divergence for older samples. The declining value of MZ correlations is compatible with the assumption that nonshared environmental influences are an increasingly important source of individual differences as individuals age. That is, experiences that serve to make individuals reared together different continue to occur and lead MZ twins to differ from one another as they grow older. A clear contrast between the results for heritability analyses for older adults for personality traits and intelligence may be observed in analyses of data from the Swedish Adoption/ Twin Study of Aging. Loehlin (1992, p. 91), for example, obtained median heritability estimates of .30 for several self-report measures of personality within this study. These estimates are marginally lower than those typically obtained from younger adult samples and are dramatically lower than estimates for the heritability of intelligence based on data collected from the same sample.

This analysis indicates that personality phenotypes, latent traits, and genotypes are not as congruent as the comparable relationships for intelligence. This lack of comparability may be a result of inadequate measurement procedures, or it may reflect something that is intrinsic to the nature of personality traits.

CONSTANCY AND CHANGE IN DISPOSITIONS

Intelligence

Intelligence changes dramatically over the life span. There are continuities between measures of information processing obtained in the first year of life and intelligence in early childhood (Bornstein, 1989). Longitudinal stabilities in intelligence represent relationships in the rank ordering of individuals at different periods on items that are based on measures that may be quite different if they derive from performance in early childhood or from performance at later ages.

Intelligence also declines with age. Schaie (1980) used longitudinal analyses of samples, adjusted for dropouts that tend to occur among individuals who exhibit intellectual declines over the life span, to demonstrate that fluid intelligence, a component of intelligence that is isomorphic with g (see Gustafsson, 1988), declines over the adult life span from age 25 to age 81 by approximately 1.52 SDs (Brody, 1992). The changes may be attributable to the influence of a biological aging process or to the cultural experiences associated with aging in the population. This probably underestimates the decline, because Schaie's analyses are based on middle class samples who are alert enough to maintain contact with psychologists. There is no doubt that the phenotype for intelligence is measured in different ways at different ages and that fluid intelligence and g decline over the life span.

Behavioral genetic analyses provide results that are germane to an understanding of genetic influences on change and continuity in intelligence. The evidence already reviewed for increasing heritability of intelligence over the life span implies that changes in the phenotype and latent trait in intelligence over the life span increase the relationship between phenotype and genotype. This analysis implies that genotypes continue to influence the way in which intelligence changes in individuals. Genetic influences on aging may influence changes in intelligence. In addition, genotypes may influence the way individuals respond to the diverse cultural opportunities that influence the development of intelligence over the life span. The net effect of these influences over the life span is to increase the heritability of phenotypes for intelligence. The data for older adults in the Swedish study may be taken as paradigmatic. Individuals with the same genotypes (MZ twins whether reared apart or together) end up with relatively similar phenotypes for intelligence, implying that they tend to change in tandem over the life span. DZ twins with similar but not identical genotypes tend to drift apart over the life span, implying that they do not change in performance in a comparable way. Thus, changes in intelligence over the life span continue to be influenced by genotypes.

Evidence for the process of genetic influences on changes in intelligence is observed in both the Louisville Twin Study and in the Texas Adoption Study. Wilson (1983) used data obtained in the Louisville Twin Study to demonstrate that change scores for intelligence were heritable. MZ twin correlations for change scores were higher than DZ twin correlations. Similarly, Loehlin et al., (1989) indicated that changes from an initial to a second assessment of intelligence in the Texas Adoption Study provided evidence that the changes that occurred were primarily attributable to the influence of genes not expressed at the time of the initial assessment.

Genetic influences also contribute to the underlying stability of the phenotype for intelligence. Data obtained in adoption studies may be used to estimate the contribution of genetic factors to stability in the phenotypes for intelligence. Correlations between biological parents and their adopted children are a function of three parameters: the narrow (additive) heritability of intelligence for the adoptee at a particular age, the narrow heritability of intelligence for the biological parent of the adoptee, and the continuity between the genotypes that influence intelligence at the ages of the adoptee and his or her biological parent. DeFries, Plomin, and LaBuda (1987; see also Phillips & Fulker, 1989) used data obtained in the Colorado Adoption Project to estimate the contribution of genotypic continuity to phenotypic continuity in intelligence. They estimated phenotypic correlations between intelligence measured at ages three and four and adult intelligence to be .4 and .5, respectively. The genetic contribution from childhood IQ to adult IQ was estimated as .18 and .28 for ages three and four, respectively. These analyses imply that approximately half of the phenotypic continuity in IQ between childhood and adulthood is attributable to the continuing influence of genes that affect both childhood and adult intelligence. The remaining influences are probably attributable to environmental influences or to differences in the genotypes that influence intelligence in children and adults.

This brief review of the behavioral genetics of change and continuity in intelligence suggests that genotypes contribute both to continuity and change in intelligence.

Personality

Continuity

Phenotypic measures of personality traits are relatively stable during the adult years (McCrae & Costa, 1990). Conley (1984) analyzed data for longitudinal studies of personality and intelligence and concluded that test–retest correlations for personality traits were only marginally lower than test–retest correlations for intelligence. The year-to-year error free stability of personality traits was .98. The comparable value for measures of intelligence was .99. If change occurs at a constant rate, these numbers when extrapolated imply that 40-year stabilities for personality traits would be approximately .45. Although personality traits may be relatively stable over the life span, these data tell us little about the stability of latent traits for personality.

Personality traits also exhibit continuities for measures obtained in childhood and during the young adult period. S. Caspi, Elder, and Bem (1987) found that ratings based on mothers' reports of temper tantrums were related to indexes of occupational status and occupational stability in a 20-year longitudinal study. Children who were rated as ill-tempered were most likely to be downwardly mobile and to be occupationally unstable. Similarly, Huesmann, Eron, Lefkowitz, and Walder (1984) obtained relationships between peer ratings of aggressive behavior in the third grade and indexes of adult criminal and antisocial behavior in a longitudinal study. They estimated that the hypothetical correlation for a latent trait of male aggressiveness in their 22-year longitudinal study was .50. Continuities of latent traits can also be studied by comparing time lagged heteromethod correlations with contemporaneous heteromethod correlations for comparable measures. Here are two studies that exemplify this approach. Funder, Block, and Block (1983) obtained two behavioral measures of delay of gratification in a sample of 4-year-old children. For male children, the correlation between a behavioral aggregate score and ratings of overcontrol was − .31. The time-lagged correlations between the behavioral aggregate and ratings obtained at ages 7 and 11 were − .47 and − .43, respectively.

Because the time-lagged correlations are not lower than the contemporaneous correlations, these data imply that the latent trait that accounts for the relationship between the behavioral measure and the ratings does not change between ages 4 and 11. A comparable analysis may be performed on data collected by Conley (1985) for the correlation between aggregate peer ratings of Neuroticism, Impulsivity, and Extraversion obtained for young adults and self-report measures of these traits obtained contemporaneously and 20 years later. The time-lagged heteromethod correlations were only marginally lower than the contemporaneous correlations. The relationships between time-lagged and contemporaneous correlations imply that approximately 60% to 80% of the true score variance on the latent traits remained invariant for the 20-year longitudinal study.

Genetics of Change

Studies of longitudinal stability and change for personality traits provide us with little information about the reasons for both stability and change in personality. Behavioral genetic analyses of change for personality traits, for the most part, provide relatively little evidence for genetic influences on stability or change in personality. Personality ratings for twins observed at different ages in the Louisville Twin Study indicate that change scores were heritable. The median correlation for change scores for several periods was .50 for MZ twins and .18 for DZ twins (Loehlin, 1992). These data suggest that changes in personality during early childhood are influenced by genotypes.

Analyses of personality ratings by adopted parents in the Texas Adoption Study also provide evidence for changes in personality that may lead phenotypes to resemble genotypes. The biological mothers of adoptees scored higher in Neuroticism than the adopted mothers of these children. At the initial assessment, personality ratings by adopted mothers of their adopted children indicated that the children were perceived as being comparable in Neuroticism to the natural children of adopted parents. At the second assessment, ten years later, adopted children had increases in Neuroticism relative to their biologically unrelated siblings who were the natural children of the adoptive parents. These data are compatible with the assertion that phenotypic changes in adopted children increased the relationship between their phenotype and their genotype (Loehlin, Willerman, & Horn, 1987).

Studies of personality changes in older adults provide little or no evidence for a continuation of this process. For example, Eaves and Eysenck (1976) obtained Neuroticism scale scores for twins in a longitudinal study. For the two-year period investigated, they found no evidence that changes in personality trait scores were heritable. MZ correlations for change scores were not higher than DZ correlations for change scores. These data imply that changes in Neuroticism were attributable to nonshared environmental influences.

After childhood, there is relatively little change in the relationship between genotypes and phenotypes for personality over the adult life span. We know little or nothing about the relationship between genotypes and latent traits for personality. Our ignorance of this relationship derives from the paucity of studies of the behavior genetics of adult personality using measures other than self-reports. There is some tentative evidence that changes in phenotypes for personality may be influenced by latent personality traits. A. Caspi and Moffitt (1991) argued that dispositional continuities in personality were enhanced by responses to novel, stressful, and unexpected events. They studied the responses of adolescent girls to the onset of early menarche. They found that girls who scored high in Neuroticism prior to the onset of menarche tended to increase in Neuroticism after the onset of early menarche. Girls who had not exhibited behavior problems prior to the onset of early menarche did not exhibit a dramatic increase in behavior problems. Thus, the onset of this novel and stressful event tended to exaggerate and increase preexistent phenotypic differences in personality traits. One might interpret these data by asserting that the changes that occurred increased the relationship between phenotypic characteristics and latent traits. Individuals changed by becoming more like themselves.

Block and Robins (in press) studied the relationship between changes in phenotypes and personality characteristics. They studied changes in self-esteem from ages 14 to 23 in a longitudinal study. These changes were then correlated with Q-sort ratings of the personalities of the subjects, made by psychologists who had interviewed them and administered a battery of tests to them when the subjects were 14. Changes in self-esteem among males were inversely related to Q-sort ratings that were indicative of Neuroticism. Self-esteem ratings declined in males who were rated as exhibiting Neurotic tendencies. Changes in self-esteem among females were correlated with a broader range of Q-sort characteristics that included items that appear to be reflective of traits of Agreeableness and Extraversion, as well as Neuroticism. Self-esteem ratings tended to decline in females whose Q-sort ratings indicated that they were Introverted, Neurotic, and Disagreeable. These data indicate that changes in an index of adjustment or personal satisfaction that may be construed as a marker for Neuroticism are predictable from trait ratings obtained prior to the occurrence of the changes. The changes also appear to increase the congruity between latent personality traits and phenotypic characteristics. The Block and Robins study appears to be an additional instance of change in personality that is analogous to the process postulated by A. Caspi and Moffitt (1991). Although the generality of this process remains to be ascertained in other studies, it is possible that these results are paradigmatic of many changes in personality phenotypes. In addition, if one assumes that latent dispositions and genotypic characteristics are related, it is possible that changes in personality phenotypes may be analogous to changes in intelligence. That is, the changes in personality phenotypes may increase their similarity to hypothetical latent traits and genotypes for personality traits. Although such a model of change appears to be required for intelligence, studies of the heritability of personality do not provide evidence for this process. The available data, based substantially on self-report measures of personality, contradict the model and support a model of changes in personality that either decreases the relationship between phenotypes and genotypes, or leaves the relationship constant over the adult life span. This implies that change in personality dispositions is attributable to nonshared environmental influences.

INDUCED CHANGE

Intelligence

Planned Intervention

The relationship between genotypes, latent traits, and phenotypes is contingent on the environment that individuals encounter. In principle, it is always possible to modify the relationship between phenotypes and genotypes by environmental interventions even for traits that are highly heritable. What is true in principle may or may not be true in practice. Attempts have been made to change phenotypes for intelligence for young children, for school-age children, and for aged adults. There is little or no evidence that these attempts result in substantial and enduring changes in phenotypic measures or in latent traits.

Several different attempts to increase intelligence for preschool-age children exhibit a common pattern, that is, early and moderately substantial changes that are not sustained. Royce, Darlington, and Murray (1983) summarized the results of longitudinal analyses of Headstart programs. These studies reported a median gain in IQ at the conclusion of the project of approximately 0.5 SD. These differences declined to 0.20 SD 3 years after the conclusion of the projects and reached zero for a final IQ assessment 7 to 10 years after the conclusion of the project. These data indicate that preschool interventions of one to two years have little or no enduring influence on phenotypes for intelligence.

More intensive preschool interventions also provide evidence for gains in intelligence that fade over time. The Abercederian Project provided intensive preschool interventions for a group of children believed to be likely to exhibit low scores on intelligence tests starting at three months of age. The university-based intervention continued throughout the preschool period. Compared with children who were randomly assigned to a control group, children in the experimental group had Stanford-Binet IQs that were approximately 1 SD higher at age 3. By age 8, the last age for which IQ scores have been reported, children in the experimental group had IQs that were 0.33 SD higher than children in the control group (Ramey, Lee, & Burchinal, 1990).

Garber (1988) reported results for a comparable project initiated in Milwaukee in which 20 children in an experimental group were exposed to intensive intellectual intervention beginning prior to six months of age and continuing up to age six. At various points during the repeated testing of experimental and control children in the project, the children in the experimental group had IQs that were 2.92 SDs higher than children in the control group. At age 14, the last age for which IQ scores were available, the experimental group had IQs that were 0.87 SDs higher than the control group. Although these differences are relatively large, there is some reason to believe that the effects are inflated. Children may have been taught material that is close to that actually presented on the test. The changes in intelligence might not be matched by comparable changes in the latent trait for intelligence because the $0.87 = SD$ difference was not sustained on measures of academic achievement. Normally, differences in IQ are related to differences in academic achievement. Whether or not the phenotypic differences obtained in the Milwaukee Study reflect true differences of the same magnitude in the latent trait for intelligence, there is no doubt that the dramatic gains decreased after the end of the intervention. There is no way of knowing if the declines in the effects of the intervention would or would not continue after age 14.

There have been several attempts to increase intelligence of individuals during their school years. Blagg (1991) reported the outcome of attempts to increase intelligence by use of the techniques advocated by the Israeli psychologist, Feuerstein (1979). The program was instituted in four secondary schools in England and involved an intervention with a mean duration of 112 hours. There were no significant effects on intelligence.

Kvashchev (Stankov, 1986) provided Romanian high school students with training in creative problem solving for three to four hours per week for three years. He reported gains in intelligence for these students one year after the conclusion of intervention of 5.66 points. The gains were slightly larger on measures of fluid ability, suggesting that the latent trait for intelligence may have increased as much as 0.5 SD 1 year after the end of the intervention. The enduring effects of the intervention are not known.

Attempts have been made to increase intelligence test performance in older adults. Baltes, Kliegl, and Dittmann-Kohli (1988) gave 10 hours of training in solving fluid intelligence problems to a sample of adults who varied in age between 63 and 87. The group given specific training had test scores that averaged 0.41 *SD* higher after training than before training on two tests that are considered good markers for fluid ability, the Ravens and the Cattell Culture Fair Test. A control group that retook these tests without intervention increased in performance 0.5 *SD*. These results suggest that there were no benefits of specific training in this study.

Schaie and Willis (1986) trained a sample of older adults, who exhibited declines in intellectual abilities during the previous 14 years, in either reasoning or spatial problems for 5 hours. These subjects exhibited gains of approximately 0.8 *SD* on the ability for which they were trained. The training effects were ability-specific. Gains on the ability for which training had not been included increased between 0.2 and 0.3 *SD*. Controls for the effects of retesting were not included and the enduring effects of the interventions are not known.

This brief review of attempts to increase intelligence by planned interventions suggests that there is little or no credible evidence that either the phenotype or the latent trait for intelligence is substantially changed by the interventions that have been used. The available data are compatible with the assertion that the upper bound estimate of the malleability or reaction range for the planned interventions that have been tested is approximately 0.5 *SD*. If we knew the enduring effect of the interventions that have been currently tested over the life span, my guess is that the effects would be less than 0.5 *SD* in magnitude. Although changes of this magnitude are not insignificant, they are small compared with both naturally occurring variations in intelligence and changes that are attributable to the influence of genotypes. In quantitative terms, $0.5 = SD$ effect accounts for approximately 6% of the naturally occurring variance in the phenotype, or approximately one eighth of a conservative estimate of the influence of genotypes on the phenotype.

Adoption

Adoption studies provide additional information about changes in intelligence that occur as a result of changes in the family environment. Analyses of adoption studies are complicated by evidence that indicates that the impact of family environment on intelligence declines with age. Perhaps the strongest evidence of possible effects of family rearing on intelligence is provided by Capron and Duyme's (1989) cross-fostering study in which French adoptees whose biological parents were either high or low in socioeconomic status were adopted by families whose socioeconomic status was either high or low. Adopted children whose biological parents differed in socioeconomic status differed in IQ by 15.6 points at age 14.

Children whose adoptive parents differed in socioeconomic status differed in IQ by 11.7 points. Children adopted by families with high social status had higher IQs than children adopted by families with low social status. Turkheimer (1991) reanalyzed these data using estimates of between-groups and within-group variability to present a regression analysis that could be used to estimate the effects of parental educational background on the IQ of adopted children. His reanalysis suggests that adoptee IQ increases by one point per year of adopted parent education and two points per year of biological parent education. The sample size is small ($N = 38$) and therefore these estimates have large standard errors. The effect sizes associated with adoption in this study should be contrasted with results obtained for adult samples in the Swedish and Minnesota studies of adults reared apart. These studies, which contain an adoption component and report data for adult samples, indicate that the effects of variation in the educational background of adopted families have a vanishingly small influence on the IQs of adult adoptees. There is considerable uncertainty surrounding estimates of the enduring effects of adoption on intelligence (Locurto, 1990). Studies providing evidence for increases in intelligence as a result of adoption are also influenced by restrictions in range of talent among adoptive families. Although adoptive families differ in education and social class background, most are middle class, and few families included in behavioral genetic studies are among the least privileged families in society. Estimates of the influence of adoption on intelligence are likely to vary as a function of the age of the adoptees and the variations in the social background of adoptive families. An estimate of 0.5 *SD* for the enduring influence of adoption on the intelligence of adoptees whose biological parents have low IQs or are low in social status who are adopted by parents who have high IQs and social privilege is probably close to the effects that are obtained in current studies.

There are cohort effects on intelligence (Flynn, 1987). Intelligence has increased by approximately 1 *SD* in many industrialized countries during the past 50 years. We do not know how to explain these changes. They may be attributable to nutritional influences or to educational changes that provide better schools for larger segments of modern societies (Lynn, 1990; Teasdale & Owen 1989). Apart from these secular changes that are not well understood, there is little evidence that phenotypes or latent traits for intelligence can be altered by planned interventions. The enduring effects of adoption are also relatively small.

Personality

Adoption studies are, at best, marginally relevant to a discussion of the effects of interventions on personality dispositions. Contemporary behavioral genetic analyses of personality imply that virtually all of the environmental influences on phenotypic measures of personality traits are nonshared ones that act to make children reared in the same family different from one another (Loehlin, 1992). Since between-family environmental influences are vanishingly small, adoption is not likely to have a profound influence on personality dispositions. This assertion is based on the assumption that children reared in the same family are not likely to develop similar personality dispositions as a result of the experiences they share. Although children reared in the same family undoubtedly share many environmental experiences, these shared experiences do not lead to the development of similar personality dispositions.

Planned Interventions

Therapeutic interventions designed to modify psychopathological states may be construed as attempts to modify personality traits, or, more generally, Neuroticism. It is difficult to obtain a quantitative estimate of changes in Neuroticism from an examination of therapy outcome research for several reasons. First, it is not clear that the goal of therapeutic interventions is to modify a latent Neurotic disposition. Second, outcome studies rarely provide information about the enduring influences of therapy. Few studies include follow-up data that extend beyond a six-month period. Many of the studies in the literature use small samples, fail to include placebo controls, deal with samples of solicited subjects rather than clinical populations who are likely to be higher in Neuroticism, and fail to include heteromethod assessments to provide an index of changes in latent traits. Meta-analyses provide one way of circumventing the limitations of individual studies. Meta-analyses of therapy outcome research often include studies with very different focuses and methodologies and may often involve aggregation of studies of differential relevance to changes in personal dispositions (Brody, 1983, 1990).

Current estimates of the effects of therapy relative to placebos based on meta-analyses obtain effect sizes close to .5 (Smith, Glass, & Miller, 1980). These outcomes should be compared with evidence of continuities in various psychopathologies. Consider, for example, the results of the NIMH Collaborative clinical trial of outcomes of various therapeutic interventions for depression against evidence for the enduring influence of depressive dispositions. Elkin et al. (1989) reported the results of a multisite clinical trial of the treatment of depression. Depressed patients were randomly assigned to either a psychotherapy treatment group, a behavior therapy treatment group, a drug therapy treatment group, or a managed care group that provided individual support and placebo drug treatment. The latter group was not a pure placebo treatment because it included minimal support services for depressed patients. Four different measures of outcome were used, two based on self-reports and two based on psychiatric ratings. Aggregated across measures and across groups, subjects assigned to the treatment groups were approximately 0.32 SD better than subjects assigned to the managed care groups. The effects of intervention in this study should be compared with evidence of the enduring effects of depression. Lewinsohn, Zeiss, and Duncan (1989) studied 2,046 individuals from community-based samples who scored high in depression. They obtained retrospective information about the probability of relapse in depression following the occurrence of a single episode of depression. The probability of having one or more depressive episodes following the onset of a single depressive episode was estimated to be .89.

Pathological Continuities

There are other studies demonstrating the enduring significance of psychopathological conditions. For example, Mannuzza et al. (1991) studied two samples of 18-year-old former patients who had been treated for hyperactivity by drugs or by behavorial interventions between ages 6 and 12. These subjects and control subjects who were selected from the community without regard to prior psychiatric diagnosis were evaluated by a psychologist. Forty percent of the proband group were diagnosed as having an attentional deficit disorder at age 18. The frequency of attentional disorder in the proband group was over 11 times higher than the frequency of this diagnosis for subjects in the control group. Fifty percent of the probands received a diagnosis from the third edition of the *Diagnostic and Statistical Manual of Mental Disorders* (DSM–III; American Psychiatric Association, 1980), compared with 16.5% of subjects in the control groups. These data indicate that individuals who receive a psychiatric diagnosis at one point in their life are at increased risk for receiving a comparable diagnosis several years after completion of treatment for the disorder. Although attentional deficit disorder may be construed as a neurologically influenced condition, the data for the Lewinsohn et al. (1989) study on relapse rates in depression suggest that other conditions not thought to be explicitly tied to neurological deficits may also exhibit comparable enduring influences on persons.

Neuroticism as assessed by self-report questionnaires is related to the occurrence of symptoms of psychological distress. Levenson, Aldwin, Bosse, and Spiro (1988) reported the results of a 10-year longitudinal study of a sample of 1,890 male subjects who were administered a brief version of the Eysenck Personality Questionnaire. Ten years later, 1,324 subjects remaining in the sample filled out the Hopkins Symptom Checklist. Neuroticism and Extraversion scores accounted for approximately 25% of the variance in indexes of psychological distress in this 10-year longitudinal study. Most of this influence was attributable to the effects of Neuroticism. We can use the results of this study to compare quantitative indexes of the enduring influence of Neuroticism on psychological distress. In order to make this comparison, it is necessary to make some assumptions that are highly speculative. The speculative account is useful in a general sense because it illustrates something about the relative magnitudes of effects of enduring dispositions and psychological interventions. Let us assume that therapeutic interventions do result in real treatment effects of approximately 0.5 SD. Translated to percent variance accounted for indexes, differences of this magnitude suggest that treatment accounts for approximately 6% to 7% of the variance in individual differences in outcomes. These effects may endure for several months after therapy. The enduring effects of such interventions over the life span are unknown. The Levenson et al. study suggests that Neuroticism accounts for approximately four times as much variance in a 10-year longitudinal study than the effects of treatments for psychological distress. Viewed against the magnitude of the enduring significance of Neuroticism in a person's life, effect sizes for planned interventions in Neuroticism appear small and of limited significance in changing the influence of Neuroticism over the life span.[1]

Breadth of Influence of Genotypes and Latent Traits

In analyzing the influence of Neuroticism on psychological distress, it is useful to consider the generality of treatment effects compared with the breadth of influence of Neuroticism and other kinds of psychopathological conditions. Many psychiatric conditions are comorbid, that is, they tend to co-occur (see Klerman, 1990). Indeed, comorbidity among DSM–III conditions may be more the rule than the exception.

Comorbidities may be attributable to the influence of genotypes. The genes that influence one disorder may be the same as the genes that influence a second disorder. Martin and Jardine (1986) studied relationships between Neuroticism and state-dependent measures of Anxiety and Depression in a large sample of Australian twins. MZ correlations among these measures were higher than DZ correlations. A genetic covariance analysis indicated that approximately 79% of the additive genetic influence on the three measures was common to all of them. These analyses support the hypothesis that the genetic influences that partially determine individual differences in Neuroticism scores are substantially the same as the genetic influences

---

[1]It should be noted that the changes that do occur as a result of therapeutic interventions may have clinical significance and lead, at least in the short run, to discernible reductions in an individual's level of distress. In this chapter I am not concerned with the clinical significance of psychological interventions but with the question of the magnitude of change that may be obtained by interventions relative to evidence for the continuity of dispositions and of the magnitude of the influence of genotypes on change and continuity in dispositions. It should be apparent that change, continuity, and the relative influence of interventions and genotypes are all, in principle, subject to analyses in terms of a common metric. Thus, statements about the magnitude of various interventions should not be construed as providing an evaluation of the costs and benefits associated with interventions.

that influence the probability of experiencing anxiety states and depressive states.

Studies of genetic influences among comorbidities of various psychological disorders show different results for different conditions, even for different conditions that are similar to each other. For example, Kendler, Neale, Kessler, Heath, and Eaves (1992) reported the results of a genetic covariance analysis of phobias for a large sample of female twins. Their analyses indicate that the genetic influences on animal phobias are those that tend to be shared with the genetic influences on other phobias. The genetic influences on agoraphobia, by contrast, are substantially specific to this type of phobia. The discussion of the relationship between genetic covariances and comorbidities of psychological distress is beyond the scope of this chapter (but see Cloninger, 1986). It is probably fair to say that there are genetic comorbidities for some psychological disorders. This implies that there are latent dispositions for some psychological disorders that are related to genotypes. These genotypically influenced latent dispositions are related to several different types of psychopathological phenotypes. Analyses of the effects of planned psychological interventions should not only compare the magnitude of changes with the evidence for continuities in dispositions but should also consider the breadth of influence of changes resulting from treatment compared with the breadth of influence of latent dispositions and genotypes that may affect several comorbid phenotypes.

CONCLUSION

Intelligence and personality traits are personal dispositions that have enduring influence on individuals' lives. Dispositions also change over the life span. Some of these changes are related to a person's dispositions at an earlier period of the person's life. That is, change itself is not invariably random and unpredictable. Moreover, some changes in personal dispositions may be heritable. Although dispositions may change over the life span, these changes appear to have an autonomous character that is not easily modified by our current methods of intervention.

REFERENCES

American Psychiatric Association. (1980). *Diagnostic and statistical manual of mental disorders* (3rd ed.). Washington, DC: Author.

Baltes, P. B., Kliegl, R., & Dittmann-Kohli, F. (1988). On the locus of training gains in research on the plasticity of fluid intelligence in old age. *Journal of Educational Psychology, 80,* 392–400.

Blagg, N. (1991). *Can we teach intelligence? A comprehensive evaluation of Feuerstein's instrumental enrichment program.* Hillsdale, NJ: Erlbaum.

Block, J., & Robins, R. W. (in press). A longitudinal study of consistency and change in self-esteem from early adolescence to early adulthood. *Child Development.*

Bornstein, M. H. (1989). Stability in early mental development: From attention and information processing in infancy to language and cognition in childhood. In M. H. Bornstein & N. A. Krasnegor (Eds.), *Stability and continuity in mental development* (pp. 145–170). Hillsdale, NJ: Erlbaum.

Bouchard, T. J., Jr., Lykken, D. T., McGue, M., Segal, N. L., & Tellegen, A. (1990). Sources of human psychological differences: The Minnesota Study of Twins Reared Apart. *Science, 250,* 223–228.

Brody, N. (1983). Where are the emperor's clothes? *Behavioral and Brain Sciences, 6,* 303–308.

Brody, N. (1990). Behavior theory versus placebo: Comment on Bowers and Clum's meta-analysis. *Psychological Bulletin, 107,* 106–107.

Brody, N. (1992). *Intelligence* (2nd ed.). San Diego, CA: Academic Press.

Capron, C., & Duyme, M. (1989). Assessment of effects of socio-economic status on IQ in a full cross-fostering study. *Nature, 340,* 552–554.

Caspi, A., & Moffitt, T. E. (1991). Individual differences are accentuated during periods of social change: The sample case of girls at puberty. *Journal of Personality and Social Psychology, 61,* 157–168.

Caspi, S., Elder, G. H., Jr., & Bem, D. J. (1987). Moving against the world: Life-course patterns of explosive children. *Developmental Psychology, 23,* 308–313.

Chipuer, H. M., Rovine, M. J., & Plomin, R. (1990). LISREL modeling: Genetic and environmental influences on IQ revisited. *Intelligence, 14,* 11–29.

Cloninger, C. R. (1986). A unified biosocial theory of anxiety and its role in the development of anxiety states. *Psychiatric Developments, 3,* 167–226.

Conley, J. J. (1984). The hierarchy of consistency: A review and model of longitudinal findings on adult individual differences in intelligence, personality, and self-opinion. *Personality and Individual Differences, 5,* 11–26.

Conley, J. J. (1985). Longitudinal stability of personality traits: A multitrait–multimethod–multioccasion analysis. *Journal of Personality and Social Psychology, 49,* 1266–1282.

DeFries, J. C., Plomin, R., & LaBuda, M. C. (1987). Genetic stability of cognitive development from childhood to adulthood. *Developmental Psychology, 23,* 4–12.

Digman, J. M. (1990). Personality structure: Emergence of the five-factor model. *Annual Review of Psychology, 41,* 417–440.

Eaves, L., & Eysenck, H. J. (1976). Genetic and environmental components of inconsistency and unrepeatability in twins' responses to a neuroticism questionnaire. *Behavior Genetics, 6,* 145–160.

Elkin, I., Shea, T., Watkins, J. T., Imber, S. D., Sotsky, S. M., Collins, J. F., Glass, D. R., Pilkonis, P. A., Leber, W. R., Docherty, J. P., Fiester, S. J., & Parloff, M. (1989). National Institute of Mental Health Treatment of Depression Collaborative Research Program. *Archives of General Psychiatry, 46,* 971–982.

Feuerstein, R. (1979). *The dynamic assessment of retarded performers: The learning potential assessment device. Theory, instruments, and techniques.* Baltimore, MD: University Park Press.

Flynn, J. R. (1987). Massive IQ gains in 14 nations: What IQ tests really measure. *Psychological Bulletin, 101,* 171–191.

Funder, D. C., Block, J. H., & Block, J. (1983). Delay of gratification: Some long-term correlates. *Journal of Personality and Social Psychology, 44,* 1198–1213.

Garber, H. L. (1988). *The Milwaukee Project: Preventing mental retardation in children at risk.* Washington, DC: American Association of Mental Retardation.

Gustafsson, J. E. (1988). Hierarchical models of individual differences. In R. J. Sternberg (Ed.), *Advances in the psychology of human intelligence* (Vol. 4, pp. 35–71). Hillsdale, NJ: Erlbaum.

Heath, A. C., Neale, M. C., Kessler, R. C., Eaves, L. J., & Kendler, K. S. (1992). Evidence for genetic influences on personality from self-reports and informant ratings. *Journal of Personality and Social Psychology, 63,* 85–96.

Huesmann, L. R., Eron, L. D., Lefkowitz, M. H., & Walder, L. O. (1984). Stability of aggression over time and generations. *Developmental Psychology, 20,* 1120–1134.

Jackson, D. N., & Paunonen, S. V. (1985). Construct validity and the predictability of behavior. (1985). *Journal of Personality and Social Psychology, 49,* 544–570.

Jensen, A. R. (1980). *Bias in mental testing.* New York: Basic Books.

Kendler, K. S., Neale, M. C., Kessler, R. C., Heath, A. C., & Eaves, L. J. (1992). The genetic epidemiology of phobias in women: The interrelationship of agorophobia, social phobia, situation phobia, and simple phobia. *Archives of General Psychiatry, 49,* 273–281.

Klerman, G. L. (1990). Approaches to the phenomena of comorbidity. In J. D. Maser & C. R. Cloninger (Eds.), *Comorbidity of mood and anxiety disorders* (pp. 13–37). Washington, DC: American Psychiatric Press.

Levenson, M. R., Aldwin, C. M., Bosse, R., & Spiro, A. III. (1988). Emotionality and mental health: Longitudinal findings from the Normative Aging Study. *Journal of Abnormal Psychology, 97,* 94–96.

Lewinsohn, P. M., Zeiss, A. M., & Duncan, E. M. (1989). Probability of relapse after recovery from an episode of depression. *Journal of Abnormal Psychology, 98,* 107–116.

Locurto, C. (1990). The malleability of IQ as judged from adoption studies. *Intelligence, 14,* 275–292.

Loehlin, J. C. (1989). Partitioning environmental and genetic contributions to behavioral development. *American Psychologist, 44,* 1285–1292.

Loehlin, J. C. (1992). *Genes and environment in personality development.* Newbury Park, CA: Sage.

Loehlin, J. C., Horn, J. M., & Willerman, L. (1989). Modeling IQ change: Evidence from the Texas Adoption Project. *Child Development, 60,* 993–1004.

Loehlin, J. C., Willerman, L., & Horn, J. M. (1987): Personality resemblance in adoptive families when the children are late-adolescent or adult. *Journal of Personality and Social Psychology, 53*, 961–969.

Lynn, R. (1990). The role of nutrition in secular changes in intelligence. *Personality and Individual Differences, 11*, 273–285.

Mannuzza, S., Klein, R. G., Bonagura, N., Malloy, P., Giampino, T. L., & Addalli, K. A. (1991). Hyperactive boys almost grown up. *Archives of General Psychiatry, 48*, 77–83.

Martin, N., & Jardine, R. (1986). Eysenck's contributions to behaviour genetics. In S. Modgil and C. Modgil (Eds.), *Hans Eysenck: Consensus and Controversy* (pp. 13–47). Philadelphia: Falmer.

McCartney, K., Harris, M. J., & Bernieri, F. (1990). Growing up and growing apart: A developmental meta-analysis of twin studies. *Psychological Bulletin, 107*, 226–237.

McCrae, R. R., & Costa, P. T., Jr. (1990). *Personality in adulthood.* New York: Guilford Press.

McGue, M. (1992, August). Behavioral genetics of cognitive ability: A life span perspective. In G. E. McLearn (Chair), *Nature/nurture: Cognitive abilities and disabilities.* Symposium conducted at the 100th Annual Convention of the American Psychological Association, Washington, DC.

Pederson, N. L., Plomin, R., Nesselroade, J. R., & McClearn, G. E. (1992). A quantitative genetic analysis of cognitive abilities during the second half of the life span. *Psychological Science, 3*, 346–353.

Phillips, K., & Fulker, D. W. (1989). Quantitative genetic analysis of longitudinal trends in adoption designs with application to IQ in the Colorado Adoption Project. *Behavior Genetics, 19*, 621–658.

Ramey, C. T., Lee, M. W., & Burchinal, M. R. (1990). Developmental plasticity and predictability: Consequences of ecological change. In M. H. Bornstein & N. A. Krasnegor (Eds.), *Stability and continuity in social development* (pp. 217–234). Hillsdale, NJ: Erlbaum.

Royce, J. M., Darlington, R. B., & Murray, H. W. (1983). Pooled analyses: Findings across studies. In Consortium for Longitudinal Studies (Ed.), *As the twig is bent . . . lasting effects of preschool programs* (pp. 411–459). Hillsdale, NJ: Erlbaum.

Schaie, K. W. (1980). Age changes in intelligence. In R. L. Sprott (Ed.), *Age, learning, ability, and intelligence* (pp. 88–111). New York: Van Nostrand Reinhold.

Schaie, K. W., & Willis, S. L. (1986). Can decline in adult intellectual function be reversed? *Developmental Psychology, 22*, 223–232.

Small, S. A., Zeldin, S., & Savin-Williams, R. C. (1983). In search of personality traits: A multimethod analysis of naturally occurring prosocial and dominance behavior. *Journal of Personality and Social Psychology, 51*, 1–16.

Smith, M. L., Glass, G. V., & Miller, T. I. (1980). *The benefits of psychotherapy.* Baltimore, MD: Johns Hopkins University Press.

Spearman, C. (1904). "General Intelligence" objectively determined and measured. *American Journal of Psychology, 15,* 201–293.

Stankov, L. (1986). Kvaschev's experiment: Can we boost intelligence? *Intelligence, 10,* 209–230.

Teasdale, T. W., & Owen, O. R. (1989). Continuing secular increases in intelligence and a stable prevalence of high intelligence levels. *Intelligence, 13,* 255–262.

Turkheimer, E. (1991). Individual and group differences in adoption studies of IQ. *Psychological Bulletin, 110,* 392–405.

Wilson, R. S. (1983). The Louisville Twin Study: Developmental synchronies in behavior. *Child Development, 54,* 298–316.

Wilson, R. S. (1986). Continuity and change in cognitive ability profile. *Behavior Genetics, 16,* 45–60.

II

THEORY AND MEASUREMENT

5

PERSONALITY CHANGE: METATHEORIES AND ALTERNATIVES

ROGER D. DAVIS and THEODORE MILLON

Change has emerged as a new focus for many adjacent sciences. In nonequilibrium physics, Gregoire Nicolis and nobelist Ilya Prigogine (1989) speak of a "new dialogue of man with nature," of new properties and "a new vision of matter, one no longer passive, as described in the mechanical view, but associated with spontaneous activity" (p. 3) and emergent complexity. In evolutionary theory, Eldrege and Gould (1972) have written about the sudden emergence of evolved forms after long periods of evolutionary stasis, called *punctuated equilibrium*. Indeed, the very vocabulary of science has changed, and is changing. Words like *chaos, fractals, bifurcations, dynamical systems, stochastic phenomena, irreversibility,* and *organization* are becoming more common. These constructs have demonstrated usefulness in such wide-ranging areas as weather prediction and population biology. In a world where specialization threatens to render the disciplines of science increasingly insular, the study of change is allowing researchers to transcend their preoccupations with horizontal refinements in order to see and seek out processes that integrate all the sciences. As noted by Nicolis and Prigogine, the dichotomy between the "hard" and "soft" sciences has narrowed considerably. Paradoxically, it is ubiquity of change, not constancy, that affords the widest vista on nature's phenomena.

Throughout its history, pyschology has often taken its cue from the neighboring sciences, especially physics. Such a paradigm shift, then, would seem quite exciting for psychologists. Though the generality of the constructs of the new science of change has yet to be demonstrated across all the sciences, such concepts often translate readily into the vocabulary of personality. With a little luck, perhaps the methods can be adapted as well. If these new developments in the adjacent sciences are any guide, then genuinely transformative personologic change, not merely quantitative change confined to a single variable, but molar-level change, change in the whole patterning of personality variables, would appear possible, at least in principle. At this crucial moment, it might be helpful to take two, maybe three, steps back and examine the fundamental assumptions that bias our conceptions of personality and personality change. In the first part of this chapter, we compare and contrast paradigms (T. S. Kuhn, 1970) or metatheories of personality and personality change. As we discuss, different assumptions entail starkly different methodologies and results. In the second part of the chapter, we look at a synthesis of these views, one consonant with the new science of change, and, we believe, quite promising.

THEORY AND TAXONOMY

First, some fundamental questions. What is personality? And what is change? Is change continuous, dimensional, an increment or decrement in the absolute quantity of some trait? Or, must traits be viewed configurally, so that each modifies the expression of the others, personality change being change in relative proportions of the traits? Can personality change discontinuously, categorically, as a qualitative change of personality type? Or, can change combine aspects of dimensionality and discontinuity, as in the idea of stages, a linear progression of qualitative changes? Beyond these questions lie issues concerning the sources of change. What are the bases of personality change? Is change propelled primarily by inner forces (nature) or outer context (nurture)? Are the necessary and sufficient conditions for personality change universal? What are the essential structures and processes underlying personality change? Is a unified science of personality change possible? Or must a science of personality change be content to rest on a seemingly limitless universe of minitheories?

One problem in answering these questions is that there are so many different ways of approaching personality. Psychologists lack a common vocabulary. The term *personality* is used so broadly that almost anything can be construed as personality, with the result that almost any kind of change can be construed as personality change. Paradoxically, it is a poverty of riches: Needs, motives, schemas, traits, attributions, goals, and other units ensure that personality phenomena can be conceptualized in a myriad of ways. In fact, these largely uncoordinated perspectives argue that the vocabulary of personality may be richer than its reality. Perhaps each represents something of the truth. But if so, each is but a partial truth, capable perhaps of internal explanatory consistency, but incapable of explanatory completeness, and therefore unsatisfying to all except the most dogmatically eclectic. But perhaps this is all that can be hoped for.

Metatheoretical chapters, of course, thrive on such breadth, inconsistency, and confusion. Accordingly, no definition of personality is offered. Nor does this chapter provide final answers to the above questions. That is not our goal. We do contend, however, that the answers given covary in some interesting ways and that these questions cannot be asked and answered independently or brought together randomly to form a coherent body of knowledge. Behaviorism and quantitative change hang together. Stage theories and qualitative change hang together. But the combination of behaviorism and qualitative change makes no sense at all. Why so? A chapter on psychological metatheory should try to answer this question. Pervin (1990), in his introduction to the *Handbook of Personality*, offered a short history of personality theory that briefly discusses many of the "perennial problems" of the field, including the idiographic–nomothetic issue, the external–internal issue, and the nature–nurture issue. Each is relevant to personality change, if only because it is impossible to give a complete treatment of change without consideration of each.

The crucial task here, however, is not merely to enumerate or list various metatheoretical problems or polarities, but to find out how the metatheoretical pie is sliced, so to speak, to discover the optimal metatheoretical schema, one that "carves nature at its joints" (Hempel, 1965). Of course, such an attempt carries with it a set of assumptions of its own, namely that such an edifice is discovered rather than constructed, that knowledge derives from an objective structure in nature knowable through some methodology, and that knowledge is not merely the product of social interaction, at least not the complete product. We must be aware of these assumptions, but we proceed as if the structure of metatheory can be known and theories classified. In so doing, what is desired is explanation, not just description. The philosopher of science Carl Hempel clearly distinguished between natural and artificial classifications. The difference, according to Hempel, is that natural classifications possess "systematic import." Hempel wrote the following:

> Distinctions between "natural" and "artificial" classifications may well be explicated as referring to the difference between classifications that are scientifically fruitful and those that are not: in a classification of the former kind, those characteristics of the elements which serve as criteria of membership in a given class are associated, universally or

with high probability, with more or less extensive clusters of other characteristics. . . . a classification of this sort should be viewed as somehow having objective existence in nature, as "carving nature at the joints." (pp. 146–147)

The biological sexes, male and female, and the periodic table of elements are both examples of classification schemes that can be viewed as possessing objective existence in nature. However, the items that we seek to classify in this chapter are not genders or chemical elements, but psychological theories and what they have to say about personality change. In doing so, we seek the ideal of a classification scheme or taxonomy that is natural, that is, one that inheres in the subject domain, not one imposed on it. Such a taxonomy exists apart from the vicissitudes of human purpose, and so asserts its necessity, not merely its instrumentality, its "the-ness" rather than its "a-ness."

How does one arrive at such a taxonomy? Many philosophers of science agree that the system of kinds undergirding any domain of inquiry must itself be answerable to the question that forms the very point of departure for the scientific enterprise: Why does nature take this particular form rather than some other? The goal of science is to explain the objects and events found in the world, and (to prefigure a philosopher who is introduced shortly) among the objects found in the world are classification systems for objects themselves. Thus, applied to a taxonomy, the question is rephrased: "Why this particular system of kinds rather than some other?" By this question, one cannot just accept any set of kinds or classes as given. Instead, a taxonomic scheme must be justified, and to be justified scientifically, it must be justified theoretically. Taxonomy and theory, then, are intimately linked. Quine (1977) made a parallel case:

One's sense of similarity or one's system of kinds develops and changes . . . as one matures. . . . And at length standards of similarity set in which are geared to theoretical science. The development is away from the immediate, subjective, animal sense of similarity to the remoter objectivity of a similarity determined by scientific hypotheses . . . and constructs. Things are similar in the later or theoretical sense to the degree that they are . . . revealed by science. (p. 171)

THE METAPHILOSOPHY OF STEPHEN C. PEPPER

What metatheoretical schema "carves nature at its joints"? One approach seems especially promising. In 1942, Stephen C. Pepper, in the culmination of a "consuming personal desire to know the truth" (p. vii), published World Hypotheses. According to the dust jacket of the 1970 edition, the purpose of his taxonomy was to provide no less than "a prolegomena to systematic philosophy and a complete survey of metaphysics" (quoted in Houts, 1991).

World Hypotheses

Pepper (1942, p. 1) began his book by noting that "among the variety of objects which we find in the world are hypotheses about the world itself." Such world hypotheses are different in kind from the hypotheses of the more restricted fields of knowledge that form the particular sciences, such as physics or biology. Such fields of inquiry are circumscribed by their content. A biologist may reject certain problematic issues as not biological in nature, that is, as not being within the explanatory domain of his or her science proper. For a world hypothesis, however, all facts are relevant, none can be dismissed. World hypotheses are, by definition, hypotheses about "the world itself," about the entire universe of "fact." They are theories of everything.

Root Metaphor Theory

Pepper (1942) desired to investigate world hypotheses as "objects existing in the world, to examine them empirically as a zoologist studies species of animals" (p. 2). Pepper contended that the voluminous metaphysical literature generated across the ages by philosophers and other thinkers derived from various combinations of seven or eight so-called "root metaphors," some adequate for cognitive purposes (e.g. mechanism), others inadequate (e.g., animism). This "root metaphor theory" formed the theoretical basis for his methodology:

> A man desiring to understand the world looks about for a clue to its comprehension. He pitches upon some area of commonsense fact and tries if he cannot understand other areas in terms of this one. This original area becomes then his basic analogy or root metaphor. (p. 91)

Thus, according to Pepper (1942), scientific activity has its origin in common sense. World theories do not step out of the vacuum fully formed. Unfortunately, however, common sense is rather unrefined for scientific purposes. Some means must be provided to bridge the two. Pepper noted two ways that knowledge may be refined, which he called multiplicative and structural corroboration:

> There are two types of corroboration and accordingly two types of critical evidence. There is corroboration of man with man, and corroboration of fact with fact. Let us call the first "multiplicative observation" and the second "structural corroboration." And let us call the products of multiplicative corroboration "data," and the products of structural corroboration "danda." (pp. 47–48)

> Whichever I do, my belief is clearly based on a cumulative corroboration of evidence. But the nature of the corroboration differs with the two methods employed. In the first . . . it consists in what may roughly be called a repetition of the same fact. I agree with myself in many repeated

observations, and my friends agree with me. . . . In the second, the corroboration comes from the agreement of many different facts in the determination of the nature of one central fact. (p. 49)

Pepper's modes of corroboration are analogous to reliability and validity, here expressed as reliability over occasions and over raters (multiplicative corroboration), and convergent validity (structural corroboration). Like any scientist, then, Pepper sought a theory, and from his theory generated a taxonomy of kinds by which to group the manifestations of the subject domain, for him the "unrestricted hypotheses" that purport to explain the world itself.

Pepper's Schema

The "Quineian" maturation (Quine, 1977) of Pepper's own sense of kinds evolved into a metatheoretical schema consisting of four world hypotheses: formism (realism), mechanism, contextualism, and organicism. Whether Pepper's system in fact "carves nature" is a question that must be left to the informed judgment of philosophers. Nevertheless, the schema does appear to possess considerable heuristic value. Interestingly, Pepper (1942) himself, writing years before Hempel, remarked that

there is a certain symmetry about the disposition of the relatively adequate world hypotheses which may itself possess a cognitive significance. Just as in the field of data the table of chemical elements exhibited an order long before the grounds for that order were established by further data and hypothesis, so possibly here in the field of danda. (p. 141)

Pepper's (1942) typology is based on two polarities: (a) kind of evidence considered, analytic–synthetic; and (b) kind of organization, dispersive–integrative. Understanding these polarities is fundamental to an appreciation of Pepper's model in its strongest (but admittedly dogmatic) reading. As with personological taxonomies, these polarities lend the model a holistic, cohesive structure that facilitates the comparison and contrast of groups along fundamental axes, thus sharpening the meanings of the constructs employed. This point cannot be stressed too much. Pepper described these polarities as follows:

These four hypotheses arrange themselves in two groups of two each. The first two are analytical world theories; the second two, synthetic. Not that the analytical theories do not recognize and interpret synthesis, and the synthetic theories analysis; but the basic facts or danda of the analytical theories are mainly in the nature of elements or factors, so that synthesis becomes a derivative and not a basic fact, while the basic facts or danda of the synthetic theories are complexes or contexts, so that analysis becomes derivative. There is thus a polarity between these two pairs of hypotheses.

There is also a polarity between the members of each pair, and the polarity is of the same sort in each pair. Formism and contextualism are dispersive theories, mechanism and organicism, integrative theories. So, analysis is treated dispersively by formism and integratively by mechanism, and synthesis is treated dispersively by contextualism and integratively by organicism. (p. 142)

Pepper also commented on the relative strength and weakness of the world theories:

[In the dispersive theories] facts are taken one by one from whatever source they come and so are left. The universe has for these theories the general effect of multitudes of facts rather loosely scattered about and not necessarily determining one another to any considerable degree. The cosmos for these theories is not in the end highly systematic— the very word "cosmos" is not exactly appropriate.

For the categories of mechanism and organicism . . . a concept of cosmic chance is inherently inconsistent and is veiled or explained away on every occasion that it threatens to emerge. If nothing better can be done with it, it is corraled in certain restricted areas of the world where the unpredictable is declared predictable, possibly in accordance with a *law* of probability. For these two theories the world appears literally as a cosmos where facts occur in a determinate order, and where, if enough were known, they could be predicted, or at least described, as being necessarily just what they are to the minutest detail.

From this parallelism another follows: that the type of inadequacy with which the dispersive theories are chiefly threatened is indeterminateness or lack of precision, whereas the type of inadequacy with which the integrative theories are chiefly threatened is lack of scope. (pp. 142–143)

The taxons or families of world hypotheses revealed by the root metaphor theory, then, were not merely found and left isolated, but were instead brought together or coordinated in order to form a coherent conceptual system. Rather than being just an aggregation of taxons, they form a true taxonomy. Elsewhere in his thesis Pepper (1942) was somewhat tentative about this undergirding schema, but he was also obviously intrigued. Undoubtedly, a deductive presentation would have made for the strongest exposition of his ideas, but would also have created a metaphilosophical dogmatism, the worth of which, as Pepper himself noted, could only be judged by the fully adequate world theory that we do not yet possess. Putting himself in the middle ground between skepticism and dogmatism, Pepper apparently desired something more than empirical regularity, but less than deductive necessity.

Pepper's work did not receive attention from psychologists until 1970, when Reese and Overton (1970) in a seminal paper borrowed his ideas as a means of "understanding the tensions produced by the shift from a learning-theory-based child psychology to a cognitive developmental one" (Morris, 1988, p. 290), that is, the shift from the mechanistic to the organismic metamodel. Interest in the role of paradigms or metamodels in developmental theory has since burgeoned, with the result that a considerable body of scholarship in this area is now available.

How is metaphilosophy relevant to personality change? One way has already been described. Pepper's (1942) schema gives us a nonarbitrary means of sectioning the metatheoretical space. Moreover, the world hypotheses described by Pepper need not be applied to personality theory merely by way of analogy. Instead, these theories can be projected onto any domain of cognitive scrutiny. In fact, that is their virtue. Paradigms provide a means of getting from nowhere to somewhere by prescribing certain relations between phenomena while proscribing supposed irrelevancies (Ford & Lerner, 1992). Although scholars may disagree about the comparative worth of paradigms, paradigms themselves are ubiquitous. After all, who knows what nature is, all paradigms aside? Indeed, modern philosophers of science are rediscovering the embeddedness of scientific explanation in metaphysical assumptions (e.g., Railton, 1989).

From a practical point of view, knowledge about paradigms or metatheories is heuristic because it provides a means of thinking outside of theory, whether to expose implicit assumptions or as a guide in theory construction. Paradigmatic knowledge is as essential for the architects of theory as it is for the critics of theory. Although we can never be free of assumptions, we can at least be aware of them. A metatheoretical schema informs our thinking by suggesting what would otherwise remain implicit. As for the embedded theories themselves, they are best viewed prototypically. A few approximate exemplars, but most are eclectic mongrels. Nevertheless, all embedded theories bear a family resemblance (Reese & Overton, 1970), and tend to function and dysfunction in characteristic ways. Below we describe Pepper's world theories in detail. The paradigms differ widely in their preferred units of analysis, the prescriptions and proscriptions they make concerning structure and process, their view of personality and of the nature of personality change, and the bases of change and constancy.

FOUR WORLD HYPOTHESES

Formism: The Analytical–Dispersive World Hypothesis

The root metaphor of formism is similarity (Pepper, 1942). Formism is associated with, among others, Plato, Aristotle, and the philosophical tradition known as realism. In psychology, formism is mainly associated with both traits and taxonomies, including psychiatric taxonomies (Lyddon, 1989). A taxonomy is essentially a system of kinds, and, by definition, everything within a kind is similar. Writing on "natural kinds," Quine (1977) noted that

> the notion of a kind and the notion of similarity or resemblance seem to be variants or adaptations of a single notion. Similarity is immediately definable in terms of kind; for, things are similar when they are two of a kind. (p. 157)

Although Pepper (1942) regarded formism as the weakest of the world hypotheses, he noted that no other world theory possesses as compelling a root metaphor. Quine (1977) referred to an "animal" sense of similarity, and observed that the ability to distinguish things similar and different in one's environment has been an important component of the evolutionary process. Even such basic behavioral notions as generalization and discrimination have their roots in similarity. In the first, two objects or conditions come to be seen as belonging to the same kind, whereas in the second they are eventually seen as different.

Categories of Formism

According to Pepper (1942) there are two sources of the formistic categories in common sense, and these produce two variants of the world theory, immanent and transcendent formism. Immanent formism is derived from the commonsense observation of similar things in the world. Its categories are (a) characters, (b) particulars, and (c) participation. Every object or particular has associated with it certain qualities or characters. Participation is simply a means of tying characters and particulars together: Qualities participate in their object. In the statement "A is yellow," an uncharacterized object "A" is characterized by the quality yellow through the verb "is." Transcendent formism can be derived from two ideas, the idea of living objects growing according to a plan (Aristotle), or the idea of an artisan working according to a plan (Plato). In either case, the form exists beyond or outside its instantiations. The categories of transcendent formism are (a) norms, (b) matter for the exemplification of the norms, (c) and a principle of exemplification that materializes the norms (Pepper, 1942).

Immanent and transcendent formism differ in the way the instances of a form or kind are realized in nature, that is, the characters or qualities of a form manifest differently depending on which kind of formism is embraced. In immanent formism, class membership implies "the immanent and full appearance of the characters concerned in any particular thing which has them" (Pepper, 1942, p. 164). In transcendent formism, however, the essence of the thing can be conceptualized, as in Platonic idealism, as existing apart from or outside the thing itself. Accordingly, transcendent formism holds that nature never expresses itself in a pure form. Although a thing may approximate the norm or plan, it rarely exemplifies the norm.

Examples of Formism

Both immanent and transcendent formism have found strong use in psychiatric taxonomy. Immanent formism represents the classical model of categorization used for the second edition of the *Diagnostic and Statistical Manual of Mental Disorders* (DSM–II; American Psychiatric Association, 1968). This model assumes that diagnostic categories possess discrete boundaries and that each category member possesses all the clinical attributes of the category (Frances & Widiger, 1986). Each psychiatric illness is expressed in its pure form. The move from the classical or monothetic model of *DSM–II* to the polythetic model of the third edition of the *Diagnostic and Statistical Manual of Mental Disorders* (DSM–III; American Psychiatric Association, 1980) can be looked at as a transition in category assumptions, from immanent to transcendent formism. In this model, nature never expresses itself in its pure form. Accordingly, no single diagnostic attribute is necessary or sufficient to diagnose a disorder. This open and permissive taxonomic structure of transcendent formism is consonant with the natural fuzziness of conceptual boundaries (Cantor & Genero, 1986; Wittgenstein, 1953). Unfortunately, formistic assumptions, deeply ingrained in language and thought, encourage researchers to conceptualize psychiatric illnesses as insidious, unitary disease entities, foreign essences that displace or corrupt the individual's healthy functioning, his or her true essence. This is especially troublesome for the personality disorders, which are not medical diseases or disease entities, but disorders of the entire person.

Personality and Personality Change

There is a connection between formism and trait psychology, best seen in the parallel relation of characters and object, and trait and person. Much as characters participate in objects, traits may be seen as qualities that participate in the individual. Moreover, some problematic characteristics of formism seem to have been played out in the history of trait psychology. Recall that formism is a dispersive theory. As such, its scope is adequate, but "facts are taken one by one from whatever source they come" (Pepper, 1942, p. 142), ultimately leaving them loosely scattered about. Historically, trait psychology has certainly had its difficulties in terms of being a multitude of traits loosely scattered about. The scope, in terms of the sheer number of traits, has been adequate, but precision has been lacking. Historically, trait psychology has been unable to clarify which traits are fundamental and which are derivative. Undoubtedly, the correlational nature of much of the research in trait psychology is primarily responsible. When two traits are moderately correlated, for example, the result is inherently ambiguous. Do the two traits correlate so highly that they are effectively the same trait? Or, are they two related, but distinct, traits?

Frustrated with this ambiguity or lack of precision, researchers have sought to derive the structure of trait terms through factor analysis, resulting in models such as the so-called five-factor or Big Five model. In this conception the horizontal cacophony of traits is replaced by a hierarchical organization in which broad, superordinate traits subsume numerous more specific traits at lower levels. Thus, unwilling to let the reality of any trait vanish under the collective weight of all traits, researchers rediscovered essentialism in the form of a trait hierarchy. Whatever reality any lower order trait possesses, it obtains by participation in this absolute hierarchy, by loading on the superordinate factors. True to the metatheory, however, "there is some disagreement about the precise nature of these domains" (Goldberg, 1993, p. 27). Goldberg, in an article on the historical development of the five-factor model, described the current state of the literature:

> At present, one could argue that there are two five-factor models. . . . Much is the same in both models: (a) The number of dimensions is identical, namely five; (b) the content of Factor IV is essentially the same, although it is oriented in the opposite direction in the two models and is thus so labeled (Emotional Stability vs. Neuroticism); and (c) there is considerable similarity, although not identity, in the content of Factor III (Conscientiousness). On the other hand, at least two of the differences between the models are quite striking: (a) The locations of Factors I and II are systematically rotated so that warmth is a facet of Extroversion in [one model], whereas it is a facet of Agreeableness in the [other] model; and (b) Factor V is conceived as Openness to Experience in [one] and as Intellect or Imagination in the [other]. (1993, p. 30)

The issue Goldberg was referring to can be expressed in a single question: "Will the real five-factor model please stand up?" Given the imprecision predicted by the metatheory, it is likely that if one model achieves preeminence, it will do so through a kind of Kuhnian process in which a particular group of researchers persuade their fellows rather than because it is an indubitable model of reality.

If by this point we are satisfied that formism has something interesting to say about personality, what does formism say about personality change? If personality taxonomy is conceptualized from the perspective of transcendent formism, then descriptive or manifest change would be represented as an increase or decrease in prototypicality, a change in the degree to which the particular essence is realized. Alternately, a more radical kind of change would be represented in change from one essence to another, discrete latent change. Such language as "one essence to another" admittedly borders on the absurd, but it is consistent with the paradigm and lays the discreteness of types out in the open. Another possibility is change in the way an underlying essence (latent type) or character (latent trait) is realized: manifest change, latent constancy. One might argue, for example, that being an antisocial (type) or being antisocial (trait) as a teenager entails a different constellation of behaviors than being an antisocial at age sixty. The taxon or trait is the same, but the attributes required to reliably infer the trait or taxon have changed. A more inventive solution is to extend the idea of latent personality types longitudinally. What were essential personality types now become latent pathways of manifest personality change; types become an artifact of cross-sectional research. Should these pathways be conceptualized as being more or less discrete, they might more aptly be called channels rather than pathways.

Criticism

Formism can be criticized in a variety of ways. Any world theory can. Most often such criticism occurs in terms of the categories of other world theories. Because each world hypothesis is presumably internally consistent, these arguments ultimately boil down to arguing that the world just is not the way this or that particular world theory supposes it to be. An organicist, for example, might argue that the dispersive universe of the formist, a cacophony of traits, is absurd. For the organicist, personality change is qualitative, occurring through the operation of a final cause. Thus, whereas the formist would consider change in an individual's standing on a single trait to represent genuine personality change, the organicist would argue that, because only qualitative change is real, such a conception risks trivializing the concept of change, that only integrative change is truly meaningful.

Organicism: The Synthetic–Integrative World Hypothesis

As a synthetic world theory, "no ordinary common-sense term offers a safe reference to the root metaphor" (Pepper, 1942, p. 280) of organicism. Pepper offered "organism" and "integration" as first approximations.

Categories of Organicism

Pepper (1942) further discussed seven categories of organicism. These categories work as a dialectical interplay between appearance and reality, always in the direction of increasing integration:

> These [categories] are (1) fragments of experience which appear with (2) *nexuses* or connections or implications, which spontaneously lead as a result of the aggravation of (3) *contradictions,* gaps, oppositions, or counteractions to resolution in (4) in *organic whole,* which is found to have been (5) *implicit* in the fragments, and to (6) *transcend* the previous contradictions by means of a coherent totality, which (7) *economizes,* saves, preserves all the original fragments of experience without any loss. (p. 283)

Or, translated into terms more easily recognized: (a) Observations of a subject domain lead the observer to (b) note relationships between various observations. These inchoate theoretical propositions automatically produce (c) aggravating and ostensibly irreconcilable inconsistencies that are resolved through (d) a complete unified theory. On investigation, the unified theory is (e) found to have been implicit in our observations all along; thus, it (f) transcends the initial, naive, inconsistencies among observations by reconceptualizing these observations in terms of a new coherent theoretical model, one that (g) integrates all the evidence according to these new terms. Thus, "a datum is a fragment with a nexus which leads to a contradiction that is resolved by an integration" (p. 303).

Undoubtedly, even this translation is a lot to digest. The key to organicism lies in the first approximation to its root metaphor, integration. Science can be considered a body of explicit theories. But our conceptualization of nature does not begin with science; it begins in common sense, which can be considered a body of implicit theories. As these implicit theories are formalized, they inevitably become enmeshed in contradictions. Eventually, a new theory is found that unifies disparate observations and theories. What was believed to be a contradiction is discovered not to have been a contradiction at all, but a by-product of previous misconceptions transcended in the new conceptualization. With each new integrative formulation, the very significance or meaning of the data is transformed, embedded in new theoretical terms. Thus, according to organicism, science moves inexorably toward greater approximations of reality. The limit of this series (Pepper, 1942) is truth itself, the integration into what physicists have called the theory of everything, what philosophers have called the absolute. In this ultimate transformation of naive commonsense observations, "logical necessity would become identified with ultimate fact" (p. 301). Nothing would remain unassimilated; everything would be harmonized with everything else.

In organicism, science cannot be merely a descriptive venture that consists of observing, categorizing, and cross-correlating various phenomena at their face value, but instead proceeds by establishing latent theoretical principles that unify the manifestations of a subject domain by explaining why these particular observations obtain rather than others. More than anything else, it is this question, "Why this rather than that?" that underlies the force toward integration in this worldview. In its most radical form, this argument holds that even if reliable observations of great positive predictive power could be made through some infallible methodology, these observations would stand simply as isolated facts unassimilated as scientific knowledge until unified through some theoretical basis. Predictive power alone does not make a science. Scientific explanations appeal to theoretical principles that operate below the level of superficialities, principles that are sufficient because they predict, necessary because they explain.

Facts that cannot be assimilated or accounted for, or facts that can only be accounted for in an arbitrary way, challenge organicism at its root metaphor, integration. The kind of inadequacy that threatens organicism, then, is inadequacy of scope (Pepper, 1942). Unassimilated facts the organicist constantly plays down, relying instead on the accumulated momentum and explanatory power of past integrations as a promissory note that someday, the ultimate integration, the absolute truth, will be achieved. As Pepper noted, being an integrative theory, organicism is "constantly tempted to throw facts out into the unreal" (p. 145).

Examples of Organicism

In psychology, organicism has been especially prominent in Piaget's cognitive development theory (Inhelder & Piaget, 1958). Whereas the exposition of the organicist categories given above in Pepper's example represents the phylogenetic expression of organicism, its course in the lifetime of a science, Piaget's theory may be considered as an ontogenetic expression of organicism, its course in the lifetime of a single individual. The epistemology is essentially the same. In both, the scientist and the individual are engaged in an "extended meaning-making enterprise" (D. Kuhn, 1992, p. 221) driven by a desire for greater coherence or theoretical unity, and against discrepancy between theory and reality. In both, these discrepancies are successively reduced through integrative theoretical transformations. In both, these transformations (stages) are putatively irreversible, bringing mind and reality into greater coordination and equilibrium. And in both, development is teleological, directed toward a final end point. For a science, this end point is knowledge of the absolute or the theory of everything; for the individual it is the achievement of formal operational thought.

Personality and Personality Change

Organicism emphasizes the organism over the context in which he or she exists. The person is construed as relatively active; the context as relatively passive and undifferentiated. Given the emphasis on integration, personality is best conceptualized personologically: The whole is more than the sum of its parts, and the parts find their meaning only in the context of the whole in which they are embedded (Reese & Overton, 1970).

Both organicism and personology share essentially the same unit of analysis, the whole organism or the whole person. Loosely speaking, if types are to space or populations what stages are to the individual or time, then many of the admonitions of personologists come into sharper focus. Accordingly, a variable-centered approach, aggregation over persons (Epstein, 1980), falsely abstracts the variable or part from the context that endows it with meaning, bringing the part into the foreground as if it possessed some legitimate existence in and of itself apart from its embodiment in the context of structures and functions that constitute personality. Such a dimensional approach is implicitly monotaxonic, approaching personality as if all persons come in only one kind. By this logic, an exclusively domain- or trait-focused program of study would then be meaningless unless controlled for type, because it is only in the context of the type that the trait finds its meaning, much in the same way that Axis I symptoms find their meaning in the context of the Axis II personality style. No single trait or behavior can be made to stand on its own.

This analysis allows us to diagnose an important tension in personality assessment, a tension between the formistic interpretation of a single inventory scale and the organicistic interpretation of the personality profile. For the formist, each trait may be interpreted singly. The meaning of any one trait is not transformed by an individual's standing on any other. For the organicist, however, the profile forms an integrated whole: The expression of any trait must be transformed by the individual's standing on every other. Thus, two psychologists, looking at the same personality inventory, form diverse impressions of the same individual, impressions embedded in their metatheoretical predilections.

Obviously, these metatheoretical assumptions have important consequences for the study of personality change when personality is operationalized through a personality inventory, or, more generally, through any set of multiple continuous variables. Should personality change be studied as change in an individual's standing on some isolated trait, or as change in the profile as a whole? From the perspective of the organicist, the formist risks trivializing personality change by fractionating the integrity of the personality structure, by limiting change to change on a single trait, and leaving these changes unintegrated. From the perspective of the formist, the organicist risks complicating the study of change beyond the capacity of human reason, by insisting that each trait first be considered in the context of every other before the true baseline or reference point is revealed. The organicist in turn may rebut that only two traits, not an inventory, are required to refute the formist. Should the standing on any one trait modify the expression of any other, then the formist's inadequacy of precision (Pepper, 1942) is exposed. The formist may in turn reply that such modifications are but intellectual abstractions, possessing no reality and impossible to model methodologically. And so on, ad nauseam. Such metatheoretical debates are infinite, but they embody real issues for the study of personality change.

Numerous personality theories are at least partially embedded in organicism, inheriting a kind of family resemblance. Freud's (1908/1953) psychosexual, Erikson's (1950, 1963, 1963) psychosocial, Kohlberg's (1986) moral, Bowlby's (1969) attachment, and Millon's (1969, 1981, Millon & Davis, in press) neuropsychological theories each represent theories of personality development. All propose that personality change is teleological, seeking some end point or end stage, the limit of the series. All propose that personality change occurs in stages, that is, that change is qualitative rather than dimensional. All propose that change takes place as a result of the resolution of some kind of conflict, be it overt conflict or discrepancy reduction. And finally, all the concerns or resolutions of previous stages are transformed by later ones. With regard to Erikson's theory, for example, Cantor and Zirkel (1990, p. 139) stated that "those general concerns which do endure through several life stages will take on new and different meaning as the particular features of life change across time."

Because organicism posits that change is in a forward direction only, irreversible and inexorable, personality change in these theories is almost synonymous with personality development. When it is not, personality change is pathological change. In other words, individual differences in organicism are longitudinal, not cross-sectional. These are differences of rate, not of kind. Because development is to a final end point, individual differences are trivialized. Novel outcomes are impossible, a principle that has been referred to as *predetermined epigenesis* (Gottlieb, 1983). Two salient terms in psychopathology reference pathological differences in personality development. Persons whose psychological development has been retarded as a result of developmental traumas or inadequacies are said to be *fixated*. The behavior of these individuals remains dominated by the concerns of earlier developmental epochs. Those who have matured psychologically, only to fall back into behavior dominated by the concerns of a prior developmental stage, are said to be *regressed*. And finally, one term in psychopathology gets directly at the root metaphor of organicism. Sometimes the entire personality structure crumbles utterly, for example, as a result of prolonged intense stress. Such individuals are said to be *decompensated*. The personality structure, to use Pepper's (1942) term, "fragments."

Criticisms

Organicism has been criticized in a number of ways. The fundamental question, as with any paradigm, is whether nature really works in the supposed way. Because only the whole is really "real," organicism tends to deny reality to parts or components. Thus, organicism prototypally denies true componential change, denies dimensional change. By the same reasoning, the idea of latent stages may not adequately address the complexity of organisms, representing a kind of reduction to the whole, rather than to the part, as in mechanism. Here again one sees the kind of inadequacy organicism is faced with—inadequacy of scope (Pepper, 1942). The question is not so much whether the complexity of personality can be adequately modeled by some stage theory or system of types, but whether it can be explained by it.

As a further point of critique, the precise nature of the latent stages in stage models of qualitative change are by no means clear. Stage theories derived from different domains or developed by different authors often do not coordinate with each other. Obviously these theories deal with different content domains, or with the same domain at different levels of abstraction, but the promise of organicism is, as we have seen, that of a single, underlying, integrative theory. Perhaps one of these theories is true. Or perhaps all are fragments to be transcended by some integrative theory that awaits discovery.

Mechanism: The Analytical–Integrative World Hypothesis

The "root metaphor" of mechanism is the machine (Pepper, 1942). The precise instantiation of this world hypothesis, however, depends on the type of machine that serves as metaphor, which often depends in turn on the state of human technology. The lever, wheel, pendulum, mechanical pump, and steam engine have all been historically useful in one way or another. The computer metaphor has been a recent favorite among cognitive psychologists. Regardless of type of machine in vogue, mechanistic theories have much in common.

Categories of Mechanism

Pepper (1942) illustrated six categories of mechanism through the lever as a simple machine. Three are discussed here. The first category is *location*. A lever "specifies and magnifies the push-and-pull efficacy of nature, or efficient casual structure" (p. 187). For the parts of a machine to work together, one must be able to specify the location of the parts in space. Should the location of the parts be indeterminate, then they will not be able to work together by exerting forces on one another. The second category consists of the *primary qualities*. These, however, are not really qualities at all, but quantities, those necessary to specify the efficient functioning of the machine. Thus, if a rock rests on the lever, only its weight and its distance from the fulcrum are important, both of which can be expressed as numerical quantities. The fact that it is a rock and not some other body is irrelevant. The mathematics necessary to describe the operation of an elbow and a crowbar are the same, though their compositions are radically different. Once the locations and quantities have been specified, all that remains is to formalize the interactions among the parts of the machine. The primary quantities can be related to each other by means of mathematical equations that express the operation of universal natural *laws*.

Mechanism is an inherently reductionistic world theory. Although a machine indeed functions as an integrative unit, as a machine, such integration does not lend the machine novel and unpredictable qualities. Scientific explanation becomes a search for the essential parts and the laws by which they function. The organism possesses no emergent qualities beyond those predicable to the efficient operation of the parts themselves. Deutsch (1951) summarized mechanism concisely:

> The classical concept or model of mechanism implied the notion of a whole which was completely equal to the sum of its parts; which could be run in reverse; and which would behave in exactly identical fashion no matter how often those parts were disassembled and put together again, and irrespective of the sequence in which the disassembling or re-assembling would take place. It implied consequently the notion that the parts were never significantly modified by each other, nor by their own past, and that each part once placed into its appropriate position with its appropriate momentum, would stay there and continue to fulfill its completely and uniquely determined function. (p. 234)

Personality Change

The reductionistic and deterministic qualities of mechanism have important implications for personality change. Although a machine functions as an integrative unit, integration in mechanism is epiphenomenal or derived. The whole is equal to the sum of its parts; the whole can be reduced to the parts without remainder. A reductionistic explanation is thus a complete explanation. In mechanism, personality is not really real at all, but merely an epiphenomenal whole whose workings can be explained by chains of stimulus–response bonds or the interaction of neuroanatomical structures and neurochemical pathways; thus, in mechanism, personality is a construct destined to be decomposed. This emphasis on elementary units is fundamentally incommensurable with the inherently holistic flavor of personality.

Summary and Future of Mechanism

Unlike the other world hypotheses, the verdict on mechanism would seem to be in. From Newton until the beginning of this century mechanism reigned as the world hypothesis of physics. But physics has since moved on, and mechanism, although yielding many discoveries (and even influencing religious thought, principally through deism), has fallen on rather hard times. As noted above, mechanism and organicism, as integrative theories, are constantly threatened by chance. There is here a faith, expressed most notably in Cronbach's (1957) presidential address to the American Psychological Association (Houts, 1991), that if one could only isolate all influences on the object of study, error variance would disappear completely. As noted in Houts (1991), this represents an epistemic conception of error, whereby error is regarded as a reflection of our ignorance of crucial independent variables, as opposed to an ontic conception, which holds that chance is a fundamental aspect of nature. Physics has moved in this direction. At a quantum level, mechanistic determinism breaks down in the face of quantum statistical laws and the uncertainty principle. Whereas "contextualism is constantly threatened with evidences for permanent structures in nature" (Pepper, 1942, pp. 234–235), mechanism has been deposed by the opposite. Mechanism, it would seem, has been consistently undermined by evidence that chance itself is fundamental to nature.

Moreover, modern physicists are discovering that chance is not limited to the realm of the very small. As noted by Deutsch (1951) earlier in this section, one of the cardinal features of mechanism is that operations must be reversible across time, or time-invariant. If the present is known, then the machine can be run backward or forward as desired to obtain a complete picture of the past or future. Nicolis and Prigogine (1989) cited numerous macrolevel instances of nonmechanistic and nonreversible change, including chaotic change and the indeterministic evolution of nonlinear dynamic systems. Accordingly, mechanism cannot exhaust past and future.

Contextualism: The Synthetic–Dispersive World Hypothesis

Contextualism is a synthetic theory, and, like organicism, its root metaphor is difficult to communicate. Context is inherently more allied with ground than figure. Consequently, explaining exactly what contextualism is involves a figure–ground reversal that risks making it into something determinate and circumscribed. Pepper (1942) adopted the historical event as a first approximation to the root metaphor of contextualism:

> By the historic event, however, the contextualist does not mean primarily a past event, one that is, so to speak, dead and has to be exhumed. He means the event alive in its present. What we ordinarily mean by history, he says, is an attempt to *re-present* events, to make them in some way alive again. The real historic event, the event in its actuality, is when it is going on now, the dynamic dramatic, active event. We may call it an "act," if we like, and if we take care of our use of the term. But it is not an act conceived as alone or cut off that we mean; it is an act in and with its setting, an act in its context. (p. 232)

Contextualism is rooted in the philosophy of Pierce, James, Dewey, and Mead, and, as might be imagined, is intimately related to pragmatism and instrumentalism.

Categories of Contextualism

Pepper is unusually opaque in presenting the specific categories of contextualism; therefore, no detailed exposition of these categories is given. Of interest here is Pepper's publication in 1966 of a revised or perfected form of contextualism called selectivism, in which intentional action replaces the historical event as the root metaphor of the current world theory. Apparently Pepper's own thinking on contextualism continued to evolve.

Rather than condense what is already opaque, we merely present some characteristics of the paradigm, without linking these with the specific categories.

Perhaps the foremost characteristic of contextualism is that absolutely nothing is necessary. Change itself is categorical (Morris, 1988), so radically so, in fact, that "in this theory nothing shall be construed as denying that anything may happen in the world" (Pepper, 1942). Pepper stated,

> disorder is a categorical feature of contextualism, and so radically so that it must not even exclude order. That is, the categories must be framed as not to exclude from the world any degree of order it may be found to have, nor to deny that this order may have come out of disorder and may return into disorder again—*order being defined in any way you please, so long as it does not deny the possibility of disorder or another order in nature also.* (p. 234)

Accordingly, "contextualism is constantly threatened with evidences for permanent structures in nature" (Pepper, 1942, pp. 234–235). Whereas organicism holds that nature is integrated and thus determinate and permanent in its structure, contextualism asks us to suspend such beliefs. After all, integration is only an assumption about the ultimate structure of nature. As such, what order that exists in the contextualist's world takes the form of local regularities or minitheories. Even these, however, are not a necessary feature of the universe; if the clock could be turned back, things might be different the second time around. Thus, there is no necessary reason or explanation that particular regularities should exist rather than others, for there are no necessary truths in contextualism. Pepper stated,

> contextualism is accordingly sometimes said to have a horizontal cosmology in contrast to other views, which have a vertical cosmology. There is no top nor [sic] bottom to the contextualistic world. In formism or mechanism or organicism one has only to analyze in certain specified ways and one is bound, so it is believed, to get to the bottom of things or to the top of things. Contextualism justifies no such faith. (p. 251)

Congruent with its emphasis on scope rather than precision, it would seem that sufficiency is the most a contextualistic science can hope to achieve. If this seems like a radical concept, it is because contextualism has its roots in intentional human action. "The basic assumption of the contextualist perspective is that human acts or 'events' are active, dynamic, and developmental moments of a continuously changing reality" (Jaeger & Rosnow, 1988, p. 65). Human action is embedded in the context of a world that is itself just as changing and variable: Both organism and context are active. Individuals actively construe reality according to their present purposes, and these purposes are embedded in an open matrix of ecological settings and changing concerns. Because humankind's relation with nature is instrumental, contextualism embraces partial theories rather than necessary truths, and actively encourages theoretical pluralism. Every acute idea contains some legitimacy (Jaeger & Rosnow, 1988). Each should inform others, but none represents ultimate knowledge. Accordingly, scientific activity in contextualism does not consist of attempts at theory falsification (Popper, 1972), as in the deterministic world hypotheses, but rather of efforts to determine the boundaries and conditions within which each partial theory applies (Jaeger & Rosnow, 1988). If more general theories are discovered in the process, all the better, but the promissory note of organicism, the ultimate integration of everything into a single unified theory, is rejected. All forms of investigation are necessary to scientific activity, but none is sufficient to exhaust the myriad and changing forms of nature. Nature is too fluid and complex to be captured in any single theory or proposition.

Personality Change

In the most radical versions of contextualism, only context is active. Here persons serve as mere passive vessels of environmental events. Presumably then, the patternedness of personality would be proportional to the patternedness of the environment, and contextual changes would inevitably be followed by commensurate personality changes. Morris (1988), for example, regarded contextualism, not mechanism, as the metatheory of operant behaviorism. Such radical definitions would appear to rely on other meanings of the word *context*, departing substantially from the classical instrumental notions of Pierce and James.

Less radical versions of contextualism, such as interactionism, emphasize a circularity of influence or organism–context relationships (e.g., Endler & Magnusson, 1976). The great trait debate (e.g. Epstein, 1980; Mishel, 1968) is a testimony, not to the primacy or poverty of traits or contexts, but to the role of both organismic and contextual factors as behavioral constraints. Whatever one's judgment of traits, moderate contextualism does remind us that to exist is to exist within an environment and that both the organism and the environment provide sources of inputs for the constraints on change. These interactions create a unique history for the organism, a history that itself facilitates some directions of change, while constraining others.

Because change is categorical, contextualism emphasizes that the personality system is open (Lerner, 1984) to change, and the multidimensionality or multidirectionality (Baltes, 1987) of change. Individuals may be pulled in diverse directions and in diverse ways over the life course. In contrast to organicism, which minimizes individual differences through the idea of a final cause, a terminal qualitative stage of development, contextualism is dispersive, and argues for increasing individual differences across time. Because contextualism emphasizes human action, contextual researchers are likely to embrace events as a basic unit of analysis, and to discover personality change throughout the life course. Humans are always embedded in context.

Criticism

Numerous critics have commented on the faddish and fragmented state of modern psychology, undoubtedly due, in part, to the dispersive nature of the current world theory. As demonstrated here, whether one accepts contextualism versus an integrative worldview depends on whether one believes the world is ultimately integrated, and if integrated, whether its structure can be fully known. Lerner, Hultsch, and Dixon (1983, p. 109) noted that "contextualism has been criticized as overintellectualized eclecticism." There is little doubt that the raw data of the world are transformed by our naive category system in the act of cognition. Just as assuredly there are other constraints on epistemology of a social, genetic, and cultural nature. Perhaps these constraints so transform the substance of the world that it cannot be known objectively, or, perhaps these biasing influences will wash out over decades of scientific discourse.

Interim Summary

Although noting that change is emerging as the focus of some adjacent sciences, in this chapter we have taken a step back from this purely empirical observation to ask what metatheoretical assumptions bias conceptions of personality and personality change. Rather than impose some arbitrary structure on the area of psychological metatheory, we have instead asked whether psychological metatheory might possess some kind of inherent structure of its own. We have argued that the fundamental questions of personality change do not fall out randomly, but instead cohere in certain ways that suggest an underlying structure valuable beyond the purpose of the present chapter.

In seeking this end, we have drawn heavily on the metaphilosophy of Stephen C. Pepper (1942) and the work of developmental theorists. We have presented Pepper's four adequate world hypotheses or paradigms; noted their basis in metaphor; and, where possible, described their categories, associated philosophical systems, types of evidence considered, structural characteristics, and theory of truth. These are summarized in Figure 1. Given that these world theories make assumptions that cut across all domains of knowledge, across all sciences, it is impossible that psychology would remain insulated from the influence of metatheory. We have therefore attempted to track out some of the more prototypal influences of each of these world theories on the field. And finally, we have asked what each of these world theories has to say about personality and personality change, and recorded a variety of answers. We hope our exposition has been lucid

Evidence Type

	Analytical	Synthetic
Dispersive	**FORMISM** Root Metaphor: Similarity Associated Philosophies: Realism, Platonic Idealism Strength: Scope Causality: Material Theory of Truth: Correspondence Ultimate Structure: Indeterminate Change: Unknown	**CONTEXTUALISM** Root Metaphor: History Associated Philosophies: Pragmatism Strength: Scope Causality: Formal Theory of Truth: Operationalism Ultimate Structure: Indeterminate Change: Any
Integrative	**MECHANISM** Root Metaphor: Machine Associated Philosophies: Naturalism, Materialism Strength: Precision Causality: Efficient Theory of Truth: Causal Adjustment Ultimate Structure: Determinate Change: Quantitative	**ORGANICISM** Root Metaphor: Integration Associated Philosophies: Absolute Idealism Strength: Precision Causality: Final Theory of Truth: Coherence Ultimate Structure: Determinate Change: Qualitative

(Left margin vertical label: Organization)

Figure 1: Pepper's (1942) world hypotheses, schematically conceived. From Houts (1991) and Kaye (1977). Adapted with permission.

enough to allow the reader to pick out these assumptions in other chapters of this volume.

In the second section of our chapter, we ask whether some synthetic perspective might exist that does not make such highly paradigmatic pre-scriptions and proscriptions on personality and personality change as do Pepper's (1942) world hypotheses.

TOWARD A SYNTHETIC VIEW: DEVELOPMENTAL CONTEXTUALISM AND LEVELS OF ORGANIZATION AS SOURCES OF CHANGE

For Pepper (1942), each world hypothesis represented a monolithic edifice uninterpretable in terms of the categories of any other world theory. Indeed, because each paradigm entails different truth criteria, it is unclear how any two world theories could be assimilated, or how the result would be judged (Reese & Overton, 1970). Although eclecticism may offer some short-term gain in coverage, Pepper argued that it ultimately contains the seeds of its own inconsistency: "The dangers of eclecticism arise from its interference with the processes of structural corroboration" (p. 341). Pepper did, however, advocate a "postrational eclecticism," distinct from "irra-tional eclecticism," noting that it is no less dogmatic to reject a world theory than it is to embrace a world theory. Consequently, one should seek to inform all of one's cognitive efforts by asking what each of the world hypotheses has to say about the matter at hand. Nevertheless, in Pepper's postrational eclecticism, the world hypotheses remain separate entities. We have more to say on this point in the final section of the chapter.

Whatever one's judgment on eclecticism, developmental theorists have continued to labor toward synthetic approaches, motivated by deficiencies produced through the assumptions of the classical paradigms. Radical contextualism, for example, is infinitely dispersive: Because no necessary connection exists between past and future (Ford & Lerner, 1992), that is, because the emphasis on novelty is so strong, it is not clear how contextualism can specify, of the infinite number of possible worlds that might exist, why ours exists as it does. Accordingly, contextualism, unless somehow moderated, is inadequate either as a theory of personality development or as a theory of personality change. The converse problem holds for organicism. Pure organicism is radically determined, through the notion of final cause and its unfolding in an invariant stage sequence. With regard to populations, one tends toward infinite individual differences, and the other tends toward zero individual differences.

One possible solution to this problem is to synthesize the two models, as represented in developmental contextualism (Ford & Lerner, 1992; Lerner, 1978, 1984, 1986, 1989). Whereas Pepper's (1942) classical world theories exclude certain sources or kinds of change paradigmatically, developmental contextualism does not (Ford & Lerner, 1992). Both qualitative and quantitative change are admissible, and both the organism and the environment are accepted as sources of change. Thus, the determinism of organicism constrains the dispersiveness of contextualism, and the extreme dispersiveness of contextualism is reigned in by the determinism of organicism (Ford & Lerner, 1992), resulting in neither static determinism nor absolute chaos, but relative plasticity. That is, the person is neither confined to one and only one pathway of change, nor confronted with an infinite number, but is constrained to some scope of alternatives, to plasticity. Both organism and its contexts set the scope of the changes that can occur. Neither quantitative nor qualitative change are paradigmatically proscribed; both are possible. Some changes, then, will have a forward or qualitative or organismic character, whereas others will have a lateral or dimensional character.

This analysis, however, is not entirely faithful to developmental contextualism. It maintains the independence of organism and context, of persons and situations. Developmental contextualism holds that individuals are fused with their contexts (Ford & Lerner, 1992). Accordingly, person and context form a single unit of analysis, the person-in-context. This allows a new kind of causality to come into the foreground, reciprocal causality. From a part perspective, each organismic component accepts certain inputs and yields certain outputs, so that reciprocal causality has an efficient aspect. However, from the perspective of the whole, the overall dynamic process yields emergent properties that cannot be predicated to the parts themselves, yet that constrain the behavior of the parts. In this sense, reciprocal causality also possesses a formal aspect. Reciprocity, of course, occurs not only between part and whole within an organism, but also across an organism and its multilevel and sequential context, as was noted in Millon (1981):

> Numerous biogenic and psychogenic determinants covary to shape personality, the relative weights of each varying as a function of time and circumstance. Further, this interaction of influences persists over time such that the course of later characteristics is related intrinsically to earlier events. Personality development must be viewed, therefore, as a process in which organismic and environmental forces display not only a mutuality and circularity of influence but an orderly and sequential continuity throughout the life of the individual.
>
> Biological and experimental determinants combine in an inextricable interplay throughout life. Thus constitutional dispositions not only shape the character of experience but are themselves modified in a constant interchange with the environment. The sequence of biogenic–psychogenic interaction creates a never-ending spiral; each step in the interplay builds upon prior interactions and creates, in turn, new potentials for future reactivity and experience. (p. 67)

Recognition of reciprocal causality as a novel and legitimate form of causality involved in both personality change and personality constancy has important methodological implications. Because of the possibility, if not the prominence, of nonlinear interactions and novel results, the application of the general linear model to the social sciences would appear to be limited, perhaps quite limited. In short, the idea of a linear interaction coheres with the mechanistic paradigm that, as noted above, has been debunked by modern physics: Subject and context come together to produce an effect, but maintain their independence throughout their interaction, emerging essentially unchanged (Riegel, 1976), in much the same way as two billiard balls may career off each other, interacting, but remaining billiard balls. As noted, mechanism proscribes change. True novelty requires that both person and context be transformed by their interaction, a process more properly referred to as a transaction than an interaction (Lerner, 1978). Accordingly, the independence assumption cannot be rigorously maintained (though factorial designs will undoubtedly continue to be used for lack of a more generally accepted methodology). The conclusion is that persons are as much fused with contexts as contexts with persons. Interested readers are referred to Houts (1991) for a discussion of contextualism's implications for empirical science methodology.

Thus far we have addressed developmental contextualism as a synthesis of organicism and contextualism, a fusion of organism and context. But organisms are not merely empty vessels covered by a skin, and contexts are not just undifferentiated, homogeneous physical environments. Both are structured, in the form of levels of organization (Ford & Lerner, 1992). These levels represent a means of talking about the sources of personality change, of separating out the sources of change in a nonarbitrary way. Part of the beauty of Pepper's (1942) schema, in its strongest reading, is that it "carves nature at its joints." Not only does it group things together in a way that is convenient for the present purpose, but it also serves a generative function. The concept of levels accomplished must do the same thing with respect to the sources of change. Novikoff (1945), as quoted in Lerner and Tubman (1991), on the nature of levels:

> The concept of integrative levels recognizes as equally for the purpose of scientific analysis both the isolation of the parts of a whole and their integration into the structure of the whole. It neither reduces phenomena of a higher level to those of a lower one, as in mechanism, or describes the higher level in vague nonmaterial terms which are but substitutes for understanding, as in vitalism. Unlike other "holistic" theories, it never leaves the firm ground of material reality. . . . The concept points to the need to study the organizational interrelationships of parts and whole. (p. 209)

What are these levels? Chemical, genetic, cellular, organ, organism, family, community, society, and culture could all be considered levels of organization that influence personality. Each is hierarchically embedded in the next. Although constraints between adjacent levels may be more obvious than those operating between distal levels, causality does not flow exclusively from the bottom up or from the top down. Instead, each level potentially influences every other, and all levels continue to transact throughout the life span (Ford & Lerner, 1992). Lewontin (1981), for example, pointed out that although each influences the others, the influence of higher levels may actually feed back and relieve constraints imposed by lower levels. Human beings, for example, are not born with the faculty of flight, or the ability to project their words into the minds of others over distances of thousands of miles, but nevertheless have developed technologies, the airplane and telephone, that overcome these limitations. The human genome project, perhaps the beginning of the ultimate feedback loop, is fundamentally an attempt to bring genetic-level constraints under higher level control. Although consciousness itself is a result of the evolution of our species, its direction and quality may soon be influenced by conscious decisions. Divisive ethical issues will no doubt be raised as accumulating knowledge about the genome enables scientists to intervene to such an extent that the very potentialities and possible pathways of personality development are fundamentally altered.

Interestingly, the idea of levels of organization offers a means of testing Pepper's (1942) hypothesis that the world hypotheses can be projected to any domain of cognitive engagement. By randomly selecting two levels of organization and projecting one of the paradigms onto the pair, to prescribe and proscribe certain formal relationships, it should be possible to spin off approaches to a discipline ad hoc, ad lib, ad nauseam. Projecting organicism onto persons and societies, for example, would lead to consideration of a society as an active entity possessing emergent properties that transcend a mere collective of persons, thereby giving the society a cohesiveness and consistency across time. Each society would evolve through a number of stages toward some final end state. Alternately, projecting mechanism onto persons and societies would lead one to embrace society as an ephiphen-omenom that must be reduced to the interaction of its constituent parts in order to be understood. Connecting more distant levels of organization, one might argue for the bidirectional influence of genes and society, and perhaps thereby derive the possibility, though not the content, of Jungian archetypes on the one hand, and sociobiology on the other.

Developmental contextualism represents each level as a potential source of personality change (Ford & Lerner, 1992). Unlike other formu-lations, which for the most part deal with influences derived from a par-ticular level of organization, a main effects approach to change, develop-mental contextualism incorporates all sources or influences in a single integrative theory. Change, then, cannot be reduced to influences ema-nating from any one level in isolation, but instead represents the interaction of a structurally differentiated matrix of multiple causes and outcomes, each of which possesses both quantitative and qualitative aspects.

One might ask, for example, how a cultural level constrains personality constancy and change. E. B. Taylor (1874, p. 1) defined culture as "that complex whole which includes knowledge, belief, art, morals, law, custom, and any other capabilities and habits acquired by man as a member of society." Culture is specific to human beings, and it has no doubt played an important role in human evolution by exerting selection pressures in favor of those with the capacity to profit by and through a social medium while selecting against those who could not. Indeed, Cole (1992) argued that the effects of environment and biology do not interact directly, but are mediated through culture. Thus, "cultural knowledge defines the course of development more specifically than the constitution of the organism itself would require" (Dannefer, 1984, p. 108).

Humans are contextually embedded in cultural throughout life, from conception to death. Cultures differ, for example, in terms of whether the parents accommodate the child's inherent biological schedule or vice versa, in terms of what foods children eat, the degree to which they are readily integrated with adults versus left with caretakers, and so on. Culture prescribes and proscribes social roles according to such subject variables as sex, race, class, birth order, and religion, thereby influencing the pattern of contexts with which any one individual will interact. In this sense, people are constrained objectively through the availability of socially defined roles, that is, what they can become, and subjectively, through their transactionally-developed expectations of the future self, or what they think they can become, in other words a phenomenological constraint. There is evidence that culture mediates some kinds of cognitive development, such as logical reasoning, and it would not be unreasonable to hypothesize that the development of postformal operational cognitive stages, should they in fact exist, might be culture-specific. Some stages of development, notably adolescence, are apparently culturally specific, the transition to adulthood in some other cultures being accomplished through social rituals that create comparably discrete boundaries between role obligations. Senescence, too, can be construed as a culturally invented stage, a stage created by a feedback of modern medical knowledge and technology, allowing many people to live to extreme biological old age.

Finally, the numerous and ongoing cultural shifts of our own society leave no doubt that culturally prescribed roles modify dispositional characteristics. Moreover, it appears that the characteristics of some cultures may protect against the development of certain forms of psychiatric illness, including personality disorders, while encouraging development of others. The increase in the prevalence rate of borderline personality disorder, for example, may be due in part to increasing cultural pluralism and consequent identity diffusion as persons are torn between the belief systems of disparate reference groups (Millon, 1987). Furthermore, patterns of diagnosis change within a culture across time, as well. Hysteria, very much a sex-stereotyped disorder, is now much less common than in the Victorian era.

SYSTEMS AND TRANSFORMATIONS

As is apparent to even the most casual observer, organisms are systems. A recent approach suggests that the study of life itself, of what is required for life to exist, may offer certain constraints on personality. Ford (1987) discussed people as a special kind of system, a living system. Ford and Lerner (1992) embedded living systems theory within developmental contextualism, dubbing the result developmental systems theory. Congruent with life span developmental psychology, this approach draws heavily on the adjacent sciences. Life is, after all, a physical, chemical, biological, familial, and, for humans, sociocultural, phenomenon.

Personality has often been conceptualized as a totality. However, although the idea of a totality is very appealing conceptually, and although references to the personality as a totality (e.g., Magnusson, 1990) are common in the literature, it appears that nature prefers a variation on this theme. A totality does not adequately separate out influences derived from multiple levels of organization; it potentially represents part–whole integration as existing only at one level. Living systems, however, are constructed hierarchically, with fewer components existing at higher levels than at lower levels: There are fewer molecules than there are atoms, fewer macromolecules than molecules, fewer cells than macromolecules, and fewer organs than cells. Indeed, the numerical inequality of higher and lower level structures may be another example of a broken symmetry that characterizes organized and irreversible processes (Nicolis & Prigogine, 1989). Apparently, life cannot exist if there are as many organs as atoms. A living system is, first and foremost, a functional–structural unit, a dynamic, open system whose purpose is to maintain life by dissipating entropy into its environment. Apparently, this physical necessity requires a hierarchical organization.

The open systems notion makes certain predictions about personality change. Obviously, one of the requirements of a living system is to remain close to homeostasis. Contextual demands disturb or perturb the system, pulling it away from equilibrium. Such demands are ubiquitous in daily life, varying from the mundane, such as getting up in the morning, to the not-so-mundane, such as missing one's flight. Phenomenologically, such perturbations are often felt as stress and anxiety. Individuals field these perturbations in different ways, depending on their coping styles. To the extent that the organism–context mismatch is small, focal, transient, or expected, the personality system, acting as the psychological equivalent of the immune system, will compensate easily, engaging protective mechanisms whose influence is temporary or reversible. These are best described as *state changes* rather than personality changes, in that they represent temporary departures from system equilibrium that do not permanently affect the quality of intraorganismic functional–structural relations. The distinction between state and trait anxiety (Spielberger, 1966), for example, is well-established.

However, if the organism–context mismatch tends to be large, pervasive, enduring, and unexpected, then the demands may exceed the organism's adaptational competencies or coping skills. Such mismatches stand a greater chance of producing radical transformational change. Numerous terms refer to processes of transformational change, including religious conversion, brainwashing, rehabilitation, and decompensation. Other terms refer to the results of radical change, such as posttraumatic stress, and perhaps, "a change of heart." Not all of these are changes for the worse. Some represent disintegrations, that is, movement from higher to lower levels of organization. Others, however, represent movement to a higher level of organization, or to a kind of organization that is simply different.

The goals of psychotherapy can be understood in a similar way through the systems model. Structurally, psychotherapy resembles Eldrege and

Gould's (1972) idea of punctuated equilibrium, with periods of stasis, change, and consolidation. New time-limited (e.g., Strupp & Binder, 1984) psychotherapies would seem especially congruent with a systems model, reflecting frustration with the implicit gradualism of other approaches. These psychotherapies all stress the importance of actively, though carefully, perturbing the client's organization or character structure. Apparently, some threshold amount of anxiety is necessary to precipitate reorganization, below which the therapist's attempts at clarification and suggestion will simply be dissipated by the defenses of the personality system. However, all time-limited approaches recognize that a certain level of personality organization (e.g., a critical amount of ego strength) is a prerequisite to time-limited psychotherapy. Apparently, some integration or structural integrity is required for reintegration, without which decompensation becomes a threat. Furthermore, classical terms in psychotherapy refer to change and stasis. Insight can be conceptualized as a phenomenological reorganization, whereas resistance represents efforts by the system to perpetuate its present structure despite new information or experiences.

The principle that individuals adapt, of which psychotherapy may be considered a self-conscious example, makes a number of predictions for personality change. The most mundane prediction is simply that the personality of individuals who are adapted to their physical and social environments should remain relatively constant. Given good adaptation, there is simply no reason for change. However, this prediction may be more true for the population than the individual. The idea that perfect adaptiveness results exclusively through contextual constancy undoubtedly has its limitations. Perfect adaptedness must be subjectively defined. Whereas contextual invariance may help those of a dependent style feel safe and secure, those of a more active disposition are likely to regard constancy as boring. For these individuals constancy is more a press than a need. Their inherent nature is to transform their surrounds according to their desires. In this sense, a passive or dependable contextual base that offers few constraints may in fact shift the interactive balance toward the person, leading him or her to become an active producer of his or her own personality change by releasing intrinsic actualizing tendencies. For some persons, then, contextual constancy may actually set in motion idiographic processes that allow them to develop in unique directions. The opposite may also be true. Extremely hostile environments, such as those experienced during the Holocaust, may lead some to search profoundly for meaning in life (Frankl, 1969) while others give up in existential despair. Whether the capacity to find meaning under the assault of contextual extremities has itself been magnified by selection pressures or whether it is an inevitable result of the capacity for self-reflection is a matter of speculation.

The opposite of contextual invariance is invariance in the personality system. In some cases, the organism itself becomes a significant constraint on the flexibility of organism–context interactions and resists change. Such constraints may lie primarily in a single functional domain, such as interpersonal skills, or may be systemwide. Obviously, the former is much easier to remedy than the latter, through, say, focal psychotherapy. To the extent that adaptive deficits are systemic, however, by definition the organism will be adaptively inflexible across contexts, tend to foster self-perpetuating vicious circles, and possess tenuous emotional stability under stress (Millon, 1981). Such individuals may properly be considered to possess a pathological personality pattern, in that it is the properties of the system itself that are primarily responsible for poor ecological fit relative to others, despite a predictable range of environments. These are individuals who do not change or accommodate when others would.

SUMMARY AND CONCLUSIONS

We have attempted to show how metatheoretical assumptions constrain conceptions of personality change by appealing to the metaphilosophy of Stephen C. Pepper. We then briefly touched on a new developmental metamodel termed developmental contextualism (Ford & Lerner, 1992; Lerner, 1978, 1984, 1986) and its concepts of levels of organization to draw ideas concerning the sources of personality change together into a coherent system. What are we to make of these various schemes in the final analysis?

We are tempted to believe that Pepper's (1942) metaphilosophy represents the "true structure of things." It is difficult to read Pepper without feeling that one is discovering something about the essential nature of reality. Language such as "carves nature at its joints" definitely encourages such a feeling. For better or for worse, however, each world theory possesses its own truth criteria, and thus implies a different philosophy of science. Accordingly, the metaphilosophy itself can be criticized in terms of the categories of the various world theories. Thus, the very idea that theories about the world can be grouped together according to certain shared relationships evokes the root metaphor of formism, similarity. The idea that we have at least gotten beneath the world of appearances to discover the true structure of metatheory evokes organicism: We have finally transcended the fragments of metatheory and tied the loose ends together in a single coherent schema. A thoroughgoing contextualist might be impressed with Pepper's ideas, but only as a partial theory ultimately circumscribed in its application. However, one possible truth criterion not included in the depiction of the world theories might serve to validate Pepper's ideas: beauty. *World Hypotheses* is an inarguably elegant work.

Certainly it is difficult not to fall into one or another of the world theories when appraising *World Hypotheses*. Pepper (1942) himself believed that the adequacy of any individual world theory could only be judged by the fully adequate world theory, which, he stated, we do not yet possess. Obviously, then, he did not regard his own schema as the fully adequate theory. Moreover, in the final section of his book Pepper attempted to anticipate and field a number of questions, one of which is "Why four world theories?" His reply: "Because there have appeared so far only four root metaphors capable of generating theories with a high degree of structural corroboration" (p. 340).

Undoubtedly, this leaves open the possibility that other paradigms may rise to prominence, perhaps featuring an entirely different set of categories and constraints on personality and personality change, or subsuming the constraints of the four world theories under a more fully adequate world hypothesis. Given the symmetry of Pepper's thesis, it is difficult to believe that these categories and constraints will simply be shuffled in a different way. Mechanism and qualitative change, for example, do not cohere. Evolution may represent such an emerging metaphor, one that will embrace the other world hypotheses in order to form the basis for the fully adequate world theory. Developmental contextualism and its embedded theory, developmental systems theory (Ford & Lerner, 1992), represent strong attempts in this direction. Whether these theories will prove adequate or eclectic can only be known in time.

REFERENCES

American Psychiatric Association. (1968). *Diagnostic and statistical manual of mental disorders* (2nd ed.). Washington DC: Author.

American Psychiatric Association. (1980). *Diagnostic and statistical manual of mental disorders* (3rd ed.). Washington, DC: Author.

Baltes, P. B. (1987). Theoretical propositions of life-span developmental psychology: On the dynamics between growth and decline. *Developmental Psychology, 23,* 611–626.

Bowlby, J. (1969). *Attachment and loss. Vol. 1: Attachment.* New York: Basic Books.

Cantor, N., & Genero, N. (1986). Psychiatric diagnosis and natural categorization: A close analogy. In T. Millon & G. L. Klerman (Eds.), *Contemporary directions in psychopathology: Towards the DSM–IV* (pp. 233–356). New York: Guilford Press.

Cantor, N., & Zirkel, S. (1990). Personality, cognition, and purposive behavior. In L. A. Pervin (Ed.), *Handbook of personality: Theory and research* (pp. 135–164). New York: Guilford Press.

Cole, M. (1992). Culture in development. In M. H. Bornstein & M. E. Lamb (Eds.), *Developmental psychology: An advanced textbook* (3rd ed., pp. 731–789). Hillsdale, NJ: Erlbaum.

Cronbach, L. J. (1957). The two disciplines of scientific psychology. *American Psychologist, 12,* 671–684.

Dannefer, D. (1984). Adult development and socialization theory: A paradigmatic reappraisal. *American Sociological Review, 49,* 100–116.

Deutsch, K. W. (1951). Mechanism, organicism, and society. *Philosophy of Science, 18,* 230–252.

Eldrege, N., & Gould, S. (1972). Punctuated equilibria: An alternative to phyletic gradualism. In T. Schopf (Ed.), *Models in paleobiology.* San Francisco: Freeman.

Endler, N. S., & Magnusson, D. (1976). *Interactional psychology and personality.* Washington, DC: Hemisphere.

Epstein, S. (1980). The stability of behavior: II. Implications for psychological research. *American Psychologist, 35,* 790–806.

Erikson, E. H. (1950). *Childhood and society.* New York: Norton.

Erikson, E. H. (1963). *Childhood and society* (2nd ed.). New York: Norton.

Erikson, E. H. (1968). *Identity: Youth and crisis.* New York: Norton.

Ford, D. H. (1987). *Humans as self-constructing living systems: A developmental perspective on personality and behavior.* Hillsdale, NJ: Erlbaum.

Ford, D. H., & Lerner, R. M. (1992). *Developmental systems theory: An integrative approach.* Newbury Park, CA: Sage.

Frances, A., & Widiger, T. A. (1986). Methodological issues in personality disorder diagnosis. In T. Millon & G. L. Klerman (Eds.), *Contemporary directions in psychopathology: Towards the DSM–IV* (pp. 347–362). New York: Guilford Press.

Frankl, V. E. (1969). *The doctor and the soul.* New York: Bantam Books.

Freud, S. (1953). Character and anal eroticism. In J. Riviere (Trans.), *Collected papers* (Vol. 2, pp. 45–50). London: Hogarth Press. (Original work published 1908)

Goldberg, L. R. (1993). The structure of phenotypic personality traits. *American Psychologist, 48,* 26–34.

Gottlieb, G. (1983). The psychobiological approach to developmental issues. In M. M. Haith & J. J. Campos (Eds.), *Handbook of child psychology: Infancy and developmental psychobiology* (4th ed., pp. 1–26). New York: Wiley.

Hempel, C. (1965). *Aspects of scientific explanation.* New York: Free Press.

Houts, A. C. (1991). The contextualist turn in empirical social science: Epistemological issues, methodological implications, and adjusted expectations. In R. Cohen & A. W. Siegel (Eds.), *Context and development* (pp. 25–54). Hillsdale, NJ: Erlbaum.

Inhelder, B., & Piaget, J. (1958). *The growth of logical thinking from childhood to adolescence.* New York: Basic Books.

Jaeger, M. E., & Rosnow, R. L. (1988). Contextualism and its implications for psychological inquiry. *British Journal of Psychology, 79,* 63–75.

Kaye, H. (1977). Early experience as the basis for unity and cooperation of "differences." In N. Datan & H. W. Reese, (Eds.), *Life-span developmental psychology: Dialectical perspectives on experimental research* (pp. 343–364). San Diego, CA: Academic Press.

Kohlberg, L. (1986). *The psychology of moral development.* New York: Harper & Row.

Kuhn, D. (1992). Cognitive development. In M. H. Bornstein & M. E. Lamb (Eds.), *Developmental psychology: An advanced textbook* (3rd ed., pp. 211–272). Hillsdale, NJ: Erlbaum.

Kuhn, T. S. (1970). *The structure of scientific revolutions* (2nd ed.). Chicago: University of Chicago Press.

Lerner, R. M. (1978). Nature, nurture, and dynamic interactionism. *Human Development, 21,* 1–20.

Lerner, R. M. (1984). *On the nature of human plasticity.* Cambridge, England: Cambridge University Press.

Lerner, R. M. (1986). *Concepts and theories of human development* (2nd ed.). New York: Random House.

Lerner, R. M. (1989). Developmental contextualism and the life-span view of person–context interaction. In M. Bornstein & J. S. Bruner (Eds.), *Interaction in human development* (pp. 217–239). Hillsdale, NJ: Erlbaum.

Lerner, R. M., Hultsch, D. F., & Dixon, R. A. (1983). Contextualism and the character of developmental psychology in the 1970's. *Annals of the New York Academy of Sciences, 412,* 101–128.

Lerner, R. M., & Tubman, J. G. (1991). Developmental contextualism and the study of early adolescent development. In R. Cohen & A. W. Siegel (Eds.), *Context and development* (pp. 183–210). Hillsdale, NJ. Erlbaum.

Lewontin, R. C. (1981). On constraints and adaptation. *Behavioral and Brain Sciences, 4,* 244–245.

Lyddon, W. J. (1989). Root metaphor theory: A philosophical framework for counseling and psychology. *Journal of Counseling and Developmental Psychology, 67,* 442–448.

Magnusson, D. (1990). Personality development from an interactional perspective. In L. A. Pervin (Ed.), *Handbook of personality: Theory and research* (pp. 193–222). New York: Guilford Press.

Millon, T. (1969). *Modern psychopathology.* Philadelphia: W. B. Saunders.

Millon, T. (1981). *Disorders of personality.* New York: Wiley.

Millon, T. (1987). On the genesis and prevalence of the borderline personality disorder: A social learning thesis. *Journal of Personality Disorders, 1,* 354–372.

Millon, T., & Davis, R. D. (in press). Development of personality disorders. *Handbook of Development.*

Mischel, W. (1968). *Personality and assessment.* New York: Wiley.

Morris, E. K. (1988). Contextualism: The world view of behavior analysis. *Journal of Experimental Child Psychology, 46,* 289–323.

Nicolis, G., & Prigogine, I. (1989). *Exploring complexity: An introduction.* San Francisco: Freeman.

Novikoff, A. B. (1945). The concept of integrative levels in biology. *Science, 62,* 209–215.

Pervin, L. A. (1990). A brief history of modern personality theory. In L. A. Pervin (Ed.), *Handbook of personality: Theory and research* (pp. 3–20). New York: Guilford Press.

Pepper, S. C. (1942). *World hypotheses.* Berkeley: University of California Press.

Pepper, S. C. (1966). *Concept and quality: A world hypothesis.* Peru, IL: Open Court.

Pepper, S. C. (1970). *World hypotheses: A study in evidence.* Berkeley: University of California Press. (Original work published 1942)

Popper, K. (1972). *Objective knowledge: An evolutionary approach.* London: Oxford University Press.

Quine, W. V. O. (1977). Natural kinds. In S. P. Schwartz (Ed.), *Naming, necessity, and natural groups* (pp. 155–175). Ithaca, NY: Cornell University Press.

Railton, P. (1989). Explanation and metaphysical controversy. In P. Kitcher & W. C. Salmon (Eds.), *Minnesota studies in the philosophy of science: Vol. XIII. Scientific explanation* (pp. 220–252). Minneapolis: University of Minnesota Press.

Reese, H. W., & Overton, W. F. (1970). Models of development and theories of development. In L. R. Goulet & P. B. Baltes (Eds.), *Life-span developmental psychology: Research and theory* (pp. 115–145). San Diego, CA: Academic Press.

Riegel, K. F. (1976). The dialectics of human development. *American Psychologist, 31,* 689–700.

Spielberger, C. D. (1966). Theory and research in anxiety. In C. D. Spielberger (Ed.), *Anxiety and behavior* (pp. 3–20). San Diego, CA: Academic Press.

Strupp, H. H., & Binder, J. L. (1984). *Psychotherapy in a new key: A guide to time-limited dynamic psychotherapy.* New York: Basic Books.

Taylor, E. B. (1874). *Primitive culture: Researches into the development of mythology, philosophy, religion, language, art, and custom.* London: J. Murray.

Wittgenstein, L. (1953). *Philosophical investigations.* Oxford, England: Basil Blackwell.

6

ASSESSING CONSTANCY AND CHANGE

JOHN R. NESSELROADE and STEVEN M. BOKER

INTRODUCTION

> He perfect, stable; but imperfect We, Subject to Change, and diff'rent
> in Degree. (John Dryden, *Palamon and Arcite: The Knight's Tale From
> Chaucer*).

> A party of order or stability, and a party of progress or reform, are both
> necessary elements of a healthy state of political life. (John Stuart Mill,
> *On Liberty*).

Constancy and change are necessary complements of each other. Without a stable reference frame, the assessment of change is not possible. Conversely, without change events, there would be no need for a concept of constancy. Students of personality are obligated to account for both the constant and the changing properties of its order and organization. Although each kind of property has its peculiar features to be respected, constancy

The authors thank the MacArthur Foundation Research Network on Successful Aging for support of the work described herein and two anonymous reviewers for their comments on an earlier version of the chapter. We are also grateful to Chris Hertzog for his thoughtful remarks on a number of issues discussed herein.

and change are advantageously considered together, rather than in isolation from, or in opposition to, each other (Nesselroade, 1990).

Students of personality have had an enduring interest in both constancy and change (Brim & Kagan, 1980). On the side of change, central concepts such as learning, development, growth, and emotion, all of which represent one or another kind of change or intraindividual variability, are inherent to the study of personality. Without such change-laden concepts, our field would be exceedingly dull and impoverished.

Constancy also has a high value placed on it for several reasons. At a popular level, people like to see constancy in the behavior of others, perhaps because it makes them more predictable. At the same time, however, most people do not want to be thought of by their fellows as being predictable. Probably one of the most important reasons stability is valued by psychologists is because of the long-standing emphasis on activities such as prediction, classification, and diagnosis. These activities are pointless unless there are some relatively constant features of behavior on which to base them. Putatively stable interindividual differences in a great variety of attributes have been assigned the largest role of providing the constancy demanded by prediction and classification activities. For example, human abilities, broadly defined, and general dispositional traits such as extraversion and anxiety have tended to be the work horses of psychometrics-based prediction schemes. But more or less stable aspects of change are also candidates for the role of predictor. For example, when someone is seen as volatile or emotional, the implication is that he or she is consistently distinct from others with respect to these inherently changeable dimensions.

Constancy and change also play important roles in the development of theory. The level of stability of interindividual differences, be it high, medium, or low, provides important information on which to base inferences about mechanisms, both endogenous and exogenous, hypothesized to be involved in development and change over the life span.

It is easy to oversimplify both concepts, or, perhaps more accurately, both sets of concepts, of constancy and change. Mortimer, Finch, and Kumka (1982), for example, pointed out that one of the problems inherent in clarifying issues of constancy and change with regard to the study of development is that there are at least four different conceptualizations of stability found in the literature. These include (a) structural invariance or the degree of continuity in the phenomenon under investigation, (b) normative stability or the persistence of relative amounts of an attribute across time, (c) level stability or maintenance of the absolute amounts of an attribute over time, and (d) ipsative stability or maintenance of an ordering of attributes (e.g., with respect to salience) within the individual over time. Similarly, change is by no means a single concept. Cattell (1966b), for example, in the area of personality research, distinguished between trait change and state fluctuation. Fiske and Rice (1955) identified and discussed many different kinds of intraindividual variability.

Suffice it to say that psychologists studying personality need to become more adept at using concepts of constancy and change, to elaborate the definition, measurement, and use of concepts that are suited to the complexity of our subject matter. Moreover, it is necessary to do so with the precision and rigor of mathematical formulations. Until such rigorous representations are implemented, much of what psychologists aspire to know and understand about personality will continue to be elusive.

In the following section, we selectively review some issues pertinent to assessing constancy and change and highlight some aspects that we believe can be attended to more effectively. In the section following that, we examine the potential of some alternative ideas for helping to deal with some of those issues.

CURRENT APPROACHES

The need to assess both change and stability has had a broad influence on the shaping of current research and data analysis methodologies. Two very general developments that have helped to forge the array of tools with which both constancy and change are presently assessed are (a) longitudinal designs and (b) multivariate methods. The effects of these two major lines of development can be witnessed in the areas of measurement, research design, and data analysis and modeling.

Longitudinal Research Designs

The history of longitudinal research designs has been reviewed elsewhere (e.g., Baltes & Nesselroade, 1979; Goldstein, 1979; Kruse, Lindenberger, & Baltes, 1992). Longitudinal designs appear in many forms and enjoy a certain mystique, especially in the context of developmental research. Particularly during the past three decades, simple longitudinal designs, longitudinal sequences, panel studies, intensive measurement of individual cases, and so on, have all found substantial application in the conduct of behavioral research. Their use has led to both the sharpening of issues and a much fuller understanding of such phenomena as stability, developmental change, time of measurement effects, cohort differences, and short-term intraindividual variability.

In psychology, for example, the general developmental model of Schaie (1965; see also Baltes, 1968) raised serious questions about the usefulness of simple longitudinal designs involving a single birth cohort of individuals. Instead, Schaie, Baltes, and others argued for carefully structured, sequential designs if individual change was to be distinguished from other key manifestations such as sociocultural change. These ideas helped to regenerate and strengthen a nearly dormant focus on psychological development across the life span, a focus that, once renewed, has influenced personality research in important ways over the past three decades. These developments have paralleled important work on the life course deriving from a more sociological tradition (e.g., Elder & Caspi, 1990; Featherman, 1985).

Multivariate Methods

The systematic development and use of multivariate methods began around the turn of this century (see Baltes & Nesselroade, 1973; Cattell, 1966a, for discussions of the multivariate orientation). The development of multivariate analysis theory and methods and the articulation of several aspects of substantive theory have been closely intertwined. For example, in measurement, the development of concepts and theories of human abilities has closely paralleled the development of factor-analytic modeling procedures.

Multivariate methods have enhanced capabilities for defining and elaborating concepts in several ways. A key question in personality research is, How many variables are needed to identify, define, and measure a concept? For example, rather than selecting one exemplar from a substantive domain of many variables, a subset of variables can be used in concert to represent the domain. Anxiety, for example, represents a broad domain of content with putative indicators ranging from self-report and clinical ratings through respiration rate to handwriting pressure. When one is trying to use anxiety level as either an input variable or an outcome, it is risky to put all the "eggs in one basket" by choosing only one of the many possible indicators of anxiety. When definitions rest on a vector of several variables, the options for identifying concepts include focusing on what the multiple measures have in common as well as defining particular patterns of relationships across several variables. These multivariate capabilities, teamed with concepts such as factorial invariance (Meredith, 1964), have enabled researchers to provide rigorous definition and meaning to conceptually appealing notions such as *qualitative* versus *quantitative* changes as well as to elaborate concepts of stability, reliability, and so on, and to separate more effectively error from true variance in estimating the structural parameters of models.

Current concepts in and approaches to assessing constancy and change rely heavily on both multivariate approaches and longitudinal research designs. Together, they have provided a means for revamping change and stability concepts through the development and use of latent variable structural modeling (Bentler, 1980; McArdle, 1988). Descriptions of some of the most current methods can be found in publications by Collins and Horn (1991), Molenaar (1985), and Millsap & Meredith (1988), among others. These methods deserve more extensive trial and further development as students of personality continue to wrestle with the difficult problems of assessing constancy and change. Along with improvements in assessment, necessary enhancements of working definitions of constancy and change are likely to develop.

Some Limitations

The gains accruing from longitudinal research designs and multivariate research methods have not been preceded, accompanied, or succeeded uniformly by improvements in the conceptualization of other pertinent issues. This has been especially true in the areas of measurement and research design. Some examples are presented in this chapter to illustrate the problems.

Measurement

Within the domain of human abilities, where attributes were thought to represent rock stable interindividual differences, it was rather natural that concerns with stability of interindividual differences tended to dominate the development of measuring instruments. Test–retest correlations, for example, are advocated for estimating reliability (e.g., Nunnally, 1967) and, therefore, the psychometric adequacy of measures. This seems appropriate when the attributes being measured reflect no, or only minimal, intraindividual change. But test–retest correlations can confound matters of method and substance (e.g., measurement unreliability and process-based changes) and, therefore, can fail as indicators of the goodness of a measure designed for assessing changeable phenomena such as states of anxiety and depression (Cattell & Scheier, 1961; Nesselroade, 1988; Spielberger, Gorsuch, & Lushene, 1969). Moreover, even measures of human abilities can show patterns of relatively short-term but coherent changes when studies are designed to look for them (Horn, 1972), a finding that suggests that personality researchers sometimes oversimplify matters of constancy and change.

Research Design

Poor measurement is not the only blot on the record of studies of constancy and change issues in personality. Innovations in research design have not always kept pace with other developments. The use of high speed, large capacity computational machinery has raised the possibility that the quality and power of methods may have begun to exceed the quality and comprehensiveness of much of the data collected in the typical investigator-initiated research study.

Some of the critical ways that data collection can be improved have been reviewed and discussed at length elsewhere (Nesselroade, 1983, 1991a). The general issue is the need to pay more direct attention to the fact that data are inherently multimodal (i.e., they reflect selection with respect to persons, variables, and occasions of measurement). The resources for any research project are limited, a constraint that dictates that there must be trade-offs in the breadth of representation that is given to the different data modalities. The exact nature of these trade-offs should be determined by the research questions and concerns regarding generalizability of the findings. The assessment of both constancy and change, for example, implies the need for multiple occasions of measurement. Sampling of persons, no matter how carefully and completely it is done, does not compensate for narrow and inadequate selection of occasions of measurement in those cases in which generalization is focused across occasions (e.g., on constancy or change). The most precisely constructed representative sampling of people does not yield information about degree of stability or amount of change in the attributes of concern if members of the sample are measured only once.

As a basis for sampling or selection in planning research, occasions unfortunately do not represent a highly homogeneous universe. Therefore, matters of duration and spacing of repeated measurements are critical aspects of longitudinal research design. However, simply including multiple occasions of measurement in the design does not adequately compensate for ill-defined selection of duration and spacing. Periodic phenomena in particular can generate extremely misleading results when analyzed with test–retest correlations and fixed-interval lags. In a fixed-interval lag design all of the intervals between assessments are equal, therefore they are perfectly correlated with each other. If the frequency of the periodic phenomenon under study is also correlated with the lag interval, the test–retest correlation will be artificially high, giving an overestimate of stability and an underestimate of intraindividual variability. Later in this chapter, we provide an example of this type of error, which is known as *aliasing error* in the fields of signal processing and computer graphics.

A second way to improve research design, and thereby data collection, involves attending as carefully to the selection of measurement instruments as to the selection of persons to study. Multivariate measurement batteries are indispensable for pinpointing concepts and patterns and for allowing the researcher to develop estimates of structural parameters that are not attenuated due to errors of measurement. However, not just any multivariate battery works as well as any other one. For example, using anxiety measures x, y, and z because they are more convenient, or shorter, or were developed by close colleagues, can yield remarkably different estimates of the relationship between anxiety as a latent variable and other latent variables than would have been the case if anxiety measures a, b, and c had been used. Such choices must be informed by knowledge of the domain, the nature of focal concepts, and concerns about generalizability.

Consistency in Variability

There is another issue that becomes salient if one takes seriously the notion of looking at constancy and change as complementary. It is that constancy can be a relatively stable characteristic or attribute of changeable phenomena. For example, the broadcasts of an AM (amplitude modulation) radio station represent a high degree of variability (the amplitude of the carrier wave), but the frequency of the carrier wave must remain within a very tight tolerance or the station's license will be revoked. Thus, the station is locatable at a highly predictable spot on the AM dial, but superimposed on that highly stable frequency is a substantial amount of variability. Both are integral to the broadcasting process and the station might just as easily be denoted in terms of a stable feature of variability—"the one that plays all the good rock music"—as in terms of constancy—"the one at 1450 on the AM dial."

In a similar vein, the parameters of intraindividual variability distributions may carry important and stable interindividual differences information that can be used to bolster our predictive and explanatory schemes significantly (Nesselroade, 1991a). Indeed, concepts such as rhythmicity, volatility, and unpredictability are characterizations of intraindividual variability dimensions that are presumed to represent more or less stable differences among persons. There is also support for the importance of intraindividual variability as a component of behavior when it is examined in a multivariate, longitudinal framework such as by P-technique factor analysis (Cattell, 1963; Jones & Nesselroade, 1991; Luborsky & Mintz, 1972). Locus of control, work values, creativity, and self-concept are included among attributes that are typically regarded as stable and traitlike yet that manifest patterns of systematic, short-term, intraindividual variability (Nesselroade, 1991b).

Within a given occasion of measurement, intraindividual variability on some measure that is asynchronous across individuals cannot be disentangled from stability among interindividual differences. The two are hopelessly confounded in cross-sectional data. Hampson (1990) showed that women perform differentially better or worse on spatial and verbal ability tasks as a function of their estrogen levels at a given point in their monthly cycle. The pattern of changes was consistent with gender differences in performance on such tasks in that, in relation to their own levels, women performed better on verbal tasks when estrogen levels were highest and better on spatial tasks when estrogen levels were lowest. A one-shot, cross-sectional study involving women at different stages of their monthly cycles would not distinguish between the variation that is due to such cycle-related sources and the variation that is due to relatively stable differences in spatial and verbal ability. If the variation among individuals at one occasion of measurement were computed for such data, it would be an overestimate of the magnitude of stable interindividual differences and, by implication, would lead to an underestimate of the relative magnitude of intraindividual variability. Further methods and techniques are needed by which constancy in patterns of intraindividual variability can be exploited in the pursuit of more accurate accounts of both the constancy and the change characteristics of behavior.

The Trait–State Distinction

The trait–state distinction in personality research (Allen & Potkay, 1981, 1983; Cattell & Scheier, 1961; Nesselroade, 1988; Spielberger et al., 1969; Zuckerman, 1983) is a useful vehicle for organizing some of the key issues and concepts related to the topics of constancy and change (e.g., Hertzog & Nesselroade, 1987). The distinction has a long history (Eysenck, 1983) but is not without controversy. One exchange (e.g., Allen & Potkay, 1981, 1983; Zuckerman, 1983) was focused on the arbitrariness of the distinction between trait and state. In this section, we do an "end run" around that controversy to some extent by recognizing a conceptual distinction between state and trait and the likelihood of different patterns of antecedents and correlates for them. In the next section, however, for purposes of illustration, we formalize the difference between trait and state in terms of period lengths.

In any event, we do not regard the dichotomy as comprehensive or exhaustive, but we have found the labels useful for conveying the essence of a distinction between relatively stable interindividual differences dimensions (traits) and dimensions of relatively short-term, intraindividual variability (states). The former also evince intraindividual change, but it is of much slower, less reversible character. Cattell (1966a), for example, referred to this kind of change as trait change. For the purposes of this chapter, we use the terms *trait* and *state* to label these two kinds of dimensions.

We assume the following generalized model to represent the score of individual i on observed variable Y at a given point in time t.

$$Y_{ti} = T_{ti} + S_{ti} + E_{ti} \quad , \tag{1}$$

where T_{ti} = individual i's trait component at time t, S_{ti} = individual i's state component at time t, and E_{ti} = an error of measurement for individual i on observed variable Y at time t. Several points should be explicitly noted about this representation.

1. The observed score has both a trait and a state component at a given point in time. This means that the variance of a

distribution of scores for many persons, all measured at time *t*, potentially consists of both trait and state components.

2. Whereas the notion of trait conveys the idea that a given individual has a characteristic value at a given point in time, the notion of a state implies a hypothetical distribution of values for the individual at a given point in time, although, at a specific instance, the individual will have a particular value from that distribution.

3. Measuring individuals only once does not eliminate the state variance contribution from the observed scores; it merely ensures that it will be hopelessly confounded with the trait variance contribution.

The history of personality research reflects a strong emphasis on rather straightforward, linear, and additive representations of both constancy and change. In many respects, these have served the science well, but it seems fair to say that novel forms of representation should be sought even as researchers continue to explore the limits of current ones. It is our belief that there are potentially important alternatives to be explored, some of which seem well-suited to the extension of constancy and change concepts in new directions. We return to this point in the final sections of this chapter.

TWO SIMULATIONS AND THEIR OUTCOMES

To explore more systematically some of the issues pertinent to assessing constancy and change, we have constructed two simulations that rest on the trait–state distinction as represented in the model described above. We present the outcomes of the simulations in familiar terms: test–retest correlation estimates of stability. These two simulations are designed to illustrate the potential for erring in the overestimation or underestimation of stability when using test–retest correlations as stability indicators. The simulations rest on equations suggesting considerable regularity. This, admittedly, is an oversimplification, and it would not be difficult to program some shocks into the system. To do so, however, would unnecessarily complicate the presentation.

Prior to presenting the simulations, we develop the bases on which they rest. These include a generic equation to represent various functional relationships between personality attributes and time and an examination of the role of measurement spacing and duration in studying personality constancy and change.

A Generic Curve for Representing Traits and States

We start with the difference equation that is used to describe the motion of a linear spring as dampened with a linear force (Hubbard &

West, 1991; Wylie, 1979), very much the same equation that describes the behavior of the springs on one's car as they are dampened by shock absorbers:

$$\frac{\Delta^2 y}{\Delta x^2} + \zeta \frac{\Delta y}{\Delta x} + \eta y = 0 \quad , \tag{2}$$

where Δx and Δy represent the finite change in the variables x and y, respectively, η represents a frequency parameter, and ζ represents a dampening parameter.

We hasten to assure the reader that Equation 2 is not as formidable as it may appear. A difference equation simply states that the future trajectory of a system can be predicted from its present and recent state and from its present and recent rates of change over some finite interval of time (Wylie, 1979). Thus, we explicitly quantify expectations regarding future behavior based on measurements of current behavior and measurements of behavior in the recent past.

We have chosen Equation 2 not because we believe that personality is appropriately represented as a spring, but because of the equation's precise and adaptive utility for the several points we wish to make. We note in passing that the notions of frequency and dampening do not seem incompatible with ideas of socialization and control on the one hand, and social support and buffering on the other that act to keep the organism functioning within some set of boundaries. Before introducing the simulations, we identify and discuss in some detail the model represented by Equation 2 and its parameters.

The Δx and Δy in Equation 2 represent differences in values across time or changes in the variables x and y. To give an intuitive feel for the two parameters, ζ and η, they have been assigned a series of values and the resulting equations plotted, as shown in Figure 1. By holding one parameter constant and varying the other parameter, one can see how changes in the parameters influence the precise shape of the curve.

The curves used to represent traits in these simulations are actually cyclic functions that decay within the first cycle. In Figure 1, parts 1a–1d illustrate various trait curves that are obtainable from Equation 2 by increasing the value of η while holding ζ constant: an *increasing cyclic frequency*. Notice that there is a secondary effect of a decrease in total amplitude of the first cycle of the trait curve as η is increased. This secondary effect is an important signature of the difference Equation 2.

In Figure 1, parts 2a–2d illustrate different state curves obtainable from the same general equation by decreasing the value of η while holding ζ constant: a *decreasing cyclic frequency*. Thus, η can be regarded as a term that controls the frequency of both the trait and state curves.

In Figure 1, parts 3a–3d show the effect of increasing ζ while holding η constant: a *greater dampening* of the trait curve. These trait curves are all

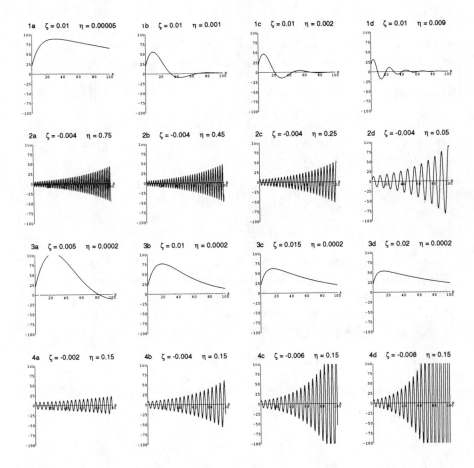

Figure 1: Varying the parameters of the state and trait curves. 1a–1d: Increasing η increases the frequency of the trait curve. 2a–2d: Decreasing η decreases the frequency of the state curve. 3a–3d: Increasing ζ increases the variance dampening of the trait curve. 4a–4d: Increasing negative ζ increases the variance growth of the state curve.

dampened within the first cycle, so it is difficult to recognize them as being from the same family of curves as the state curves. Using this equation, the degree of nonlinearity in the decay of the trait curve can be controlled by balancing a decreasing frequency against an increasing decay.

In Figure 1, parts 4a–4d show the effect of varying a negative value of ζ while holding η constant. When ζ is negative, its effect is one of negative variance decay, that is, an effect of variance growth. As ζ is made to be a larger negative number, the variance growth becomes more rapid. Thus, one can interpret ζ as a parameter that controls the dampening of the trait or state curves.

Thus, the curves shown in Figure 1 illustrate how very flexible Equation 2 is in that it can be used to describe prototypic trait and state curves simply by varying the parameters ζ and η. An aspect that we want to emphasize here is that by means of Equation 2 trait and state concepts are both cases of a more general representation of constancy and change.

Example Trait Curve

In Figure 2, an example trait curve is presented that was produced by setting $\zeta = .01$ and $\eta = .0002$. Thus, the score on trait T for individual i at time t follows the expression

$$\frac{\Delta^2 T_{ti}}{\Delta t^2} + .01 \frac{\Delta T_{ti}}{\Delta t} + .0002 T_{ti} = 0 \quad . \tag{3}$$

This curve has a period approximately equal to two human lifetimes and is 99% dampened within that period. If the x-axis in Figure 2 is taken to represent time in years and the y-axis to represent level of attribute (shown here on a scale of 0 to 100), the general shape of the curve bears more than a cursory resemblance to the way fluid intelligence is portrayed to change over the human life span (Cattell, 1957).

Example State Curve With Decreasing Variance

For the example state curve shown in Figure 3, parameter values of $\zeta = .005$ and $\eta = 3.85$ were given to Equation 2. These values produce

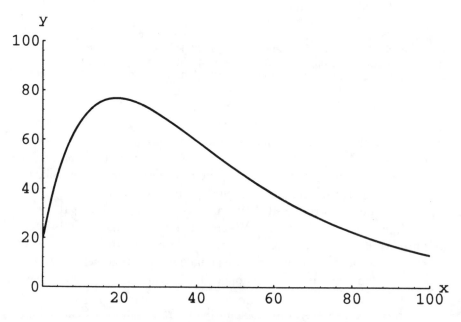

Figure 2: State curve with decreasing variance.

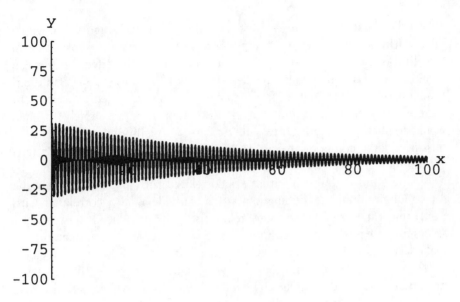

Figure 3: Example trait curve.

a curve with a period of 1 and a dampening force such that the fluctuation is 99% dampened within 200 periods. With the exception of the two parameter values, this example state curve and the preceding example trait curve are mathematically identical.

If the x-axis in Figure 3 represents time in years and the y-axis represents some personality attribute measured on a scale of 0 to 100, then the following is true for individual i:

$$\frac{\Delta^2 S_{ti}}{\Delta t^2} + .005 \frac{\Delta S_{ti}}{\Delta t} + 3.85 S_{ti} = 0 \quad . \tag{4}$$

This state curve illustrates variability in some personality attributes that is correlated with the change in seasons, the magnitude of which variability diminishes with age. Something like seasonal affective disorder, for example, the amplitude of which wanes with increasing age or under a lengthy treatment regimen, exemplifies the basic idea.

A set of measurements of this state curve would show *aliasing artifacts* (Shannon, 1975) if measurements were performed at approximately the same day of the year for each wave of a panel study. In other words, if an individual's state score were correlated with the season of the year and measurements were always performed during that season, one would underestimate the intraindividual variability and overestimate the stability of the score. In an extreme case such as the idealized state curve that is perfectly correlated with the day of the year, if measurements were always performed on the same day of the year, one would estimate the state variance to be zero and estimate perfect test–retest reliability when in actuality one would have entirely missed a large component of state variance. Illustrative of this kind of cyclicity but for a different time scale is the effect of estrogen level on various ability measures described by Hampson (1990) and mentioned earlier. Extrapolating from Hampson's data, repeated measurement built around equal measurement lags of one month on a sample of women would tend to produce high test–retest correlations in ability scores while missing a large component of state variability occurring within the intervening months.

The point is that if a variable is correlated with any time scale and a set of longitudinal measurements of that variable is also correlated with that same time scale, a spurious relationship is introduced between the scores and measurement occasions. It is common practice, for example, to make longitudinal measurements with equal lag times. This, in some cases, unfortunate practice ensures that the measurements are perfectly correlated with that time scale. Hence, any cyclic phenomenon whose period is also correlated with that time scale will be mismeasured in one way or another unless the spurious relationship due to the common time scale is taken into account.

Figure 4 shows a 10-year interval of the state curve from Figure 3 for one hypothetical individual. In this panel study, each individual is measured on the state function at three points (e.g., $a1$, $a2$, $a3$) that are spaced

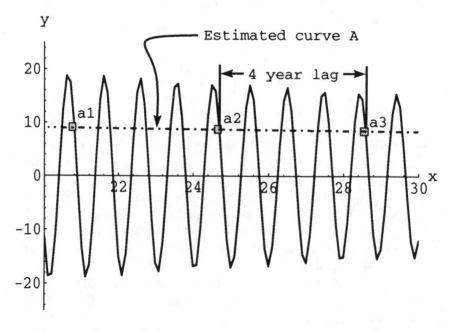

Figure 4: Measurement lag as a multiple of the cyclic period.

exactly four years apart. It can be assumed that individuals' curves, even though they are the same shape, are somewhat asynchronous across time. When some people are high, others are low, and vice versa. Because the measurement lag is an exact multiple of the period of the state, the curve A that would be estimated from these measurements for each individual would manifest no change in level. Thus, the average curve would also be flat, but a high test–retest measure of stability, computed over individuals, would be found.

Figure 5 shows the same 10-year interval of the state curve from Figure 3. Suppose a panel study were designed to measure the state at three points (e.g., b1, b2, b3) that are spaced four years and three months apart. Again, it can be assumed that the state function of each individual is described by the same curve but that the individual curves are somewhat asynchronous. Because the measurement lag is a near multiple of the period of the state curve, a linear effect is seen for each individual's curve, but because of the asynchronicity of the curves, a low test–retest stability coefficient would be found, computed over individuals. If the individuals' curves were nearly in phase, then a linear effect and a high test–retest stability would prevail.

One way to avoid these aliasing artifacts is to use a random measurement lag. By choosing a uniform random distribution of lags, the selection of the measurement lag is guaranteed to be uncorrelated with the period of a cyclic phenomenon, no matter what period that cyclic phenomenon

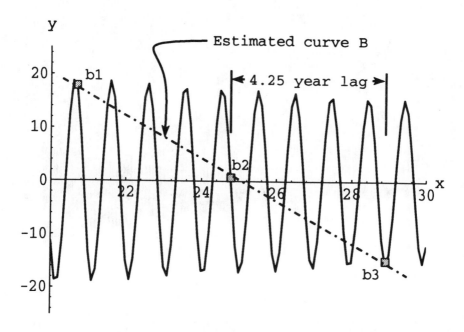

Figure 5: Measurement lag as a near multiple of the cyclic period.

may have. This technique turns the former problem into an advantage. Because the selection of lag is now uncorrelated with the period of a cyclic phenomenon, after removing the overall correlation between all of the scores, a partial correlation between the scores at lags that share common divisors can now be attributed to the period of a cyclic phenomenon. This technique gives much the same result as would a Fourier transform (Bracewell, 1978), but does not require sampling within the so-called *Nyquist limit*, that is, sampling with a lag less than half the period of the cyclic phenomenon.

Example State Curve With Increasing Variance

Figure 6 shows an example state curve with increasing variance. Here we have used Equation 2, with parameter values $\zeta = -.004$ and $\eta = 3.85$. These values produce a curve with a period of 1 and a negative dampening force such that the magnitude of intraindividual variability increases as x increases (e.g., increasing variability in health status with advancing age).

Specifically, if the x-axis in Figure 6 represents time in years and the y-axis represents some behavior or personality attribute measured on a scale of 0 to 100, for individual i

$$\frac{\Delta^2 S_{ti}}{\Delta t^2} - .004 \frac{\Delta S_{ti}}{\Delta t} + 3.85 S_{ti} = 0 \quad . \tag{5}$$

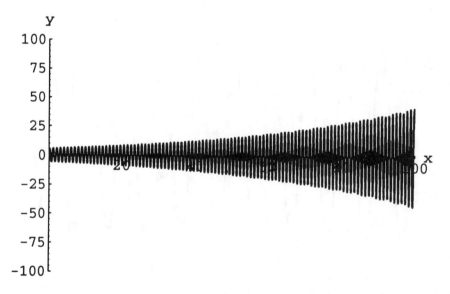

Figure 6: State curve with increasing variance.

Generally, the kind of intraindividual variability pattern portrayed in Figure 6 might be illustrated by the gradual blossoming of some full-blown cyclic dysfunction or the gradual erosion of emotional self-control, although a somewhat higher degree of regularity is implied by the curve than might be expected with psychological or behavioral attributes.

Example Compound Trait and State Curve

Figure 7 is the sum of the trait curve from Figure 2 and the state curve with increasing variance from Figure 6. The result is a linear combination of T_{ti} from Equation 3 and S_{ti} from Equation 5 such that Equation 1,

$$Y_{ti} = T_{ti} + S_{ti} + E_{ti} \quad , \tag{6}$$

holds where $E_{ti} = 0$. Performance on a fluid intelligence measure, for example, influenced in part by increasing intraindividual variability in motivation to do well on the test with increased age would be expected to show such a compound curve.

Simulation 1: Random Trait Curves and Equal Lag Intervals

In this simulation, we emulated the sampling of 100 individuals on one variable in a three-wave panel study design of the kind mentioned

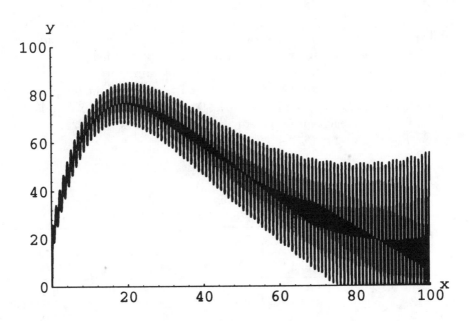

Figure 7: Compound trait and state curve with increasing state variance.

earlier. We constructed a population of 100 individuals who each have compound trait and state curves such that the trait curves vary randomly from individual to individual, but the state curves for each individual are identical to the state curve in Figure 6. The trait curves were individualized by adding a normally distributed random number to ζ and η from Equation 3. Thus, $\zeta = .01 + R_\zeta$ where $\bar{R}_\zeta = 0.0$ and $\sigma(R_\zeta) = .003$, and $\eta = .0002 + R_\eta$, where $\bar{R}_\eta = 0.0$ and $\sigma(R_\eta) = .00006$.

The difference equations were then iterated over $0 \le t \le 100$ with a step size $\Delta t = 0.1$ to produce a population of 100 compound trait and state curves. An age of measurement t_{i1} for the first wave of measurement was independently generated for each individual i as a normally distributed random number $t_{i1} = R_{ti1}$, where $\bar{R}_{ti1} = 40$ and $\sigma(R_{ti1}) = .3$. The second and third ages of measurement for each individual were generated as $t_{i2} = t_{i1} + 5$ and $t_{i3} = t_{i2} + 5$.

Each individual's score Y_{ti} at each measurement time t_{i1}, t_{i2}, t_{i3} was then sampled from the population of compound trait and state curves, and standard test–retest correlations were computed. The results are summarized in Table 1.

These stability coefficients reflect a rock solid attribute. Indeed, they are so high that the wary reader might suspect we intend to use them to make a point. In fact, this is the case, as we show shortly.

Simulation 2: Common Trait and State Curves

Random Lag Intervals

Next, we selected the compound trait and state curve of one of the individuals from the study population to simulate a panel study with random lags. We performed three waves of measurement on this individual curve 100 times using the same method as in Table 1 to find the age t_{n1} of each measurement n for the first wave. The second age for each measurement n was generated as $t_{n2} = t_{n1} + R_{tn1}$, where $\bar{R}_{tn1} = 5$ and $\sigma(R_{tn1}) = .3$. Similarly, the third age for each measurement n was generated as $t_{n3} = t_{n2} + R_{tn2}$, where $\bar{R}_{tn2} = 5$ and $\sigma(R_{tn2}) = .3$.

TABLE 1
Random Trait Curves Sampled at Equal Lag Intervals

	Correlation Matrix		
	Wave 1	Wave 2	Wave 3
Wave 1	1.00000	0.98561	0.94050
Wave 2	0.98561	1.00000	0.98434
Wave 3	0.94050	0.98434	1.00000

TABLE 2
Single Trait Curve Sampled at Random Lag Intervals

	Correlation Matrix		
	Wave 1	Wave 2	Wave 3
Wave 1	1.00000	−0.09183	0.02435
Wave 2	−0.09183	1.00000	0.23998
Wave 3	0.02435	0.23998	1.00000

In this way we attempted to capture the state variability of just one of the compound trait and state curves from the study population. The variability in Table 2 is almost entirely due to the state component, because the trait curve, which was the same for all individuals, is nearly linear in the target age range. When these correlations are compared with the correlations in Table 1, it becomes clear that the equal lag interval method used earlier to measure the random trait curves has missed an important source of variability and has therefore substantially overestimated the stability of the measure.

Equal Lag Intervals

To illustrate how the overestimation of test–retest stability occurs, we selected the compound trait and state curve of one of the individuals from the study population and performed a panel study with fixed-interval lags. To simulate 100 records for the panel study, we conducted three waves of measurement on this individual curve 100 times using the same method used earlier to find the age t_{n1} of each measurement n for the first wave. The second and third ages for each measurement n were generated as $t_{n2} = t_{n1} + 5$ and $t_{n3} = t_{n2} + 5$. Table 3 shows what happens to the intraindividual variability when we use the fixed lag method for our panel design study.

The individuals represented in Table 3 whose attributes seem truly set in stone are the same individuals who were portrayed in Table 2 with a

TABLE 3
Single Trait Curve Sampled at Fixed Equal Lag Intervals

	Correlation Matrix		
	Wave 1	Wave 2	Wave 3
Wave 1	1.00000	0.99510	0.98080
Wave 2	0.99510	1.00000	0.99527
Wave 3	0.98080	0.99527	1.00000

large degree of variability. The measuring instrument is the same and we have assumed an ideal case with zero measurement error. The difference between these two correlation matrixes is due entirely to the randomization of lag intervals.

Seen in this light, the same population of random trait curves whose correlation matrix in Table 1 looked so stable just moments ago now seems to cast a lengthy shadow of doubt regarding the degree of stability. Indeed, one would be wise to consider the potential for periodic phenomena in one's data before announcing the discovery of stability in a set of population parameters.

DYNAMICAL SYSTEMS

In this, the penultimate section of the chapter, we examine some relatively new ideas and some of their implications for further work in the area of personality research. We focus on the field of dynamical systems theory, the vocabulary and mathematics of which are powerful tools that promise to better equip behavioral scientists to deal with some of the issues of constancy and change.

The preceding simulation examples were formulated in the terms of difference equations. To review, a difference equation states that the future trajectory of a system can be predicted from its present and recent state and from its present and recent rates of change over some finite interval of time (Wylie, 1979). We find this to be a convenient set of concepts for explicitly quantifying expectations regarding future behavior, based on measurements of current behavior and behavior in the recent past.

A conceptualization of deterministic change based on difference equations may not seem to be rich enough to account for the apparently unpredictable nature of much of human behavior. However, in recent years relatively simple systems of difference equations have been shown to be at once entirely deterministic and yet unpredictable in their trajectories after some small amount of time has elapsed (Parker & Chua, 1989; Ruelle & Takens, 1971; Thompson & Stewart, 1986). Systems that exhibit this type of deterministic unpredictability are said to be *chaotic*, a term that has seen much use and abuse in recent popular culture (Ruelle, 1990). A chaotic system exhibits a behavior that is called *sensitive dependence on initial conditions*. What this means is that an infinitesimal change in the current state or current rate of change will cause an unpredictably large change in the system after some finite amount of time has elapsed. Awareness of the potential for chaotic behavior is one consequence of adopting the dynamical systems perspective on constancy and change.

Cyclic or periodic behavior can be expressed simply and flexibly with difference and differential equations. Differential equations represent change as an instantaneous quantity rather than over a finite time lag as do difference equations. Periodic behavior can be quite stable and its stability is well expressed in terms of the predictability of its difference equations. Tools such as *phase space embedding* are commonly used to reveal the nature of the stability of periodic and quasi-periodic phenomena that are studied as dynamical systems (Seydel, 1988). At the risk of oversimplification, phase space embedding is a technique for representing a dynamical system in which a vector in a D dimensional phase space corresponds to the state of the dynamical system at D equal intervals of time. One finds that the dimension of the embedding space used to examine a dynamical system can be a critical factor in the apparent predictability of a set of sampled data. We used this fact to guide the creation of the simulation examples in the previous section. What may look like measurement error when viewed in an embedding space of one dimensionality may be perfectly correlated with something else when viewed in an embedding space of another dimensionality.

Another surprising finding resulting from dynamical systems theory is the existence of sets of deterministic difference equations that, although appearing quite stable, can exhibit sudden jumps or changes in the nature of their behavior (Glass & Mackey, 1988). These sudden changes in the nature of the behavior of a dynamical system are known as *bifurcations.* This characteristic of bifurcating systems of difference equations is an intriguing one for psychologists who are interested in representing and understanding mechanisms that produce sudden changes in patterns of human behavior.

In fact, observed intraindividual variability might not progress smoothly and continuously between states as indicated in our simulations; it might well proceed in apparently discontinuous jumps. There is some evidence that a cognitive time has an internal representation that is composed of discrete intervals rather than a continuum (Boker, 1993). Analysis of the degree of predictability of these bifurcations between relatively stable states represents a promising model for the process of change and constancy within an individual (Abarbanel, Brown, & Kadtke, 1990; Casdagli, 1989; Farmer & Sidorowich, 1987; Frank, Lookman, & Nerenberg, 1990; Packard, Crutchfield, Farmer, & Shaw, 1980; Sugihara & May, 1990).

If one's current personality is thought of as a set of mechanisms, built from one's genetic predispositions and past experiences, which translates current experience and current physiology into future behavior, then one is already working within a dynamical systems perspective (see, e.g., Cattell, 1980). Although applications of this methodology to the study of behavior are in their infancy, there is a clear promise that the use of the formal tools of differential equations and dynamical systems will result in a more precise communication of models of personality concomitant with increased awareness of the implications of such models.

DISCUSSION

Students of personality stability and change are entitled at this point to ask, "So what do we do to design future studies more optimally?" The material presented in this chapter has several notable implications for personality research. We focus primarily on two classes of implications; one having to do with general issues of research design, and the other with research on development and other kinds of changes.

In the course of the simulations presented here, we have made substantial use of the trait–state distinction, a conception that we believe to be a useful device for integrating ideas about constancy and change into one framework. Like most dichotomies, the label does not convey all the subtleties and gradations between constancy and the idealized change represented by a pure state. It does, however, force a consideration of more structured possibilities than just stable traits and noise or error. The distinction has enabled us to define and present some prototypic aspects of both constancy and change and to focus on what seem to be some key issues that students of personality should examine as they pursue their objectives.

1. Implications for the Design of Research Studies

The assessment of both constancy and change continues to be a desirable, but demanding, activity. Stability and change information is among the most carefully sought and interpreted information concerning personality. Although the practice of designing research studies to answer questions having to do with both stability and change has been improved in many ways during the past several decades, there is room for still further improvement.

For example, the use of both multivariate approaches to assessment and longitudinal measurement has strengthened research efforts in important ways. Measurement devices, however, are still often composed of little more than a few ad hoc items stuck together with a little dab of face validity. Slavish adherence to past practices has maintained a high premium on such criteria as internal consistency and high test–retest correlation when other concerns such as sensitivity to change and ability should also be duly weighted if an instrument is ultimately to be valid.

Moreover, using longitudinal design in itself is not sufficient to guarantee accurate information about process, change, and stability. There are many different kinds of longitudinal designs, and as the simulations presented here have shown, the most common approaches may not be the most valid or useful ones.

Research design concerns must be weighted carefully in relation to selection issues. Whereas psychologists generally have been trained to think about selection issues with respect to people, this is less true when it comes to variables, and even less so in the case of occasions of measurement. Although this chapter has not focused directly on multivariate issues, it is clear that research design needs to take into account selection effects in all modes of data classification and selection, people, variables, occasions of measurement, and so on. The simulations presented here have pointed to the central importance of selection of occasions of measurement. For example, when it is defined too narrowly (e.g., measure every five years on the same data as nearly as possible), the apparent rigor and orderliness of the design may in fact jeopardize the conclusions regarding stability and change that can be drawn from the resulting data.

More generally, the examples presented here suggest that selection of occasions of measurement is a multifaceted issue. If one is to attend seriously to shorter term intraindividual variability, one needs a sufficient number of assessments in relatively quick succession to provide estimates of intraindividual variability parameters (e.g., amplitude, periodicity, and latency). In addition, if one seeks information about longer term stability and change (e.g., trait change), one needs to distribute assessments across an appropriate portion of the life span. As recommended elsewhere (Nesselroade, 1991a), optimal designs may require the implementation of bursts of measurements, the bursts being separated by appropriately long intervals in order to capture short-term intraindividual variability, longer term intraindividual change patterns, and interindividual differences in the patterns of intraindividual changes. Longer term intraindividual change patterns can include the parameters of intraindividual variability distributions as well as trait levels.

2. Implications for the Conceptualization of Developmental Phenomena

Plotting the course of developmental change is a valuable preliminary to the explication of changes including the identification of their underlying mechanisms. The simulations presented in this chapter suggest that distinguishing among kinds of intraindividual change dimensions (e.g., changes in traits versus state changes) can provide much more variety and texture to the descriptive phase of developmental work.

The integration of constancy and change will remain a general objective for researchers interested in developmental phenomena, whether from a more traditional or from a life span perspective. It may seem odd to encourage developmentalists to concern themselves explicitly with constancy, but, to the extent that constancy in some form is part of the target phenomena, it needs to be accounted for also. To act as though constancy is self-explanatory while seeking to account for change is a statement about one's biases. Moreover, the simulation outcomes suggest that it will be profitable for researchers to concern themselves explicitly with both constancy and change if each is to be better understood and if the rich complexities of our subject matter are to be appropriately represented.

REFERENCES

Abarbanel, H., Brown, R., & Kadtke, J. (1990). Prediction in chaotic nonlinear systems: Methods for time series with broadband Fourier spectra. *Physical Review A, 41*(4), 1782–1807.

Allen, B. P., & Potkay, C. R. (1981). On the arbitrary distinction between states and traits. *Journal of Personality and Social Psychology, 41*, 916–928.

Allen, B. P., & Potkay, C. R. (1983). Just as arbitrary as ever: Comments on Zuckerman's rejoinder. *Journal of Personality and Social Psychology, 44*, 1087–1089.

Baltes, P. B. (1968). Longitudinal and cross-sectional sequences in the study of age and generation effects. *Human Development, 11*, 145–171.

Baltes, P. B., & Nesselroade, J. R. (1973). The development of analysis of individual differences on multiple measures. In J. R. Nesselroade & H. W. Reese (Eds.), *Life-span developmental psychology: Methodological issues* (pp. 219–251). San Diego, CA: Academic Press.

Baltes, P. B., & Nesselroade, J. R. (1979). History and rationale of longitudinal research. In J. R. Nesselroade & P. B. Baltes (Eds.), *Longitudinal research in the study of behavior and development* (pp. 1–39). San Diego, CA: Academic Press.

Bentler, P. M. (1980). Multivariate analysis with latent variables: Causal modeling. *Annual Review of Psychology, 31*, 419–456.

Boker, S. M. (1993). *Foundations for a quantum theory of the perception and mnemonic representation of time and temporal structure.* Unpublished manuscript, University of Virginia, Psychology Department, Charlottesville.

Bracewell, R. N. (1978). *The Fourier transform and its applications.* New York: McGraw-Hill.

Brim, Jr., O. G., & Kagan, J. (Eds.). (1980). *Constancy and change in human development.* Cambridge, MA: Harvard University Press.

Casdagli, M. (1989). Nonlinear prediction of chaotic time series. *Physica D, 35*, 335–356.

Cattell, R. B. (1957). *Personality and motivation: Structure and measurement.* New York: World Book.

Cattell, R. B. (1963). The structuring of change by P- and incremental-R techniques. In C. W. Harris (Ed.), *Problems in measuring change* (pp. 167–198). Madison: University of Wisconsin Press.

Cattell, R. B. (1966a). Guest editorial: Multivariate behavioral research and the integrative challenge. *Multivariate Behavioral Research, 1*, 4–23.

Cattell, R. B. (1966b). Patterns of change: Measurement in relation to state–dimension, trait change, lability, and process concepts. In R. B. Cattell (Ed.),

Handbook of multivariate experimental psychology (pp. 355–402). Chicago: Rand McNally.

Cattell, R. B. (1980). *Personality and learning theory* (Vol. 2). New York: Springer.

Cattell, R. B., & Scheier, I. H. (1961). *The meaning and measurement of neuroticism and anxiety.* New York: Ronald Press.

Collins, L., & Horn, J. L. (Eds.). (1991). *Best methods for the analysis of change: Recent advances, unanswered questions, future directions.* Washington, DC: American Psychological Association.

Elder, G. H., & Caspi, A. (1990). Studying lives in a changing society: Sociological and personological explorations. In A. I. Rabin, R. A. Zucker, R. A. Emmons, & S. A. Frank (Eds.), *Studying persons and lives* (pp. 201–247). New York: Springer.

Eysenck, H. J. (1983). Cicero and the state–trait theory of anxiety: Another case of delayed recognition. *American Psychologist, 38,* 114.

Farmer, J., & Sidorowich, J. (1987). Predicting chaotic time series. *Physical Review Letters, 59*(8), 845–848.

Featherman, D. L. (1985). Individual development and aging as a population process. In J. R. Nesselroade & A. von Eye (Eds.), *Individual development and social change: Explanatory analysis* (pp. 213–241). San Diego, CA: Academic Press.

Fiske, D. W., & Rice, L. (1955). Intraindividual response variability. *Psychological Bulletin, 52,* 217–250.

Frank, G., Lookman, T., & Nerenberg, M. (1990). Chaotic time series analyses of epileptic seizures. *Physica D, 46*(3), 427.

Glass, L., & Mackey, M. (1988). *From clocks to chaos, the rhythms of life.* Princeton, NJ: Princeton University Press.

Goldstein, H. (1979). *The design and analysis of longitudinal studies.* San Diego, CA: Academic Press.

Hampson, E. (1990). Estrogen-related variations in human spatial and articulatory-motor skills. *Psychoneuroendocrinology, 15,* 97–111.

Hertzog, C., & Nesselroade, J. R. (1987). Beyond autoregressive models: Some implications of the trait-state distinction for the structural modeling of developmental change. *Child Development, 58,* 93–109.

Horn, J. L. (1972). State, trait, and change dimensions of intelligence. *British Journal of Educational Psychology, 42,* 159–185.

Hubbard, J. H., & West, B. H. (1991). *Differential equations: A dynamical systems approach.* New York: Springer-Verlag.

Jones, C. J., & Nesselroade, J. R. (1991). Multivariate, replicated, single-subject design and P-technique factor analysis: A selective review of intraindividual change studies. *Experimental Aging Research, 16,* 171–183.

Kruse, A., Lindenberger, U., & Baltes, P. B. (in press). Longitudinal research on human aging: The power of combining real-time, microgenetic, and simulation approaches. In D. Magnusson (Ed.), *Methodological and research strategical issues in longitudinal research.* Cambridge, England: Cambridge University Press.

Luborsky, L., & Mintz, J. (1972). The contribution of P-technique to personality, psychotherapy, and psychosomatic research. In R. M. Dreger (Ed.), *Multivariate personality research: Contributions to the understanding of personality in honor of Raymond B. Cattell* (pp. 387–410). Baton Rouge, LA: Claitor's Publishing Division.

McArdle, J. J. (1988). Dynamic but structural equation modeling of repeated measures data. In J. R. Nesselroad & R. B. Cattell (Eds.), *Handbook of multivariate experimental psychology* (2nd ed., pp. 561–614). New York: Plenum Press.

Meredith, W. (1964). Notes on factorial invariance. *Psychometrika, 29,* 177–185.

Millsap, R. E., & Meredith, W. (1988). Component analysis in cross-sectional and longitudinal data. *Psychometrika, 53,* 123–134.

Molenaar, P. C. M. (1985). A dynamic factor model for the analysis of multivariate time series. *Psychometrika, 50,* 181–202.

Mortimer, J. T., Finch, M. D., & Kumka, D. (1982). Persistence and change in development: The multidimensional self-concept. *Life-Span Development and Behavior, 4,* 263–313.

Nesselroade, J. R. (1983). Temporal selection and factor invariance in the study of development and change. In P. B. Baltes & O. G. Brim, Jr. (Eds.), *Life-span development and behavior* (Vol. 5, pp. 59–87). San Diego, CA: Academic Press.

Nesselroade, J. R. (1988). Sampling and generalizability: Adult development and aging research issues examined within the general methodological framework of selection. In K. W. Schaie, R. T. Campbell, W. Meredith, & S. C. Rawlings (Eds.), *Methodological issues in aging research* (pp. 13–42). New York: Springer.

Nesselroade, J. R. (1990). Adult personality development: Issues in assessing constancy and change. In A. I. Rabin, R. A. Zucker, R. A. Emmons, & S. Frank (Eds.), *Studying persons and lives* (pp. 41–85). New York: Springer.

Nesselroade, J. R. (1991a). Interindividual differences in intraindividual changes. In J. L. Horn & L. Collins (Eds.), *Best methods for the analysis of change: Recent advances, unanswered questions, future directions* (pp. 92–105). Washington, DC: American Psychological Association.

Nesselroade, J. R. (1991b). The warp and woof of the developmental fabric. In R. Downs, L. Liben, & D. S. Palermo (Eds.), *Visions of aesthetics, the environment, and development: The legacy of Joachim F. Wohlwill* (pp. 213–240). Hillsdale, NJ: Erlbaum.

Nunnally, J. C. (1967). *Psychometric theory.* New York: McGraw-Hill.

Packard, N. H., Crutchfield, J. P., Farmer, J. D., & Shaw, R. S. (1980). Geometry from a time series. *Physical Review Letters, 45*(9), 712–716.

Parker, T. S., & Chua, L. O. (1989). *Practical numerical algorithms for chaotic systems.* New York: Springer.

Ruelle, D. (1990). Deterministic chaos: The science and the fiction. *Proceedings of the Royal Society London A, 427,* 241–248.

Ruelle, D., & Takens, F. (1971). On the nature of turbulence. *Communications on Mathematical Physics, 20,* 167–192.

Schaie, K. W. (1965). A general model for the study of developmental problems. *Psychological Bulletin, 64,* 92–107.

Seydel, R. (1988). *From equilibrium to chaos: Practical bifurcation and stability analysis.* New York: Elsevier Science.

Shannon, C. E. (1975). *The mathematical theory of communication.* Urbana: University of Illinois Press.

Spielberger, C. D., Gorsuch, R. L., & Lushene, R. (1969). *The State–Trait Anxiety Inventory (STAI) test manual, Form X.* Palo Alto, CA: Consulting Psychologists Press.

Sugihara, G., & May, R. (1990). Nonlinear forecasting as a way of distinguishing chaos from measurement error in time series. *Nature, 334,* 734–741.

Thompson, J. M. T., & Stewart, H. B. (1986). *Nonlinear dynamics and chaos.* New York: Wiley.

Wylie, C. R. (1979). *Differential equations.* New York: McGraw-Hill.

Zuckerman, M. (1983). The distinction between trait and state scales is not arbitrary: Comment on Allen and Potkay's "On the arbitrary distinction between traits and states." *Journal of Personality and Social Psychology, 44,* 1083–1086.

7

USING GROWTH CURVE ANALYSES TO ASSESS PERSONALITY CHANGE AND STABILITY IN ADULTHOOD

A. GEORGE ALDER and STEVEN J. SCHER

One of the central issues debated among personality psychologists has been the degree to which personality changes throughout adulthood. Although some theorists have argued strongly that change in personality should be an expected attribute of normal, adult development (e.g., Erikson, 1950; Levinson, 1986), empirical investigations of this question have often reported little if any change in personality in adulthood (e.g., Conley, 1984; Costa & McCrae, 1988; Kelly, 1955; Siegler, George, & Okun, 1979). These findings have led to a growing acceptance of the view that personality in adulthood is characterized much more by stability than by change (Conley, 1985; Field & Milsap, 1991; Kogan, 1990; McCrae & Costa, 1990; see Costa & McCrae, chapter 2 in this volume for a comprehensive summary). However, uncritical adoption of this view may be somewhat premature, at least in part because of important methodological and conceptual factors that can preclude a direct interpretation of the results of existing research on change in personality.

149

The study of personality development demands an interest in the analysis and measurement of individual change, an area that has long perplexed behavioral researchers (Bryk & Raudenbush, 1987). One complication arises due to frequent ambiguities resulting from the specific terminology used, often rather imprecisely, by various investigators. For example, terms like *continuity* and *stability* have been used interchangeably to indicate the lack of certain types of change in personality characteristics over time (cf. Shanan, 1991). This lack of precision has especially important consequences for research on personality development because, as we illustrate below, different types of stability can be assessed only through certain types of data analyses.

TYPES OF STABILITY

Several authors (e.g., Caspi & Bem, 1990; Ozer & Gjerde, 1989) have noted that the term *stability* can take on different meanings when applied to personality research. One important distinction differentiates between absolute stability and relative stability. *Absolute stability* refers to a lack of change in the absolute level of the measured attribute(s) over time. *Relative stability* typically refers to the consistency of the rank order of individuals within a group on some individual-differences measure across time.[1]

Assessing Absolute Stability

An examination of absolute stability requires the analysis of a set of repeated measures of a personality attribute obtained from individuals over time. The changes in each individual's score on those measures allow an assessment of the degree of absolute stability for each individual.

However, absolute stability has often been assessed not at this individual level, but at an aggregate level. That is, stability has been assessed by comparing the mean value for a group of individuals measured at one time with the mean for the same group measured at a later time (e.g., Costa & McCrae, 1978; Siegler et al., 1979; see Caspi & Bem, 1990, for a review of this issue). However, the finding that the mean level of some personality attribute does not change over time does not necessarily indicate that there is no change at the individual level. If individual changes were random and both positive and negative, they could be canceled out by the process of averaging, thereby resulting in no mean change being observed. Thus,

---

[1] Relative stability as it is used here has been alternatively referred to as *stability of individual differences* (Costa & McCrae, 1986), *covariance stability* (Hertzog & Nesselroade, 1987), and *differential stability* (Caspi & Bem, 1990), among others.

the examination of change in the average level of a measured personality attribute may be uninformative regarding the degree of change at an individual level.

Assessing Relative Stability

Whereas the evaluation of absolute stability has sometimes mistakenly been assessed with cross-sectional data (e.g., Costa et al., 1986), the assessment of relative stability requires the collection of longitudinal data. The retest correlation coefficient (i.e., correlation between values at two times) is frequently used as the measure of relative stability (Costa & McCrae, 1989). Research using this methodology to assess relative stability suggests that there is considerable stability for a variety of different personality measures (see Caspi & Bem, 1990, for a summary).

Reliability and Estimates of Relative Stability

There are several problems with the use of the retest correlation coefficient as an estimated stability coefficient. First, this correlation is only an estimate of the true stability coefficient, one that will be attenuated by any unreliability of measurement. The retest correlation coefficient can be corrected for reliability-related attenuation using an estimate of the reliability of the measurement instrument. Using this approach, near-perfect stability estimates have been reported on several personality attributes (e.g., Costa & McCrae, 1988).

However, one problem in the use of this method is determining an appropriate estimate of reliability. This problem is quite serious, because in some cases the formula to correct correlations for attenuation due to low reliability of measurement may result in estimated correlation coefficients that are greater than one (see Ghiselli, Campbell, & Zedeck, 1981, p. 242, for one hypothetical example).

This fact makes two commonly used methods of estimating reliability problematic. One method depends on the use of reliability estimates supplied with published tests. This method is not recommended (e.g., Anastasi, 1988) because typically, the sample used to generate the reliability estimates is not comparable with that to be included in the current study. Of particular importance is the heterogeneity of the samples involved. When a reliability estimate is obtained from a homogenous sample, the range of scores on the test will be restricted, resulting in a necessarily lower estimate of the reliability than if a more heterogeneous sample were used. And, the lower the reliability estimates, the more likely it will be that the test–retest correlation (i.e., the stability index) will be greater than one when corrected for attenuation. A seemingly preferable method would be to estimate reliability from a separate sample taken from the same population as the sample that is the focus of the research. However, this alternative may still yield an estimated correlation that is greater than one.

Another solution is to estimate reliability of the personality measure based on the sample of individuals for which the stability coefficient is to be calculated. Of course, if only two waves of data are available, the reliability estimate must be some form of internal-consistency measure, because the test–retest correlation (i.e., the Time 1–Time 2 correlation) is precisely the statistic of substantive interest.

Other Methods for the Analysis of Relative Stability

In instances in which the personality attribute has been measured on three or more occasions, or when there is more than one indicator of the personality attribute assessed at each of two times, several alternative procedures exist for estimating relative stability. Although there are some specific differences among these procedures, they are all based on the assumption that individual development follows a first-order autoregressive model. Such models assume that an individual's current status is dependent only on that individual's previous status plus some random component (for an accessible introduction to these models, see Kenny & Campbell, 1989). That is, these methods model a person's score at time $t + 1$ by regressing the $t + 1$ score on that individual's score at time t. Thus, only the previous measure (i.e., the score at time t) is seen to directly influence the current score (i.e., the score at time $t + 1$). Further, these models have traditionally only allowed for linear relationships between the data over time.

Processes that follow first-order autoregressive models produce correlation matrixes that have a simplex structure, that is, a structure characterized by a matrix in which the elements of the matrix decrease in magnitude as they increase in distance from the main diagonal, and in which the elements along the subdiagonals are approximately equal (Jöreskog, 1970).[2] It has been suggested that such models are appropriate in longitudinal studies in which the same variable is measured for the same individuals over several occasions (Jöreskog & Sörbom, 1986).

From this general perspective, Heise (1969) has developed a procedure for use in situations in which there are three waves of data. This procedure allows one to estimate the reliability of the measurement instrument (which is assumed to be equal across occasions of measurement) and correct retest correlations for attenuation using this estimate. Costa, McCrae, and Arenberg (1980) adopted this procedure and reported stability coefficients greater than 0.80 for the scales of the Guilford-Zimmerman Temperament Survey over a 12-year period.

---

[2]For an example of a simplex-like correlation matrix (although one that is not necessarily derived from an autoregressive model), see Table 1, Sample 1.

Based on a similar model, when there are multiple indicators of a given personality attribute obtained on at least two occasions of measurement, it is possible to fit a latent structure model to the data using techniques for covariance structure analysis (e.g., EQS, Bentler, 1989; and LISREL, Jöreskog & Sörbom, 1986). Relative stability is examined by estimating the correlations between the latent variables representing the personality attribute at each time of measurement.

RELATIVE STABILITY, ABSOLUTE STABILITY, AND THE RATE OF CHANGE

Although the above procedures can be used to provide improved estimates of relative stability, it is important to remember that they do not provide any information with regard to absolute stability. Because estimates of relative stability are necessarily based on correlation coefficients, they essentially discard any information regarding differences in absolute levels of the variable across time. In the simplest case, a perfect linear relationship that increases in time would show perfect relative stability (i.e., the retest correlation would be equal to one), but could show a great deal of absolute change, whether assessed at an individual or at a group level.

In a slightly more complex situation, consider a case in which individuals, on average, become more introverted over time. If those who are most introverted at the time of first measurement increase in introversion more (or at a faster rate) than those who were initially the least introverted (i.e., if there is a positive correlation between initial degree of introversion and increase in introversion over time), then this situation would result in perfect relative stability, but also absolute change at both the individual and the group level.

In other cases, however, differences in the rate of change of a variable over time can result in less than perfect relative stability. If the situation described above is reversed, and it is assumed that those who start out the least introverted have the fastest rate of change (i.e., there is a negative correlation between initial level of introversion and rate of change), it is easy to imagine a situation in which those who start out at the lower end of the introversion scale (relative to others in the group) could catch up to, and perhaps even surpass, those at the upper end. This situation would indicate low relative stability (as well as low absolute stability).

This discussion suggests that change should be conceptualized somewhat differently than has historically been the case. In the past, change has been conceptualized as some type of discrete increment or decrement in behavior occurring between two occasions of measurement (Willett, 1988). As a result, the most frequently used measure of individual change was the difference score. However, a substantial and often confusing literature arose regarding this measure (e.g., Cronbach & Furby, 1970; Harris, 1963; Linn & Slinde, 1977). The predominantly unfavorable appraisal of the difference score, and the implicit implication that it is an unsuitable measure of individual change, gained widespread acceptance that resulted in both a decrease in the use of difference scores by many investigators and a corresponding reluctance of some journal editors to publish results that were based on analyses of difference scores (Schaie & Hertzog, 1985).

More recently, however, something of a counter movement has appeared in the psychometric literature that reevaluates the issues related to assessing individual change and provides an important new perspective on many of the previously presented problems with measuring individual change (see, e.g., Rogosa, Brandt, & Zimowski, 1982; Willett, 1988). The foundation of this alternative perspective is the belief that individual change or growth should be viewed not as a discrete process (e.g., as change), but as a continuous process (e.g., as growth) that underlies development. The change perspective has been called "unnatural" (Willett, 1988, p. 347) and has been seen as the source of many of the problems related to the measurement of change or growth.

For example, it has been argued that the conceptualization of change as a discrete process has promoted the reliance on two-wave longitudinal data as the basis for assessing change. Such two-occasion designs are limited in that they do not provide adequate data for analyzing and comparing individual differences in change (Bryk & Weisberg, 1977; Nesselroade, Stigler, & Baltes, 1980; Rogosa et al., 1982). Furthermore, even when data have been obtained on more than two occasions, the incremental conception of change has resulted in researchers often dividing the data into pairs of waves for purposes of analysis (e.g., Calsyn & Kenny, 1977; Eisdorfer & Wilkie, 1973).

When development is conceptualized as a continuous process, on the other hand, models for individual growth become the basis for the description and analysis of change (Rogosa et al., 1982). More specifically, under this approach, multiple waves of longitudinal data (preferably more than two) are collected from a sample of individuals, and an explicit model of individual development is specified and fitted to these observations. The parameters from the collection of individual growth curves then become the focus for subsequent statistical analyses.

It is possible to select from a wide variety of mathematical models to represent individual status as a function of time. These models range from the simple (e.g., conceptualizing growth as a linear function of time) to the comparatively complex (e.g., assuming growth follows some form of exponential or logistic pattern over time), with the choice of the individual growth curve model being made on either theoretical or empirical grounds.

The preferred alternative is to select a model for individual growth so that the parameters from the individual growth curves are rationally interpretable (i.e., they make sense in terms of what is theoretically known about the processes that underlie development; Willett, 1988). This approach has been used extensively in research investigating physical growth (e.g., Tanner, 1988). The strength of this approach relates to the fact that the parameters from the individual growth curves have real interpretive value. However, in the social sciences, models are typically derived empirically, using the polynomial model of the lowest degree necessary to provide an adequate fit to the data (Bryk & Raudenbush, 1987; Willett, 1988). Such empirical curve fitting is often used when there is little knowledge regarding the underlying mechanisms of growth (Guire & Kowalski, 1979; Willett, 1988).

Viewing change as a continuous process, and bearing in mind our earlier comments about the ways that rate of change can affect relative stability, it is clear that neither a measure of relative stability nor a measure of absolute stability alone provides a complete description of the nature of change at the individual level. It is preferable to have some way of describing and assessing both levels of absolute change and individual differences in the rate and pattern of individual change. The examination of growth curves described above (and more fully explained below) provides such a method. The choice of the model to fit the growth curves represents an examination of or decision about the pattern of change. Further, in the linear case, the rate of change can be assessed by examination of the individual slopes of the growth curves. In nonlinear cases, the parameters of the specified functions can be interpreted to obtain a variety of types of information regarding the change.

GROWTH CURVE ANALYSES

As discussed earlier, the first step in the analysis of growth curves is the adoption of an appropriate model to describe the nature of the change. One of the most commonly adopted models is the linear growth curve. Under this model it is assumed that individual development is a linear function of time, which can be represented as follows:

$$Y_{it} = \pi_{0i} + \pi_{1i}t + \epsilon_{it} \quad . \tag{1}$$

Equation 1 simply provides the mathematical description of a straight line with respect to time (t) for a specific individual i. As such, Y_{it} represents the observed score for individual i at time t; the intercept π_{0i} represents the true level of Y for individual i at time 0; the slope π_{1i} represents a growth parameter, that is, the true rate of change in Y for individual i; and the term ϵ_{it} represents random error in the measurement of Y for individual i at time t.[3]

Suppose, for example, introversion is measured for a sample of individuals at several different times. Individual linear growth curves can then be fit to these data by regressing the observed introversion scores on the times of measurement. The growth curve parameters, π_{0i} and π_{1i}, represent the intercept and slope, respectively, from these individual linear regressions. In terms of analyzing individual rates of change, the important parameter is the regression slope, π_{1i},[4] that provides us with an idiographic measure of the rate of change in introversion over time. Those people for whom the estimated slope is zero can be said to exhibit absolute stability over time. On the other hand, those individuals with estimated nonzero slopes show change in introversion over time, with positive slopes indicating growth, and negative slopes indicating decline in the level of introversion.

Further, the mean of the slopes provides a summary measure of the average amount of change for the sample of individuals, with a mean slope of zero indicating absolute stability at the group level and mean slopes other than zero indicating change in the average level of introversion over time. Similarly, the variance of the slopes provides an index of interindividual differences in individual change. In instances in which every individual's rate of change is the same (i.e., π_{1i} is constant across individuals), the variance of the slopes will be zero. When, on the other hand, the variance of the slopes is greater than zero, there are differences between individuals in the rate of change over time.

When individual development is modeled using individual growth curves, the matter of assessing relative stability is not as straightforward as with other approaches (e.g., Kenny & Campbell, 1989). Although this might seem to be a shortcoming of the growth curve approach, it is, instead, a strength, because a richer description of change at the individual level is provided. Specifically, if individual change is assumed to follow a linear model, then relative stability can exist in one of two ways. First, if every individual demonstrates the same rate of change over time (or, conversely, no change over time), then the variance of the individual slopes will be zero. This is a situation in which one would observe perfect relative stability. However, relative stability is also possible when individuals show different rates of change (recall, for example, our discussion earlier, in which the most introverted individuals at Time 1 change at a faster rate than less

---

[3]It is commonly assumed that ϵ is normally distributed for all individuals and all times of measurement and that the ϵs are uncorrelated across time. However, it is possible to relax the assumption of uncorrelated errors if the appropriate procedures to estimate the individual growth curves are used.

[4]With only two waves of data, the individual slopes are proportional to the observed difference scores.

introverted people, resulting in high relative stability). In this situation the variance of the individual slopes will necessarily be greater than zero. In such cases, relative stability can be assessed by examining the correlation between the individual slopes and the individual intercepts (i.e., by examining the relationship between rate of change and initial position on the attribute being measured). If the absolute value of this correlation is one (or close to one), then the rank ordering of individuals for the variable under investigation is consistent over time, and, thus, the group of individuals demonstrates relative stability on the measured characteristic.

ASSESSMENT OF SYSTEMATIC INDIVIDUAL DIFFERENCES IN CHANGE

The use of the correlation between the estimates of the individual slopes and the individual intercepts as an index of relative stability represents an example of a general strategy that can be used with growth curve analyses in order to identify systematic individual differences in change. One of the advantages of adopting a growth curve perspective is that it provides a logical and tractable approach to dealing with a wide variety of questions that have traditionally been associated with correlates of change. This is an important advantage because many of the perceived problems with difference scores have been raised specifically in relation to their use as criterion variables in correlation research (e.g., Kessler, 1977).

Two main concerns have been raised with regard to the use of difference scores in this context. First, it has been argued that difference scores are intrinsically less reliable that their component scores (e.g., Linn & Slinde, 1977). Along these lines, Rogosa et al. (1982) have shown that the reliability of the difference score is a function of three factors: (a) the precision of measurement for the component scores (i.e., the reliability of the Time 1 and Time 2 measures), (b) the length of time between the two measurements, and (c) the variability in the true individual changes. The most critical of these components is the variability of the true changes. In fact, when there are substantial between-individual differences in within-individual change, it has been demonstrated that the difference score can be more reliable than the component scores (Rogosa & Willett, 1983; Zimmerman & Williams, 1982). Conversely, when there are only minor between-individual differences in within-individual change, the reliability of the difference score will necessarily be low (Rogosa et al., 1982). The crucial point is that when there are no substantial differences in true, between-individual change, then the observed difference score is an unreliable measure of between-individual change (Rogosa, 1988).

The second main criticism of the use of difference scores as criteria in correlational studies is that the correlation between the difference scores and the initial status gives an advantage to individuals with certain initial scores (e.g., Bereiter, 1963; O'Connor, 1972; Plewis, 1985). This seems to be an invalid criticism, however, because the observed difference score is an unbiased, albeit fallible, estimate of true individual change (Rogosa et al., 1982). Further, Willett (1988) has argued convincingly that there may indeed be a correlation between true individual change and true initial status. Consider, for example, a situation in which all individuals are changing linearly over time (although at different rates), and a personality attribute (e.g., introversion) is assessed at more than two times. Given equal Time 1 scores, individuals who exhibit rapid growth will necessarily have higher Time 2 scores than those who grow less rapidly. If these patterns of individual growth continue unchanged, there will be a positive relationship between Time 2 scores and change, whether change is defined as the total amount of change between Time 1 and Time 3 or between Time 2 and Time 3. Thus, in situations in which individuals are changing over time it would appear that individual change and individual status would necessarily be related. A correlation between initial status and change, therefore, may reflect a true relationship, rather than an artifact of the measurement procedure.

The correlation between the difference score and initial status can take on any value from -1.00 to 1.00 (Rogosa et al., 1982; Rogosa & Willett, 1985b). Rogosa and his colleagues (Rogosa et al., 1982; Rogosa & Willett, 1985b) have argued that the frequent finding of a negative correlation between observed initial status and observed change is, at least in part, a function of the negative bias that exists in using the observed correlation between initial status and change to estimate the correlation between true initial status and true change. This bias results from the fact that the measurement error associated with the observed initial score is present, with the opposite sign, in the observed difference score.[5] Thus, in situations in which there is a positive correlation between true change and true initial status, it is possible for the correlation based on the observed quantities to be zero or negative (e.g., R. L. Thorndike, 1966). In addition, the common practice of standardizing a variable so that it has a constant variance over time restricts the possible values of the correlation between change and initial status so that this correlation must necessarily be negative (Rogosa et al., 1982). Thus, the standardization of scores over time and the frequent reliance on the observed correlation between change and initial score as the estimate of the true relationship have both contributed to the

---

[5]The negative bias that arises in using the correlation between observed initial status and observed change to estimate the correlation between true initial status and true change has long been recognized (e.g., E. L. Thorndike, 1924), and several alternative procedures exist for dealing with this negative bias (Blomqvist, 1977; Thomson, 1924; Zieve, 1940). Unfortunately, however, these adjustment procedures have seldom been used in empirical investigations.

misperception that change and initial status are necessarily negatively related.

Several of the proposed alternatives to the difference score as a measure of individual change have been derived to explicitly obtain measures of change that are uncorrelated with initial status. A somewhat confusing variety of residual change scores has emerged in the psychometric literature (e.g., the residual change score, DuBois, 1957; and the base-free measure of change, Tucker, Damarin, & Messick, 1966) and have been adopted for use in numerous empirical investigations (e.g., Arenberg, 1978). Interestingly, the psychometric properties, especially the reliabilities, of the various residual change scores are not that different from those for the simple difference score (Williams, Zimmerman, & Mazzagatti, 1987).

In addition, there are severe logical and interpretational problems associated with the use of the various residual change scores. Residual change scores attempt to determine what the observed or true change would have been for a specific individual if all of the individuals in the sample had had equal initial scores (Rogosa et al., 1982). But, as explained earlier, there may actually be a relationship between initial status and change. Thus, answering this question discards information about "some genuine and important change in the person" (Cronbach & Furby, 1970, p. 74). Given these interpretational ambiguities, and a lack of clear improvement in the psychometric properties, residual difference scores cannot be considered to be better measures of individual change than simple difference scores.

The growth curve perspective suggests that the shortcomings of the difference score are not a result of any inherent deficiency with the difference score as a measure of individual change per se. Rather, this perspective leads to the realization that these shortcomings arise from the limitations imposed by the paucity of information provided with the common two-wave longitudinal design; two-wave data provide limited information, and do not allow for a comparison of individual differences in the rate or pattern of change.

Adoption of the growth curve perspective suggests that the development of models for individual change based on growth curves is the appropriate focus for the assessment of individual change and that the estimation of these models necessarily requires multiple waves of data.

The growth curve approach allows the examination of a wide variety of questions that deal with determinants of between-individual differences in individual change. These questions are formulated in terms of a second mathematical model, one that relates between-individual differences in the parameters of the individual growth curves to individual characteristics. The assessment of relative stability by examining the correlation between the individual slopes and intercepts is just one example of this general strategy. More specifically, individual growth parameters can be modeled as follows:

$$\pi_{ki} = \beta_{k0} + \beta_{k1}X_{k1i} + \ldots \beta_{kp-1}X_{kp-1i} + U_{ki} \quad , \qquad (2)$$

where there are $p - 1$ measured individual characteristics (X_{kp}), β_{kp} represents the effect of X_{kp} on the growth parameter π_{ki}, and U_{ki} is random error.[6]

STATISTICAL ESTIMATION OF GROWTH CURVES

The two models represented in Equations 1 and 2 can be combined into a single, two-level model in order to investigate a diverse and rich variety of research questions that deal with individual change and systematic determinants of individual change. Models of this kind have been investigated under a variety of names within the statistical literature, including random coefficient regression models (e.g., Rosenberg, 1973), multilevel models (e.g., Goldstein, 1989), and hierarchical linear models (e.g., Sternio, Weisberg, & Bryk, 1983). Further, several possible alternative procedures have been developed in order to estimate such multilevel models. These vary from the relatively straightforward procedures outlined by Willett (1988) for use in estimating simple versions of such models to the more comprehensive estimation procedures, with their related computer software, that can be used for estimating more complex versions of the above models (e.g., Bryk, Raudenbush, Seltzer, & Congdon, 1988; Longford, 1986; Rasbash, Prosser, & Goldstein, 1989). Regardless of the estimation procedure used, however, these procedures provide an important alternative for use with longitudinal data, an alternative that has heretofore been largely ignored in the study of personality change in adulthood.

SIMULATED DATA FOR ANALYTIC COMPARISON

In order to demonstrate the potential utility of addressing questions of stability in longitudinal data from a growth curve perspective, several artificial data sets were generated. With artificial data the relationships among the true scores can be specified in advance, and random errors of measurement are added to these true scores in order to simulate observed scores. One of the inherent advantages of using artificial data is that various statistical techniques can be applied to the observed scores in order to

---

[6]Equation 2 can be altered to incorporate nonlinear relationships between the parameters of the individual growth curves and individual characteristics.

determine how well they capture the nature of the underlying relationships among the true scores. A brief description of the simulation procedures precedes the presentation of the results from both conventional analyses and growth curve analyses.

Four hypothetical populations of 5,000 individuals were created under the assumption that, over time, levels of introversion change in a linear fashion. The true individual slopes and true initial values were sampled from a multivariate normal distribution. The populations differed in terms of the degree of relative stability imposed in the data. That is, the correlation between the true rates of growth and the true initial scores varied, with the correlations set to 0.00, 0.30, 0.60, and 0.90 for Populations 1 to 4, respectively. In each of the populations, the initial values were set to have a mean of 100 and a variance of 400, whereas the slopes were distributed with a mean of 0 and a variance of 25. Further, four waves of data were simulated using each of the populations by setting the times of observation as Time 1 = 0, Time 2 = 1, Time 3 = 2, and Time 4 = 3, and obtaining true scores corresponding to each time of observation through application of the individual growth curve equations.[7] Random errors of measurement were drawn independently from a normal distribution with a mean of 0 and a variance of 71 and added to each of the true scores in order to produce, for each population, a set of observed scores, with the reliability of the Time 1 scores being equivalent to 0.85.[8] Finally, a random sample of 300 was obtained from each of the four populations to serve as the data for the following analyses.

Traditional Analyses of Stability

The bases for more traditional analyses of stability in longitudinal data are between-wave summary statistics. Table 1 provides the means, standard deviations, estimated reliabilities,[9] and the between-wave correlation matrixes for each of the samples of 4-wave data. Inspection of the summary statistics reveals several of the common attributes of longitudinal data, including increased variability with time (e.g., Krauss, 1980) and, with the exception of Table 1d, the simplex-like correlation matrix in which the correlations decrease with increased distance from the main diagonal.

A common method of addressing questions related to absolute stability of mean level over time is to subject longitudinal data of the kind simulated

---

[7]For example, if an individual had a true initial value of 100 and a true slope of 5, then that person's true scores for the four occasions of observations would be 100, 105, 110, and 115.
[8]The data were simulated so as to have a constant error variance across occasions of observation rather than a constant reliability.
[9]The estimated reliabilities were obtained by subtracting the variance of the error scores (i.e., 71) from the variance of the observed scores and calculating the ratio of this difference (i.e., the estimated true score variance) over the variance of the observed scores.

TABLE 1
Between-Wave Summary Statistics for Four Samples of Hypothetical Growth Data

(a) Sample 1

	Time 1	Time 2	Time 3	Time 4
Time 1	1.000	**0.980**	**0.902**	**0.786**
Time 2	0.830	1.000	**0.975**	**0.907**
Time 3	0.775	0.845	1.000	**0.996**
Time 4	0.684	0.796	0.886	1.000
M	97.26	97.34	96.97	96.89
SD	21.05	22.09	24.19	26.80
Reliability	0.840	0.854	0.879	0.901

(b) Sample 2

	Time 1	Time 2	Time 3	Time 4
Time 1	1.000	**0.961**	**0.925**	**0.874**
Time 2	0.833	1.000	**0.981**	**0.961**
Time 3	0.814	0.873	1.000	**0.991**
Time 4	0.776	0.863	0.903	1.000
M	99.13	97.60	98.45	99.51
SD	22.30	23.99	27.04	29.90
Reliability	0.857	0.877	0.903	0.920

(c) Sample 3

	Time 1	Time 2	Time 3	Time 4
Time 1	1.000	**0.998**	**0.955**	**0.923**
Time 2	0.854	1.000	**0.992**	**0.973**
Time 3	0.827	0.882	1.000	**0.995**
Time 4	0.809	0.875	0.906	1.000
M	98.97	99.05	99.23	100.17
SD	20.68	24.20	26.83	30.15
Reliability	0.833	0.878	0.901	0.921

(d) Sample 4

	Time 1	Time 2	Time 3	Time 4
Time 1	1.000	**0.997**	**0.998**	**0.995**
Time 2	0.877	1.000	**0.948**	**0.991**
Time 3	0.891	0.910	1.000	**0.999**
Time 4	0.895	0.915	0.937	1.000
M	100.01	100.60	98.40	99.48
SD	22.28	26.94	31.88	35.94
Reliability	0.857	0.9021	0.930	0.945

Note: The numbers in boldface represent the observed between-occasion correlation coefficients, corrected for attenuation using the estimated reliabilities.

here to a repeated-measures analysis of variance (ANOVA). There were no significant main effects for time of observation for any of the four different samples, indicating that there were no significant changes, over time, in introversion. This is not surprising, given that the data were generated so that there would be no change in the average level over time (i.e., the expected values of the slopes are equal to zero).

The observed between-occasion correlation coefficients, corrected for attenuation using the estimated reliabilities, appear in boldface print above the main diagonals in Table 1. Using these corrected correlations as measures of relative stability (see earlier discussion of reliability and estimates of relative stability), one would arrive at the mistaken impression that in each of the four samples, introversion shows almost perfect relative stability.

With four waves of data it is also possible to adopt some of the aforementioned covariance-structure-based strategies to assess relative stability. By assuming that introversion changes according to a first-order autoregressive model (see earlier discussion), it is possible to fit a model to the data using a program for covariance structure analysis (e.g., LISREL). The program estimates the parameters of a prespecified model, and, assuming that the data appear to adequately fit the model, these parameters can be used to assess relative stability.

Specifically, it has been assumed that the true scores on introversion followed a first-order autoregressive model and that the observed scores, therefore, produced a quasi-simplex structure (i.e., a simplex model that allows for measurement errors; Jöreskog & Sörbom, 1986). In addition, equal error variances across occasions were assumed.

This model was fit to each of four samples using LISREL (see Jöreskog & Sörbom, 1986, pp. III.70–III.81 for a detailed example). The program successfully produced estimates of the parameters for the autoregressive model for the data from the first three samples. The program was unable to estimate the model for the sample from the fourth population.[10]

Table 2 presents a summary of the goodness-of-fit indexes provided by LISREL for Samples 1 through 3. The autoregressive model appears to fit the data from Populations 2 and 3 fairly well, and, considering the sample size, provides an approximate fit to the data from the first population.

Among the parameters estimated by the program are the standardized regression coefficients (i.e., the β_i^*s) between the latent variables (i.e., the true introversion scores) at each time of measurement. These coefficients are equivalent to test–retest correlations between the corresponding latent variables, and the correlation between any two nonadjacent variables is equivalent to the product of the intervening β_i^*s (Werts, Linn, & Jöreskog, 1977). Alternately, these parameter estimates can be viewed as

---

[10]This is likely due to the high degree of collinearity among the underlying true scores that was produced by the correlation of 0.9 between the initial score and the slope.

TABLE 2
Summary of Goodness-of-Fit Indexes From LISREL Analyses

Sample	GFI	AGFI	RMSR	χ^2	p
1	0.983	0.914	0.011	10.77	0.005
2	0.992	0.960	0.006	4.88	0.087
3	0.999	0.993	0.002	0.81	0.668

Note: GFI = goodness-of-fit index; AGFI = adjusted goodness-of-fit index; RMSR = root-mean-square residual; χ^2 = chi-square goodness-of-fit test statistics each with 2 *df*s; p = probability associated with chi-square test.

correlations between the observed variables, with the attenuation due to the less than perfect reliability of measurement corrected. These parameters, therefore, can be used as estimates of relative stability.

These stability estimates for our simulated introversion data appear in Table 3. They suggest that there is considerable relative stability in introversion over time.

In sum, application of these commonly used approaches to address questions of stability of personality in longitudinal data would lead to the conclusion that there is a high degree of both absolute and relative stability in introversion for each of the four populations. A somewhat different conclusion is reached when the same data are analyzed from a growth curve perspective.

Growth Curve Approach to the Assessment of Stability

As discussed earlier, growth curve analysis begins with the specification and estimation of a model of change for each respondent. From this per-

TABLE 3
LISREL Estimates of Stability Coefficients

Sample 1	Time 1	Time 2	Time 3
Time 2	0.888		
Time 3	0.803	0.904	
Time 4	0.757	0.852	0.942
Sample 2	**Time 1**	**Time 2**	**Time 3**
Time 2	0.912		
Time 3	0.874	0.958	
Time 4	0.860	0.942	0.984
Sample 3	**Time 1**	**Time 2**	**Time 3**
Time 2	0.931		
Time 3	0.898	0.964	
Time 4	0.887	0.953	0.989

TABLE 4
Means and Variances for Parameter Estimates From Individual Growth Curves

Sample	Statistic	Intercept	Slope[a]
1	M	97.47	−0.15
	Variance	415.66	42.38 (29.21)
	Reliability	0.87	0.69
2	M	98.34	0.20
	Variance	436.61	37.80 (22.71)
	Reliability	0.88	0.60
3	M	99.34	0.38
	Variance	389.93	34.91 (21.00)
	Reliability	0.877	0.60
4	M	99.81	−0.38
	Variance	440.32	38.66 (23.91)
	Reliability	0.90	0.62

Note: [a]Values in parentheses are estimates of variance of true slopes.

spective, interest lies in the various parameters that are estimated from the individual growth curves.

In the present case it was assumed that change in introversion followed a linear model, and, as such, separate linear regression lines were fit to each individual's observed scores. The means and variances of the parameters from this model (i.e., slopes and intercepts) are reported in Table 4.

However, the observed slopes and intercepts are estimated with error. As such, the variances of these parameters are overestimates of the variance of the true parameters[11] (Willett, 1988). One advantage of adopting the growth curve perspective is that when change is assumed to follow a linear model, and when there are more than two waves of data, it is possible, using procedures outlined by Willett (1988, pp. 402–404), to obtain estimates of the error variances, allowing a direct calculation of the variability of the true parameters. Further, once these estimates have been obtained, it is possible to estimate the reliabilities of the individual slopes and intercepts by calculating the ratio of the estimates of the variances of the true values to the corresponding observed values. Estimates of these quantities also appear in Table 4.

In order to assess average levels of absolute stability from the growth curve perspective, one examines the mean value of the individual slopes. As is evident in Table 4, the average value of the individual slopes in each of the four samples is quite low, with none of these average slopes being significantly different from zero. These results accurately reflect the nature

---

[11]The inclusion of error does not affect the mean values because of the assumption that the expected value of error is equal to zero.

of the populations and are consistent with those obtained from the more traditional analyses reported above (i.e., the repeated measures ANOVAs), in which it was concluded that there was absolute average stability across time.

To assess relative stability from the growth curve perspective, one must first examine the variability of the estimated individual slopes. And, although there is no commonly accepted procedure for testing whether or not a sample variance is significantly different from zero, an examination of the variances of the estimated slopes in Table 4 would seem to suggest a considerable degree of heterogeneity, with this heterogeneity being indicative of between-individual differences in within-individual change (e.g., the rates of change in introversion are different for different individuals).

Given these between-individual differences, relative stability can be assessed by examining the relationship between the estimates of the parameters of the individual growth curves (i.e., the estimates of the slope and the intercept for each individual). The observed correlations between these estimates appear in Table 5. However, these correlations are not only attenuated by the unreliability of the slopes and intercepts, they are, as noted above, negatively biased estimates. In order to obtain unbiased estimates of disattenuated correlation coefficients, a maximum likelihood procedure for estimating the population regression coefficient of the true rate of change (i.e., slope) on the true initial status (i.e., intercept) was applied to the present data (cf. Blomqvist, 1977). A 95% interval estimate of the true regression coefficient was obtained and the estimated regression coefficients were subsequently converted to correlation coefficients, producing the interval estimates of the correlation coefficient shown in the third column of Table 5. The correlation coefficients between true slopes and true initial value that were calculated directly from the simulated true scores for the various samples used appear in the fourth column of the table.

TABLE 5
Observed, Corrected, and True Correlation Coefficients Between Initial
Value and Slopes

Sample	Observed	Est. Range[a]	True[b]
1	0.035	0.070–0.345	−0.0025
2	0.259	0.353–0.636	0.313
3	0.414	0.538–0.816	0.548
4	0.729	0.900–1.134	0.918

Note: [a]Estimated range of true correlation coefficient.
[b]True correlation coefficient obtained from correlation between true scores obtained in simulations.

Inspection of Table 5 reveals that the interval estimates of the true correlations contain the true correlation for Samples 3 and 4, and come close to capturing the correlation in the other two instances. What is perhaps most problematic with this approach is that in all instances the true correlation coefficient is located near, or beneath, the lower limit of the range of estimated true correlations. This suggests that Blomqvist's (1977) procedure might provide an over correction; however, further work using these procedures would have to be conducted in order to substantiate this view.

Despite this possible shortcoming, it can be argued that the growth curve analyses produced a more accurate description of the nature of the relationships among the underlying true scores than did the more traditional analyses. Specifically, for the samples from Populations 1 and 2 (in which the correlations between the true slopes and intercepts were set to 0.00 and 0.30, respectively), the interval estimates of the slope–intercept correlations indicated low to moderate relationships between the observed initial level of introversion and the observed rates of change, a result consistent with the comparatively low levels of relative stability imposed on the artificial data. For the third sample, the estimated correlation between the slope and intercept ranged from 0.54 to 0.82. This result quite closely reflects the moderate level of stability present in the simulated data (in which the correlation between true slopes and intercepts was set to 0.60). Finally, the interval estimate of 0.90 to over 1.0 for the slope–intercept correlation that was obtained from the growth curve analysis of the sample from the fourth population quite accurately reflected the high degree of relative stability that was present in the artificial data (in which the true initial value–slope correlation was .90). These results stand in strong contrast to the traditional analyses reported earlier, which indicated high levels of relative stability for all four samples.

Summary of Analyses of the Simulated Data

The results presented here suggest that the growth curve analyses provide an accurate description of the nature of the relationships among the true scores. Specifically, these analyses were able to detect high levels of relative stability when such stability was imposed on the underlying distributions from which the samples were obtained. Further, and perhaps more important in terms of assessing stability and change in personality data, the growth curve analyses were comparatively sensitive in terms of detecting heterogeneity in the underlying growth curves when that heterogeneity was in fact present. These results are quite different from the results based on the more traditional approaches that seemed to overemphasize the degree of relative stability that was present in the underlying data. It seems warranted to wonder how much of the generally high degree of stability found in personality research is attributable to the method of analysis rather than to true stability.

OTHER BENEFITS OF GROWTH CURVE ANALYSES

The present results suggest the potential usefulness of adopting a growth curve perspective in terms of evaluating stability and change in longitudinal research in general, and in personality data in particular. Further, not all of the strengths of the growth curve approach were emphasized in the data simulations. Among the more common difficulties that arise in collecting real longitudinal data are (a) that some individuals are inevitably unable to be measured on all occasions and (b) that the logistics of collecting longitudinal data frequently preclude the measurement of all individuals at the same time. The first problem has often been dealt with by deleting individuals with missing data (a far from desirable solution), whereas the second problem has often resulted in violations of the time-invariant assumption of certain statistical techniques (e.g., ANOVA). Growth curve analyses can readily handle both of these situations (Laird & Ware, 1982).

Recently, Kenny and Campbell (1989) suggested that the investigator who is interested in assessing questions of change and stability in personality is confronted with the choice between two alternative classes of models: growth curve models and autoregressive models. After some consideration of these two models, Kenny and Campbell concluded that autoregressive models have certain advantages that merit their use. Interestingly, one of the shortcomings noted with regard to the potential use of growth curve analyses is that "growth curve modelers discount individual change and assume perfect stability" (Kenny & Campbell, 1989, p. 448). This conclusion not only seems to be at odds with the present results, but also appears to be a misinterpretation of the essence of growth curve analysis that is fundamentally based on the assessment of individual change.

Further, Kenny and Campbell's (1989) recommendation that investigators adopt autoregressive models is also challenged by the present results. These authors suggested that use of autoregressive models can be predicated, at least in part, on the basis of how well they fit the observed data (Kenny & Campbell, 1989, p. 447). However, unilateral adoption of autoregressive models based solely on their goodness of fit to the observed data seems unwise. As Rogosa and Willett (1985a) have noted, and as demonstrated in several of the LISREL analyses in this chapter, data that are generated from nonautoregressive models (as in the constant rate of growth model adopted as the basis for the data simulations here) can often conform to a simplex correlation pattern. Thus, although not wanting to totally discount the usefulness of autoregressive models, we would argue that growth curve analyses also have their place in the assessment of stability and change in personality—a role that has to date, we believe, been underemphasized.

SUMMARY AND CONCLUSIONS

In this chapter, we have attempted to explain how the techniques of growth curve analysis can be applied to longitudinal personality data. We began by clarifying the definitions of two types of stability, absolute stability and relative stability. The former refers to the amount of stability in the absolute level of a trait over time; the latter refers to the degree of stability in the rank order of the trait over time.

After reviewing several approaches to measuring these two types of stability, we argue that several problems in the measurement of change could best be solved by adopting a different perspective on change than has usually been adopted. Rather than focusing on discrete jumps (or drops) in a measured attribute, we argue that it may be preferable to conceptualize change as a continuous process for each individual. That is, we can think of personality change as forming a continuous function in time for each individual. Growth curve analysis proceeds by attempting to uncover the nature of this function for each individual, and questions about the degree of stability in the population are examined by aggregating the various parameters that describe these individual functions.

Through simulated data, we have shown that several of the methods of analysis discussed were able to accurately capture the level of absolute stability in the data. However, of the methods used, growth curve analysis was the only one that came close to accurately indicating the level of relative stability in the data. These findings suggest that further comparative study of these methods is clearly needed.

In the meantime, however, these findings lead us to suggest that we should be cautious in offering an answer to the question in the title of this book. Although a fairly large research literature supports the notion that personality is stable in adulthood (see Costa & McCrae, this volume), this literature is based largely on data analyzed with the techniques that, if our simulations are to be believed, tend to overestimate the degree of relative stability present.

What conclusion, then, can we reach? We would suggest that caution be exercised when choosing a method of analysis for future research on personality change. When designing studies, it is desirable to obtain measurements on more than two occasions in order to allow the use of growth curve analysis.[12] At the very least, data from studies of personality change

---

[12]More than two measurement occasions are necessary or desirable for many of the other techniques described, as well.

should be analyzed with several of these techniques. If different techniques suggest different conclusions about the degree of personality stability, then the question must remain open. However, when multiple techniques yield the same conclusions, then we can truly feel confident about an answer to the question, Can personality change?

REFERENCES

Anastasi, A. (1988). *Psychological testing* (6th ed.). New York: Macmillan.

Arenberg, D. (1978). Differences and changes with age in the Benton Visual Retention Test. *Journal of Gerontology, 33*, 534–540.

Bentler, P. M. (1989). *EQS: Structural equations program manual.* Los Angeles: BMDP Statistical Software.

Bereiter, C. (1963). Some persisting dilemmas in the measurement of change. In C. W. Harris (Ed.), *Problems in measuring change* (pp. 3–20). Madison: The University of Wisconsin Press.

Blomqvist, N. (1977). On the relation between change and initial value. *Journal of the American Statistical Association, 72*, 746–749.

Bryk, A. S., & Raudenbush, S. W. (1987). Application of hierarchical linear models to assessing change. *Psychological Bulletin, 101*, 147–158.

Bryk, A. S., Raudenbush, S. W., Seltzer, M., & Congdon, R. T. (1988). *An introduction to HLM: Computer program and users' guide* (Version 2). Chicago: University of Chicago Department of Education.

Bryk, A. S., & Weisberg, H. I. (1977). Use of the nonequivalent control group design when subjects are growing. *Psychological Bulletin, 84*, 950–962.

Calsyn, R. J., & Kenny, D. A. (1977). Self-concept of ability and perceived evaluation of others: Cause or effect of academic achievement. *Journal of Educational Psychology, 69*, 136–145.

Caspi, A., & Bem, D. J. (1990). Personality continuity and change across the life course. In L. A. Pervin (Ed.), *Handbook of personality: Theory and research* (pp. 549–575). New York: Guilford Press.

Conley, J. J. (1984). Longitudinal consistency of adult personality: Self-reported psychological characteristics across 45 years. *Journal of Personality and Social Psychology, 47*, 1325–1333.

Conley, J. J. (1985). Longitudinal stability of personality traits: A multitrait-multimethod-multioccasion analysis. *Journal of Personality and Social Psychology, 49*, 1266–1282.

Costa, P. T., Jr., & McCrae, R. R. (1978). Objective personality assessment. In M. Storandt, I. C. Siegler, & M. F. Elias (Eds.), *The clinical psychology of aging* (pp. 119–143). New York: Plenum Press.

Costa, P. T., Jr., & McCrae, R. R. (1986). Personality stability and its implications for clinical psychology. *Clinical Psychology Review, 6*, 407–423.

Costa, P. T., Jr., & McCrae, R. R. (1988). Personality in adulthood: A six-year longitudinal study of self-reports and spouse ratings on the NEO Personality Inventory. *Journal of Personality and Social Psychology, 54,* 853–863.

Costa, P. T., Jr., & McCrae, R. R. (1989). Personality continuity and the changes of adult life. In M. Storandt & G. R. VandenBos (Eds.), *The adult years: Continuity and change* (pp. 45–77). Washington, DC: American Psychological Association.

Costa, P. T., Jr., McCrae, R. R., & Arenberg, D. (1980). Enduring dispositions in adult males. *Journal of Personality and Social Psychology, 38,* 793–800.

Costa, P. T., Jr., McCrae, R. R., Zonderman, A. B., Barbano, H. E., Lebowitz, B., & Larson, D. M. (1986). Cross-sectional studies of personality in a national sample: 2. Stability in neuroticism, extroversion, and openness. *Psychology and Aging, 1,* 144–149.

Cronbach, L. J., & Furby, L. (1970). How we should measure "change"—or should we? *Psychological Bulletin, 74,* 68–80.

DuBois, P. H. (1957). *Multivariate correlational analyses.* New York: Harper.

Eisdorfer, C., & Wilkie, F. (1973). Intellectual changes with advancing age. In L. F. Jarvik, C. Eisdorfer, & J. E. Blum (Eds.), *Intellectual functioning in adults* (pp. 21–29). New York: Springer.

Erikson, E. H. (1950). *Childhood and society.* New York: Norton.

Field, D., & Milsap, R. E. (1991). Personality in advanced old age: Continuity or change? *Journal of Gerontology: Psychological Sciences, 46,* P299–P308.

Ghiselli, E., Campbell, J. P., & Zedeck, S. (1981). *Measurement theory for the behavioral sciences.* San Francisco: Freeman.

Goldstein, H. (1989). Models for multilevel response variables with an application to growth curves. In R. D. Bock (Ed.), *Multilevel analysis of educational data* (pp. 107–125). San Diego, CA: Academic Press.

Guire, K. E., & Kowalski, C. J. (1979). Mathematical description and representation of developmental change functions on the intra- and interindividual levels. In J. R. Nesselroade & P. B. Baltes (Eds.), *Longitudinal research in the study of behavior and development* (pp. 89–110). San Diego, CA: Academic Press.

Harris, C. W. (Ed.). (1963). *Problems in measuring change.* Madison: University of Wisconsin Press.

Heise, D. R. (1969). Separating reliability and stability in test–retest correlation. *American Sociological Review, 34,* 93–101.

Hertzog, C., & Nesselroade, J. R. (1987). Beyond autoregressive models: Some implications for the trait–state distinction for the structural modeling of developmental change. *Child Development, 58,* 93–109.

Jöreskog, K. G. (1970). Estimation and testing of simplex models. *British Journal of Mathematical and Statistical Psychology, 23,* 121–145.

Jöreskog, K. G., & Sörbom, D. (1986). *LISREL VI program manual.* Chicago: International Educational Services.

Kelly, E. L. (1955). Consistency of the adult personality. *American Psychologist, 10,* 659–681.

Kenny, D. A., & Campbell, D. T. (1989). On the measurement of stability in over-time data. *Journal of Personality, 57,* 445–481.

Kessler, R. C. (1977). The use of change scores as criteria in longitudinal survey research. *Quality and Quantity, 11,* 43–66.

Kogan, N. (1990). Personality and aging. In J. E. Birren & K. W. Schaie (Eds.), *Handbook of the psychology of aging* (3rd ed., pp. 330–346). San Diego, CA: Academic Press.

Krauss, I. K. (1980). Between- and within-group comparisons in aging research. In L. W. Poon (Ed.), *Aging in the 1980s: Psychological issues* (pp. 545–551). Washington, DC: American Psychological Association.

Laird, N. M., & Ware, J. H. (1982). Random-effects models for longitudinal data. *Biometrics, 38,* 963–974.

Levinson, D. J. (1986). A conception of adult development. *American Psychologist, 41,* 3–13.

Linn, R. L., & Slinde, J. A. (1977). The determination of the significance of change between pre- and posttesting periods. *Review of Educational Research, 47,* 121–150.

Longford, N. T. (1986). *Statistical modelling of data from hierarchical structures using variance component analysis.* Lancaster, England: Centre for Applied Statistics, Lancaster University.

McCrae, R. R., & Costa, P. T., Jr. (1990). *Personality in adulthood.* New York: Guilford Press.

Nesselroade, J. R., Stigler, S. M., & Baltes, P. B. (1980). Regression toward the mean and the study of change. *Psychological Bulletin, 88,* 622–637.

O'Connor, E. F., Jr. (1972). Extending classical test theory to the measurement of change. *Review of Educational Research, 42,* 73–97.

Ozer, D. J., & Gjerde, P. F. (1989). Patterns of personality consistency and change from childhood through adolescence. *Journal of Personality, 57,* 483–507.

Plewis, I. (1985). *Analyzing change: Measurement and explanation using longitudinal data.* New York: Wiley.

Rasbash, J., Prosser, R., & Goldstein, H. (1989). *ML3: Software for two-level analysis, users' guide.* London: Institute of Education.

Rogosa, D. R. (1988). Myths about longitudinal research. In K. W. Schaie, R. T. Campbell, W. Meredith, & S. C. Rawlings (Eds.), *Methodological issues in aging research* (pp. 171–209). New York: Springer.

Rogosa, D. R., Brandt, D., & Zimowski, M. (1982). A growth curve approach to the measurement of change. *Psychological Bulletin, 90,* 726–748.

Rogosa, D. R., & Willett, J. B. (1983). Demonstrating the reliability of the difference score in the measurement of change. *Journal of Educational Measurement, 20,* 335–343.

Rogosa, D. R., & Willett, J. B. (1985a). Satisfying a simplex structure is simpler than it should be. *Journal of Educational Statistics, 10,* 99–107.

Rogosa, D. R., & Willett, J. B. (1985b). Understanding correlates of change by modeling individual differences in growth. *Psychometrika, 50,* 203–228.

Rosenberg, B. (1973). Linear regression with randomly dispersed parameters. *Biometrika, 60,* 61–75.

Schaie, K. W., & Hertzog, C. (1985). Measurement in the psychology of adulthood and aging. In J. E. Birren & K. W. Schaie (Eds.), *Handbook of the psychology of aging* (2nd ed., pp. 61–92). New York: Van Nostrand Reinhold.

Shanan, J. (1991). Who and how: Some unanswered questions in adult development. *Journal of Gerontology: Psychological Sciences, 46,* P309–P316.

Siegler, I. C., George, L. K., & Okun, M. A. (1979). Cross-sequential analysis of adult personality. *Developmental Psychology, 15,* 350–351.

Sternio, J. F., Weisberg, H. I., & Bryk, A. S. (1983). Empirical Bayes estimation of individual growth-curve parameters and their relationship to covariates. *Biometrics, 39,* 71–86.

Tanner, J. M. (Ed.). (1988). *Auxology 88: Perspectives in the science of growth and development.* London: Smith-Gordon.

Thomson, G. H. (1924). A formula to correct for the effect of errors on the measurement on the correlation of initial values with gains. *Journal of Experimental Psychology, 7,* 321–324.

Thorndike, E. L. (1924). The influence of chance imperfections upon the relation of initial score to gain or loss. *Journal of Experimental Psychology, 7,* 225–232.

Thorndike, R. L. (1966). Intellectual status and intellectual growth. *Journal of Educational Psychology, 57,* 121–127.

Tucker, L. R., Damarin, F., & Messick, S. (1966). A base-free measure of change. *Psychometrika, 31,* 121–127.

Werts, C. E., Linn, R. L., & Jöreskog, K. G. (1977). A simplex model for analyzing academic growth. *Educational and Psychological Measurement, 37,* 745–756.

Willett, J. B. (1988). Questions and answers in the measurement of change. *Review of Research in Education, 15,* 345–422.

Williams, R. H., Zimmerman, D. W., & Mazzagatti, R. D. (1987). Large sample estimates of the reliability of simple, residualized, and base-free gain scores. *Journal of Experimental Education, 52,* 116–118.

Zieve, L. (1940). Note on the correlation of initial scores with gains. *Journal of Educational Psychology, 31,* 391–394.

Zimmerman, D. W., & Williams, R. H. (1982). Gain scores in research can be highly reliable. *Journal of Educational Measurement, 19,* 149–154.

8

IF BEHAVIORS CHANGE, CAN PERSONALITY BE FAR BEHIND?

CARLO C. DiCLEMENTE

The question, Can personality change?, is most succinctly answered by, It depends. It depends on how one defines personality and how one defines change. It depends on whether one examines constellations of behaviors, imputed characteristics, or inherited temperament and dispositions. It depends on when and how often one examines the phenomenon called personality. It depends on how one understands stablity and the process of change. This equivocal response reflects more the complexity of the question than any attempt to avoid a definitive response.

LEARNING FROM ADDICTIONS

In this chapter, these issues are examined from the perspective of addiction and change. Addiction and addictive behaviors provide provocative data and interesting dilemmas to enrich the discussion about personality and change. The objective of this analysis is to ponder issues and questions that addiction researchers and clinicians have been exploring for years that relate to the question, Can personality change?

175

The analysis provides intriguing information for proponents of stability of personality as well as for those who embrace a more dynamic change perspective.

The term *addiction* appears, at times, almost synonymous with the term *personality*. Addicts are individuals who appear to be locked into stable, persistent, long-term patterns of behavior. Often these patterns of behavior are hypothesized to be the result of stable, internal dynamics and inherited dispositions (Tarter, 1988). There is currently a consensus among researchers that searching for a single pattern of personality traits or dimensions common to all addicts is a simplistic and unachievable goal (Sutker & Allain, 1988). However, classification of alcohol and drug abusers into subtypes based in part on personality attributes (Labouvie & McGee, 1986), pathological characterological dimensions (Graham & Strenger, 1988; Morey & Skinner, 1986), and other early childhood dimensions (Alterman & Tarter, 1986) continues to provide some support for a link between personality and addiction. Hence, personological variables represent one dimension that has been important in the study of addictions that seems to support a stability perspective.

In contrast to this stability, however, is the fact that addictive behavior change is a well established phenomenon. Although there has been a great deal of pessimism expressed about the possibility and probability of changing addictive behaviors, there is ample and reliable evidence that change does occur. The critical issue here, as with all discussions of personality change, is the time frame taken by the observer. Cross-sectional views and short-term perspectives can be discouraging. At any one point in time, attempts to change are much more likely result in relapse and failure than in success (Cohen et al., 1989; Hunt, Barnett, & Branch, 1971; Schachter, 1982). However, long-term follow-up and natural history perspectives reveal quite a different picture (Armor, Polich, & Stambul, 1978; Moos, Finney, & Cronkite, 1990; Vaillant, 1983). Change happens, not always, but often. At times the change or changes are dramatic. More often they occur over long periods of time in less dramatic fashion (Prochaska, DiClemente, & Norcross, 1992; Schachter, 1982).

It is difficult to accurately assess how much change in addictive behaviors occurs over time. Both population and an individual perspective are needed to paint the complete picture. The most accurate and comprehensive figures relate to nicotine addiction. Prevalence of cigarette smoking has decreased from 42% of the population in the early 1960s to approximately 26% of the population in 1992. Some of this decline is related to fewer individuals adopting the habit. However, it is estimated that more than 38 million Americans have quit smoking over the past 25 years (U.S. Department of Health and Human Services [USDHHS], 1990a). Initiation usually occurred during teenage years and cessation 15 to 30 years later; thus, most of them had been addicted, daily smokers who smoked for many years. Surveys of drinkers show that the proportion of heavy drinkers drops dramatically as drinkers get older (Cahalan, 1987). Long-term success rates for dependent drinkers with serious problems that require treatment average from 30% to 50% when death and dropout of subjects has been taken into account (Fillmore, 1974; Moos et al., 1990). With estimates that there are approximately 1.4 million clients in treatment during a year (USDHHS, 1990b), the ultimate success of this cohort measured 10 or more years later would represent over a half million individuals who achieved successful modification of their problematic pattern of use. However, there are also clear signs of stability. In a 20-year longitudinal study of American college youth, about half of the individuals who were problem drinkers in their thirties or forties showed signs of problem drinking in their college days. During extended follow-up periods, approximately 15% of the sample population will have died due to causes associated with their alcohol abuse. This is a much higher rate than that of community controls (Moos et al., 1990). Estimates of behavior change with the cessation of illegal drug use are more difficult to make. The high levels of drug use in the 1960s have subsided and the outcome success of drug treatment seems comparable or somewhat lower than the success of alcoholism treatment. However, there are few long-term outcome studies of drug abusers. Although the picture is not completely clear, addictive behaviors—including smoking, drinking, and illegal drug use—are modifiable, and a large number of individuals have demonstrated stable success in the modification of these behaviors.

In fact, current research in the addictions is focused more on the patterns and processes of addictive behavior change than on the question of whether or not change can occur. Marlatt and Gordon (1985) have focused on the phenomenon of recidivism and explored the relapse process and its role in the process of change. Prochaska and DiClemente (1984, 1992a) have developed a *stages-of-change* perspective that conceptualizes the process of addictive behavior change as a staged phenomenon that, they estimated, takes 7 to 10 years. Moos and colleagues (1990) have developed a multidimensional evaluation paradigm that includes client and life context factors, both pre- and posttreatment, and they use this paradigm for short-term and long-term outome evaluations. This process perspective is beginning to yield an understanding of the patterns of addiction and change that can enrich the discussion of whether personality can change.

A PROCESS PERSPECTIVE

Addiction and change seem to be opposing processes. Addiction represents fixation and stability over a considerable period of time. Definitions of addiction encompass physiological and psychological dependence as well as the sense that the behavior is out of the control of the individual. Failure to change in the face of negative consequences is yet another way of describing addiction (*Diagnostic and Statistical Manual of Mental Disorders*, 3rd ed., rev. [DSM–III–R]; American Psychiatric Association, 1987). The most problematic individuals typically engage in these behaviors for long periods of time, measured in decades, not years, before ever considering any attempt at change or seeking help to do so (Kissin, 1977). These reasons, as well as the fact that often individuals can be addicted to multiple substances either simultaneously or sequentially, encourage the view that there are some underlying personality dimensions that account for such stability. Whether one accepts the construct of an addiction-prone personality or not, addictive behaviors are repetitive, stable, difficult to modify constellations of behaviors, attitudes, and affects that become a cardinal focus in the individual's life space and life work. This description appears to capture many of the definitional elements of the term personality. Thus, understanding how addictions develop and how individuals change with respect to these addictive behaviors would be quite relevant to the discussion of whether personality can change.

Initiation and cessation of addictive behaviors include periods of stability alternating with periods of change. It is not simply a matter of turning a switch on or off. Becoming addicted and breaking free from addiction is a gradual, often subtle, and quite frustrating experience that seems best understood from a process of change perspective. Initiation, for example, includes a sequence of behaviors extending from first use, to experimentation, to casual use, to regular use, and finally to dependence. The initiating behaviors related to alcohol or drug consumption are quite unstable for a time, until they become consolidated into a stable pattern of use called dependence. In turn, this condition called dependence, which has both psychological and physiological components, often lasts for long periods of time and appears as a stable characteristic of the individual. Hence, the label *addict* is given. The addict is described as being controlled by the substance and, as a result, quite different from the person he or she was prior to becoming "hooked" on the alcohol or drugs. Stealing, lying, and criminal activity often occur only after an individual becomes addicted. Thus, the course of initiation brings changes not only in substance use behaviors but in multiple areas of the addict's life (Huba & Bentler, 1984; Newcomb & Bentler, 1988).

From this more stable state of repeated dependent use, individuals can make the transition through a series of stages of change leading to cessation and eventually to another stable state called maintenance, which represents sustained, long-term change. However, maintained change, even if continued for years, does not appear to simply reinstate the preaddiction state of the individual (Moos et al., 1990). There is substantial shifting of attitudes and behaviors from the time of the initiation of the addictive behavior to the time of its successful cessation and a discontinuity between factors involved in initiation and those related to cessation (DiClemente & Prochaska, 1985).

The patterns of addiction and change seem to be best represented by a period of instability (initiation), followed by a period of rather stable dependence, followed by another period of instability (cessation), and then another period of stable abstinence or nonproblematic use. Both onset and modification involve multiple areas of an individual's functioning, relationships with others, and sense of self. Of course, this entire pattern applies only to those individuals who become addicted and then successfully modify that behavior. A number of individuals die either in the process of becoming addicted (overdose, consequences of use, or accident) or before being able to achieve stable abstinence.

A recent model of intentional behavior change has conceptualized the process of change as movement through a series of five stages. These stages identify constellations of attitudes, behaviors, and tasks related to the course of successful modification of an addictive behavior (Prochaska & DiClemente, 1984, 1992a, 1992b). From this perspective, individuals who engage in dependent or problematic substance use and have no intention of and have given no serious consideration to changing that behavior pattern are considered precontemplators of change. Serious consideration of change with no proximal intentions to take action marks the contemplation stage. Preparation stage individuals are planning to change in the near future. In the action stage, individuals use behavioral coping skills to stop the pattern of use. In maintenance, individuals who have been successful for three to six months in the action stage begin to ensure the long-term stability of the new pattern of sobriety or nonproblematic use. As outlined in Table 1, these stages appear to capture the process of cessation of addictive behaviors and may be useful for understanding initiation (Prochaska et al., 1992). In addition, these same authors have envisioned five levels of conflicts or of problem involvement that can either be the focuses of change or represent factors related to the process of change. These stages and levels of change are used to explain the issues of addiction and change in this chapter.

From the onset, it is important to note that this model is one of intentional change in which the individual is an active participant in the process of change. Because addictions require the active consumption or use of a substance and the cooperation of the individual in the cessation process, the application of this model appears quite appropriate. There are other types of changes (e.g., developmental, environmental, or imposed) that are, in large measure, beyond the control of the individual but can certainly influence the process of intentional change, particularly in the arena of addictive behaviors.

TABLE 1
A Stages of Change Perspective of Initiation and Cessation of Addictive Behaviors

Substance Abuse	Stages of Change				
	Precontemplation	Contemplation	Preparation	Action	Maintenance
Initiation	No Experimentation No Intention to Use	Considering Use Some Initial Experimentation	Some Use Positive Expectancies/Pros Over Cons	Regular Use & Abuse Consequences Ignored	Dependence Integrated Into Life-style
Cessation	Little or No Interest Little or No Interest in Change	Pros & Cons in Balance Deliberating About Problem and Change	Developing Network of Users Some Attempts to Change	Social Support for Use Serious Efforts to Modify Behaviors	Precontemplation for Change Life-style Change
	Not a Problem—Under Control	Ambivalence	Intention to Change in the Near Future	Preventing Relapse	Increasing Self-efficacy
	Pros Higher Than Cons	Pros & Cons in Balance		Recycling & Modifying Social Network	Addressing Other Problem Levels

A LEVELS-OF-CHANGE PERSPECTIVE

Nathan (1988) has argued that the addictive personality is the behavior of the addict. His point is that it has been difficult, if not impossible, to find personality factors that can reliably differentiate alcohol abusers from others. Much of the work he critiqued involves the search for measures of maladaptive personality characteristics that would uniformly predict alcohol abuse and dependence. Few measures or single characteristics have been able to consistently predict later use or dependence (Sutker & Allain, 1988). Multiple factors related to childhood and adolescent behaviors, however, have been associated with the emergence of alcohol and drug abuse. Studies have indicated a possible contributing role in the severity or level or substance use for anxiety, depression, and low self-esteem (Blau, Gillespie, Felner, & Evans, 1989); for dissatisfaction and lack of compliance with parental rules (Vicary & Lerner, 1983); and for difficult temperament characteristics, including negative mood, slow adaptability, withdrawal, and high intensity of reactions to situations (Lerner & Vicary, 1984).

There are multiple identifiable patterns of substance use, based on age of initiation and level of use from ages 10 to 30 (Tubman, Vicary, von Eye, & Lerner, 1990). These authors examined longitudinal data for these different patterns of use. Childhood aggessiveness, disobedience in the home, depression, academic problems, and excess parental physical punishment were some of the factors that predicted later use of tobacco, alcohol, marijuana, and polysubstance abuse. Not all factors were predictive for each specific substance (Tubman et al., 1990). These same authors reported that early heavy alcohol use, on the other hand, predicted adjustment, academic, and psychiatric problems. There appears to be a reciprocal relationship between substance use, psychosocial functioning, and psychological adjustment.

Multidimensionality and complexity characterize the current status of research into the precursors and predictors of addiction. Instead of examining global traits or dispositions that can predict the patterns of initiation of addictions, it may be more fruitful to examine specific areas of functioning that increase the risk of adoption of drug use, and then study the impact that the process of initiation or cessation of addictive behaviors has on these various aspects of personal functioning. This perspective parallels efforts by Mischel (1990) and others in personality research to shift the unit of study from global traits to identifiable subfunctions that represent both products and ongoing processes. Establishing and modifying the pattern of behaviors called addictions involves multiple areas of an individual's life and can produce rather stable patterns of functioning in many of these areas over certain periods of time.

One of the advantages of studying addictive behaviors is that there is a specific target behavior (be it alcohol consumption, cigarette smoking, or illegal drug use) that is readily quantifiable. However, initiation and cessation of this behavior and the sequelae of these changes involve multiple levels of functioning that include biology, self-perception, and interpersonal and environmental interactions as well as the more historical and profound sense of self (Newcomb & Bentler, 1988). In an attempt to isolate some specific areas of change, Prochaska and DiClemente (1984, 1992b) have enumerated five levels of change in their transtheoretical model of intentional change: (a) symptomatic/situational, (b) maladaptive cognition, (c) interpersonal conflicts, (d) family and systems conflicts, and (e) intrapersonal conflicts. These five levels isolate distinct areas of conflict or problems that can be the target or the consequence of the change process. For the purpose of this chapter, these levels are used to isolate areas of functioning that are important in the etiology and modification of addictive behaviors (see Table 2). Because this model has been developed to assist clinicians in changing problematic behaviors, the levels usually focus on conflicts or maladaptive behaviors.

The first level is called the symptom/situational level, and it encompasses the concrete behavior patterns and immediate environmental influences that surround the addictive behavior. Behavioral treatments such as counterconditioning, stimulus control, and reinforcement management are directed at problems at this level. The second level isolates maladaptive cognitions, thus including self-statements as well as behavior-specific expectations and beliefs. These types of cognitions have been identified as crucial or contributing problematic issues in many theories of psychotherapy, including those of Ellis

TABLE 2
Levels of Change Involved in Initiation and Cessation of Addictive
Behaviors

Level of Change	Areas of Functioning
I. Symptomatic/Situational	Substance Use Pattern
	Micro and Macro Environmental Factors
II. Maladaptive Cognition	Expectancies
	Beliefs
	Self-evaluation
III. Interpersonal Conflicts	Dyadic Interaction
	Hostility
	Assertiveness
IV. Family and Systems Conflicts	Family of Origin
	Legal
	Social Network
	Employment
V. Intrapersonal Conflicts	Self-esteem
	Self-concept
	Antisocial Personality

(1973), Beck (1991), and Adler (1927), and are an integral part of Bandura's (1986) social cognitive theory. These first two levels, in essence, represent the focus of current cognitive–behavioral interventions.

The third and fourth levels concentrate on interpersonal functioning and problems. Dyadic interactions that are problematic or contribute to problematic behaviors represent the third level of change. For example, interpersonal hostility, passivity, and dependence; marital abuse; and poor interpersonal communication and lack of assertiveness would be focal problems at this level. More extensive systemic social relationships and family of origin interactions or conflicts, such as those involving familial relations, social networks, employment, courts, and prisons, are considered at the family/systems level. Family and systems therapies and community-oriented interventions tend to focus on the types of organizational and environmental contextual problems at this level.

The fifth level isolates intrapersonal conflicts, which again can either be the focal problem or the problematic groundwork contributing to other problems. Self-concept, self-esteem, sexual orientation, and personal meaning and identity are some areas of conflict that seem more appropriately labeled intrapersonal. This level often represents the most firmly embedded and most difficult to change aspects of an individual's functioning. Psychodynamic and existential therapies have focused on problems at this level.

Traditionally, characteristics at the intrapersonal conflicts level would be considered as personality dimensions. However, stable characteristics assessed in psychopathology or personality research have been identified at many of these levels. For example, a sense of inferiority, an irrational need for love, interpersonal hostility and aggressiveness, passivity, helplessness and depression, pathological attachment to a parent, low self-esteem, impulsivity, and identity confusion are all characteristics that have been identified as personality dimensions or characteristics that contribute to personality disorders and could be conceptualized as representing several levels of change. The levels offer a multidimensional framework with which to examine individuals and their problems, including addictions, as they are presented to clinicians and can represent areas of functioning that are a focus of intervention. Various theories of therapy have chosen different levels as the primary ones at which to conceptualize addiction problems and the appropriate interventions (Blane & Leonard, 1987). In the transtheoretical model, these levels provide the framework to explore multiple areas of functioning and examine how they can hinder or promote the process of change.

EVIDENCE FOR A LEVELS UNDERSTANDING OF ADDICTION AND CHANGE

At the symptom/situational level the psychopharmacology of the substance being abused, the stimulus cues that trigger use, the immediate drug taking environment, and the potent reinforcing effects of the drug tend to be the critical dimensions identified by researchers both as etiological factors and points of intervention (Galizio & Maisto, 1985). Peer influences and adjustment problems are important factors in the establishment and maintenance of substance abuse problems (Shedler & Block, 1990). Recovery from alcohol or drug dependence involves managing situational cues and changing a variety of behaviors linked to the drug or alcohol use (Moos et al., 1990; Prochaska, Velicer, DiClemente, Guadagnoli, & Rossi, 1991). Thus, at this symptom/situational level, addictive behaviors are related to biochemical reactions, to clusters of other behaviors, and to multiple situational cues that influence and are influenced by initiation and cessation.

Addicts have also been characterized as having distorted expectancies and beliefs about the abused substance. Efforts to understand outcome expectancies for alcohol and drug use have generated much research (Brown, Goldman, Inn, & Anderson, 1980; Connors, O'Farrell, Cutter, & Logan-Thompson, 1986). There is some evidence that certain types of expectancies and beliefs about the effects of alcohol influence problematic substance use (Goldman, Brown, & Christiansen, 1987). Subjective distress and maladaptive self-statements have been identified as contributors to the initiation of drug use and abuse (Kaplan, Martin, & Robbins, 1984; Shedler & Block, 1990). In the cessation of substance abuse and dependence, efficacy expectations have been demonstrated to shift during the course of change and remain rather stable when long-term maintenance has been established (DiClemente, Fairhurst, & Piotrowski, in press; DiClemente, Prochaska, & Gibertini, 1985). In addition, cognitive mechanisms are a critical component of the relapse model proposed by Marlatt and Gordon (1985). Cognition and shifts in attitudes and beliefs contribute to the process of initiation and cessation of addictions.

Interpersonal influence, lack of interpersonal skills, and tendencies to codependency represent yet another set of problems that seem best characterized at the interpersonal conflict level. Shedler and Block (1990) described the adolescent frequent drug user as "interpersonally alienated, emotionally withdrawn and manifestly unhappy" (p. 617). Interpersonal effectiveness, or lack of it, is often described as an important precipitant of the maladaptive coping represented by substance abuse (Shiffman & Wills, 1985). Interpersonal relationship problems clearly play a role in the initiation and cessation of addictive behaviors, from alcohol consumption and cigarette smoking to cocaine and heroin use (Kaplan et al., 1984; Moos et al., 1990; USDHHS, 1988, 1990b).

Familial history of alcoholism and transmission of alcoholism through family traditions (Steinglass, Bennett, Wolin, & Reiss, 1987) represent a family/system level of understanding alcohol problems and treatment. There is ample evidence that both genetics and environment are involved in the process of the development of addictions, particularly abuse of alcohol

(Tarter, 1991; USDHHS, 1990b). Parenting variables, such as being unresponsive, underprotective, hostile, and pressuring, have been identified by Shedler and Block (1990) as important predictors of adolescent drug use. Recovery, on the other hand, has dramatic implications for the spouse and the children (Moos et al., 1990; Zweben, 1986). The work of Steinglass, Bennett, and colleagues (1987) is particularly intriguing in that the transmission route is assumed to be family rituals or traditions that are adopted or discarded. These rituals include meals, celebrations, and holiday traditions. Relationships to larger social networks such as legal, health, and employment systems are also critical subfunctions affected by initiation and cessation of addictive behaviors (USDHHS, 1990b). Alcoholic subjects who were stably in remission at a 10-year follow-up reported more family cohesion, less family conflict, more physical comfort, and less pressure at work than their relapsed counterparts (Moos et al., 1990).

Finally, a variety of evidence indicates that intrapersonal factors are important for understanding addictions. For example, psychodynamic therapists have often identified serious early oral stage conflicts as a key to understanding addictions. Contemporary views also incorporate an intrapersonal perspective for the initiation and cessation of addictions (Bean & Zinberg, 1981). Alcoholics Anonymous, for example, views the basic problem of addiction to alcohol as one of character (DiClemente, 1993a). Longitudinal studies have identified an ego control factor that contributes to drug use as well as other intrapsychic variables (Shedler & Block, 1990). However, Vaillant and Milofsky (1982) have made the opposite case: They conclude that the substance dependence (alcoholism in this study) is responsible for the development of passive dependent personality traits, introversion, and other personality characteristics. Although arguments continue (Zucker & Gomberg, 1986), the interaction of addiction and intrapersonal adjustment and characteristics is quite well established (Newcomb & Bentler, 1988). When it comes to cessation, it is also clear that abstinence or recovery after a long period of alcohol and drug abuse or dependence is associated with shifts in values as well as personal and social functioning, so that recovered long-term substance abusers do not look much different from their peers who have never been addicted (Valliant, 1983; Moos et al., 1990).

Addictions, it seems, involve multiple levels of functioning. If these levels represent varied aspects and areas of individual functioning, then change at any one level would affect all levels. If the cocaine addict stops using cocaine, for example, brain chemistry, cues, self-perceptions, interpersonal relationships, and, in time, self-esteem and identity are affected. This represents a holistic perspective not very different from that espoused by Rogers (1961) and Maslow (1970). Change at any level has implications for all levels. As has been demonstrated, multiple factors at multiple levels are associated with the initiation of addictive behaviors. In order to integrate these multidimensional aspects, some have suggested a developmental perspective, others have called for a biopsychosocial approach to understanding the process of becoming addicted (Zucker & Gomberg, 1986). The same is true for recovery from addictions (Donovan & Marlatt, 1988). Although there continues to be some controversy about what constitutes recovery, it is clear that changes in cognition, affect, environment, and behavior are needed to bring about cessation. Cessation of addictive behaviors, in turn, creates changes in cognition. affect, environment, and other behaviors. This interaction across levels of change, in fact, is what characterizes the process of change (Prochaska & DiClemente, 1984, 1992b).

From a levels-of-change perspective, the development of a problematic, dependent use of a substance and the cessation of that use most often require changes at all levels. However, changes that take place at multiple levels do not occur as an immediate result of the regular use or cessation of use, but more like distant ripples made by a stone tossed into the middle of a still pond. The process of change takes time, occurs in stages, and requires a longitudinal perspective. Some discussion of this process, with examples, will clarify the interaction between levels and stages of change.

THE PROCESS OF ADDICTION AND CHANGE

Initiation

The process of initiation of an addiction is quite variable. Some individuals appear to be able to use addictive substances like cigarettes, alcohol, and cocaine, at quite low levels for long periods of time. Others appear to become addicted dependent users rather easily and quickly. Some of these differences can be due to the drug, the route of administration, and the personal dimensions of the individual. Moreover, chances of becoming addicted seem better if there is a family connection that is either genetic or environmental, or both. Individuals who begin use early in their developmental history usually develop less effective coping skills for dealing with life's problems (Huba & Bentler, 1984). Social networks of regular users quickly become saturated with the substance and with other substance abusers. For those who become addicted, then, environmental, family, and personal factors interact to create a durable, dependent relationship with the abused substance.

The process of addiction is multifaceted and involves multiple levels of problems and influences. Which factors constitute the necessary and sufficient causes is an elusive question. Creating typologies based on the amount of use over time (Tubman et al., 1990); examining reciprocal influences between substance abuse and psychosocial adjustments; creating subgroups using level of dependence on a single substance or multiple substances; and examining associated problems or consequences such as psychiatric, legal, and marital issues (Babor & Lauerman, 1986) may offer some answers. For certain subgroups of users, multiple determinants, including ones identified as personality dimensions like impulsiveness or sociopathy, can be involved in the initiation of addiction over the course of time, from first use to dependent use or from the stage of precontemplation of initiation to a solidly maintained habit (Prochaska & DiClemente, 1992a; Prochaska et al., 1992).

Becoming addicted also requires some restriction of behaviors. The repertoire of other reinforcing behaviors becomes constricted (Barrett, 1985). Social networks shrink or become predominantly substance abuse determined. The life-style of the individual becomes more and more defined in relation to the consumption of the addictive substance. Individual choices appear directed to enhancing the drug taking behaviors that in turn become a dominant thema organizing the life of the individual. This process of initiation takes time, at minimum six months to a year. Most often it takes years to become a confirmed, dedicated addict with solid expectancies and beliefs about the personal benefits of the substance and to develop a life-style and self-concept that supports the addiction. Being a drinker, a smoker, or a cocaine user becomes more than a moment by moment self-description and more of an established, personal characteristic. Changes in the rate and amount of consumption of the substance are acompanied by and create changes in multiple levels of functioning including the intrapersonal problem level.

Addiction

Once an individual is addicted, dependence on the substance can extend over a long period of time. In several treatment studies the mean length of time individuals engaged in problematic use prior to seeking treatment was 20 years for smoking (DiClemente et al., 1991) and 15 years for drinking (Paredes, Gregory, Rundell, & Williams, 1979). Addiction usually represents an extended period of a recurrent pattern of dependent, problematic use of the substance. Although there can be fluctuations and slight alterations in the exact pattern of use over time, for the addicted individual the pattern seems more stable than variable and is not responsive to change simply as a result of negative consequences. Often the behavior seems immune even to catastrophic consequences. If anything, the addict appears to prefer to change the environment at the situational, interpersonal, or systems level rather than change the behavior. This stability and resistance to the suppression or extinction of the behavior appears to be the basis for seeking an underlying stable personality dimension that could explain addiction. The stability and solidity of the habit or addiction seem to demand an underlying personal characteristic that drives the habit.

However, as described in the levels-of-change section, this stability could be due to the fact that substance use becomes embedded in multiple areas of the individual's functioning so that continuing use is less problematic than attempting to change (DiClemente & Prochaska, 1985). From a stages-of-change perspective, individuals who have achieved a well-established addiction become precontemplators of the process of cessation.

Cessation

The cycle of change or modification of an addiction begins with the individual firmly established in a pattern of dependent use of the addictive substance. The addict in this precontemplation stage represents either a satisfied customer who would rather fight than switch or an entrenched and embattled user who is unwilling or feels unable to change. All the centrifugal and centripetal forces in the individual's life seem to be supporting stability and to be resisting change. The course and process of change is usually more lengthy and difficult than the process of initiation. In order to modify the addictive behavior pattern, the person moves through the distinct stages of change identified in the transtheoretical model, from the stage of precontemplation to contemplation, preparation, action, and maintenance (Prochaska & DiClemente, 1992a, 1992b; Prochaska et al., 1992).

Movement into the contemplation stage of change is marked by an evaluation of the decisional considerations for and against change, as well as greater openness to information and experiences that can become part of this evaluation (DiClemente & Prochaska, 1985; DiClemente et al., 1991). Movement into preparation is marked by increased commitment, preparatory activities, and proximal intentions to change (DiClemente et al., 1991; Prochaska & DiClemente, 1992a). The action stage is marked by cessation activity and the initial phase of breaking the addiction and establishing cessation or sobriety. After three to six months of successful action, the individual enters the maintenance phase in which change becomes solidified in self-evaluations and life-style.

These stages of change provide a detailed view of the movement from a stable pattern of addiction through a process of instability or change that ends in another period of stability. However, the process is usually not a linear one and most often takes a substantial period of time to accomplish. Estimates are that the time required from the initial movement from pre-contemplation into contemplation to the final goal of maintained change can take 7 to 10 years (Prochaska & DiClemente, 1992a).

The period of instability involved in addictive behavior change is marked by cyclical movement through the stages of change multiple times (Prochaska et al., 1992). Schachter (1982) and others (Cohen et al., 1989) have estimated that individuals who have successfully changed an addictive behavior make at least three to five unsuccessful attempts before being successful. Relapse is the rule rather than the exception in the addictive behaviors (Brownell, Marlatt, Lichtenstein, & Wilson, 1986; Marlatt & Gordon, 1985). Thus, achieving long-term sustained change requires repeated efforts and substantial periods of time even for a single behavior, like cigarette smoking.

This cyclical pattern of individual change has provided confusion and discomfort for researchers, clinicians, and addicts (DiClemente, 1993b). Short-term follow-up studies, three to six months posttreatment, demonstrate a substantial failure rate depending on the conservativeness or stringency of the outcome measure (Cohen et al., 1989). In any treatment program, the percentage of outcome success is at best moderate for brief cessation activity that lasts 24 or 48 hours, decreases for short-term abstinence of a week or more, and gets quite small for long-term, continuous abstinence (Brownell et al., 1986). When followed for extended periods of time, individuals demonstrate different patterns of outcome success (Mermelstein, Gruder, Karnity, Reichman, & Flay, 1991; Swan & Denk, 1987). Some abstain completely, others slip or lapse with varying regularity, and others quickly return to the substance. For example, at 6, 12, and 18 months posttreatment, individuals will enter and exit abstinence so that the percent of individuals at the point of prevalence of abstinence at any one time point will include different individuals (Gottheil, Thornton, Skoloda, & Alterman, 1982; Marlatt & Gordon, 1985). However, over time an increasing number will recycle through the preaction and action stages until they achieve maintenance (Prochaska et al., 1992).

Only extended time frames and long-term longitudinal examinations will yield a solid understanding of this process of change, as demonstrated by the work of Vaillant (1983) and Moos et al. (1990). In the latter group's study 77% of the patients who were in remission at two years were also classified as in remission eight years later. On the other hand, 33% of the patients who were relapsed at two years were in remission at the 10-year follow-up. With long-term remission these authors found increases in positive life context and better functioning, even if measured from the 2- to the 10-year time points. They concluded some successful maintainers can resume essentially normal patterns of functioning. Stable, maintained change of addictive behaviors is not easy to achieve but brings with it positive changes in many areas of functioning.

Maintenance or Termination

Controversy surrounds the question of whether individuals once addicted can ever become nonaddicted. In many ways the two sides of this controversy mirror the two poles of the issue of whether personality can change. There are two camps, one that seems to support fluidity and change, and the other that endorses stability and permanence. The issue centers around whether addiction either results from or becomes a permanent characteristic of the individual so that even years of sobriety will not change this susceptibility, or whether longer term sobriety brings with it so many changes at multiple levels that sobriety creates a new nonaddicted individual. From a process of change perspective, the question is whether addicted individuals can ever emerge from the cycle of change to a point at which the prior addictive behavior becomes a nonissue or whether they must remain forever in a more vigilant, maintenance stage of change.

From the perspective of Alcoholics Anonymous, an alcoholic who quits drinking is always recovering, but can never be fully recovered. It is as though the alcoholic dimension, which is conceived of as characterological, cannot change and will be a potent force for addiction whether 2, 10, or 20 years postcessation. This perspective is considered protective in that individuals who have been addicted should never consider themselves recovered lest they be tempted to stray from absolute abstinence. Other perspectives are represented by less absolutist injunctions (Gottheil et al., 1982; Marlatt & Gordon, 1985). Some offer the possibility that at least for certain substance, like cigarette smoking, individuals could exit from, or terminate, this cycle of change (Prochaska & DiClemente, 1992a).

Whether the perspective is one of long-term maintenance or of termination from the cycle of change, both require multiple changes in an individual's life. In fact, current thinking is that maintenance for cessation of addictive behaviors requires major life-style changes, which implies shifts in social relationships, the central values controlling life-style, and the perceptions of self. Thus, changes in a network of attitudes, behaviors, and environment are needed to support sobriety instead of drug involvement. Clearly, for a single pattern of addiction, the requirements for maintenance of cessation are extensive in the amount, depth, and breadth of the changes needed at the various levels and the length of time needed to accomplish these changes.

IMPLICATIONS FOR PERSONALITY CHANGE

This examination of addictive behavior change reveals a variety of interesting and important implications for the question of whether personality can and does change. The following points summarize these implications. However, the bottom line of this analysis of the initiation and cessation of addictive behaviors seems to point to a response best articulated as, "If addictive behaviors change, can personality be far behind?"

1. Theories of addiction provide a heuristic model for conceptualizing human functioning in patterned sets of behaviors. Initiation and cessation of addictions represent alternating behavior patterns reflecting change and

stability. These periods of change and periods of stability interact over long periods of time, well beyond the traditional one- or two-year longitudinal study. Extensive longitudinal perspectives are needed in order to fully capture this process of change. Even three or four time points over a five-year period could yield a picture of stability of drinking, for example, and miss the periods of sobriety and shifts in readiness to change that would be important components of the process of change. Maintained change takes years to accomplish. Estimates based on shorter time frames would err in the direction of premature stability.

2. Neither addiction nor cessation is inevitable. These processes of change require participation on the part of the individual. Without that participation, change does not occur. The majority of individuals who experiment with or use alcohol or drugs do not become addicted, and, with alcohol, it is the vast majority who do not move from use to abuse to dependency. In contrast, some individuals do become addicted and remain stuck in the addictive behavior pattern until they die. However, it is also possible to change or modify the addictive behavior, as millions of people have done regarding abuse of alcohol, cigarettes, and other drugs. Individual differences in negotiating the path into and out of addiction are critical for understanding change. Not all individuals who are addicted will change. However, it would be circular to argue that individuals who do not change, cannot. Nor is it reasonable to assume that only individuals who do not change have a stable addictive personality. There are more parsimonious explanations. For individuals who see the use of the addictive substance as integral to their life or inevitable for them, the addiction will appear as steady and stable as many a personality trait. However, age and the ravages of the consequences of use have often moved even the most inveterate addict into a process of change that has led to decades of sobriety. Change and stability are the point and counterpoint of the process that may represent a model for understanding personality and change.

3. Cessation of an addictive behavior does not follow a linear path. Relapse and recycling through the stages of change is the rule rather than the exception. There is a cyclical, spiral nature to the process of successful change (Prochaska et al., 1992). Cessation is not a single event but a series of events that culminates in sustained, long-term change and the absence of the entire pattern of behaviors that once dominated the thoughts, emotions, and life space of the addicted individual.

The importance of examining the lifetime of the individual, developing individual change curves, assessing motivational dimensions related to the change, and understanding the cyclical nature of the process of change are all lessons from studies of addictions. Some personality researchers have already adopted a longitudinal, life-course perspective in order to understand continuity and change (Caspi & Bem, 1990). It is hoped that lessons from studies of addictions will support and enhance this perspective and contribute to a better understanding of how people and personality can change.

4. Establishing and changing the stable patterns of behavior called addictions clearly involve multiple levels of personal functioning. Although an addiction is often a behavioral pattern of consumption of a single substance, which is generalized across many situations and engaged in to excess, there are few aspects of the individual's life that are unaffected. Expectancies, beliefs, values, relationships with family and friends, social networks, self-esteem, self-control, and self-concept are all implicated in the initiation and successful cessation of the addictive behavior. These changes reverberate throughout the levels of an individual's life space. Do they actually reach the constructs that researchers call temperament or basic dispositions? This is still an unanswered question. However, even if the dispositions like impulsivity or risk taking are not changed at their deepest level, their manifestations often seem permanently modified by the shift from addiction to stable sobriety. Anecdotal reports that individuals who become addicted or achieve sobriety after being addicted are changed persons appear to be getting support in longitudinal studies.

Can personality change directly, or only through behavioral change? The question is an intriguing one. Lessons from the addictions seem to support the statement that if addictive behaviors change, change of personality dimensions or subfunctions cannot be far behind. Often with addictive behaviors, sobriety precedes changes in intrapersonal self-constructs. From a levels-of-change perspective, intrapersonal change most often occurs as a result of changes at symptom/situational and cognition levels. Changes in personality dimensions seem to occur at the outer edges of the concentric circles that spread beyond the point of impact of the stone tossed into the center of the pond.

5. Personality change is probably best understood as part of the aftereffects of the process of change, rather than more direct and immediate changes. Usually individuals move through initiation, then struggle to stop circumscribed patterns of behavior like addictions, and finally find that many other aspects of their lives either change or need to change as a result. There are probably times when individuals make changes at deeper levels, changing personal dispositions and intrapersonal problems first, then changing their addictive behaviors. This type of change, which is not seen in therapy very often, seems to come from the bottom up rather than the top down and can be the result of some conversion process. At times, it appears that individuals who are addicted are waiting for this more basic change or conversion to happen or, possibly, for some form of magic, in order to make a change. However, the psychoactive nature of the abused substances and the compulsive pattern of the drug taking behavior make bottom-up change quite difficult. The current state of knowledge and experience indicates that the more common path is for addicted individuals

to focus on the most problematic behavior and use energy and skills to change that behavior. In the course of these efforts, multiple changes at multiple levels seem to accompany that process, particularly if those changes are necessary for, or related to, the long-term modification of the target behavior.

6. In order to answer definitively the questions surrounding personality change and addictive behaviors, the designs and methodologies of studies need to change. Most analytic procedures are static and more appropriate for cross-sectional designs and questions. Researchers may have found more stability, as a result of methods and time frames of observations, than has actually existed. The field of personality and addiction research needs more dynamic analytic methods, like hierarchical linear models and LISREL causal models, and research designs to examine stability and change (DiClemente, Carbonari, & Velasquez, 1992; Collins & Horn, 1991; Francis, Fletcher, Stuebing, Davidson, & Thompson, 1991). Recently, researchers from many different areas have made the same point. Individual growth or change curves, survival analyses that allow for the study of multiple periods of abstinence or relapse, linear and causal models that are longitudinal, and event models that can look backward as well as forward are all needed in order to examine the question of change at multiple levels of individual functioning. These new techniques will allow researchers to research the nature of the entire phenomenon in question that includes stability and change. If this need for new methodologies and analytic techniques is so apparent for addictive behavior change, it should be even more urgent in order to examine change as it pertains to personality.

CONCLUSION

Addictions offer a view of individual functioning that is unique. How and why specific substance use behaviors become problematic for only a subgroup of individuals who engage in that behavior is an intriguing question that can only be answered using a multidimensional perspective and a process of change paradigm. The same is true for understanding the cessation of long-term patterns of problematic, dependent use of the substance. The correspondence between the insights garnered from our current understanding of addictions and recent considerations of stability and change in personality research may represent a significant leap forward in the sophistication and precision with which the phenomena of stability and change are addressed. It is hoped that this discussion of behavior change and personality change from an addiction perspective will offer rich food for thought supporting both stability and change at multiple levels of personal functioning.

REFERENCES

Adler, A. (1927). *The practice and theory of individual psychology.* New York: World Book.

Alterman, A. I., & Tarter, R. E. (1986). An examination of selected typologies: Hyperactivity, familial, and antisocial alcoholism. In M. Galanter (Ed.), *Recent developments in alcoholism* (Vol. 4, pp. 169–189). New York: Plenum Press.

American Psychiatric Association. (1987). *Diagnostic and statistical manual of mental disorders* (3rd ed., rev.). Washington, DC: Author.

Armor, D., Polich, J., & Stambul, H. (1978). *Alcoholism and treatment.* New York: Wiley.

Babor, T. F., & Lauerman, R. J. (1986). Classification and forms of inebriety: Historical antecedents of alcoholic typologies. In M. Galanter (Ed.), *Recent developments in alcoholism* (Vol. 4, pp. 113–144). New York: Plenum Press.

Bandura, A. (1986). *Social foundations of thought and action: A social cognitive theory.* Englewood Cliffs, NJ: Prentice Hall.

Barrett, R. J. (1985). Behavioral approaches to individual differences in substance use. In M. Galizio & S. A. Maisto (Eds.), *Determinants of substance abuse* (pp. 125–175). New York: Plenum Press.

Bean, M., & Zinberg, N. E. (1981). *Dynamic approaches to the understanding and treatment of alcoholism.* New York: Free Press.

Beck, A. T. (1991). Cognitive therapy as the integrative therapy. *Journal of Psychotherapy Integration, 1*(3), 190–194.

Blane, H. T., & Leonard, K. E. (1987). *Psychological theories of drinking and alcoholism, Research Institute on Alcoholism.* New York: Guilford Press.

Blau, G. M., Gillespie, J. F., Felner, R. D., & Evans, E. G. (1989). Predispositions to drug use in rural adolescents: Preliminary relationships and methodological considerations. *Journal of Drug Education, 18,* 13–22.

Brown, S. A., Goldman, M. S., Inn, A., & Anderson, L. R. (1980). Expectations of reinforcement from alcohol: Their domain and relation to drinking patterns. *Journal of Consulting and Clinical Psychology, 48,* 419–426.

Brownell, K. D., Marlatt, G. A., Lichtenstein, E., & Wilson, G. T. (1986). Understanding and preventing relapse. *American Psychologist, 41*(7), 765–782.

Cahalan, D. (1987). *Understanding America's drinking problem.* San Francisco: Jossey-Bass.

Caspi, A., & Bem, D. J. (1990). Personality continuity and change across the life span. In L. A. Pervin (Ed.), *Handbook of personality theory and research* (pp. 549–575). New York: Guilford Press.

Cohen, S., Lichtenstein, E., Prochaska, J. O., Rossi, J. S., Gritz, E. R., Carr, C. R., Orleans, C. T., Schoenbach, V. J., Biener, L., Abrams, D., DiClemente, C., Curry, S., Marlatt, G. A., Cummings, K. M., Emont, S. L., Giovino, G., & Ossip-Klein, D. (1989). Debunking myths about self-quitting:

Evidence from ten prospective studies of persons who attempt to quit smoking by themselves. *American Psychologist, 44*(11), 1355–1365.

Collins, L. M., & Horn, J. L. (1991). *Best methods for the analysis of change: Recent advances, unanswered questions, future directions.* Washington, DC: American Psychological Association.

Connors, G. J., O'Farrell, T., Cutter, H. S. G., & Logan-Thompson, D. (1986). Alcohol expectancies among male alcoholics, problem drinkers, and non-problem drinkers. *Alcoholism: Clinical and Experimental Review, 10,* 667–671.

DiClemente, C. C. (1993a). Alcoholics Anonymous and the structure of change. In B. S. Brady & W. R. Miller (Eds.), *Research on Alcoholics Anonymous: Opportunities and alternatives* (pp. 79–97). New Brunswick, NJ: Rutgers Center of Alcohol Studies.

DiClemente, C. C. (1993b). Changing addictive behaviors: A process perspective. *Current Directions in Psychological Science, 2*(4), 101–106.

DiClemente, C. C., Carbonari, J. P., & Velasquez, M. M. (1992). Alcoholism treatment mismatching from a processing change perspective. In R. R. Watson (Ed.), *Drug and alcohol abuse reviews: Vol. 3. Alcohol abuse treatment.* Totowa, NJ: Humana Press.

DiClemente, C. C., Fairhurst, S. F., & Piotrowski, N. A. (in press). The role of self-efficacy in the addictive behaviors. In J. Maddux (Ed.), *Self-efficacy, adaptation and adjustment theory, research and application.* New York: Plenum Press.

DiClemente, C. C., & Prochaska, J. O. (1985). Processes and stages of change: Coping and competence in smoking behavior change. In S. Shiffman & T. A. Wills (Eds.), *Coping and substance abuse* (pp. 319–344). San Diego, CA: Academic Press.

DiClemente, C. C., Prochaska, J. O., Fairhurst, S. K., Velicer, W. F., Velasquez, M. M., & Rossi, J. S. (1991). The process of smoking cessation: An analysis of precontemplation, comtemplation, and preparation stages of change. *Journal of Consulting and Clinical Psychology, 59*(2), 295–304.

DiClemente, C. C., Prochaska, J. O., & Gibertini, M. (1985). Self-efficacy and the stages of self-change of smoking. *Cognitive Therapy and Research, 9*(2), 181–200.

Donovan, D. M., & Marlatt, A. (1988). *Assessment of addictive behaviors.* New York: Guilford Press.

Ellis, A. (1973). *Humanistic psychotherapy: The rational–emotive approach.* New York: McGraw-Hill.

Fillmore, K. M. (1974). Drinking and problem drinking in early adulthood and middle age: An exploratory 20-year follow-up study. *Quarterly Journal of Studies of Alcohol, 35,* 819–840.

Francis, D. J., Fletcher, J. M., Stuebing, K. K., Davidson, K. C., & Thompson, N. M. (1991). Analysis of change: Modeling individual growth. *Journal of Consulting and Clinical Psychology, 59*(1), 27–37.

Galizio, M., & Maisto, S. A. (1985). *Determinants of substance abuse: Biological psychological and environmental factors.* New York: Plenum Press.

Goldman, M. S., Brown, S. A., & Christiansen, B. A. (1987). Expectancy theory: Thinking about drinking. In H. T. Blane & K. E. Leonard (Eds.), *Psychological theories of drinking and alcoholism* (pp. 181–226). New York: Guilford Press.

Gottheil, E., Thornton, C. C., Skoloda, T. E., & Alterman, A. I. (1982). Follow-up of abstinent and nonabstinent alcoholics. *American Journal of Psychiatry, 139*(5), 560–565.

Graham, J. R., & Strenger, V. E. (1988). MMPI charateristics of alcoholics: A review. *Journal of Consulting and Clinical Psychology, 56*(2), 197–205.

Huba, G. J., & Bentler, P. M. (1984). Causal models of personality, peer culture characteristics, drug use, and criminal behaviors over a five-year span. In D. W. Goodwin, K. T. VanDusen, & S. A. Mednick (Eds.), *Longitudinal research in alcoholism* (pp. 73–94). Boston: Klower-Nijhof.

Hunt, W. A., Barnett, L. W., & Branch, L. G. (1971). Relapse rates in addiction programs. *Journal of Clinical Psychology, 27,* 455–456.

Kaplan, H. B., Martin, S. S., & Robbins, C. (1984). Pathway to adolescent drug use: Self-derogation, peer influence, weakening of social controls, and early substance use. *Journal of Health and Social Behavior, 25,* 270–289.

Kissin, B. (1977). Theory and practice in the treatment of alcoholism. In E. B. Kissin & H. Begleiter (Eds.), *Treatment and rehabilitation of the chronic alcoholic* (pp. 1–51). New York: Plenum Press.

Labouvie, E. W., & McGee, C. R. (1986). Relation of personality to alcohol and drug use in adolescence. *Journal of Consulting and Clinical Psychology, 54,* 289–293.

Lerner, J. V., & Vicary, J. R. (1984). Difficult temperament and drug use: Analyses from the New York longitudinal study. *Journal of Drug Education, 14,* 1–8.

Marlatt, G. A., & Gordon, J. R. (Eds.). (1985). *Relapse prevention: Maintenance strategies in the treatment of addictive behaviors.* New York: Guilford Press.

Maslow, A. H. (1970). *Motivation and personality* (3rd ed.). New York: Harper & Row.

Mermelstein, R., Gruder, C. L., Karnity, T., Reichman, S., & Flay, B. (1991, April). *Assessment of change following a cessation attempt: Description of new smoking outcome categories.* Poster presented at the 12th Annual Meeting of the Society of Behavioral Medicine, Washington, DC.

Mischel, W. (1990). Personality dispositions revisited and revised: A view after three decades. In L. A. Pervin (Ed.), *Handbook of personality theory and research* (pp. 111–134). New York: Guilford Press.

Moos, R. H., Finney, J. W., & Cronkite, R. C. (1990). *Alcoholism treatment: Context, process and outcome.* New York: Oxford University Press.

Morey, L. C., & Skinner, H. A. (1986). Empirically derived classification of alcohol-related problems. In M. Galanter (Ed.), *Recent developments in alcoholism* (Vol. 4, pp. 145–168). New York: Plenum Press.

Nathan, P. E. (1988). The addictive personality is the behavior of the addict. *Journal of Consulting and Clinical Psychology, 56*(2), 183–188.

Newcomb, M. D., & Bentler, P. M. (1988). *Consequences of adolescent drug use.* Newbury Park, CA: Sage.

Paredes, A., Gregory, D., Rundell, O. H., & Williams, H. L. (1979). Drinking behavior, remission and relapse: The Rand Report revisited. *Alcoholism: Clinical and Experimental Research, 3*(1), 3–10.

Prochaska, J. O., & DiClemente, C. C. (1984). *The transtheoretical approach: Crossing the traditional boundaries of therapy.* Homewood, IL: Dorsey Press.

Prochaska, J. O., & DiClemente, C. C. (1992a). Stages of change in the modification of problem behavior. In M. Hersen, R. Eisler, & P. M. Miller (Eds.), *Progress in behavior modification* (Vol. 28, pp. 184–214). Sycamore, IL: Sycamore.

Prochaska, J. O., & DiClemente, C. C. (1992b). The transtheoretical approach. In J. C. Norcross & M. R. Goldfried (Eds.), *Handbook of psychotherapy integration* (pp. 300–334). New York: Basic Books.

Prochaska, J. O., DiClemente, C. C., & Norcross, J. C. (1992). In search of how people change: Applications to addictive behaviors. *American Psychologist, 47*(9), 1102–1114.

Prochaska, J. O., Velicer, W. F., DiClemente, C. C., Guadagnoli, E., & Rossi, J. S. (1991). Patterns of change: Dynamic typology applied to smoking cessation. *Multivariate Behavioral Research, 26*(1), 83–107.

Rogers, C. R. (1961). *On becoming a person.* Boston: Houghton Mifflin.

Schachter, S. (1982). Recidivism and self-cure of smoking and obesity. *American Psychologist, 37,* 436–444.

Shedler, J., & Block, J. (1990). Adolescent drug use and psychological health. *American Psychologist, 45*(5), 612–630.

Shiffman, S., & Wills, T. A. (1985). *Coping and substance abuse.* San Diego, CA: Academic Press.

Steinglass, P., Bennett, L. A., Wolin, S. J., & Reiss, D. (1987). *The alcoholic family.* New York: Basic Books.

Sutker, P. B., & Allain, A. N. J. (1988). Issues in personality conceptualizations of addictive behaviors. *Journal of Consulting and Clinical Psychology, 56,* 172–182.

Swan, G. E., & Denk, C. E. (1987). Dynamic models for the maintenance of smoking cessation: Event history analysis of late relapse. *Journal of Behavioral Medicine, 10*(6), 527–554.

Tarter, R. E. (1988). Are there inherited behavioral traits that predispose to substance abuse? *Journal of Consulting and Clinical Psychology, 56,* 189–196.

Tarter, R. E. (1991). Developmental behavior: Genetic perspective of alcoholism etiology. In C. Galenter (Ed.), *Alcoholism* (pp. 71–88). New York: Plenum Press.

Tubman, J. G., Vicary, J. R., von Eye, A., & Lerner, J. V. (1990). Longitudinal substance use and adult adjustment. *Journal of Substance Abuse 2,* 317–334.

U.S. Department of Health and Human Services. (1988). *The health consequences of smoking: Nicotine addiction. A report of the Surgeon General* (DHHS Publication No. CDC 88-8406). Washington, DC: U.S. Government Printing Office.

U.S. Department of Health and Human Services. (1990a). *The health benefits of smoking cessation* (DHHS Publication No. CDC 90-8416). Washington, DC: U.S. Government Printing Office.

U.S. Department of Health and Human Services. (1990b). *Seventh special report to the U.S. Congress on alcohol and health* (DHHS Publication No. ADM 281-88-0002). Washington, DC: U.S. Government Printing Office.

Vaillant, G. E. (1983). *The natural history of alcoholism: Causes, patterns, and paths to recovery.* Cambridge, MA: Harvard University Press.

Vaillant, G. E., & Milofsky, E. (1982). The etiology of alcoholism: A prospective viewpoint. *American Psychologist, 37,* 494–503.

Vicary, J. R., & Lerner, J. V. (1983). Longitudinal perspectives on drug abuse: Analyses from the New York Longitudinal Study. *Journal of Drug Education, 13,* 275–285.

Zucker, R. A., & Gomberg, S. L. (1986). Etiology of alcoholism reconsidered: The case for a biopsychosocial process. *American Psychologist, 41*(7), 783–793.

Zweben, A. (1986). Problem drinking and marital adjustment. *Journal of Studies on Alcohol, 47,* 167–172.

III

CHANGE AND THE LIFE CYCLE

9

PERSONALITY CHANGE IN ADULTHOOD

RAVENNA HELSON and ABIGAIL STEWART

Personality change in adulthood is a relatively new topic in personality psychology, and our first point is that some of the assumptions, definitions, and research designs that may be useful for the study of personality in the present or over short intervals are not adequate for a study of personality over the life course. Second, we consider components of personality and agents of change that seem profitable to study. Third, we illustrate findings on personality change from three programs of longitudinal research; and finally, we offer some recommendations.

Over short periods of time it is clearly desirable to demonstrate some degree of consistency of personality. Reliability is generally assumed to be a necessary feature of scientific constructs. Though the consistency of personality has been questioned (Mischel, 1968; Ross & Nisbett, 1991), the evidence for it is substantial (Block, 1971; Conley, 1985a; Costa & McCrae, 1980; and many others) and now seems quite sufficient (Kogan, 1990).

Over long periods of time, the expectation that personality will remain entirely the same is highly questionable. The issue here is not the scientific

This work was supported by National Institute of Mental Health Grant 43948.

legitimacy of personality constructs, but the extent to which adult personality is malleable or adaptable through various periods of life and in various social contexts.

A BIAS AGAINST CHANGE

To questions of malleability of adult personality, personality and developmental psychology bring some long-standing biases. Twenty years ago, in *Lives Through Time*, Block (1971) discussed the focus on stability to the neglect of change:

> The dominant conceptualizations of the basis and laws of personality development—psychoanalysis, reinforcement theory, and the constitutional–genetic viewpoint—concur in construing later personality as the result primarily of an orderly unfolding of capacities and qualities intrinsic to an individual or laid down earlier. (p. 11)

Thus, change over time

> disappoints the investigator, for he is prevented from the visible accomplishment of predicting the future. . . . Inconstancy over time is viewed as indicative of poor psychological measurement or as due to an unanalyzable, irreducible, random component in human behavior or as evidence of the unimportance of the variable involved.

This bias against finding change persists. A recent review essay by Caspi and Bem (1990), titled "Personality Continuity and Change Across the Life Course," described in detail many mechanisms that promote continuity of personality, with only casual references to possible mechanisms of change. The authors said that "a claim of systematic change requires a theory that specifies in what way the observed absence of continuity is systematic" (p. 569). But when the term *change* appears in the literature, they continued, it most frequently denotes merely the absence of continuity. We find it puzzling that there continues to be a scarcity of theories about personality change. Caspi and Bem said that they preferred a research strategy in which personality variables refer to "genotypic features of the human organism rather than to hybrid features of the person and the culture" (p. 556). By keeping person variables and cultural variables clearly distinct, they said, their integration into an interactional theory of personality is facilitated. The usefulness of this strategy would seem to be illustrated in their own excellent work on the persistence of maladaptive interpersonal styles (Caspi, Bem, & Elder, 1989). However, to clearly separate personality and cultural variables pushes toward a narrow conceptualization of personality. Caspi's (1993) assumption that personality change requires extraordinary force and all-out effort would seem to reflect a conception of personality in terms of genotypic features of the organism that almost by definition do not change.

McCrae and Costa (1990) defined personality in terms of five broad traits (neuroticism, extraversion, openness, agreeableness, and conscientiousness) that they believe do not change after age 30. These researchers have done a valuable service in showing that important aspects of personality show impressive rank order stability over long periods. But here again, a narrow definition of personality in terms of unchangeable components is linked to a research design that is biased against the demonstration of change. In their most ambitious study of personality over time, Costa and McCrae (1988) studied a large sample of adults from ages 20–96, at two times six years apart, apparently assuming that if personality changed, age should produce the same effect on everyone through most of adulthood. They did not build in or identify factors that might be associated with change, except at the abstract level embodied in cross-sequential and time-sequential designs, and their criteria for evaluating the evidence for change enabled them to dismiss it all as error variance (Helson, 1993). We think that their research design permits them to draw conclusions about stability rather than change.

There are different kinds of stability and different kinds of change (Block, 1971; Mortimer, Finch, & Kumka, 1982). Experts in the measurement of personality tend to think of stability in terms of consistency of the rank order of individual differences as assessed by correlation coefficients. But in the study of change, differences in means at different times of testing are of great importance. Though it is surprising to many, there is no relation between rank order stability and mean-level change (Ozer, 1986). If one's five children each progress from one grade in school to the next, the order of their grades remains the same, but the mean level of grades has increased. Change in the mean level of personality characteristics does not suggest any lack of reliability in the measurement of personality, and high reliability does not indicate that mean levels have not changed.

To insist that mean levels of all major dimensions of personality remain the same over adult life, as McCrae and Costa (1990) do, suggests a degree of rigidity in personality that does not characterize adaptive phenomena. It either ignores evidence of the impact of life experience of various kinds or assumes that there is no pattern in the impact of these experiences (that they are random or unpredictable). To emphasize the coherence of personality, as Caspi and Bem (1990) sometimes do, makes more place for change, because the claim is only that important features of the organization of personality have not changed. (Personality is said to be coherent when behaviors, even though phenotypically different, are manifestations of the same underlying personality characteristic or structure.) Nevertheless, attention is directed to processes of assimilation rather than to processes of both assimilation and accommodation (Block, 1982).

The notion of coherence of personality may be fruitfully explored in terms of integrative personality components like the self, and the experimentalists who study the self (Cantor & Kihlstrom, 1987; Greenwald, 1980; Markus & Kunda, 1986; Swann, 1987; and others) are often concerned with personality change. They have many interesting ideas, but their methodology often leads them to a choice of phenomena too complicated or contrived to translate into life span terms. It may be, in part, for this reason that some of this group also exaggerate stability. Thus, Swann (1987) emphasized how difficult it is to create the conditions that would lead someone to negotiate a different identity, yet he mentioned conditions that are quite common in life span research, such as moving from one environment to another in which a person is regarded in new ways.

It is important to be aware of the way that traditional contexts of research are biased against the finding of personality change. In order to have a fair chance at finding life span change, it is necessary, first, to avoid restrictive conceptualizations of personality in terms of unchangeable components. Let personality be defined as a relatively enduring structure of motivations and resources (in which resources include characteristics such as intelligence, competence, and likability). Second, it is necessary to design studies to enable assessment of big, long-term factors that might be expected to produce change over time.

WHAT CHANGES, WHAT STAYS THE SAME?

In this section we make the point that virtually all classes of components of personality that personality psychologists study have been shown to change over the life span, or to change with educative efforts. After illustrating this point, we discuss hierarchies of stability and the selection of measures particularly suited to the study of change. Among components of personality that change are traits and personality configurations (such as scripts, life-styles, or the creative personality), cognitive and expressive styles, defense and coping mechanisms, motives, interests, values, and, of course, developmental themes and tasks.

As a first example, the personality of outstandingly creative individuals is, for a complex of reasons, generally regarded as highly stable (Albert, 1975; Cox, 1926). Dudek and Hall (1991) readministered the California Psychological Inventory (CPI; Gough, 1957/1987) and Adjective Check List (ACL; Gough & Heilbrun, 1983) to architects studied by MacKinnon (1965) 25 years after his original landmark investigation. The highly creative subgroup was still the most strongly motivated, spontaneous, and independent, and the least creative retained their tendencies toward social conformity. However, the consistency of creative personality was not the whole picture. The sample as a whole showed changes attributable to aging, such as reduced impulsiveness and flexibility. This and other studies show that careers and creative products change character at different points in the life course (Gruber, 1989; Jaques, 1965; McCurdy, 1940; Simonton, 1989), and evidence often indicates that changes in personality, such as decreasing impulsivity and increasing cognitive control or expertise, are involved.

McClelland (1985) viewed social motives, such as needs for power, achievement, and affiliation, as resulting from many years of associations among expectations, affects, and outcomes. Once a network of associations has been built up around natural incentives, the motive becomes a "recurrent concern about a goal state that drives, orients, and selects behavior" (p. 183). There is considerable evidence for the long-term stability of such motives (McClelland, 1966; Skolnick, 1966), and Franz (in press) found both consistency and change in motives over 10 years. Both men and women decreased in the need for achievement and increased in the need for affiliation between ages 31 and 41. Finally, McClelland (1985) demonstrated motive change in response to specific interventions. He designed a set of experiences that created a new associative network around the natural incentive of success among entrepreneurs drawn from a wide range of settings.

Psychoanalytic theory (Freud, 1937) suggests that ego defenses emerge and decline over the life course. In two longitudinal studies (Haan, 1972; Vaillant, 1976), mature defenses, such as sublimation and suppression, were found to be used more frequently in middle age than in adolescence or early adulthood, whereas the use of immature defenses, such as acting out, fantasy, and projection declined. Why do defenses become more mature? Discussing core conflictual themes, Luborsky et al. (1985) said that wishes remain the same but the rigidity of their expression may lessen as their consequences are understood, as better means are found for gratifying them, and as responses from others and from the self become more positive. These ideas were explored by Thorne and Klohnen (1993).

Hierarchies of Stability

Several researchers have attempted to order components of personality in terms of stability, using this stability hierarchy to construct models of personality change over the life span (Conley, 1985b; Kimmel, 1974; Lachman, 1988; Whitbourne, 1989). In Conley's system, personality traits, such as extraversion and neuroticism, are most stable, followed by values and personal styles, such as those identified by Spranger (1928), Allport and Vernon (1931), Jung (1924), and others. A third category of components consists of personal formations, which encompass roles, identities, and opinions, including well-being and self-esteem. Although influenced by the more basic strata and not nearly so stable, the organization of the lower order phenomena is important, Conley said, because it is the locus of interactions between changing environmental conditions and personality.

He believes that a person is likely to have several personal formations during adulthood, the succession influenced by the normative life cycle, nonnormative life events, and sociocultural changes. He illustrates his schema with a case of a middle-aged man in whom a change along a dimension of personal style (critical–acceptant) was an important aspect of the shift from one personal formation to another.

Another structural model of personality that attends to issues of stability and change is the hierarchy and network of schemas in cognitive–experiential self-theory (CTS; Epstein, 1990). Basic postulates are, for example, the degree to which the world is regarded as benign or malevolent, and the degree to which the self is regarded as worthy. As one descends the hierarchy, schemas become narrower in scope, more closely related to direct experience, and easier to change. After an extremely negative event, however, even basic beliefs tend to change in an unfavorable direction, and the change does not reverse (Catlin & Epstein, 1992).

Strategies for Selection of Constructs

If one is interested in studying personality change, one strategy would be to include measures from different strata in a stability hierarchy. Another would be to use constructs from theories of adult development. These include the themes of identity, intimacy, generativity, and integrity (Erikson, 1950), or motivational patterns or tasks relevant to particular periods of life (Cantor, Norem, Niedenthal, Langston, & Brower, 1987; Havighurst, 1972; Helson, Mitchell, & Moane, 1984). Other developmental theorists discuss an increasing organization and differentiation of the self over time (Stewart & Healy, 1984; Werner, 1948; Whitbourne & Weinstock, 1979). When White (1966) described natural growth in young adulthood, using his classic case studies as data, he spoke of a stabilization of identity, a freeing of relationships, a deepening of interests, and a humanization of values. These processes represent changes in the structures of personality.

A third strategy for the study of change would be to use measures of personality characteristics that are generally important in social life, such as socialization, dominance, and tolerance. (Scales for these characteristics are contained in the CPI; Gough, 1957/1987.) The CPI was developed to assess "folk concepts" for the study of persons in society and across cultures, and its scales are often useful for evaluating social or environmental influence (see later sections).

We have cited evidence that many components of personality can change, and we have given examples of constructs and structural models that are intended or especially appropriate for the study of personality change. Stable personality traits have an important place in the structure of personality, but there is more to personality than these traits (McAdams, 1992).

Factors Affecting Personality Change in Adulthood

White (1972) said that we do not discover our selves but make them. In the previous section, we came repeatedly to the idea that personality change in adulthood involves building up or reconstructing associations around wishes or motives or basic beliefs. Here we want to suggest briefly the variety of factors that influence these processes. They include features of the social environment, which have been explored fairly extensively; aspects of personality that may tend to facilitate or impede the likelihood of change; and biological factors that may be associated with change. Biological issues have been the least thoroughly investigated by students of personality change and deserve further attention.

Social Factors

In some times and places the social world is stable. But stability cannot be assumed. Sociologists and anthropologists study upward and downward mobility, marginality, urbanization, modernity, migration, immigration, and other movements of people up and down and across the social world, leaving the place they were and demanding adaptation to a place that is new. For example, studies of modernity show how individuals move from authoritarian control to a sense of individual responsibility (Inkeles & Smith, 1974). Social events, such as wars and depressions, affect the construction of identities and life choices of individuals (Elder, 1974; Stewart & Healy, 1989) and are sometimes important in creating cohort differences (Alwin, Cohen, & Newcomb, 1991). For example, Stewart and Healy found that women raised during the Depression, who entered the paid labor force during World War II, were particularly likely (compared with cohorts just before and just after them) to develop a strong vocational identity. In turn, these women were especially likely to invoke or renegotiate these identities in the expansive 1960s, after suppressing them in the buttoned-down, sex-differentiated 1950s.

Social clock norms about the appropriateness of behaviors and goals at different ages guide people through the age–status system, structuring and monitoring their expectations, aspirations, experiences, and self-evaluations (Neugarten, 1968). During the transition to parenthood, for example, roles change (Cowan & Cowan, 1992; Grossman et al., 1980), and over time personality changes, too. Helson et al. (1984) compared repeated measures on the CPI of women who had become mothers since their senior year in college. At age 27 these women had higher scores on CPI scales for responsibility, self-control, tolerance, and femininity, and lower scores on scales for self-acceptance and sociability. Women who had not become mothers did not show this pattern of change.

Processes of socialization, which include modeling, direct teaching, and administering rewards and punishments, are important in higher education and apprenticeships, and affect personality change. In a study of the effects of liberal arts education, over time and in contrast with other forms of higher education, Winter, McClelland, and Stewart (1981) showed that it was associated with increases in leadership motivation, an instrumental personal style, and the ability to construct arguments that successfully integrate information and perspectives. Processes that alleviate or revise earlier learnings are the concern of psychotherapists and self-help groups of various kinds. The consciousness-raising groups associated with the women's movement are an interesting example of a technique for encouraging personal change in the context of a social movement.

The occupancy of roles affects one's relation to others and the kind of experience one gains in life. Kohn and Schooler (1983) showed that, over time, complexity of work affected cognitive skills, confidence, self-concept, and interests outside the work setting. "Doing substantively complex work," Kohn (1980) wrote, "tends to increase one's respect for one's own capacities, one's valuation of self-direction, one's intellectuality (even in leisure time pursuits), and one's sense that the problems one encounters in the world are manageable" (p. 205).

Some social controls exert their influence through primary group relationships. Thus, Sampson and Laub (1990) found that attachment to a partner led some young men out of delinquency and crime. Choice of partners like one's self may help one to remain the same (Caspi & Herbener, 1990), but partners, lovers, children, friends, and bosses can also be catalysts for change (Helson & Roberts, 1992; Josselson, 1992).

Changes in roles and relationships can also produce personality change. Healy (1989) showed that immediately after a divorce both men and women had reduced capacities to integrate complex information, though performance on other cognitive tasks was unaffected. This disorganizing effect of divorce may have been the first stage in a process of reorganization, because Bursik (1991) showed that over a longer period divorce resulted in increases in ego development in some women.

Psychological Factors

Psychological factors influence personality change in many ways. Personality affects the life situations one chooses or has to accept, the reactions one elicits from others, and cumulative life outcomes. Caspi et al. (1989), Costa and McCrae (1980), and Scarr and McCartney (1983) have made this point, but they deemphasized or did not pursue the question of how one's experiences may change one's personality.

Block (1982) adapted the Piagetian concepts of assimilation and accommodation for conceptualizing processes of both consistency and change in personality. Assimilation occurs when people use existing personality structures to organize new experience, and accommodation occurs when people change their schemas to admit new experience. Both processes work together in personality development, and individual differences in preference for one process over the other may mould personality and predict personality change. Runyan's (1978, 1980) model of stage–state sequences over time extends the familiar idea of person–situation interaction to the life course. Skolnick (1986) used it to describe sequences of positive and negative personal relationships from infancy to adulthood. A simple version of attachment theory, she said, would predict continuity in positive or negative relationships, because of pervasive effects of early attachment patterns on personality. However, she found considerable variety in stage–state sequences in relational histories.

Research participants with advantages in personality resources often increase their advantage over time. However, Clausen (1993) found that personalities of planfully competent adolescents changed less than those of their less competent peers over 45–50 years of adulthood. In the Institute of Human Development (IHD) samples he studied, planful adolescents, especially males, made sensible decisions that enabled them to do well and maintain stability. On the other hand, Block (1971) found in the same samples that women he typed as cognitive copers were not well adjusted in adolescence but changed positively over time. Thus, a variety of personality patterns may influence the amount and nature of personality change, depending on contextual factors.

Among structural psychological factors affecting change, one factor may be that the self becomes more firmly consolidated with experience, so that stability of individual differences increases (Finn, 1986), and radical change becomes more difficult and is less often contemplated (Gould, 1972). On the other hand, cognitive and integrative skills increase from late adolescence through middle age (Haan, Millsap, & Hartka, 1986; Labouvie-Vief, Devoe, & Bulka, 1989). Both of these changes in personality with age may be expected to influence other changes. For example, cognitive and integrative skills are surely involved in the shift from less mature to more mature coping mechanisms.

Stage theories of lives, such as those of Erikson (1950) and Levinson, Darrow, Klein, Levinson, and McKee (1978), assume a regular process of change over the life course. These theories are too broad and complex for easy empirical tests, and results continue to be mixed, partial, or indirect (Costa & McCrae, 1980; Roberts & Newton, 1987; Stewart, Franz, &

Layton, 1988; Whitbourne & Waterman, 1979). Some recent versions of stage theory use the metaphor of narrative. For example, McAdams (this volume) says that one's subjective life story is one's identity and that identity development consists of formulating increasingly adequate stories about the self.

Few personality theorists have delineated individual differences in patterns of change in adulthood. Those who have include Loevinger (1976) and Kernberg (1980). Kernberg described processes through which narcissistic individuals deteriorate in middle age. Awareness of the limits of their achievements, he said, produces feelings of envy and rage that lead to defensive devaluation of others and reduce external and internal sources of support. Lacking a normal capacity to integrate the good and the bad, they become more introverted in a world that comes to be seen as hostile and devoid of meaning. In a partial test of Kernberg's ideas within a normal sample of women, Wink (1992) showed that extraverted narcissists (who most resembled the familiar conception of this syndrome) were buoyant in their late 20s but had relational failures, did not maintain the careers they started, and failed to grow in personality as their age-mates did from the late 20s to early 40s.

Biological Factors

The study of behavior genetics over the life span is in its early stages. According to the current view (Plomin, Chipuer, & Loehlin, 1990), genetic factors are substantially involved in age-to-age personality change during childhood, and changes that occur in adulthood are largely due to nonshared environmental influences. However, this is only the overall picture. Genes can turn on or off at different times, and different personality characteristics show different temporal patterns of genetic influence. Analyzing scores of the same twins at ages 20 and 30 on the Multidimensional Personality Questionnaire (Tellegen, 1982), McGue, Bacon, and Lykken (1993) found reductions in heritability for Positive Emotionality and Negative Emotionality but not for Constraint. Pedersen, Plomin, Nesselroade, and McClearn (1992) found, contrary to the general view, that heritability of general cognitive ability in twins at an average age of 65 was much higher than estimates typically found earlier in life.

On the other hand, studies also show that some biological influences in later life have been overestimated. Hormonal changes during menopause have often been assumed to constrict or rigidify women's personalities, and young women expect "the change of life" to have that sort of effect (Neugarten, Wood, Kraines, & Loomis, 1963). However, menopausal women themselves consider it of little consequence (Datan, 1986; Neugarten & Kraines, 1965), and Helson and Wink (1992) found no relation between menopausal status and personality change. For example, scores of premenopausal, currently menopausal, and postmenopausal women on the CPI Femininity/Masculinity scale all dropped between the early 40s and the early 50s.

ILLUSTRATIVE STUDIES OF PERSONALITY CHANGE IN YOUNG ADULTHOOD

We have tried to show that there are many components of personality change and that many factors affect change. Now we would like to illustrate some of the points we have been making with findings from three longitudinal studies of adult lives, chosen because they have all contextualized their findings so that inferences can be drawn about personality and life change. These are complex studies with many parts. We cannot summarize them, but we report some of their findings, focusing on issues of normative change and on roles and cohort or social climate as agents or carriers of change.

Managerial Lives in Transition

Howard and Bray (1988; see also Bray, Campbell, & Grant, 1974) followed a sample of 266 male managerial candidates at AT&T over 20 years, from the late 1950s, when they were in their 20s, to the late 1970s, when they were in their 40s.

The men were studied in assessment centers, where they were put through behavioral simulations, interviewed, and administered a variety of cognitive, personality, attitudinal, and biographical instruments. A major focus of the study was to explore career and personal development among managers. Here we describe normative personality change (change shown by most of the participants) and illustrate findings about change related to work role. The measures mentioned here are from the Edwards Personal Preference Schedule (EPPS; Edwards, 1959), variables coded from interviews, or factor scores based on several sources of inventory and assessment data.

The most dramatic change in personality and motivation was a drop on an Ambition factor score, steep over the first 8 years, but obtained again over the next 12. Though shown by both college and noncollege men, it was particularly pronounced in the college men, who had started off with higher ambitions. Interview data suggested that the drop accompanied a more realistic view of possibilities for promotion in the company. It did not connote a lack of interest in challenging jobs, because scores on the EPPS Achievement scale increased, and so did scores on EPPS Dominance and on a Leadership Motivation factor score.

Another large change was that both college and noncollege men increased over time on the Autonomy scale of the EPPS, most sharply over the first 8 years of the study, but again over the subsequent 12 years (see Figure 1). Over time the men increased in feelings of hostility and decreased in need for friendships or for the understanding of others. "It was as if their years of living from youth to middle age had propped them up for the assumption of individual responsibilities, but at the same time had hardened them into willful independence" (Howard & Bray, 1988, p. 150). "If Erikson's (1950) conceptualization of generativity as the primary task of this life stage were to be applied, it would more likely be realized in productive work than in nurturing the young" (Howard & Bray, 1988, p. 411).

The Nurturance scale showed change that was attributable to specific work roles: Scores of men on the highest career track dropped, especially from Years 8 to 20, and those of men on the lowest track increased slightly over both periods. On the basis of the interview material, Howard and Bray (1988) concluded that men with executive responsibilities focused on instrumental demands of the job by distancing themselves from emotional involvements with others.

The years from the late 1950s to the early 1970s were years of change not only in the United States at large but in the institution of AT&T. Howard and Bray (1988) provided social and institutional context for their

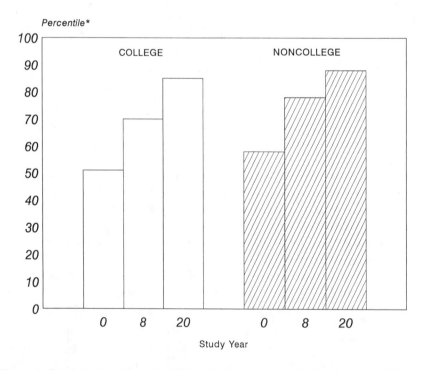

Figure 1: Change with age on the Edwards Autonomy scale. Subjects are 266 men who participated in the AT&T Managerial Potential Study over 20 years. From Howard and Bray (1988). Reprinted with permission.
*1958 Bell System Norms; $p < .005$ time effect.

findings. They began a second study in 1977 with a new sample of managerial candidates who were now both male and female and ethnically diverse. This sample has not been studied a second time. Howard and Bray believed that the younger cohort of managerial candidates was powerfully influenced by the world of the late 1960s and early 1970s, because they were adolescents at the time. They suggested that the emphasis on individual self-definition associated with those times, along with the lessened pressure for conformity, resulted in greater interindividual differentiation in the second cohort. Nevertheless, they hypothesized that the second cohort would show some similar developmental trends, such as becoming more autonomous and less ambitious.

The Mills Longitudinal Study

The Mills Study (Helson, 1967; Helson & Wink, 1992) began with 140 women who graduated from Mills College in 1958 or 1960. The women were studied first as seniors, then by mail at average ages 27, 43, and 52. Like the AT&T Study, the Mills Study began with an interest in continuity of personality, but in the last two follow-ups there has been considerable interest in change. One reason was that several studies of men's adult development had been conducted (Levinson et al., 1978; Vaillant, 1977; and others), and comparable studies of women were needed. Another was that the Mills women experienced their young adulthood and middle age in a distinctive social context that lent itself to the study of personality change. They graduated from college a few years before the beginning of the social changes affecting gender roles and women's opportunities in the labor force. The study uses a mixture of inventory, questionnaire, and open-ended or interview data.

Normative personality change has been demonstrated in the sample between ages 21 and 43 (Helson & Moane, 1987) and between ages 43 and 52 (Helson & Wink, 1992), the results generally supporting theories of adult development. Another study (Wink & Helson, 1993) dealt with normative change associated with gender roles. It explored Gutmann's theory that the major factor in personality change in adulthood is the gender-related division of labor associated with a specieswide *parental imperative* in young adulthood. Gutmann (1987) argued that young men suppress their self-indulgence and become more independent, confident, and goal-oriented, whereas women suppress their aggression and their own goals in the nurturance of husband and children. After children leave home, he said, men tend to express more passive, sentient, affiliative concerns, whereas women become more independent and concerned with their own goals. Wink and Helson compared the Mills women and their partners in the early parental and postparental periods of life, when the women were aged 27 and 52 and the partners a few years older. Figure 2 shows the results

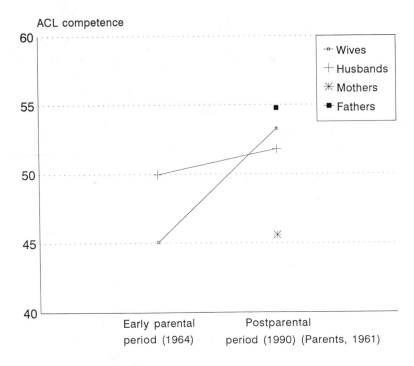

Figure 2: Means on the Competence cluster of the Adjective Check List (ACL) for women and their partners at the early parental (*n* = 65) and postparental (*n* = 48) periods, and for a subsample of the women's parents (*n* = 29 couples) at the postparental period. Data from Wink and Helson (1993).

for a Competence cluster scale derived from the Adjective Check List (ACL; Gough & Heilbrun, 1983). High scorers on Competence describe themselves as goal-oriented, that is, organized, thorough, efficient, practical, clear-thinking, realistic, and precise, and also as mature, confident, and contented. At age 27 the women scored lower on this scale than their partners, but at age 52 they scored about the same. (Figure 2 shows means based on scores of all couples for whom data were available at each time of testing; other analyses restricted to couples participating at both times also show a sharper increase on Competence for women than for men.) ACL scores for a subsample of the women's mothers and fathers had been obtained in 1961 when the parents were in their early 50s, and their scores on Competence are also shown in Figure 2. Unlike the daughters, the mothers scored lower than their husbands in the postparental period.

Thus, personality change in Mills women and their partners tends to support Gutmann's (1987) theory, but the results for parents suggest that women do not necessarily become more competent and confident with age. It depends on their social world. Another finding of this study was that the Mills women increased in competence whether they had children or not.

If there is a specieswide parental imperative, it can be suppressed by cultural factors, and literal parenting is not the major vehicle of change.

Because there was much heterogeneity in life paths among women during the late 1960s and 1970s, the Mills Study has produced several articles on the influence of social roles on personality. One of these (Helson et al., 1984) used Neugarten's (1968) concept of a system of age norms, a social clock that is superimposed on a biological clock and regulates sequential changes in behavior and self-perception over time. Helson et al. focused on norms concerning behaviors related to the big endeavors of young and middle adulthood, involving family and work, which they called social clock projects. They used the Mills data to illustrate how college-age personality characteristics influenced the project a woman chose and her success in its various phases, and they also showed how personality changed as a result of commitment to projects.

Subsequent studies have examined aspects of this theoretical picture in greater detail. The Mills sample belonged to a cohort in which a majority of women expected to marry and start a family in early adulthood, and never to have paid work as a major commitment. Helson and Picano (1990) identified four groups of women whose life stories showed different degrees of traditionality of role by their early 40s: homemakers in an intact marriage with children, and, three groups that all participated in the labor force, mothers in intact marriages (who were called *neotraditionals* because they worked), divorced mothers, and nonmothers. Scales of the CPI (Gough, 1957/1987) showed, first, that these groups had differed systematically in college in their respect for social norms (socialization), and then supported hypotheses of sociologists that the traditional role made women dependent and prone to suppress their assertive and aggressive impulses. Figure 3 shows that all three groups of women who participated in the labor force increased on the CPI Independence scale from ages 21 to 43, but homemakers did not. Also as predicted, homemakers increased to high levels of self-control. During this period of social history, said Helson and Picano, "the traditional role seems to have provided a shelter in which conscientious, competent women who were somewhat over controlled in young adulthood were becoming maladaptively so over time" (p. 318).

The Radcliffe Longitudinal Study

Both the AT&T and the Mills Longitudinal Studies permitted assessment of personality change on the same measures collected over time. In the Radcliffe Longitudinal Study (Stewart, 1978; Stewart & Vandewater, 1993) the focus has been more on processes of life change and their attendant implications for personality.

The Radcliffe Study is an ongoing study of women who graduated from Radcliffe College in 1964. They were studied during their first year

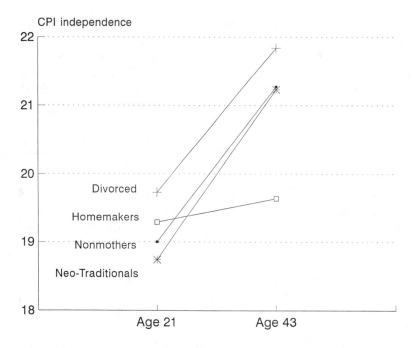

Figure 3: Means on the CPI Independence scale at ages 21 and 43 for homemakers (*n* = 17) and three groups of women with less traditional role paths: neo-traditional, *n* = 35; divorced, *n* = 26; and nonmothers, *n* = 26. Data from Helson and Picano (1990).

of college and followed up by mail at ages 31, 36, 43, and 48, with at least 100 women participating at each postcollege time of testing. Questionnaires, checklists, and Thematic Apperception Tests (TATs) are available at several ages, and California Q Deck descriptions (Block, 1978) and the CPI were obtained at midlife.

In an early study Stewart (1980) showed that women with a self-defining or instrumental personal style (assessed on the TAT at age 18) were likely to pursue career activity by age 31; they were also likely to adopt an action-oriented approach to solving life problems (Stewart, 1978). Thus, personality played an important role in shaping early life choices. These early choices have, in turn, been demonstrated to be consequential for women's later adult lives. Stewart and Vandewater (1993) found that early commitments to either careers or families or both were associated not only with many life outcomes at age 43 (such as number of children, income, educational attainment, and career success), but also with some midlife personality characteristics. For example, women who had made early commitments to families (and not careers) were more concerned about generativity issues than were women who had made commitments to careers.

Finally, Vandewater and Stewart (in press) used the Q-sort and CPI data collected when the women were in their 40s to compare the midlife personalities of (a) women who had begun careers in the 1960s, when it was unusual for women to have careers; (b) women who had initiated careers of the same type in the late 1970s and 1980s, when the culture was much more supportive; and (c) women who had never initiated careers at all (though they usually had jobs). Though the possibility that these three groups differed in personality in early adulthood could not be explored, it was clear that they differed in their 40s. The early careerists had midlife personalities characterized by extraversion and assertiveness. For such women, say Vandewater and Stewart, pathfinding may have been possible and attractive. Moreover, making their way in male-dominated fields may have enhanced these characteristics. Women who had never initiated careers were characterized by introversion and interpersonal warmth and connectedness. For such women, particularly in a disapproving social environment, careers would offer little incentive. Spending more of their time in a domestic sphere may also have supported their interpersonal ties and attention to inner life. The women who made career commitments late (only in their 30s) showed some of the characteristics of both of the other groups: They were extraverted and assertive but also interpersonally warm and connected. Perhaps these women were interested in pursuing careers only when the social–emotional price was lower than it had been in the 1960s.

This study, then, brings together the consequences of early choices, later changes in those choices (which were predicted by personality characteristics), and the cumulative effects of an individual life pattern in a larger social context.

Summary

The three longitudinal studies briefly described here give concrete examples of the influence of personality in selection of roles and of personality change in the context of roles and cohorts. It is tempting to put the findings together in a substantive discussion of male and female lives in our changing society, but other findings and studies would need to be incorporated, and such a project goes beyond our present purpose.

FINAL REMARKS

One hears it said that whether personality changes depends on the definition of personality. However, not all definitions of personality are equally adequate. Definitions that exclude motives, values, styles, scripts, task orientations, self-concepts, and coping mechanisms do not cover what personality psychologists study. In our view, they are reductionistic as well as biased against the demonstration of personality change.

Whether personality is found to change depends also on the conceptualization of change. We argue for research designs that assess the influence of hypothesized agents of change, such as personality structure, social role, or social climate, in contrast to designs that classify change as error variance. We argue against restricting evidence of personality change to change in the most stable aspects of personality, or expecting change to take place over short intervals. Shaping, enlarging, differentiating, and making new connections seem to be the common processes of change. These processes over time affect our motives, competence, identity, perspective, and appraisals of self-worth.

The study of personality change is important, both for an adequate understanding of personality and for the construction of social policy. However, it is also complicated and difficult. It offers many challenges. Models of the process of personality change are needed (Block, 1982; Emmons, King, & Sheldon, 1993; Markus & Kunda, 1986; and others). Developed theories are needed about factors that promote or inhibit personality change, as are theoretically based reasons to focus on some personality variables and life experiences rather than others.

Even if there were better theories, many studies suffer from too little data. Some of them lack reliable and repeated measures of personality, others lack information about the environment, and there can never be enough information about the many facets of research participants' lives and experiences.

More longitudinal studies and increased access to longitudinal archives, such as those of the Murray Center for the Study of Lives,[1] are necessary. Comparisons of findings across longitudinal studies or between longitudinal studies and ingeniously recruited cross-sectional samples are needed: Tomlinson-Keasey and Blurton (1992) found a match for Terman's gifted women at midlife among members of local Mensa chapters and parents of gifted children. This is hard work, seldom attempted, and tools and practice are needed for the task (Helson, 1993). Without such comparisons, personality psychologists can never evaluate the influence of social climate and cohort. When cohort is unlikely to distort results, cross-sectional studies of subjects of different ages may be useful (Neugarten et al., 1963). Short-term longitudinal studies, of which there are increasing numbers, can focus on particular life events or periods of life (Bolger, 1990). Experimental studies can make an important contribution, if they are sensitive to life span issues. Work is needed on many topics, such as how to infer personality change from life change, factors associated with the duration of change, and relations between subjective change and objective change.

Research on consistency of personality will continue to occupy a central place in the field; however, openness to the idea of personality change

---

[1]For information, contact Murray Research Center, Radcliffe College, 10 Garden Street, Cambridge, MA 02138.

offers an opportunity for enriched conceptualizations, new tools, new partnerships, and new empirical contributions.

REFERENCES

Albert, R. S. (1975). Toward a behavioral definition of genius. *American Psychologist, 30,* 140–151.

Allport, G. W., & Vernon, P. E. (1931). A test for personal values. *Journal of Abnormal and Social Psychology, 26,* 231–248.

Alwin, D. F., Cohen, R. L., & Newcomb, T. M. (1991). *Political attitudes over the life span.* Madison: University of Wisconsin Press.

Block, J. (1971). *Lives through time.* Berkeley, CA: Bancroft Books.

Block, J. (1978). *The Q-sort method in personality assessment and psychiatric research.* Palo Alto, CA: Consulting Psychologists Press. (Original work published 1961)

Block, J. (1982). Assimilation, accommodation, and the dynamics of personality development. *Child Development, 53,* 281–295.

Bolger, N. (1990). Coping as a personality process: A prospective study. *Journal of Personality and Social Psychology, 59,* 525–537.

Bray, D. W., Campbell, R. J., & Grant, D. L. (1974). *Formative years in business: A long-term AT&T study of managerial lives.* New York: Wiley.

Bursik, K. (1991). Adaptation to divorce and ego-development. *Journal of Personality and Social Psychology, 60,* 300–306.

Cantor, N., & Kihlstrom, J. (1987). *Personality and social intelligence.* Englewood Cliffs, NJ: Prentice Hall.

Cantor, N., Norem, J. K. Niedenthal, P. M., Langston, C. A., & Brower, A. M. (1987). Life tasks, self-concept ideals, and cognitive strategies in a life transition. *Journal of Personality and Social Psychology, 53,* 1178–1191.

Caspi, A. (1993). Why do maladaptive behaviors persist? Sources of continuity and change in behavioral development. In D. Funder, R. Parke, C. Tomlinson-Keasey, & K. Widaman (Eds.), *Studying lives through time: Personality and development* (pp. 343–376). Washington, DC: American Psychological Association.

Caspi, A., & Bem, D. J. (1990). Personality continuity and change across the life course. In L. A. Pervin (Ed.), *Handbook of personality theory and research* (pp. 549–575). New York: Guilford Press.

Caspi, A., Bem, D. J., & Elder, G. H., Jr. (1989). Continuities and consequences of interactional styles across the life course. *Journal of Personality, 57,* 375–406.

Caspi, A., & Herbener, E. S. (1990). Continuity and change: Assortative marriage and the consistency of personality in adulthood. *Journal of Personality and Social Psychology, 58,* 250–258.

Catlin, G., & Epstein, S. (1992). Unforgettable experiences: The relation of life events to basic beliefs about self and world. *Social Cognition, 10,* 189–209.

Clausen, J. A. (1993). *American lives: Looking back at the children of the Great Depression.* New York: Free Press.

Conley, J. J. (1985a). Longitudinal stability of personality traits: A multitrait-multimethod-multioccasion analysis. *Journal of Personality and Social Psychology, 49,* 1266–1282.

Conley, J. J. (1985b). A personality theory of adulthood and aging. In R. Hogan & W. H. Jones (Eds.), *Perspectives in personality* (Vol. I, pp. 81–116). Greenwich, CT: JAI Press.

Costa, P. T., & McCrae, R. R. (1980). Still stable after all these years: Personality as a key to some issues in aging. In P. B. Baltes & O. G. Brim (Eds.), *Life-span development and behavior* (Vol. 3, pp. 65–102). San Diego, CA: Academic Press.

Costa, P. T., & McCrae, R. R. (1988). Personality in adulthood: A six-year longitudinal study of self-reports and spouse ratings on the NEO Personality Inventory. *Journal of Personality and Social Psychology, 54,* 853–863.

Cowan, C. P., & Cowan, P. A. (1992). *When partners become parents: The big life change for couples.* New York: Basic Books.

Cox, C. M. (1926). *The early mental traits of three hundred geniuses.* Stanford, CA: Stanford University Press.

Datan, N. (1986). Corpses, lepers, and menstruating women: Tradition, transition, and the sociology of knowledge. *Sex Roles, 14,* 693–703.

Dudek, S. Z., & Hall, W. B. (1991). Personality consistency: Eminent architects 25 years later. *Creativity Research Journal, 4,* 213–232.

Edwards, A. L. (1959). *Edwards Personal Preference Schedule.* New York: Psychological Corporation.

Elder, G. H., Jr. (1974). *Children of the Great Depression.* Chicago: University of Chicago Press.

Emmons, R. A., King, L. A., & Sheldon, K. (1993). Goal conflict and self-regulation of action. In D. M. Wegner & J. W. Pennebaker (Eds.), *Handbook of mental control* (pp. 528–551). Englewood Cliffs, NJ: Prentice Hall.

Epstein, S. (1990). Cognitive-experiential self-theory. In L. A. Pervin (Ed.), *Handbook of personality theory and research* (pp. 165–192). New York: Guilford Press.

Erikson, E. (1950). *Childhood and society.* New York: Norton.

Finn, S. E. (1986). Stability of personality self-ratings over 30 years: Evidence for an age/cohort interaction. *Journal of Personality and Social Psychology, 50,* 813–818.

Franz, C. E. (in press). Do preoccupations change as individuals age? A longitudinal study of mid-life adults. In M. E. Lachman & J. B. James (Eds.), *Multiple paths of midlife development.* Chicago: University of Chicago Press.

Freud, A. (1937). *Ego and the mechanism of defense.* London: Hogarth Press.

Gough, H. G. (1987). *Manual for the California Psychological Inventory*. Palo Alto, CA: Consulting Psychologists Press. (Original work published 1957)

Gough, H. G., & Heilbrun, A. B., Jr. (1983). *The Adjective Check List manual: 1980 edition*. Palo Alto, CA: Consulting Psychologists Press.

Gould, R. (1972). The phases of adult life: A study in developmental psychology. *American Journal of Psychiatry, 129,* 521–531.

Greenwald, A. G. (1980). The totalitarian ego: Fabrication and revision of personal history. *American Psychologist, 35,* 603–618.

Grossman, F. K., Eichler, L. L., Winickoff, S. A., Anzalone, M. K., Gofseyeff, M. H., & Sargent, S. P. (1980). *Pregnancy, birth, and parenthood*. San Francisco: Jossey-Bass.

Gruber, H. E. (1989). The evolving systems approach to creative work. In D. B. Wallace & H. E. Gruber (Eds.), *Creative people at work* (pp. 3–24). New York: Oxford University Press.

Gutmann, D. L. (1987). *Reclaimed powers: Toward a new psychology of men and women in later life*. New York: Basic Books.

Haan, N. (1972). Personality development from adolescence to adulthood in the Oakland Growth and Guidance Studies. *Seminars in Psychiatry, 4,* 399–414.

Haan, N., Millsap, R., & Hartka, E. (1986). As times goes by: Change and stability in personality over fifty years. *Psychology and Aging, 1,* 220–232.

Havighurst, R. J. (1972). *Developmental tasks and education*. New York: McKay.

Healy, J. M., Jr. (1989). Emotional adaptation to life transitions: Early impact on integrative cognitive processes. In D. M. Buss & N. Cantor (Eds.), *Personality psychology: Recent trends and emerging directions* (pp. 115–127). New York: Springer-Verlag.

Helson, R. (1967). Personality characteristics and developmental history of creative college women. *Genetic Psychology Monographs, 76,* 205–256.

Helson, R. (1993). Comparing longitudinal studies of adult development: Toward a paradigm of tension between stability and change. In D. Funder, R. Parke, C. Tomlinson-Keasey, & K. Widaman (Eds.), *Studying lives through time: Personality and development* (pp. 93–119). Washington, DC: American Psychological Association.

Helson, R., Mitchell, V., & Moane, G. (1984). Personality and patterns of adherence and non-adherence to the social clock. *Journal of Personality and Social Psychology, 46,* 1079–1096.

Helson, R., & Moane, G. (1987). Personality change in women from college to midlife. *Journal of Personality and Social Psychology, 53,* 176–186.

Helson, R., & Picano, J. (1990). Is the traditional role bad for women? *Journal of Personality and Social Psychology, 59,* 311–320.

Helson, R., & Roberts, B. (1992). The personality of young adult couples and wives' work patterns. *Journal of Personality, 60,* 575–597.

Helson, R., & Wink, P. (1992). Personality change in women from the early 40s to the early 50s. *Psychology and Aging, 7,* 46–55.

Howard, A., & Bray, D. (1988). *Managerial lives in transition: Advancing age and changing times.* New York: Guilford Press.

Inkeles, A., & Smith, D. H. (1974). *Becoming modern.* Cambridge, MA: Harvard University Press.

Jaques, E. (1965). Death and the midlife crisis. *International Journal of Psycho-analysis, 46,* 502–514.

Josselson, R. (1992). *The space between us: Exploring the dimensions of human relationships.* San Francisco: Jossey-Bass.

Jung, C. G. (1924). *Psychological types.* London: Kegan Paul, Trench, & Trubner.

Kernberg, O. F. (1980). Pathological narcissism in middle age. In O. F. Kernberg (Ed.), *Internal world and external reality* (pp. 135–153). Northvale, NJ: Jason Aronson.

Kimmel, D. C. (1974). Personality processes and psychopathology. In D. C. Kimmel (Ed.), *Adulthood and aging* (pp. 289–314). New York: Wiley.

Kogan, N. (1990). Personality and aging. In J. E. Birren & S. W. Schaie (Ed.), *Handbook of the psychology of aging* (pp. 330–346). San Diego, CA: Academic Press.

Kohn, M. L. (1980). Job complexity and adult personality. In N. J. Smelser & E. H. Erikson (Eds.), *Themes of work and love in adulthood* (pp. 193–210). Cambridge, MA: Harvard University Press.

Kohn, M. L., & Schooler, C. (1983). *Work and personality: An inquiry into the impact of social stratification.* Norwood, NJ: Ablex.

Labouvie-Vief, G., Devoe, M., & Bulka, D. (1989). Speaking about feelings: Conceptions of emotion across the life span. *Psychology and Aging, 3,* 425–437.

Lachman, M. (1989). Personality and aging at the crossroads: Beyond stability versus change. In K. W. Schaie & C. Schooler (Eds.), *Social structure and aging: Psychological processes* (pp. 167–189). Hillsdale, NJ: Erlbaum.

Levinson, D. J., Darrow, C. N., Klein, E. B., Levinson, M. H., & McKee, B. (1978). *Seasons of a man's life.* New York: Knopf.

Loevinger, J. (1976). *Ego development: Conceptions and theories.* San Francisco: Jossey-Bass.

Luborsky, L., Mellon, J., Ravensway, P., Childress, A. R., Cohen, K. D., Hole, A., Ming, S., Crits-Christoph, P., Levine, F. J., & Alexander, K. (1985). A verification of Freud's grandest clinical hypothesis: The transference. *Clinical Psychology Review, 5,* 231–246.

MacKinnon, D. W. (1965). Creativity and the realization of creative potential. *American Psychologist, 20,* 273–281.

Markus, H., & Kunda, Z. (1986). Stability and malleability of the self-concept. *Journal of Personality and Social Psychology, 51,* 858–866.

McAdams, D. P. (1992). The five-factor model in personality: A critical appraisal. *Journal of Personality, 60,* 329–361.

McClelland, D. C. (1966). Longitudinal trends in the relation of thought to action. *Journal of Consulting Psychology, 30,* 479–483.

McClelland, D. C. (1985). *Human motivation.* Glenview, IL: Scott, Foresman.

McCrae, R. R., & Costa, P. T., Jr. (1990). *Personality in adulthood.* New York: Guilford Press.

McCurdy, H. G. (1940). Literature and personality: Analysis of the novels of D. H. Lawrence. Part II. *Character and Personality, 8,* 311–322.

McGue, M., Bacon, S., & Lykken, D. T. (1993). Personality stability and change in early adulthood: A behavioral genetic analysis. *Developmental Psychology, 29,* 96–109.

Mischel, W. (1968). *Personality and assessment.* New York: Wiley.

Mortimer, J. T., Finch, M. D., & Kumka, K. (1982). Persistence and change in development: The multidimensional self concept. In P. B. Baltes & O. G. Brim (Eds.), *Life-span development and behavior* (Vol. 4, pp. 264–310). San Diego, CA: Academic Press.

Neugarten, B. L. (1968). Adult personality: Toward a psychology of the life cycle. In B. L. Neugarten (Ed.), *Middle age and aging* (pp. 137–147). Chicago: University of Chicago Press.

Neugarten, B. L., & Kraines, R. J. (1965). "Menopausal symptoms" in women of various ages. *Psychosomatic Medicine, 27,* 266–273.

Neugarten, B. L., Wood, V., Kraines, R. J., & Loomis, B. (1963). Women's attitudes towards the menopause. *Vita Humana, 6,* 140–151.

Ozer, D. J. (1986). *Consistency in personality: A methodological framework.* Berlin: Springer-Verlag.

Pedersen, N. L., Plomin, R., Nesselroade, J. R., & McClearn, G. E. (1992). A quantitative genetic analysis of cognitive abilities during the second half of the life span. *Psychological Science, 3,* 346–353.

Plomin, R., Chipuer, H. M., & Loehlin, J. C. (1990). Behavioral genetics and personality. In L. A. Pervin (Ed.), *Handbook of personality: Theory and research* (pp. 225–243). New York: Guilford Press.

Roberts, P., & Newton, P. M. (1987). Levinsonian studies of women's adult development. *Psychology and Aging, 2,* 154–163.

Ross, L., & Nisbett, R. E. (1991). *The person and the situation.* New York: McGraw-Hill.

Runyan, W. M. (1978). The life course as a theoretical orientation: Sequences of person–situation interaction. *Journal of Personality, 46,* 552–558.

Runyan, W. M. (1980). A stage–state analysis of the life course. *Journal of Personality and Social Psychology, 38,* 951–962.

Sampson, R. J., & Laub, J. H. (1990). Crime and deviance over the life course: The salience of adult social bonds. *American Sociological Review, 55,* 609–627.

Scarr, S., & McCartney, K. (1983). How people make their own environments: A theory of genotype–environment correlations. *Child Development, 54,* 424–435.

Simonton, D. K. (1989). The swan-song phenomenon: Last-works effects for 172 classical composers. *Psychology and Aging, 4,* 42–47.

Skolnick, A. (1966). Motivational imagery and behavior over twenty years. *Journal of Consulting Psychology, 30,* 463–478.

Skolnick, A. (1986). Early attachment and personal relationships across the life course. In P. B. Baltes, D. L. Featherman, & R. M. Lerner (Eds.), *Life-span development and behavior* (Vol. 7, pp. 173–206). San Diego, CA: Academic Press.

Spranger, E. (1928). *Types of men.* Halle, Germany: Max Niemeyer Verlag.

Stewart, A. J. (1978). A longitudinal study of coping styles of self-defining and socially defined women. *Journal of Consulting and Clinical Psychology, 46,* 1079–1084.

Stewart, A. J. (1980). Personality and situation in the prediction of women's life patterns. *Psychology of Women Quarterly, 5,* 195–206.

Stewart, A. J., Franz, C. E., & Layton, L. (1988). The changing self: Using personal documents to study lives. *Journal of Personality, 56,* 41–74.

Stewart, A. J., & Healy, J. M., Jr. (1984). Processing affective responses to life experiences: The development of the adult self. In C. Malatesta & C. Izard (Eds.), *Emotion in adult development* (pp. 277–293). Newbury Park, CA: Sage.

Stewart, A. J., & Healy, J. M., Jr. (1989). Linking individual development and social changes. *American Psychologist, 44,* 30–42.

Stewart, A. J., & Vandewater, E. A. (1993). Career and family clocks in a transitional cohort: The Radcliffe class of 1964. In K. Hulbert & D. Schuster (Eds.), *Women's lives through time: Educated American women of the twentieth century* (pp. 235–258). San Francisco: Jossey-Bass.

Swann, W. B. (1987). Identity negotiations: Where two roads meet. *Journal of Personality and Social Psychology, 53,* 1038–1051.

Tellegen, A. (1982). *Brief manual for the Differential Personality Questionnaire.* Unpublished manuscript, University of Minnesota, Department of Psychology, Minneapolis.

Thorne, A., & Klohnen, E. (1993). Interpersonal memories as maps for personality consistency. In D. Funder, R. Parke, C. Tomlinson-Keasey, & K. Widaman (Eds.), *Studying lives through time: Personality and development* (pp. 223–253). Washington, DC: American Psychological Association.

Tomlinson-Keasy, C., & Blurton, E. U. (1992). Gifted women's lives: Aspirations, achievements, satisfaction and personal adjustment. In J. Carlson (Ed.), *Cognition and educational practice: An international perspective* (pp. 151–176). Greenwich, CT: JAI Press.

Vaillant, G. E. (1976). Natural history of male psychological health: V. Relation of choice of ego mechanisms of defense to adult adjustment. *Archives of General Psychiatry, 33,* 535–545.

Vaillant, G. E. (1977). *Adaptation to life.* Boston: Little, Brown.

Vandewater, E. A., & Stewart, A. J. (in press). Changes in women's career commitments and personality development. In M. E. Lachman & J. B. James (Eds.), *Multiple paths of midlife development.* Chicago: University of Chicago Press.

Werner, H. (1948). *The comparative psychology of mental development* (rev. ed.). Chicago: Follett.

Whitbourne, S. K. (1989). Comments on Lachman's "Personality and aging at the crossroads." In. K. W. Schaie & C. Schooler (Eds.), *Social structure and aging: Psychological processes* (pp. 191–198). Hillsdale, NJ: Erlbaum.

Whitbourne, S. K., & Waterman, A. S. (1979). Psychosocial development during the adult years: Age and cohort comparisons. *Developmental Psychology, 6,* 252–259.

Whitbourne, S. K., & Weinstock, C. S. (1979). *Adult development: The differentiation of experience.* New York: Holt, Rinehart & Winston.

White, R. W. (1966). *Lives in progress* (2nd ed.). New York: Holt, Rinehart & Winston.

White, R. W. (1972). *The enterprise of living: Growth and organization in personality.* New York: Holt, Rinehart & Winston.

Wink, P. (1992). Three types of narcissism in women from college to midlife. *Journal of Personality, 60,* 7–30.

Wink, P., & Helson, R. (1993). Personality change in women and their partners. *Journal of Personality and Social Psychology, 65,* 597–605.

Winter, D., McClelland, D. C., & Stewart, A. J. (1981). *A new case for the liberal arts.* San Francisco: Jossey-Bass.

10

DOES THOUGHT CONTENT CHANGE AS INDIVIDUALS AGE? A LONGITUDINAL STUDY OF MIDLIFE ADULTS

CAROL E. FRANZ

Although normative changes in personality during adulthood are proposed in some theoretical and empirical literature, they have seldom been researched extensively in longitudinal samples. My purpose in this chapter is to examine the question of personality change from early adulthood to midlife as reflected by the kinds of themes written in response to the research version of the Thematic Apperception Test (TAT). According to deCharms (1992),

> although the thought sampling [that is, TAT-based] technique has roots
> in the concepts of the unconscious and projection, we avoid these

I greatly appreciate the helpful comments on earlier versions of this chapter by Joel Weinberger, David McClelland, Jackie James, Abby Stewart, Todd Heatherton, Robert Bornstein, and David Buss.

Part of this research uses the *Patterns of Child Rearing, 1951–52* data set. These data were collected by R. Sears, E. Maccoby, and H. Levin, and are available through the archive of the Henry A. Murray Research Center of Radcliffe College, Cambridge, Massachusetts. The 1978 follow-up by McClelland, and the 1987 McClelland–Franz follow-up are also archived at the Murray Center.

terms in favor of construing the thought sample as a nonself-conscious description of the way a person experiences her world. (p. 326)

In a review of the literature on stability and change in personality, Lachman (1989) found considerable stability in studies of the five major personality traits: neuroticism, extraversion, openness to experience, agreeableness, and conscientiousness. Intrapsychic variables such as motives, coping styles, defenses, and self-concept were more subject to change. Most of the research has been cross-sectional, and Lachman urged more longitudinal work. Follow-ups of the now adult Sears, Maccoby, and Levin (1957) children at ages 31 and 41 provide an opportunity to examine stability and continuity in constructs assessed using the TAT during the transition to middle age. A particular focus of this chapter is on social motives such as n Power, n Achievement, n Affiliation (n signifies need), and Intimacy motivation that, according to McClelland (1985), energize, propel, and select behavior.

A THEORETICAL OVERVIEW

What kinds of changes are expected or normative for middle aged adults? Theory can be looked to for guidelines concerning age-related and normative differences. In the transition to midlife, three types of change can be anticipated: age-related (maturational or developmental), normative change in response to predictable events or change in one's social context, and nonnormative change. The maturational or developmental changes laid out by numerous theorists include Erikson's (1963) emphasis on shifts from a self-orientation to a broader other-orientation. The midlife adult becomes concerned with issues of generativity such as the well-being of others, productivity, and the well-being of the next generation. Vaillant (1977; Vaillant & Milofsky, 1980) modified Erikson's theory by adding a stage of career consolidation between the intimacy and generativity stages. Franz and White (1985) suggested that Erikson's depiction of adult stages of identity followed by intimacy then midlife generativity is problematic because of his theory's emphasis on increasing individuation since birth. Franz and White proposed that a parallel developmental path of attachment, interacting with the individuation path, was necessary for a person to develop both the internal representations and interpersonal skills necessary for intimacy and generativity. According to Franz and White, change along the individuation path during these adult years will be away from self-focused career issues toward productivity and leaving a legacy (Erikson, 1963). Development along the attachment path will move from a self-serving relationship with another person or group toward more mutual and interdependent, caring relationships with other people.

Other theorists have advanced similar notions that as adults age toward midlife they become more interdependent. Depending on the theorist, adults may shift from an institutional to an interindividual self; may change from an achieving self to an executive/responsible self; or may move toward a more stabilized ego identity, freer personal relationships, deeper interests, more humanized values, and greater caring (Kegan, 1982; Schaie, 1977–1978; White, 1966, respectively). Levinson, Darrow, Klein, Levinson, and McKee (1978) proposed that men in their 40s become more realistic; at the same time, they also become more individuated and more intensely attached. This theme of greater realism in midlife adults also emerges in the work of Buhler (1968), Buhler and Goldenberg (1968), and Gould (1980). Grandiosity and creative expansion are viewed as healthy aspects of adolescence and early adulthood. At midlife the adult becomes more realistic regarding his or her own omnipotence and invulnerability (Buhler, 1968; Buhler & Goldenberg, 1968).

According to some theorists, the midlife adult's cognitions and emotions become less dualistic and more contextualized, differentiated, and complex (Jung, 1972; Labouvie-Vief, Hakim-Larson, & Hobart, 1987; Loevinger, 1976), and more interior (Lubin, 1964; Neugarten, 1970; Rosen & Neugarten, 1964). As interiority expands, "the older person tends to respond to inner rather than outer stimuli, to withdraw emotional investments, to give up self-assertiveness, and to avoid rather than embrace challenge" (Rosen & Neugarten, 1964, p. 99). Finally, maturity, broadly defined depending on the theorist or researcher, is assumed to increase with age (cf. Erikson, 1963; Franz & White, 1985; Helson & Wink, 1992; Vaillant, 1977).

Other researchers and theorists propose that normative life events, not age, are related to changes from early adulthood to midlife. According to Gutmann, men move from an active, assertive mode to a more dependent, passive one at midlife, whereas women become more assertive (Gutmann, 1975; Neugarten, 1970). These changes occur because of predictable shifts in parenting roles for men and women at middle age; men and women function in line with different biological demands. Havighurst (1973) and Brim and Ryff (1980) outlined high-probability events in the life course that may account for similar changes within a cohort. During the transition to midlife, normative events may include moving from selecting a mate to learning to live with and relate to a mate; from child bearing and rearing to the empty nest; from choosing an occupation to striving for satisfactory performance in a job; from finding a congenial social group to achieving adult social and civic responsibility; and from feeling no physiological limits to accepting and adjusting to the physiological changes of middle age (Havighurst, 1973). Normative events may be specific to a particular cohort (Helson & Wink, 1992). For instance, mothers of young children are now highly likely to be in the work force, whereas, in 1951, very few women combined work and family responsibilities (Sears et al., 1957). To the extent that entrance into or involvement in the workplace is associated with personality change, these shifts might now be apparent in younger cohorts. Major historical events specific to a single cohort—such as the Great Depression, World War II, or the Vietnam War—may differentially affect personality (Elder, 1979; Stewart & Healy, 1989). Although the sample in this study spent formative adolescent years in the 1960s, the absence of personality data prior to the 1960s precludes examination of this type of change.

Finally, intraindividual change can occur in response to factors such as stress (Fiske & Chiriboga, 1990) or low-probability events (Brim & Ryff, 1980). When subjects from Fiske and Chiriboga's (1990) longitudinal study of adults from four different cohorts were asked how they had changed, most subjects reported that they were now "more patient, tolerant and mature" (p. 40). Other indicators showed relative stability in flexibility, rigidity, and self-concept; less continuity occurred among those subjects experiencing more stress. Among subjects in the two younger cohorts approaching midlife, philosophical and religious values stayed consistently high over the time of the follow-up. On the other hand, valuing achievement, work, and social service decreased in men, but not in women. Men remained consistent in their high valuation of ease, contentment, and seeking enjoyment. Fiske and Chiriboga concluded that continuity is the norm; health, work, and family issues appear responsible for the maintenance of this continuity.

The question of whether thought content changes over time has also been examined in personal documents, such as diaries and letters. Using a content-analytic coding system based on Erikson's (1963) theory, shifts in identity, intimacy and generativity themes have been examined in several longitudinal case studies during transition periods (Espin, Stewart, & Gomez, 1990; Franz, 1988, in press; Franz & Paul, 1986; Peterson & Stewart, 1990; Stewart, Franz, & Layton, 1988). In general, the results support Erikson's view that during adulthood subjects' thought content changed in the direction of increasing themes of intimacy and generativity over time; identity concerns decreased somewhat after early adulthood. The type of identity theme chosen by the research subjects shifted with increasing age toward a more mature, committed expression of identity, especially commitment to a career.

Veroff, Reuman, and Feld (1984) examined shifts in social motives across several different cohorts. The motives that were examined included the need to have an impact; the efficiency motive, or the desire for excellence; and the desire to establish, maintain, or restore positive relations with another person or persons (n Power, n Achievement, and n Affiliation, respectively). Veroff studied two types of power motivation: fear of weakness and, the more commonly studied, hope for power (n Power; Winter, 1992).

Until recently, motivational theory made no clear predictions concerning development of motives over the life course, with the exception of the role of childhood antecedents in the development of adult motives (McClelland & Franz, 1992; McClelland & Pilon, 1983). McAdams (1985) proposed that midlife generativity may be reflected by a balance of the need for intimacy and n power. Earlier in adulthood, though, this combination is associated with greater internal conflict (Zeldow, Daugherty, & McAdams, 1988).

Comparing a wide age range of adults from a 1957 study with those from a 1976 replication, Veroff, Depner, Kulka, and Douvan (1980) concluded that

> among men, the achievement motive has remained stable, the affiliative motive has decreased, and both power motives have increased. Among women, both motives for achievement and power as fear of weakness have increased, but there has been no change in the other two motives. (p. 1249)

Veroff (1986), one of the few motivational theorists to discuss life course dynamics in motives, proposed that, because of the different life trajectories of men and women, n Achievement peaks earlier in adulthood for men. Women, he hypothesized, are more likely to turn to jobs for self-differentiation; work, then, has a different meaning for men and for women. Veroff believed that increases in n Power between 1957 and 1978 were due, in part, to changes in the workplace toward more impact-oriented jobs. He concluded that although motivational shifts are apparent among men, these shifts are not age related, rather, they are related to normative and non-normative life experiences. These results, however, are based on cross-sectional data that can confound cohort, age, change, and developmental trends.

Veroff (1982, 1986) argued that the context of the individual needs to be incorporated into an understanding of motives in the life course. Two of Veroff's points are relevant here: First, because of age, sex, social context, and life cycle issues the meaning of a motive may vary depending on where a person is in the life cycle. Second, patterns of interactions among motives need to be assessed; that is, personality development and change will depend somewhat on the person's initial motive structure.

Many personality theorists and researchers assume that there is relative stability in personality characteristics over time among adults; developmentally oriented personality theorists highlight predictable, systematic shifts in some aspects of personality across the life course. As White wrote, "some features of life call for the broadening of experience; others require its deepening" (1966, p. 370). How can personality psychologists disentangle these possibilities for both stability and change in midlife adults? What thought contents are more stable, what changes and what conditions foster greater continuity or change?

THE PRESENT STUDY: CHANGE AND STABILITY IN MIDLIFE ADULTS

To investigate this question of continuity and change, I analyze changes in three types of thought-content measures assessed using the TAT: social motives such as n Achievement, n Power, n Affiliation, and Intimacy motivation; Psychological stance (an indicator of psychosocial maturity); and an age-related thought-content scoring system (ARTS) newly derived for this study. I describe these measures in detail in the methods sections. Based on age-oriented theoretical approaches, I predict decreases in the assertive motives and increases in affiliation or a communal orientation over the 10 years from age 31 to age 41. According to Gutmann (1975), though, sex differences in change will occur, due to dissimilar role changes for men and women. In keeping with life span theoretical approaches, maturity will increase over time.

Because of my interest in change in adulthood, I had earlier derived an explicitly Eriksonian theory-based content-analytic system (Franz, 1988, in press; Stewart et al., 1988). For a project sponsored by the MacArthur Foundation, I, along with David McClelland, developed an empirically derived scoring system for examining themes typically written by people in different age groups (Franz & McClelland, 1992). Instead of determining, a priori, what themes in stories people should be writing (e.g., more intimacy at age 31 or more generativity at age 41), I was interested in what people were writing. With regard to this new empirically derived scoring system, three categories of themes emerged. Younger adult subjects tended to write more worrisome, conflicted stories (*youthful uncertainty*) and more idealistic or grandiose themes (*idealizations*). Older adults wrote themes of planning, realistic strivings, and warm refreshing relationships that we called *grounded realistic* thinking; Youthful Uncertainty and Idealizations decreased significantly over 10 years and Grounded Realistic thinking increased (Franz, 1992). In this chapter, because of the number of variables being examined overall, I focus only on Idealizations. If Idealizations are typical and adaptive for young, but not older, people (as is suggested by Buhler, 1968, and Kohut, 1985), they will be higher among 31-year-olds and decrease significantly over time. According to Kohut (1985),

> we should not deny our ambitions, our wish to dominate, our wish to shine, and our yearning to merge into omnipotent figures, but should instead learn to acknowledge the legitimacy of these narcissistic forces. . . . We then shall be able to transform our archaic grandiosity and exhibitionism into realistic self-esteem and into pleasure with ourselves, and our yearning to be at one with the omnipotent self object into the socially useful, adaptive capacity to be enthusiastic. (p. 128)

In addition, if it is more adaptive to be more idealistic in early adulthood, Idealizations at age 31 will be associated with better life outcomes such as social and work accomplishments, and lower depression (Zung, 1965) at age 41.

Finally, I examined the current literature on change and life events to see what other researchers identified as possible factors associated with change in midlife. Factors associated with change for which I have measures in this study include stress, health problems, shifts in job status, number of children, and marital status (Caspi & Bem, 1990; Epstein, 1990; Fiske and Chiriboga, 1990; Helson, 1992; Lachman, 1989; Lerner & Ryff, 1978; Stewart, 1982; Stewart & Healy, 1989, Veroff, 1986).

Description of Sample

Only a brief introduction to the sample will be given because details of the original study and the follow-ups are reported in multiple sources. The original Sears et al. (1957) sample was composed of 379 mothers and their kindergarten-aged children, one child per mother, selected from two towns in the Boston area. The sample was all White, American-born, with an intact family in 1951; there were 202 boys and 177 girls. Details of the sample selection, interview procedure, coding, and reliabilities may be found in Sears et al.

McClelland, in 1978, followed up a subsample of the Sears et al. (1957) subjects, then aged 31, who were still living in the Boston area. Out of the 130 subjects located, 118 were interviewed. Seventy-eight of these subjects came to a second session in which they were administered a variety of personality measures that included a six-picture TAT. Pictures included a captain, a draftsman at his desk, two female scientists, a trapeze picture, a couple by a river, and a couple at a cafe. t tests of parenting and demographic measures indicate that the 1978 sample was representative of the 1951 sample (Koestner, Franz, & Weinberger, 1990; McClelland & Pilon, 1983).

The subsample studied at age 41 comprised subjects for whom there were addresses from the earlier wave of data collection in 1978.[1] Subjects were contacted by mail if they had moved beyond approximately four hours' driving distance from Boston. Of the subjects who could be located (78%) from the earlier wave, 85% of the women and 66% of the men participated in the 1987–1988 wave of data collection (n = 94; 43% men/57% women). Incomplete demographic questionnaire data excluded 5 subjects (3 men and 2 women) from analyses. Checks on the sampling indicated that the sample was representative of the 1978 sample and the original 1951 sample,

[1] I am grateful for financial support from the Seaver Institute that made the age 41 follow-up possible through a postdoctoral training grant under the supervision of Dr. David McClelland. I am also indebted to Dr. Joel Weinberger, Elizabeth Vandewater, Dr. Joseph Healy, Dr. Richard Koestner, and our highly competent group of graduate students who helped with the study: Ruth Jacobs, Elizabeth St. Lawrence, and Steve Kelner.

with the exception that the follow-up of 41-year-olds had a larger proportion of women and more middle class men than the 1951 sample (Franz, McClelland, & Weinberger, 1991; McClelland & Franz, 1992).

The final sample at age 41 included 89 White, primarily middle class, subjects: 76 married or previously married White subjects and 13 single subjects. Seventeen subjects were divorced or separated and not remarried. Nearly all (91%) of the subjects who were married or divorced had children (range = 1–6 children, M = 1.92). No subjects were yet experiencing the empty nest; no single subjects had children. All of the subjects finished high school, 50% had some college education, and 42% had pursued more education after college. At the time of the follow-up, most of the sample (92%) were working at least part-time outside the home; only six women were not working for pay. As is typically found (Rix, 1988), the men had significantly more education, worked at higher level jobs, and earned more income than the women (Franz et al., 1991). Because the focus of this chapter is on stability and change, TAT results are reported only for the 48 subjects followed-up at both times. The demographic data for this subsample is in proportion to that of the larger sample of 89 subjects.

Description of Measures

Social Motives: *n* Power, *n* Achievement, *n* Intimacy

All TATs had previously been scored for the social motives of *n* Power (Winter, 1992), *n* Achievement (McClelland, Atkinson, Clark, & Lowell, 1992), *n* Affiliation (Heyns, Veroff, & Atkinson, 1992), and Intimacy motivation (McAdams, 1992), and corrected for correlation with text length (Smith, Feld, & Franz, 1992).

Scores had been entered in 1978 as totals across six pictures; one picture at age 41, however, differed from those at age 31: The man and woman in a cafe was replaced by a picture of a man and an exotically dressed woman walking a horse through a field. Comparisons between motives at age 31 and at age 41, then, are based on a slightly different set of pictures. It should be noted, however, that the different picture at each time is one to which subjects write similar themes, that is, Intimacy motivation or *n* Affiliation (D. C. McClelland, personal communication, May, 1991).

Trained scorers coded the TATs of the age 41 sample with the same motive scoring systems as at age 31. Scorers attained an expert level of reliability with the published scoring systems (interrater reliability above 87% for presence of imagery and rho above .85 for total imagery) and an equally high level of reliability with the scores of the 1978 TATs. Details concerning the TAT measures are reported in McClelland and Pilon (1983), and McClelland and Franz (1992). Because cogent discussions of the reliability and validity of the standard TAT-based measures of social motives exist in numerous sources (cf. Lundy, 1985, 1988; McClelland, 1985; Smith, 1992; Weinberger & McClelland, 1990), these issues are not addressed here.

A TAT-based measure of maturity, called Psychological stance (Stewart, 1982, 1992; Stewart & Healy, 1992), was also coded. According to Stewart (1992), four stances—receptive, autonomous, assertive, and integrated—form a continuum depicting how well adapted the person's relationship is to his or her environment. A person's predominant stance reflects the following: the receptive individual is "entirely submerged in the environment"; the mature, integrated individual is "depicted in some stable and neutral relation to the environment" (Stewart & Healy, 1992, p. 442). The integrated person writes more themes of working and planning, mutuality and sharing in relationships with others, and complexity of emotional expression. Stewart (1992) reviewed the reliability and the 15-year history of the validity of this instrument.

In keeping with prior research by Stewart (1992), a single overall weighted score was computed for each subject at each time (1 × receptive score, 2 × autonomous score, 3 × assertive score, and 4 × integrated score/unweighted total). The total score was corrected for its correlation with text length. The Psychological stance measure can be thought of as a measure of psychosocial maturity (McClelland, 1985; Stewart & Healy, 1992) and is predicted to increase over time.

Derivation of an Age-Related Thought-Content System (ARTS)

I derived a new content-analytic coding system based on TATs of two samples of adult subjects. Using a standard criterion group approach to deriving scoring systems, TATs of five adults in their early 30s were compared with TATs of five adults in their early 40s from the Sears et al. (1957) sample. Any themes present in one group but absent in the other formed the initial scoring system.[2] Three themes were commonly written about by the younger subjects: worry that something might go wrong in the future; worry and/or conflict in interpersonal relationships such as arguments, affairs, and emotional distance; and Idealizations or grandiosity. With Idealizations, the younger subjects more often wrote stories that seemed to go beyond the picture. Subjects introduced famous characters, and idealistic wishes and activities such as the creation of devices that would save the environment or the world, of characters who pondered their place in the history of humanity, and of characters who performed unusual feats such as making love from a trapeze or, as one person wrote, "in the center ring

---

[2]My thanks to David McClelland for his role in creating this scoring system, and to graduate students in courses at Boston University, Adelphi University, and the postdoctoral training group for assistance in identifying themes.

under the big top." These images seemed to have a coherent central theme of idealistic thinking.

In order to evaluate the reliability and validity of the measure, the rudimentary coding system was then applied to a second set of TATs from a different sample of adults in which it successfully distinguished between young and old subjects. A scoring guide was then finalized with definitions, examples of themes, and scoring rules, such as the decision to score a theme no more than once in a story. Use of the ARTS system indicated that coders could attain a high level of reliability (above 87% agreement on presence of imagery).

All of the five TAT pictures in common were coded for ARTS in both time periods (78 from 1978 and 89 from 1987). Duplicate subject numbers and any cues to date were removed. Protocols were randomly placed in sets so as to minimize coder bias. In order to maximize coder reliability, the trained coder scored all stories written to a single picture by all the subjects at the same time. In keeping with the motive scores, these scores were also corrected for their correlation with text length. Only the results specific to Idealizations are reported here; results relating to other categories are reported elsewhere (Franz, 1992).

Factors Associated With Change

The association between personality change and different life experiences was also explored. For these analyses, I examined changes in marital status, work status, number of children, stress, and health in relation to the previously described personality and maturity measures. When comparable variables were available at both age 31 and age 41, simple difference scores were used (Rogosa, 1988).

Demographic information regarding occupation, marital status, and the number of children was available at both age 31 and age 41 (Franz et al., 1991; McClelland & Franz, 1992; McClelland & Pilon, 1983); change scores were computed (age 41 − age 31) for each. Because so few subjects were single, or divorced but not remarried, stability in marital status was simply an indicator of whether the subject had remained married or not from age 31 to age 41. Subjects had been administered a life events questionnaire, modified to account for women's life events at age 41, on which they checked the events that had occurred in the past year (McClelland, 1989). A count of the number of major illnesses over the past year and past 10 years was made from a listing of major illnesses experienced by the subjects. Subjects tended to be in good health (Franz et al., 1991). Major illnesses were distinguishable from minor illnesses by their chronicity, duration, intensity, and severity (McClelland, 1989).

Outcomes were assessed in three domains: social and work accomplishment, and depression (Zung, 1965). Conventional social accomplishment was developed from Vaillant's (1977) life history index of social accomplishment; childhood antecedents of and adult correlates of this measure support its validity (Franz et al., 1991; Picano, 1989). Points were given to subjects for the following kinds of social behaviors: experiencing high marital satisfaction in a marriage 10 or more years in duration, not being divorced, having children, having close friends, and engaging in activities with nonfamily members.

The work accomplishment measure assessed commitment to and involvement in industrious or work-related behaviors rather than just assessing more traditional occupational level (i.e., job status). Included in this composite are points for work satisfaction and commitment, education obtained for one's occupation, occupational status, additional jobs held, and active leisure pursuits. Women at home with children received work credits equivalent to those of a small business manager (McClelland & Franz, 1992). Finally, subjects were administered the Zung (1965) depression scale as a way of assessing their psychological well-being. There were no sex differences in any of these outcome measures.

Evidence for Stability and Change in Thought Content

Preliminary Analyses

Because a new scoring system is being introduced, it seems important to look at the overlap among the TAT-based constructs. In addition, the tendency among motive researchers has been to only present data on the specific motive under study. It may be that one underexplored area of change in the person is how the motives interrelate at different times (Veroff, 1986). In Tables 1 and 2, only within-time correlations are examined; over-

TABLE 1
Intercorrelations Among Thought Content Measures: Age 31

	1.	2.	3.	4.	5.
1. Idealizations					
2. *n* Power	.23				
3. *n* Achievement	.08	.11			
4. *n* Affiliation	−.21	−.21	.02		
5. Intimacy Motivation	−.06	.00	.20	.38**	
6. Psychological Stance	.29*	.01	.42***	−.12	−.19

*p < .05; **p < .01; ***p < .001; two-tailed. N = 49

TABLE 2
Intercorrelations Among Thought-Content Measures: Age 41

	1.	2.	3.	4.	5.
1. Idealizations					
2. n Power	.19				
3. n Achievement	−.26	−.30**			
4. n Affiliation	−.12	−.06	.05		
5. Intimacy Motivation	−.10	−.13	.16	.54***	
6. Psychological Stance	.02	−.04	.02	−.14	.01

*$p < .05$; **$p < .01$; ***$p < .001$; two-tailed. $N = 49$.

time relationships might represent shifts in the meanings of the constructs for the person.

As can be seen in Table 1, subjects high in n Intimacy were also high in n Affiliation (this relationship also held at age 41; see Table 2). N Achievement and Idealizations both correlated significantly with Psychological Stance. High Idealizations also were associated with higher levels of n Power. Idealizations, then, may represent a healthy assertive aspect of the person. Unlike Idealizations, n Power is not associated with the measure of maturity, Psychological Stance. It makes sense that motives would be associated with Stance, though, to date, there is no theory predicting these relationships. Motives such as Intimacy motivation (McAdams, 1992) and n Achievement (McClelland & Koestner, 1992), however, have independently been associated with measures of well-being.

In Table 2 it can be seen that the intercorrelations among the motives at age 41 corresponded fairly well with those at 31. Two intercorrelations seem unusual. First, even though n Achievement and n Power are both considered assertive motives, they were negatively correlated at age 41. Although Veroff (1986) hypothesized such a relationship for women, in this sample, as subjects grew older, subjects whose behavior was directed by one assertive motive tended to be significantly lower in the other. This hypothesis can be examined longitudinally. For women, if n Achievement is not impact centered, high n Achievement at age 31 will be associated with lower n Power at age 41. In fact, the correlation between n Achievement at age 31 and n Power at age 41 is significantly different for women and men, $r(29) = −.50$, $p < .01$; $r(16) = .07$, ns, respectively (z diff. $= 1.94$, $p < .05$). N Power and n Achievement were negligibly correlated at age 31, $r(29) = .06$, among women. It may be that, in this cohort of women, women who develop their sense of competence and agency through n Achievement early in life are unlikely to be motivated, as well, by power.

Second, all correlations between motives, Idealizations and Psychological Stance have reduced to nonsignificance. In general, though, it appears that the degree of overlap among the TAT-based measures is low enough that they are not tapping the same constructs.

Intraindividual Change in Thought-Content Measures

Changes in thought content were evaluated using paired t tests. As can be seen in Table 3, men's and women's stories at the age of 41 contained fewer Idealization themes and fewer themes regarding personal standards of excellence (n Achievement) than at the age of 31. Men also wrote stories that were significantly lower in themes concerning the desire to have an impact on others by the age of 41 (n Power). The scores of both men and women showed increases in concern about getting or maintaining positive relationships with others (n Affiliation). Psychological stance, an indicator of greater adaptation to the environment, increased significantly. It appears that considerable change occurs in this sample, much of it in the directions suggested by life span theorists reviewed earlier in this chapter. N Achievement and n Power can be viewed as self-assertive motives, and n Affiliation as a communal orientation toward other persons (Veroff, 1982); the decreases in self-assertion and increases in communion in this sample support the notion that in midlife there is movement away from a self-focused assertiveness and toward a more interpersonal focus. Similarly, idealizations decrease over time, indicating, perhaps, less need for grandiosity when the realistic achievements of adulthood materialize as "realistic self-esteem" (Kohut, 1985, p. 128). The results do not support Gutmann's (1975) hypothesis that women become less communal and more assertive.

Differential Stability

Systematic increases or decreases in thought content do not rule out the possibility of differential stability, that is, "the retention of an individ-

TABLE 3
Paired t-Test Comparisons of Motives, Psychological Stance, and Idealizations at Ages 31 and 41

	Age 31		Age 41		t test
	M	SD	M	SD	
n Power	6.06	4.11	5.17	3.13	1.39 ns
n Achievement	3.60	3.56	1.75	4.13	2.95 $p < .01$
n Affiliation	9.45	3.14	11.56	3.58	−3.56 $p < .01$
n Intimacy	6.33	2.91	6.70	3.63	−.65 ns
Psychological Stance	2.22	.46	2.54	.24	−5.10 $p < .001$
Idealizations	1.22	1.25	.18	.39	5.45 $p < .001$

N = 49

TABLE 4
Stability of Motives, Psychological Stance, and Idealizations: Correlations
Between Age 31 and Age 41 Measures

	Men	Women	Total
	(18)	(31)	(49)
n Achievement	.33	.33^t	.36*
n Power	−.09	.35^t	.26^t
n Affiliation	.17	.28	.24^t
n Intimacy	−.18	.48**	.29*
Psychological Stance	.65**	.36*	.50**
Idealizations	.11	−.14	−.03

$tp < .05$; *$p < .05$; **$p < .01$; two-tailed.

ual's relative placement in a group" (Caspi & Bem, 1990, p. 550). In Table 4, the degree to which subjects' scores on each measure were correlated over 10 years can be seen. N Achievement, n Intimacy, and Psychological Stance were significantly correlated with the corresponding measure over these 10 years but not n Affiliation, n Power, or Idealizations. Change and some stability, then, are apparent in this sample. Levels of both n Achievement and psychological maturity changed significantly over time, but from these analyses it can be seen that individuals retained their relative placement within the group. Greater consistency appears for Intimacy motivations; subjects tended to write as many Intimacy motivation themes at age 31 as at age 41, and maintained their relative placement in the group. Idealizations, need for power among men, and need for affiliation show the least stability. All three shifted in the predicted directions over time; subjects also varied in frequencies of use of these themes in comparison with the group at each time.

Factors Associated With Change

Correlational analyses of the relationships among stressors, the number of major illnesses reported over the past 10 years, marital stability, change in the number of children, and degree of job status change can be seen in Table 5. The specific conditions for change—children, marriage, and job status—were chosen because they have been discussed as typical of people in the 31- to 41-year-old age group. Approximately 41% of the sample changed marital status in the 10-year period, and 36% had more children; 53% of the subjects increased their job status, and 17% decreased job status. For the year prior to 41, subjects averaged 6.24 ($SD = 5.03$) life stresses. They reported an average of 1.72 (range 0 to 9; $SD = 2.06$) major illnesses in the prior 10 years; 35% of the subjects, however, reported no major illnesses.

TABLE 5
Correlations Between Factors Associated With Change and Changes in Thought Content: Age 31 to Age 41

| | Increases (T2–T1) in: | | | | | |
	Ideals	n Pow	n Ach	n Aff	n Int	Stance
# Stresses (n = 45)	−.07	−.07	.03	.28	.31*	−.16
# Major Illnesses (n = 42)	.05	.26t	.09	.09	.25t	.26t
Increased Job Status (n = 45)	−.04	.06	.35*	.05	.24t	.17
Increased # Children (n = 38)	.21	.03	.02	.05	−.26t	.16
Marital Instability[1] (n = 45)	−.12	−.06	.01	.28t	.10	−.29*

t $p < .10$; *$p < .05$; two-tailed.

Note: Marital Instability: 1 = stable; 2 = unstable.

Life stresses were most likely to be related to changes in Intimacy motivation; increases in the Intimacy motivation were significantly associated with reports of higher stress levels in the past year reported at age 41. Increases in Intimacy motivation were marginally associated with increases in job status, and higher numbers of major illnesses at age 41. It may be that such stresses increased a subject's sense of isolation from others or increased the desire for social support. Subjects who had more children between ages 31 and 41 decreased in Intimacy motivation. Earlier it was shown that a person's level of Intimacy motivation relative to the rest of the sample remained stable over time and did not change with age; it did vary, however, in association with different types of life events.

Otherwise, specific life events during this 10-year period were only weakly associated with motive changes. Subjects who increased in job status over the 10 years also increased significantly in Achievement. Having more major illnesses at age 41 was marginally associated with increased Power, Intimacy motivation, and higher levels of maturity (Psychological stance). The association between n Power and poor health concurs with other, cross-sectional, studies of motivation and health (McClelland, 1989). Subjects who stayed married over the 10 years decreased significantly in n Affiliation and increased significantly in Psychological Stance. Although Fiske and Chiriboga (1990) found greater change in personality under stressful situations, the large number of nonsignificant relationships in Table 5 suggests few changes associated with at least this group of common life events.

CONCLUSIONS

When asked to describe how one group of TAT stories differed from another, an undergraduate student summarized it by saying "These guys (pointing to the 41-year-old pile) are more boring." In a way, yes, the 41-

year-old subjects wrote fewer assertive themes, and they appeared to have lost some of that grandiosity and idealism apparent at age 31. What had replaced this drive of the early 30s? Concern with relationships, sharing and mutuality, work and planning, complex emotions, maturity . . . was this boredom? One middle aged adult, as he pondered the different types of themes evident at the two ages—especially the grandiose exuberance found in the Idealization coding scheme—wondered if there was anything positive about midlife.

Does thought content change as people age? The answer, based on results from TAT stories, appears to support the axiom that there is both change and continuity. On the one hand, despite the passage of time and life experience over 10 years, these adults were stable relative to each other in some of their motives and maturity. Subjects' levels of n Achievement, Intimacy motivation, and Psychological Stance at age 31 remained stable in comparison with those of other subjects at age 41. In spite of this continuity, differences appear in the content of their thoughts; some changes related to the passage of time, others to life experiences.

As these men and women aged, they moved toward greater maturity and greater concern with relationships. The degree to which they wrote themes of achievement and Idealizations lessened over time; themes associated with impact (n Power) were especially lower in men at age 41. These results support, in general, theoretical views of reduced self-concern and assertion and greater concern with communion and other people in middle age, of movement toward greater adaptation to the environment, and of rising interiority (Erikson, 1963; Franz & White, 1985; Gutmann, 1975; Kegan, 1982; Rosen & Neugarten, 1964; Schaie, 1977–1978; Stewart, 1992; White, 1966).

In partial support of Fiske and Chiriboga (1990), some motive instability was associated with life changes during these 10 years. Intimacy appeared most variable, increasing in the context of greater stress, more illnesses, and rising job status, and decreasing in conjunction with affiliative changes such as having more children between ages 31 and 41. In contrast with their discovery that marriage maintained stability, in this sample, marital stability was associated with greater maturity and decreasing n Affiliation over 10 years. Although Fiske and Chiriboga predicted greater change in personality among subjects experiencing more life changes, of the 30 correlations reported in Table 5, only 9 were significant above the .10 level. In this sample, then, the evidence for change due to aging appears to be stronger than that for change due to these common life changes.

Idealistic thinking such as discovering a cure for an incurable disease, saving the whales, and single-handedly creating world peace at age 31 seemed to benefit subjects at age 41, especially if it decreased as subjects aged. Men and women who were high in Idealizations at age 31 were significantly higher in social accomplishment, $r(44) = .46$, $p < .01$, and work accomplishment, $r(44) = .48$, $p < .01$, and were more psychosocially mature, $r(46) = .45$, $p < .01$, at age 41. Lower depression (Zung, 1965) at age 41 was associated with writing more themes of Idealizations at age 31, and decreasing Idealizations in men, $r(40) = -.31$; $r(14) = .50$, $p < .05$, respectively. In light of recent theorizing on the deficits of clinical narcissism (Kohut, 1977; Wink, 1992), it was interesting that this TAT-based measure of idealistic and grandiose thinking is associated with positive outcomes at midlife. These results support the sense that there are developmentally healthy aspects of idealism (Gottschalk, 1990; Kohut, 1977; Levinson et al., 1978; Wink, 1992). As Gottschalk wrote,

> People who have experienced smooth transitions from the infantile and early state of infantile narcissism (when it was appropriate to be loved and cared for unconditionally) to the more adult state of stable self-esteem (when it became understood that love from others would be more likely conditional on one's behavior and achievements) are less vulnerable than others. . . . The poor in self-love get poorer and the rich in self-love get richer. (p. 77)

To have some youthful dreams of greatness seemed to be adaptive for these subjects, and, as Gottschalk suggested, connected with life achievements such as social and work accomplishment, and greater adaptation to the environment.

Only mixed support was available for Gutmann's (1975) role-related ideas concerning gender crossover at midlife. Although men decreased in achievement and increased in affiliation over time, women did so as well. It may be that men's agency could appear more reduced than that of women because men's power motive decreased. This cohort was quite different from that examined by Guttman; men and women reaching adulthood in the 1970s could expect lives less closely constrained by social roles than those of their parents or grandparents. What Gutmann viewed as biologically determined may have reflected the cultural constraints of the generation of midlife men and women he studied during the 1960s.

In closing, the importance of the social context of this cohort cannot be underestimated. Without a second cohort it is impossible to discern whether the changed imagery was age or social history related. These subjects were born into the baby boom of the 1950s and experienced adolescence in the overturn of cultural expectancies of the 1960s. Their early adulthood during the 1970s was one in which old rules no longer applied. The emergence of new family structures, high divorce rates, feminism, more women in the workplace, the disillusionment of the war in Vietnam, Watergate, and the oil crisis all served as catalysts in a changing society. It could be that the higher needs for power, achievement, and idealizations in the age 31 stories written in 1978 reflect the uncertainty, worry, and need for self-assertion necessary to establish a sense of self and a coherent life path at that historical time. Similarly, the more content, relational stories at age 41 (in 1987) may have reflected the economic prosperity of these well-educated, middle class adults.

Based on these results, I am not yet ready to concur with Fiske and Chiriboga (1990) or McCrae and Costa (1990) that the norm in adulthood is continuity; it all depends on the ages, the measures, and the psychological qualities examined in people's lives. In this sample the evidence for change is strong, most of it in keeping with theorized age-related changes of midlife adults, some of it associated with normative life experiences. Some stability was also evident over these 10 years. With so few longitudinal studies spanning definitive periods during the adult years, personality researchers have only succeeded in taking a few snapshots of people in motion. Ultimately, the only answers to the question of what, when, and how changes occur will be found through more focused, large multitrait, multimethod, and multicohort longitudinal research. For only there can we manage to untangle the complexities of change, continuity, sex, age, cohort, and development in the midlife transition.

REFERENCES

Brim, O. G., & Ryff, C. D. (1980). On the properties of life events. In P. B. Baltes & O. G. Brim (Eds.), *Life-span development and behavior* (Vol. 3, pp. 368–387). San Diego, CA: Academic Press.

Buhler, C. (1968). The developmental structure of goal setting in group and individual studies. In C. Buhler & F. Massarik (Eds.), *The course of human life: A study of goals in the humanistic perspective* (pp. 27–54). New York: Springer.

Buhler, C., & Goldenberg, H. (1968). Structural aspects of individual's history. In C. Buhler & F. Massarik (Eds.), *The course of human life: A study of goals in the humanistic perspective* (pp. 54–63). New York: Springer.

Caspi, A., & Bem, D. (1990). Personality continuity and change across the life course. In L. Pervin (Ed.), *Handbook of personality theory and research* (pp. 549–575). New York: Guilford Press.

deCharms, R. (1992). Personal causation and the origin concept. In C. P. Smith, J. W. Atkinson, D. C. McClelland, & J. Veroff (Eds.), *Motivation and personality: Handbook of thematic analysis* (pp. 325–333). Cambridge, England: Cambridge University Press.

Elder, G. (1979). Historical change in life patterns and personality. In P. B. Baltes & O. G. Brim (Eds.), *Life-span development and behavior* (Vol. 2, pp. 117–159). San Diego, CA: Academic Press.

Epstein, S. (1990). Cognitive–experiential self-theory. In L. Pervin (Ed.), *Handbook of personality theory and research* (pp. 165–192). New York: Guilford Press.

Erikson, E. H. (1963). *Childhood and society* (2nd ed.). New York: Norton.

Espin, O. M., Stewart, A. J., & Gomez, C. (1990). Letters from V: Traumatic historical events and adolescent psychosocial development. *Journal of Personality, 58,* 347–364.

Fiske, M., & Chiriboga, D. A. (1990). *Change and continuity in adult life.* San Francisco: Jossey-Bass.

Franz, C. E. (1988). *A case study of adult psychosocial development: Identity, intimacy, and generativity in personal documents.* Unpublished doctoral dissertation, Boston University.

Franz, C. E. (1992, September). *Do preoccupations change as people age?* Paper presented at the MacArthur/Murray Center Network for Successful Midlife Development meetings, Brewster, MA.

Franz, C. E. (in press). A quantitative case study of changes in identity, intimacy, and generativity. *Journal of Personality.*

Franz, C. E., & McClelland, D. C. (1992). *Scoring manual for age-related preoccupations.* Unpublished manuscript, Boston University, Center for Health and Applied Social Science.

Franz, C. E., McClelland, D. C., & Weinberger, J. (1991). Childhood antecedents of conventional social accomplishment in midlife adults: A 36-year prospective study. *Journal of Personality and Social Psychology, 60,* 586–595.

Franz, C. E., & Paul, E. L. (1986, April). *Developmental trends in adult generativity.* Paper presented at the meeting of the Eastern Psychological Association, New York.

Franz, C. E., & White, K. W. (1985). Individuation and attachment in personality development: Extending Erikson's theory. *Journal of Personality, 53,* 224–257.

Gottschalk, L. A. (1990). Origins and evolution of narcissism through the life cycle. In R. A. Nemiroff & C. A. Colarusso (Eds.), *New dimensions in adult development* (pp. 73–90). New York: Basic Books.

Gould, R. L. (1980). Transformational tasks in adulthood. In S. I. Greenspan & G. H. Pollock (Eds.), *The course of life: Psychoanalytic contributions toward understanding personality development: Vol. 3. Adulthood and the aging process* (pp. 117–127). Washington, DC: National Institute of Mental Health.

Gutmann, D. (1975). Parenthood: A key to the comparative study of the lifecycle. In N. Datan & L. Ginsberg (Eds.), *Life-span developmental psychology: Normative life crises* (pp. 167–184). San Diego, CA: Academic Press.

Havighurst, R. J. (1973). History of developmental psychology: Socialization and personality development through the life span. In P. B. Baltes & K. W. Schaie (Eds.), *Life-span developmental psychology: Personality and socialization* (pp. 4–24). San Diego, CA: Academic Press.

Helson, R., & Wink, P. (1992). Personality change in women from the early 40s to the early 50s. *Psychology and Aging, 7,* 46–55.

Heyns, R. W., Veroff, J., & Atkinson, J. W. (1992). A scoring manual for the affiliative motive. In C. P. Smith, J. W. Atkinson, D. C. McClelland, & J. Veroff (Eds.), *Motivation and personality: Handbook of thematic analysis* (pp. 211–223). Cambridge, England: Cambridge University Press.

Jung, C. G. (1972). The transcendent function. In H. Read, M. Fordham, G. Adler, & W. McGuire (Eds.), *The structure and dynamics of the psyche: Vol. 8. The collected works of C. G. Jung* (2nd ed., 67–91). Princeton, NJ: Princeton University Press.

Kegan, R. (1982). *The evolving self: Problem and process in human development.* Cambridge, MA: Harvard University Press.

Koestner, R., Franz, C., & Weinberger, J. (1990). The family origins of empathic concern: A 26-year longitudinal study. *Journal of Personality and Social Psychology, 58,* 709–717.

Kohut, H. (1985). Thoughts on narcissism and narcissistic rage. In C. Strozier (Ed.), *Self psychology and the humanities: Reflection on a new psychoanalytic approach by Heinz Kohut* (pp. 124–160). New York: Norton.

Kohut, H. (1977). *The restoration of the self.* Madison, CT: International Universities Press.

Labouvie-Vief, G., Hakim-Larson, J., & Hobart, C. (1987). Age, ego-level, and the life-span development of coping and defense processes. *Psychology and Aging, 2,* 286–293.

Lachman, M. E. (1989). Personality and aging at the crossroads: Beyond stability versus change. In K. W. Schaie & C. Schooler (Eds.), *Social structure and aging: Psychological processes* (pp. 167–190). Hillsdale, NJ: Erlbaum.

Lerner, R. M., & Ryff, C. (1978). Implementation of the life-span view of human development: The sample case of attachment. In P. B. Baltes (Ed.), *Life-span development and behavior* (Vol. 1, pp. 1–44). San Diego, CA: Academic Press.

Levinson, D. J., Darrow, D. N., Klein, E. B., Levinson, M. H., & McKee, B. (1978). *The seasons of a man's life.* New York: Knopf.

Loevinger, J. (1976). *Ego development.* San Francisco: Jossey-Bass.

Lubin, M. I. (1964). Addendum to chapter 4. In B. L. Neugarten (Ed.), *Personality in middle and late life: Empirical studies* (pp. 102–104). New York: Atherton Press.

Lundy, A. (1985). The reliability of the Thematic Apperception Test. *Journal of Personality Assessment, 49,* 141–145.

Lundy, A. (1988). Instruction set and Thematic Apperception Test validity. *Journal of Personality Assessment, 52,* 309–320.

McAdams, D. P. (1985). *Power, intimacy, and the life story: Personological inquiries into identity.* Homewood, IL: Dorsey Press.

McAdams, D. P. (1992). The intimacy motivation scoring system. In C. P. Smith, J. W. Atkinson, D. C. McClelland, & J. Veroff (Eds.), *Motivation and per-*

sonality: *Handbook of thematic analysis* (pp. 229–253). Cambridge, England: Cambridge University Press.

McClelland, D. C. (1985). *Human motivation.* Glenview, Il: Scott, Foresman.

McClelland, D. C. (1989). Motivational factors in health and disease. *American Psychologist, 44,* 675–683.

McClelland, D. C., Atkinson, J. W., Clark, R., & Lowell, E. (1992). A scoring manual for the achievement motive. In C. P. Smith, J. W. Atkinson, D. C. McClelland, & J. Veroff (Eds.), *Motivation and personality: Handbook of thematic analysis* (pp. 153–178). Cambridge, England: Cambridge University Press.

McClelland, D. C., & Franz, C. E. (1992). Motivational and other sources of work accomplishments in mid-life. *Journal of Personality, 60,* 679–707.

McClelland, D. C., & Koestner, R. (1992). The achievement motive. In C. P. Smith, J. W. Atkinson, D. C. McClelland, & J. Veroff (Eds.), *Motivation and personality: Handbook of thematic analysis* (pp. 143–152). Cambridge, England: Cambridge University Press.

McClelland, D. C., & Pilon, D. A. (1983). Sources of adult motives in patterns of parent behavior in early childhood. *Journal of Personality and Social Psychology, 44,* 564–574.

McCrae, R. R., & Costa, P. T., Jr. (1990). *Personality in adulthood.* New York: Guilford Press.

Neugarten, B. L. (1970). Adaptation and the life cycle. *Journal of Geriatric Psychology, 4,* 71–87.

Peterson, B. E., & Stewart, A. J. (1990). Using personal and fictional documents to assess psychosocial development: A case study of Vera Brittain's generativity. *Psychology and Aging, 5,* 400–411.

Picano, J. J. (1989). Development and validation of a life history index of adult adjustment for women. *Journal of Personality Assessment, 53,* 308–318.

Rix, S. E. (1988). *The American woman 1988–89: A status report.* New York: Norton.

Rogosa, D. (1988). Myths about longitudinal research. In K. W. Schaie, R. T. Campbell, W. Meredith, & S. C. Rawlings (Eds.), *Methodological issues in aging research* (pp. 171–210). New York: Springer.

Rosen, J. L., & Neugarten, B. L. (1964). Ego functions in the middle and later years: A thematic apperception study. In B. L. Neugarten (Ed.), *Personality in middle and late life: Empirical studies* (pp. 90–101). New York: Atherton Press.

Schaie, K. W. (1977–1978). Toward a stage theory of adult cognitive development. *International Journal of Aging and Human Development, 8,* 129–138.

Sears, R. R., Maccoby, E. E., & Levin, H. (1957). *Patterns of child rearing.* Evanston, IL: Row, Peterson.

Smith, C. P. (1992). Reliability issues. In C. P. Smith, J. W. Atkinson, D. C.

McClelland, & J. Veroff (Eds.), *Motivation and personality: Handbook of thematic analysis* (pp. 126–142). Cambridge, England: Cambridge University Press.

Smith, C. P., Feld, S. C., & Franz, C. E. (1992). Methodological considerations: Steps in research employing content analysis systems. In C. P. Smith, J. W. Atkinson, D. C. McClelland, & J. Veroff (Eds.), *Motivation and personality: Handbook of thematic analysis* (pp. 515–536). Cambridge, England: Cambridge University Press.

Stewart, A. J. (1982). The course of individual adaptation. *Journal of Personality and Social Psychology, 42,* 1100–1113.

Stewart, A. J. (1992). Scoring manual for psychological stances toward the environment. In C. P. Smith, J. W. Atkinson, D. C. McClelland, & J. Veroff (Eds.), *Motivation and personality: Handbook of thematic analysis* (pp. 451–480). Cambridge, England: Cambridge University Press.

Stewart, A. J., Franz, C. E., & Layton, L. (1988). The changing self: Using personal documents to study lives. *Journal of Personality, 56,* 41–74.

Stewart, A. J., & Healy, J. M., Jr. (1989). Linking individual development and social changes. *American Psychologist, 44,* 30–42.

Stewart, A. J., & Healy, J. M., Jr. (1992). Assessing adaptation to life changes in terms of psychological toward the environment. In C. P. Smith, J. W. Atkinson, D. C. McClelland, & J. Veroff (Eds.), *Motivation and personality: Handbook of thematic analysis* (pp. 440–450). Cambridge, England: Cambridge University Press.

Vaillant, G. E. (1977). *Adaptation to life.* Boston: Little, Brown.

Vaillant, G. E., & Milofsky, E. (1980). Natural history of male psychological health: IX. Empirical evidence for Erikson's model of the life cycle. *American Journal of Psychiatry, 137,* 1348–1359.

Veroff, J. (1982). Assertive motivations: Achievement versus power. In A. J. Stewart (Ed.), *Motivation and society* (pp. 99–132). San Francisco: Jossey-Bass.

Veroff, J. (1986). Contextualism and human motives. In D. R. Brown & J. Veroff (Eds.), *Frontiers of motivational psychology: Essays in honor of John W. Atkinson* (pp. 132–145). Berlin: Springer-Verlag.

Veroff, J., Depner, C., Kulka, R., & Douvan, E. (1980). Comparison of American motives: 1957 versus 1976. *Journal of Personality and Social Psychology, 39,* 1249–1262.

Veroff, J., Reuman, D., & Feld, S. (1984). Motives in American men and women across the adult life span. *Developmental Psychology, 20,* 1142–1158.

Weinberger, J., & McClelland, D. C. (1990). Cognitive versus traditional motivational models: Irreconcilable or complementary? In R. M. Sorrentino & T. Higgins (Eds.), *Handbook of motivation* (pp. 562–597). Greenwich, CT: JAI Press.

White, R. W. (1966). *Lives in progress: A study of the natural growth of personality.* New York: Holt, Rinehart & Winston.

Wink, P. (1992). Three types of narcissism in women from college to mid-life. *Journal of Personality, 60,* 7–30.

Winter, D. G. (1992). A revised scoring manual for the power motive. In C. P. Smith, J. W. Atkinson, D. C. McClelland, & J. Veroff (Eds.), *Motivation and personality: Handbook of thematic analysis* (pp. 311–324). Cambridge, England: Cambridge University Press.

Zeldow, P. B., Daugherty, R. R., & McAdams, D. P. (1988). Intimacy, power, and psychological well-being in medical students. *Journal of Nervous and Mental Disease, 176,* 182–187.

Zung, W. K. (1965). A self-rating depression scale. *Archives of General Psychiatry, 12,* 63–70.

IV

CONCEPTIONS OF CHANGE

11

QUANTUM CHANGE: TOWARD A PSYCHOLOGY OF TRANSFORMATION

WILLIAM R. MILLER and JANET C'DEBACA

> The true way goes over a rope which is not stretched at any great height but just above the ground. It seems more designed to make people stumble than to be walked upon. (Franz Kafka 1948, p. 278)

At midnight the old man, unable to sleep, stares uneasily into the darkness beyond his bedroom window. In the rending hours ahead, he will come face to face with the way he was and is, and with the end to which his life course inexorably leads. In the dawn, he will awaken forever changed, transformed beyond his own imagining or that of those who know him. His name is Ebenezer Scrooge.

The timeless *Christmas Carol* penned by Charles Dickens (1843/1984) quickly found its way into the Western psyche. Its hopeful message is that

---

Special thanks are due to colleagues who participated in a series of discussions at the National Drug and Alcohol Research Centre in Sydney Australia, from which the plan for this research emerged: Eva Congreve, Ken Curry, Loretta Elkins, Janet Greeley, Rian McMullin, Merida N'Enyar, Robyn Richmond, Stephen Rollnick, and John Stanhope. The senior author also expresses his appreciation to Professor Nick Heather and the staff of the Centre for their hospitality during his sabbatical stay as the Maxwell Edwards Visiting Professor.

the most intransigent human hearts (and personalities) can be changed literally overnight, departing from and rising above the patterns of the past. Do such metamorphoses truly occur? Can personality be turned upside down in a matter of minutes, hours, or days?

Certainly there are numerous real-life accounts. In the first century, according to biblical records (Acts 9), a man was struck blind on the road to Damascus. When he regained his vision some days later he was transformed from Saul, a hunter and persecutor of Christians, to Paul, whose letters are revered as sacred Christian writings two millennia later. Biography and autobiography are rich with accounts of lives changed suddenly and dramatically: Jane Addams, Joan of Arc, Saint Bernadette, Buddha, Mary Baker Eddy, Søren Kierkegaard, C. S. Lewis, Martin Luther, Henry Murray, Leo Tolstoy, John Wesley, and Malcolm X.

Such changes have also been observed in clinical contexts. Barlow, Abel, and Blanchard (1977) documented the case of a carefully diagnosed transsexual who underwent a sudden, stable, and comprehensive reorganization of identity and behavior patterns. Following a single 2–3 hour prayer and healing session with a physician, he experienced an immediate shift in identity from female to male, changed his clothing and appearance from feminine to masculine, and discontinued hormonal therapy. An encounter with a second faith healer two weeks later consolidated the change. He was evaluated by Barlow's team over a period from 2.5 to 4 years after initial assessment, which had clearly confirmed transsexualism. These follow-up interviews reflected "clear reversal of gender identity," a shift from homosexual to heterosexual arousal, and periodic dating of at least 10 women. Unobtrusive behavioral observation confirmed these findings, and Barlow et al. (1977) observed, "In this case, without any instruction and presumably without familiarity with the behaviors in the checklist, all of the components of masculine motor behavior were seemingly acquired in a matter of hours" (p. 394). Their prior research (Barlow, Reynolds, & Agras, 1973) indicated that such change, if it occurs at all, would normally require over 150 intensive treatment sessions during the course of a year or more.

In some circles, discontinuous transformational experiences are accepted as factual if not commonplace. Bill Wilson, the cofounder of Alcoholics Anonymous (AA), was in the late stages of alcoholic deterioration when he was suddenly "catapulted into a spiritual experience":

> All at once I found myself crying out, "If there is a God, let Him show Himself! I am ready to do anything, anything!" Suddenly the room lit up with a great white light. I was caught up into an ecstasy which there are no words to describe. It seemed to me, in the mind's eye, that I was on a mountain and that a wind not of air but of spirit was blowing. And then it burst upon me that I was a free man. (Kurtz, 1979, pp. 20–21, 255)

Such experiences are not uncommon in AA, albeit sometimes less dramatic. They are reported to occur rapidly and abruptly, to affect a wide range of behaviors and attributes, and to yield changes that are impressively persistent. For some, the craving for alcohol is suddenly removed. These tend to be not only cognitive, but unambiguously emotional experiences. Dr. William Silkworth, a seasoned observer of alcoholics, offered the following description:

> They seem to be in the nature of huge emotional displacements and rearrangements. Ideas, emotions, and attitudes which were once the guiding forces of the lives of these [people] are suddenly cast to one side, and a completely new set of conceptions and motives begin to dominate them. (Alcoholics Anonymous, 1976, p. 27)

The interest of psychologists in sudden transforming experiences is as old as the discipline itself. William James (1902, p. 196), quoting his contemporary George A. Coe, expressed interest in transformational change "which, though not necessarily instantaneous, seems to the subject of it to be distinctly different from a process of growth, however rapid." James regarded such sudden change to be qualitatively different from ordinary, gradual change. He observed that such conversion experiences are often preceded by despair, and he hypothesized a number of personality predispositions to such sudden and permanent change. James also described, in a case example, the ability of such conversions to remove long-standing desires:

> I was effectually cured of all inclination to that sin I was so strongly addicted to that I thought nothing but shooting me through the head could have cured me of it; and all desire and inclination to it was removed, as entirely as if I had been a suckling child; nor did the temptation return to this day. (p. 217)

The occurrence of such rapid transformations has not been lost on more modern research psychologists, who similarly note the apparent difference from ordinary principles of learning. David Premack (1970) discussed experiences involving humiliation and conscience as triggers for sudden decisional shifts in behavior. Hunt and Matarazzo (1970) observed that

> too little attention has been given [to] the apparent existence of two kinds of learning—or perhaps we should say two kinds of performance or two kinds of behavioral control. One is the familiar, classical type of acquisition, with behavior developing gradually over time as a function of reinforcement. . . . The other is an immediate acquisition or suppression as a function of decision processes or attitude. (p. 84)

Obviously wary of "reinstating the forbidden but not forgotten problems of volition and will," they persisted that, "The phenomena are there. We would rather avoid the issues involved, but we will accept the risk rather than brush the behavioral phenomena under the rug" (p. 88). This sentiment was echoed by Barrett (1989, p. 97): "Conversion experiences of all kinds seem to baffle modern day psychologists or to turn them away. . . . Scientific psychology has the task of understanding the phenomenon that is described, that is, a change of behavior." Karoly (1977, p. 203) described the behavior-changing influences of "morality" and "higher-order principles of social conduct," and Orford (1985, p. 294) asserted that "spiritual change may be seen as a widespread logical change in a whole set of attitudes about right and wrong conduct. Such a sweeping change may be necessary to support a radical reversal of conduct in one particular area."

METAPHORS FOR QUANTUM CHANGE

Although psychologists have long observed and puzzled about such quantum changes, there is no conceptual system even for describing the phenomena. The applicable language has been more that of theology and religion, and its roots are ancient. First-century Christian writings used everyday Greek words (now translated as *repentance* or *conversion*) as metaphors for transformational experiences: *epistrepho* (to turn, turn away, turn around, or turn back) and *metanoia* (to change one's mind). These connotations of radical reorganization had not been part of the common usage of these terms, and represented a concept apparently foreign to ancient Greek thought (Goetzmann, 1975).

James Loder (1981) posited a topography of transformational metanoia experiences. All begin, he proposed, with a state of conflict, "a rupture in the knowing context" (p. 32), a disruption of the person's ordinary pattern of perception. This triggers a process of scanning for solutions, which can lead to "an insight, intuition, or vision [that] appears on the border between the conscious and the unconscious, usually with convincing force" (p. 32). This results in a release of energy, an "aha" and relief in which the conflict is resolved. Finally, the event is interpreted into behavior, symbols, and new thought patterns, often accompanied by a transformation of perception: "It was as if I had never seen the trees before" (p. 109).

A psychological conception of transformational shifts can be found in Milton Rokeach's classic research on values. Rokeach (1973) conceptualized a hierarchical organization of personality, with self-concept as the central and enduring core. Late in his life, Carl Rogers similarly speculated that "there is an essential person which persists through time, or even through eternity" (cited in Bergin, 1985, p. 102). Near and subordinate to this core, Rokeach maintained, are terminal and instrumental values, numbering a few dozen, that serve a central guiding role in one's life. More peripheral and malleable are attitudes, numbering in the thousands, and then specific beliefs and transient cognitions and behaviors. Rokeach suggested that whereas attitude change would not be expected to result in substantial behavior shifts, changes involving central value structures would yield widespread and enduring transformations in attitudes and behavior. His research illustrated such generalized changes resulting from seemingly innocuous value confrontations (Rokeach, 1973).

A DESCRIPTIVE STUDY OF QUANTUM CHANGE

Where would one begin in the empirical investigation of quantum change? Scientific inquiry typically starts with systematic observation to describe the phenomena to be understood. Yet prospective access to such occurrences may not be readily arranged. Quantum changes as reported in biographies are often, like Scrooge's, private, unexpected, even uninvited events. They occur on the desert road to Damascus, waiting at the curb in front of the library (Premack, 1970), lying in a hospital bed at death's door (Kurtz, 1979), or doing what one has done thousands of times before except this time it is different. Even in settings where such experiences might be more likely to occur—at AA meetings, intensive retreats, worship services, or hospitals—the wait for a single quantum change could be a long one, although studies of conversions have been conducted in such contexts (Spilka, Hood, & Gorsuch, 1985).

If radical and sudden shifts in personality do indeed occur, they pose a puzzle of great potential. Nearly all of current scientific psychology is focused on describing, understanding, or influencing gradual incremental change. Successive approximation is the accustomed pace of learning, development, psychotherapy, and behavior modification. Discrete shifts do occur, of course, as in "aha" insight learning and humor (cf. Apter, 1982). Quantum transformations, however, suggest at least a different magnitude of change. How, when, and why do they occur? What factors influence the likelihood that such shifts will endure? Are there similarities among these experiences that suggest common processes or stages? What aspects of a person are altered? These were among the initial questions that shaped our investigation of quantum change.

The first two years were spent in discussions among interested colleagues, developing perspectives on whether quantum change is a distinct phenomenon and, if so, how it might be defined and measured. In an ideal study, people about to undergo quantum change would be assessed on a broad range of variables before and then after their experiences. Lacking a means to identify the caterpillars, we settled on retrospective interviews of butterflies. It remained for us to forge a beginning definition of quantum change, in order to recruit subjects. Our two general guidelines were that such changes should be "sudden and profound" (Alcoholics Anonymous, 1976, p. 14). The first of these sine qua non criteria would be that the subjects experienced them as relatively sudden, discrete shifts, differing subjectively from ordinary change (James, 1902). As for "profound," we sought enduring changes in a broad range of behaviors and attributes (as opposed to a circumscribed behavior change, such as stopping smoking), which had lasted for at least 2 months.

Designing and Choosing Measures

A variety of assessment domains were considered, far too many to include in a study of volunteers, and so began the familiar process of winnowing dependent measures. Highest priority was given to allowing subjects first to tell their stories with minimal structuring. Recognizing this as a rich source for subsequent qualitative analyses, we decided to audiotape all interviews. A set of specific questions was developed, to be asked of all subjects regarding their experiences, drawing on commonly reported aspects of transcendent experience (James, 1902; Noble, 1987). These were sequenced to form a Quantum Experiences Retrospective Interview (QUERI), beginning with an unstructured subject narrative and progressing to specific questions not answered during the narrative (copies are available from the senior author). A self-administered "How I See It" questionnaire was designed to obtain further details regarding interviewees' subjective experiences.

Because biographical accounts of quantum change have often emphasized shifts in value structures, we used the basic assessment methodology of Rokeach (1983) to query subjects' value priorities before and after their experiences. A set of 50 values was derived, combining content adapted from Rokeach (1973) and new value dimensions, suggested by our clinical research team members, that were not represented in Rokeach's original technique. Each value label was printed on an index card, along with a brief clarification (e.g., permanence: to make a contribution that will continue after I have died). Instructions were designed to identify the 10 highest and 10 lowest value priorities—(a) before the quantum change experience, and (b) currently—with rank orderings obtained within each of these sets of 10.

Two administrations of a set of semantic differential items (Osgood, Suci, & Tannenbaum, 1978) were used to obtain subjects' self-descriptions before versus after the experience. The Life Experiences Survey (Sarason, Johnson, & Siegel, 1978) was chosen to yield information concerning life events that occurred in the year prior to the quantum change, also rating each event as positive or negative on a 7-point Likert scale. The Religious Background and Beliefs Scale (Tonigan & Miller, 1990) was selected to sample current and past religious beliefs and practices.

Finally, three personality scales were chosen to explore traits of potential interest in quantum change. Tellegen's absorption scale (Tellegen & Atkinson, 1974) measures the propensity to become absorbed in events external to oneself. A locus of control scale (Nowicki & Duke, 1974) was used to assess trait perceptions of personal versus external control. Finally, the Myers-Briggs Type Indicator (Myers & McCaulley, 1985) was administered, yielding scores on four preference styles: introversion–extraverson (I–E), sensing–intuiting (S–N), thinking–feeling (T–F), and judging–perceiving (J–P).

Recruitment of Subjects

Subjects were sought via a newspaper feature story in the *Albuquerque Journal*, asking for volunteers "who have been transformed in a relatively short period of time—who have had a deep shift in core values, feelings, attitudes or actions" (Conaway, 1991, pp. C1, C3). No specification was given as to whether such changes had been experienced as positive or negative, or as religious or spiritual events. No remuneration was offered, to remove the possibility of volunteers fabricating accounts for financial gain. A total of 89 calls were received in response to the news story and were screened by the second author for eligibility. From these, 12 were excluded based on brief telephone screening (e.g., wanted payment, unwilling to devote 3 hours, unwilling to be audiotaped), and 22 others subsequently withdrew, were unavailable, or failed to keep appointments for an interview. The remaining 55 were interviewed, of whom 52 completed all questionnaires.

Interviews

The interview sessions, which lasted on average 107 minutes, were conducted at the University of New Mexico Psychology Clinic by three clinical psychologists, four clinical psychology graduate students, a master's-level counselor, and an undergraduate honors student.[1] Interviewers participated in a training workshop on reflective listening skills (Miller & Rollnick, 1991) and conducted practice interviews before seeing study subjects.[2]

---

[1]The authors are grateful to their colleagues at the University of New Mexico who volunteered their time to conduct these interviews: Janet Brody, Nan Henderson, Dr. Mike Hillard, Dr. Dan Matthews, Henry Montgomery, Pauline Sawyers, Tracy Simpson, and Dr. Carolina Yahne. In addition, the following colleagues participated in the planning of this study: Lauren Aubrey, Skip Daniel, Katherine Grant, Jim Story, and Ann Waldorf.

[2]The research plan was reviewed and approved by the Human Research Review Committee of the College of Arts and Sciences, University of New Mexico, in August, 1991. Reapproval for a modified plan was granted in October, 1991, and extended in September, 1992.

Results

Subjects

The 31 female (56%) and 24 male interviewees ranged in age from 30 to 78 (M = 48.9), and in years of education from 12 to 27 (M = 16.1). In racial–ethnic composition, the sample comprised 49 non-Hispanic Whites, 3 Hispanics, and 3 from other minority groups. The quantum change experience identified by subjects had occurred, on average, 11.2 years prior to the interview (range = 0–39 years), at ages from 7 to 76 (M = 37.7; Mdn = 36).

A few overall clinical comments regarding the sample may be helpful here. The interviewers were impressed by the diversity of these subjects. No striking commonalities in personality or presentation were apparent. Indeed, these seemed to be diverse and largely ordinary individuals who had had extraordinary experiences. A relatively consistent impression was that these people remembered their experiences vividly, and were eager to talk about them, despite the fact that on average 11 years had passed since their occurrence. They viewed their quantum change experiences as central turning points in their lives, watersheds that divided their memories into before and after.

Characteristics of Quantum Changers

The personality characteristics of subjects following their quantum change experiences cannot be assumed to reflect those preceding change. As indicated earlier, we studied the butterflies, not the caterpillars. Comparisons can only be made with norms for the personality scales used. On the locus of control scale, subjects scored as mildly external on average (M = 10.3 ± 4.1). Scores on Tellegen and Atkinson's (1974) absorption scale were unremarkable, falling within two-tenths of a point of U.S. population means (19.8 ± 7.5 for males, 21.5 ± 6.6 for females).

On the Myers-Briggs Type Indicator, introverted (I), intuitive (N), and feeling (F) types were overrepresented relative to U.S. norms (see Table 1). The four NF personality type codes, combining intuitive and feeling preferences (INFJ, ENFJ, INFP, and ENFP) were the four most overrepresented in our sample, with NF types in general occurring at twice the adjusted population base rate (Myers & McCaulley, 1985). From a classic Jungian understanding of personality types, NF and particularly INF individuals would be most interested in and focused on the inner life. From our research design, it is impossible to determine whether the NF personality type preceded or resulted from quantum change, or simply predisposed these individuals to volunteer for the study. Table 1 presents the prevalence of each type, in comparison with expected U.S. frequencies.

TABLE 1
Myers-Briggs Type Preferences of Quantum Changers

Type	Quantum Sample	U.S. Norms[1]	Ratio
Introvert (I)	58.5%	47.5%	1.23
Extravert (E)	41.5%	52.5%	0.79
Intuiting (N)	62.3%	43.7%	1.42
Sensing (S)	37.7%	56.3%	0.67
Feeling (F)	54.7%	46.7%	1.17
Thinking (T)	45.3%	53.3%	0.85
Perceiving (P)	43.4%	40.3%	1.08
Judging (J)	56.6%	59.7%	0.95
INFJ	9.4%	3.9%	2.42
ENFJ	11.3%	4.9%	2.32
INFP	11.3%	5.7%	1.99
ENFP	13.2%	8.0%	1.66
ISTJ	18.9%	12.1%	1.56
ESTP	5.7%	4.1%	1.40
INTP	5.7%	4.8%	1.19
ISFJ	5.7%	7.8%	0.73
ENTP	3.8%	5.3%	0.72
INTJ	3.8%	5.4%	0.71
ENTJ	3.8%	5.9%	0.65
ISFP	1.9%	3.6%	0.51
ISTP	1.9%	4.1%	0.47
ESFJ	1.9%	8.1%	0.24
ESTJ	1.9%	11.7%	0.16
ESFP	.0	4.7%	0.00

Note: [1]Based on MBTI data bank norms for Form G (Myers & McCaulley, 1985), with prevalence rates weighted by gender according to the ratio (58.5% female) in our tested sample.

Characteristics of Quantum Change Experiences

A majority of subjects could still specify the date (58%) and time of day (56%) when their experience occurred, and indicated that it began suddenly (75%), took them by surprise (82%), and emanated from an external source or event (76%) rather than being something that they themselves had done. Some experiences were reported as lasting less than a minute (13%), with 64% concluding in less than 24 hours. Relatively few had visual or auditory experiences, though one in five reported that it was "as if" they were seeing or hearing something. The relative frequencies of various subjective aspects of the experience are reported in Table 2.

Emotional distress or upset prior to the experience was reported by 56% of subjects. Both females (M = 10.6 ± 9.5) and males (M = 9.7 ± 14.3) reported a moderately high level of negative life experiences in the year prior to their quantum event, roughly half a standard deviation above published norms (Sarason et al., 1978). On positive life events in the year prior to quantum change, both women (4.7 ± 5.2) and men (5.9 ± 6.9) reported relatively low levels relative to norms. About half (46%) indicated

TABLE 2
Subjective Descriptions of Quantum Change

*Just before my experience . . .

% True	Antecedent
56%	I was emotionally distressed or upset
46%	Nothing special was happening
29%	I was praying or trying to be close to God
27%	Someone else was praying for me
15%	I was experiencing physical pain
13%	I was trying to have a special experience
11%	I had been asleep

*During my experience . . .

% True	Experience
87%	An important truth was revealed to me
78%	I was relieved of a mental burden
60%	I felt completely loved
58%	I had experiences that are very difficult to explain in words
58%	I was surprised or startled
56%	I felt at one with or connected to everything around me
55%	I felt like I was in the hands of a power much greater than myself
49%	I felt a holy presence close to me
47%	I cried
46%	I was as if someone was speaking to me
27%	I felt afraid
26%	I laughed
22%	I felt like I was outside my body for a period of time
18%	Certain people or things around me seemed to glow
13%	A medical problem from which I had been suffering was healed
9%	I had trouble breathing
2%	I was asleep; the experience was a dream

*After my experience . . .

% True	Experience
95%	I saw a new meaning
95%	My life was changed
84%	The world looked different to me
75%	I felt at peace
67%	I felt joyful
67%	I was a completely different person
64%	I felt loved and cared for
29%	I was exhausted
26%	I felt confused
22%	I felt afraid
9%	I fell (or was) asleep

*Other Aspects of the Experience

%	
82%	Were surprised by the experience
75%	Experience began suddenly rather than gradually
58%	Certain of the specific date of the experience
56%	Certain of the specific time of day
33%	Someone helped guide the subject through the experience or to understand it

TABLE 2
(Continued)

*Other Aspects of the Experience

27%	Had been expecting or hoping for something like this to happen
22%	Others around the subject were having a similar kind of experience
20%	Experience ended suddenly
6%	Paid money for the experience

Did you hear anything special, like someone speaking to you?

9%	Actually heard a voice
18%	"As if" someone were speaking

Did you see anything special, like a vision or light?

4%	Actual vision
6%	"As if" seeing
16%	Other visual experiences

Did you have any special feelings in your body?

38%	Yes

Has your [significant other] ever had a similar experience?

16%	Yes

Have the changes or effects from this experience lasted, or have you tended to go back to how you were before?

80%	Completely lasted
20%	Mostly lasted
0%	Lasted somewhat
0%	Not lasted at all

Had you had experiences like this before the one you have been describing?

26%	Yes

Have you had experiences like this since the one you have been describing?

44%	Yes

At the time of your experience, were you in therapy or counseling?

20%	Yes

Note: N = 55. *Categories here are not mutually exclusive.

that nothing special had been happening just prior to their experience. A minority said they had been praying or trying to be close to God at the time of their change experience (30%), and/or had been expecting or hoping for something like this to happen (28%). The specific antecedents were amazingly varied. Among the things immediately preceding the quantum change were walking to a night club, cleaning a toilet, having an argument, being at work, lying awake in bed, watching television, driving (three cases), preparing for a morning shower, eating at a fast food restaurant, studying, working at hard physical labor, singing, smoking marijuana, having an abortion, traveling, receiving acupuncture, crying, and traveling in a foreign land. Only 20% were in therapy at the time of the experience, and of these 11 people, 8 said they thought this had played a role in their experience. For 26%, this was not the first time they had had such an experience.

Most reported that because of their quantum experience, their lives were now much better (96%), and were confident that the changes would last (93%). Of the two individuals who indicated their lives to be worse as a result of the experience, one had suffered a stroke, and the other a major financial setback. Subjective aftereffects of these quantum experiences are listed in Table 2, and were predominantly positive. Overall, the most common quality of the effects of quantum change was of liberation, deeply positive feeling, and a new kind of meaning and perception. By subjects' reports, the changes were also viewed positively by most but not all those around them: Eighteen percent of spouses or partners, 14% of family members, and 8% of friends were reported by subjects to have regarded the changes negatively.

For exploratory purposes, we computed correlations between 81 self-reported attributes of the experience (see Tables 2 and 3) and the length of time lapsed since the quantum change event had occurred, to assess whether this duration was related to subjects' perceptions of the event and its effects. Only two of these correlations exceeded $\pm.30$ ($p < .05$), indicating that temporal proximity of the event was unrelated to descriptions of the event, its antecedents, and its sequelae.

A majority (85%) of subjects currently described themselves as either religious (41%) or spiritual (44%). With respect to belief in God, 59% reported having believed in God before their experience, and 83% reported believing in God now.

Before and After

Although we could not assess these subjects prior to their experiences, we did ask for retrospective descriptions of themselves before and after their quantum changes. With familywise Bonferroni correction of alpha (critical $p = .05/4 = .0125$), subjects reported significant positive shifts on all three factors of the semantic differential (Osgood et al., 1978): evaluative, $t(53) = 6.76$, $p < .001$; potency, $t(53) = 5.08$, $p < .001$; and activity, $t(52) = 3.10$, $p < .003$.

Subjects were also asked to describe themselves on a variety of subjective dimensions (7-point Likert scales) before the quantum change experience, in the weeks immediately afterward, and now. On all nine dimensions (see Table 3), subjects reported highly significant improvement ($p < .001$) from before to immediately after their quantum change, and

TABLE 3
Ratings of Subjective States Before and After Quantum Change, and Now

	Group Means ± Standard Deviations			Change Before to After			Change Before to Now		
	Before	After	Now	t	df	p <	t	df	p <
Happiness	2.4 ± 1.6	4.5 + 1.8	5.3 ± 0.9	6.21	53	.001	10.33	49	.001
Sense of humor	3.6 ± 1.7	4.4 ± 1.7	5.4 ± 0.9	2.75	53	.008	6.84	49	.001
Desire to live	3.5 ± 2.3	5.2 ± 1.5	5.7 ± 0.6	4.76	50	.001	6.41	48	.001
Feeling of being in control of my life	2.0 ± 1.8	3.9 ± 2.0	4.8 ± 1.5	5.36	53	.001	8.08	49	.001
A sense of something missing in life	4.1 ± 2.1	1.5 ± 1.7	1.5 ± 1.9	-7.09	53	.001	-5.53	49	.001
Close and loving relationships	2.8 ± 1.9	4.3 ± 1.6	5.3 ± 0.9	4.87	53	.001	7.70	49	.001
Satisfaction with my life	2.1 ± 1.9	4.2 ± 1.9	5.2 ± 1.0	6.11	53	.001	9.48	49	.001
A sense of meaning	2.1 ± 1.9	5.0 ± 1.7	5.6 ± 0.7	8.09	53	.001	11.38	49	.001
A close relationship with God	2.1 ± 2.1	4.5 ± 2.1	4.8 ± 1.9	6.55	52	.001	6.83	48	.001

Note: All scores are from 7-point Likert scales, arranged so that higher numbers designate more of the state.

on all scales this change was reported to have maintained or increased to the present time. The largest immediate shifts were reported as increased sense of meaning; a decreased sense of something missing in life; and increased happiness, satisfaction, and sensed closeness to God.

Subjects' value hierarchies likewise reflected substantial differences in reported priorities before versus after the quantum change experience. We calculated for each of the 50 values its frequency of being chosen as one of a subject's top 10 priorities. Values were then rank ordered based on frequency of selection. When frequencies were tied for two or more values, rank order was decided by the mean ranking assigned by subjects choosing that value as one of their top 10. In four cases with lowest priorities, in which both frequency and ranking were tied, values were listed in alphabetical order. These rank order priorities for values are reported in Table 4 for men and women before and after their quantum change experiences. In general, value priorities were reported to have been largely reversed for both women and men. Men reported that prior to their experience, their five highest values were (in order) wealth, adventure, achievement, pleasure, and being respected. These values were reordered after quantum change, often relatively rapidly, falling to current priority ranks (out of 50) of 50th, 29th, 26th, 25th, and 33rd, respectively. In their place, new top priorities for men were spirituality, personal peace, family, God's will, and honesty. Women said that their top prechange priorities were family, independence, career, fitting in, and attractiveness. These were ranked 12th, 22nd, 34th, 49th, and 38th currently, displaced by new priorities of growth, self-esteem, spirituality, happiness, and generosity. After quantum change, the value priorities of women and men appeared more similar than they had been before, suggesting changes toward common value structures, sometimes from opposite sex-role-stereotyped directions. Change scores for each value are also shown in Table 4, computed as the difference between prechange and postchange rankings. A negative change score of -23, thus, reflects a drop of 23 ranks (out of 50), whereas positive change scores indicate increased priority for a value.

SAMPLES OF QUANTUM CHANGE STORIES

The summary statistics described above provide only part of the picture, and understate the richness of the idiographic accounts of these individuals. Our subjects recounted turning points in their lives, moments of change that were, in many cases, a marked beginning of a longer process of integration and change. To illustrate the variety, a few stories are summarized here, with names and identifying details altered to protect anonymity.

TABLE 4
Value Priorities Before and After Quantum Change

Value	Priority Rankings Before		Priority Rankings Now		Change Score	
	Men	Women	Men	Women	Men	Women
Achievement	3	18	26	23	−23	−5
Adventure	2	19	29	20	−27	−1
Attractiveness	10	5	46	38	−36	−33
Authority	22	34	44	47	−22	−13
Career	19	3	32	34	−13	−31
Caring for Others	38	13	30	32	+8	−19
Comfort	21	32	47	41	−26	−9
Creativity	35	22	19	10	+16	+12
Equality for All	36	20	38	36	−2	−16
Faithfulness to Others	24	11	8	16	+16	−5
Fame	14	33	45	48	−31	−15
Family	6	1	3	12	+3	−11
Fitting in	20	4	36	49	−16	−45
Forgiveness	41	50	9	8	+32	+42
Freedom	9	14	21	26	−12	−12
Friends	15	17	20	17	−5	0
Fun	7	28	37	39	−30	−11
Generosity	46	36	14	5	+32	+31
God's Will	28	38	4	19	+24	+19
Growth	30	41	6	1	+24	+40
Happiness	29	9	15	4	+14	+5
Health	17	24	13	9	+4	+15
Helpfulness	47	27	17	24	+30	+3
Honesty	27	40	5	7	+22	+33
Humility	49	45	7	14	+42	+31
Independence	13	2	48	22	−35	−20
Intimacy	50	44	12	33	+38	+11
Justice	44	23	28	21	+16	+2
Knowledge	23	6	16	13	+7	−7
Leisure	34	37	22	18	+12	+19
Be Loved	26	8	23	31	+3	−23
Loving	37	43	11	11	+26	+32
Monogamy	42	21	18	27	+24	−6
Neatness	40	26	42	42	−2	−16
Permanence	48	46	27	44	+21	+2
Personal Peace	43	48	2	6	+41	+42
Pleasure	4	25	25	15	−21	+10
Popularity	11	15	49	50	−38	−35
Power	12	42	43	45	−31	−3
Rationality	25	31	39	37	−14	−6
Be Respected	5	29	33	35	−28	−6
Risk Taking	18	35	35	30	−17	+5
Romance	16	16	40	46	−24	−30
Safety	45	12	31	29	+14	−17
Self-Control	32	7	24	28	+8	−21
Self-Esteem	8	30	10	2	−2	+28
Spirituality	31	47	1	3	+30	+44
Strength	33	49	41	43	−8	+6
Wealth	1	10	50	40	−49	−30
World Peace	39	39	34	25	+5	+14

Moment of Insight

Angie described a quantum experience that had occurred four years earlier, after she had left an anger management workshop. "I stopped and thought, 'My God, I have been in a state of shame all my life. That's why I have been so angry.'" She began crying and could not stop; "years of emotions" came to the surface. Afterward she felt a great weight lifed from her, relieved of the "responsibility of being more than human." "It was an extraordinary healing; my self-worth grew, and my anger diminished 100%. . . . It has meant everything to my parenting, and will mean everything to my children. Now I can respond to a small child in a nurturing way. I would have lost them without that transformation. Now I feel I have a future."

Time Out from Life

Barbara underwent a debilitating surgery that immobilized her for a period of two months. "I was lying there on the couch, looking at the mountains, and contemplating my life. I realized I wasn't doing any of the things I really wanted to do." Major changes followed: She quit her job, discontinued a demanding schedule of volunteer work, and went back to school. "I was spending too much time doing things for others; I stopped saying 'Yes' to everybody, and began focusing more on myself and my family, and spending more time with friends. Now [two years later] I'm more careful about where I put my energy, more focused on what I want from life."

Moment of Choice

Carl was in an alcoholism treatment center when he had his moment of truth. He had just had a fight with his wife, and he sat staring at "The Twelve Steps of AA" poster on the wall of the group room. "I kept looking at the word, 'God,' and suddenly it struck me that I could really be happy, healthy, and whole. It was a very physical feeling, intense: 'I am this way, but I can be this way [sober].' I became teachable in that moment. The choice was put there, and I accepted it." Carl reported that that moment, four years prior, changed the way he sees things, his attitudes and choices, his friends, and especially his honesty.

Spiritual Conversion

On Easter Sunday, Diane had attended a worship service at which the pastor gave an "alter call," inviting people to come forward to commit their lives to Christ. She did not go, but later while driving to her parents' house she decided to make the commitment. The conversion experience was immediate: "I went all goose-bumps, and felt like crying, and was filled with a tremendous sense of awe, peace, and joy." On that day, seven years ago, she stopped drinking and smoking, and her sadness was lifted. A long period of depression and confusion ended, and she felt able to forgive others for issues from her past, including abuse. "My sense of reality changed. I was sensitized to the pain of others, and also to the beauty around me."

Trauma

Edward, a vigorous athlete and active man who swore he would never work behind a desk, was injured in an accident that left him completely paralyzed from the neck down. As he was being taken into the emergency room (15 years ago), "I felt as if God were speaking to me: 'You take control of the physical circumstances, I'll cover everything else.' I had a special feeling of warmth and security in my body." His fast-paced, perfectionistic life was suddenly changed. One week after the accident he had an experience "that was like starting my life all over, being born again. I had to throw out everything I knew before starting all over again from scratch." Among the major changes he reported were a more compassionate and trusting sense of others, an appreciation of beauty in the world, and "a deeper, more enhanced dependence on God in controlling things we don't understand."

A Voice

Over 30 years ago, on an otherwise uneventful day, Francis was at home with his family, and walking past the fireplace when suddenly he heard a voice: "Francis, all you have to do to be happy is to do what you believe." It was a strange man's voice, not one he recognized. "I knew it was not God's voice; I knew it was in my head." He concealed the experience from his family and friends. "I felt an immediate drop in internal tension, which resulted in a peacefulness I had never experienced before—a peacefulness so overpowering that I would do nothing then or today that would result in its loss." He also commented on other changes: "My personality was reorganized and integrated. The biggest difference was *total* honesty. Also I started walking and taking my time—I used to run everywhere, and always wanted my own way by dominating in my family. I used to have trouble communicating with people, especially women outside my family. I started listening to people. My oldest son told me if I hadn't changed back then, he would have left home. My youngest would *never* come to me at bedtime, just to Mom. Right after my experience, he started coming to me to be tucked in—that really moved me. My wife disliked the change in me back then; I would get emotional easily, like she did. . . . Now my family and I enjoy each other, and I never get on people's backs. I live a life almost totally free of tension, while filled with complex activity."

Catastrophe

One morning at age 15 (11 years prior), Gina awoke realizing she was late for school. Why had her father not awakened the children for breakfast, as usual? The house was quiet. She found her parents' bodies in different rooms, victims of violence. In the nightmare that followed, she lost everything. Her extended family said they could not take in all the children, so she—as the oldest and adopted—was placed in foster care. "Every aspect of my life, from getting up and brushing my teeth to going to church to knowing who I was, was over. I remember thinking I shouldn't even have a name, because I'm not a person anymore." The family shut her out, emotionally and literally, not allowing her even to take her clothing from the house. "I just quit talking, and didn't speak a word for around a year." She began abusing sedatives, failed all of her classes at school, and once jumped from a third-floor window. Prior to this experience she had been a fairly religious person, having been raised in a church-going family. She described herself as having been a happy teenager viewing life as fun and a challenge, looking forward to each new day, planning ahead for her future. Gina now describes herself as skeptical about the future, and refuses to make plans beyond a week's time. She does not consider herself religious, believing that God created the universe but has no impact on anyone's life, no connection with people.

Switching Controls

At the time of her experience at age 35, Helen was living with her parents and going to college. "My parents were very 'thumbs-on' people, and I felt trapped. My father constantly put me down, and I felt really empty. I knew I would never be able to get a job and be happy. I knew I would never have a family because I was—well, I had passed my 20's. I was still failing at college because every time success was close, I'd just freeze up. My parents sent me to psychologists who told me that all I needed to do was leave home." Yet she saw no way that she could do that, and her life seemed to have no direction or purpose. A friend suggested that she try what she called a "soul change." Looking back (age 42 at interview), she realized that this had planted the seed that change could happen. One day she woke up, found she couldn't speak, and "I knew I wasn't with me. I could see me, but I was standing around to the side of my body." This went on for three days. "After that, I just felt really peaceful and happy and glad to be alive," a feeling that continues to increase. She says she has gained confidence, is no longer afraid, and feels direction in her life. "I feel free. If I want to go for a walk, I do it. If I want to watch TV, I watch TV." Within a year she met a man, moved in with him, and is now married and has three children. Enrolled again at the university, she uses a computer analogy for her experience: "The brain is like a computer, and whoever is at the controls runs the computer. I took a break, and for those three days, someone else was at the controls. Some people switch controls and stay switched."

IS QUANTUM CHANGE A REAL PHENOMENON?

One obvious question is whether these quantum transformations reflect another kind of change to which our accustomed models are ill suited. To be sure, discrete changes are observed in ordinary behavior. Although mean learning curves are smooth, animal and human performance curves are typically jagged, and often contain an elbow. Apter (1982) has described flip-flop shifts in behavior between qualitatively discriminable states. Perhaps the phenomena that we are calling quantum changes merely represent the extreme tail of the normal distribution of behavior change, and appear exceptional simply by virtue of their extremity.

Several factors persuade us to regard these quantum changes as outliers, rather than points on the tail of a familiar distribution. First, the rapidity and magnitude of changes reported by our subjects require a considerable stretch of imagination to be viewed as extreme examples of ordinary change. The prototypic examples of Saul, Scrooge, and Bill Wilson do not resemble the ordinary developmental processes of a midlife crisis; like the reports of many of our subjects, they were sudden and unexpected reversals of life direction.

Second, quantum changers experience their transformations as markedly different from ordinary change (cf. James, 1902). Our subjects' change experiences were salient enough to be remembered clearly—down to the date, time, and details—11 years later on average, and they remained eager, even relieved to talk with someone about their experiences. Most believed that they had had little to do with the change, but had been acted on by external forces that, in many cases, they did not understand. In a "Damascus" change experience reported by Edwards, Oppenheimer, and Taylor (1992), the subject recounted the following:

> I think I changed overnight. I honestly, truthfully do, I think that's how it happened. I didn't have any flash of light, I never thought I saw God. It happened. And that's all I can tell you. It happened, why question it? (p. 77)

Third, quantum changes frequently evidence dramatic generalization. Our subjects often reported that everything changed. It is precisely in the realm of *personality*—those enduring and presumed stable attributes that characterize people—that quantum change seems to occur. The reported shifts are in dimensions such as values, life goals, temperament, and perceptual style.

Finally, these changes appear to be not only large and generalized, but relatively enduring. Unlike Apter's (1982) bistable behaviors that shift back and forth between poles, the stories of quantum changers suggest a one-way door. Alcoholic quantum changers report sudden and complete loss of the desire to drink, persisting over a decade or more (Edwards et al., 1992; Kurtz, 1979). Generalized shifts in identity appear stable (e.g., Barlow et al., 1977).

To be sure, retrospective reports such as those from this study must be interpreted with caution, and some obvious methodological limitations must be acknowledged. Our subjects were self-selected volunteers, responding to an article describing this type of change experience. Characteristics of our sample cannot, therefore, be assumed representative of those who have undergone such experiences. Personality characteristics, for example, might reflect willingness to volunteer for an unreimbursed study, or a particular interest in the phenomena described in our news article. Long-term self-reports may be biased by a wide variety of memory and motivational factors, and prospective observation would have been preferable. We are in the process of interviewing subjects' close friends and family to determine the extent to which changes were evident to others. (We note, however, that change experiences of this type have been reported for many centuries, and documented by psychologists since the beginning of the discipline, some, by serendipity, with prospective baseline measures [Barlow et al., 1977; Edwards et al., 1992].) Further, even if retrospective reports accurately reflect subjects' conditions before and after their transformational experiences, changes between pretransformation and current status (e.g., in value priorities) could be the result of other historical and developmental processes. On all three-point inquiries, subjects reported that the changes evident in their current state had occurred soon after their quantum experiences, but again retrospective recall of when changes occurred could be influenced by a variety of biases, including knowledge of the purpose of this study.

Possible Catalysts of Quantum Change

If there is a genuinely distinct phenomenon of personality transformation, qualitatively different from the commonly understood processes of learning and development, what are its determinants? We offer four speculative mechanisms, four alternative lenses through which quantum change might be viewed.

Self-Regulation

Behavior theorists and researchers have proposed the existence of at least two types of memory (e.g., Sherry & Schacter, 1987) or behavior control (e.g., Hunt & Matarazzo, 1970; Kanfer & Gaelick, 1986; Premack, 1970). The familiar type is automatic, gradual, and operates with relatively little awareness. A second type is more consciously controlled, salient, effortful, decisional, and discontinuous. Although behaviors differ in their controllability, many (for example, driving and typing) can operate in either automatic or controlled modes. Automatic behaviors tend to continue unless self-monitoring reveals a significant discrepancy between incoming information and goal templates representing the proper or desired state of affairs. Such a discrepancy is a motivational state that disrupts automatic processing and triggers executive control, setting in motion a search for and efforts toward change (Miller & Brown, 1991; cf. Loder, 1981).

This self-regulatory process is usually described in relation to discrete and temporary behaviors. At the level of routine behavior, this occurs numerous times daily, as when in driving an automobile one suddenly becomes aware of the need for planful action. Brief interventions for problem drinkers, which have a well-established record of triggering behavior change, may operate via motivational factors that awaken such a self-regulatory process (Bien, Miller, & Tonigan, 1993). It is conceivable that quantum changes represent a major and enduring reorganization of behaviors triggered by highly significant discrepancies, involving goals that are central to meaning and identity. Such triggering of executive processes and course correction reordering may occur at various levels of behavioral organization. In this view, quantum changes would represent the higher order end of a continuum of self-regulatory shifts.

Perception Shift

A second perspective construes quantum change as a shift in perception, a salient aspect in the story of Ebenezer Scrooge. Loder (1981) likened transformation to a figure/ground reversal in Gestalt psychology. This analogy was extended by McMullin (1986), who compared quantum shifting with the familiar reversible perception figures of Gestalt psychology (e.g., vase vs. faces; old woman vs. young woman). The initial perception may dominate a subject's attention, inhibiting an alternative perspective, but in an identifiable moment the subject sees the figure in a new way, reorganizing the same stimuli into a different gestalt incompatible with the first (see Figure 1). McMullin proposed a staged description of transformational change similar to Loder's, and described 17 clinical strategies (e.g., creating dissonance, exploring the client's hierarchy of values, and storytelling) that might be useful in precipitating such perceptual shifts. Our subjects commonly reported major shifts, at the point of quantum change, in their perceptions of themselves, other people, and the world around them. Loder described the process as "two habitually incompatible frames of reference converging, usually with surprising suddenness, to compose a meaningful

Figure 1. Old woman–young woman visual analogy of transposition (Figure 1 was drawn by cartoonist W. E. Hill and was originally published in *Puck* on November 6, 1915. It was later published by E. G. Boring, 1930.)

unity" (1981, p. 32). This bears some resemblance to the intentional paradoxical tactics described by brief and family therapists for inducing rapid change (e.g., Haley, 1963; Watzlawick, Weakland, & Fisch, 1974).

Value Conflict

The above-mentioned work of Rokeach offers a third possible lens through which to view the mechanisms underlying quantum change. In a manner resembling Festinger's (1957) experiments on cognitive dissonance, Rokeach sought to induce value conflict in university students who had completed the Rokeach Value Survey (Rokeach, 1983) and who consistently rated Freedom as a higher priority than Equality. Students randomly assigned to an experimental group were given a pejorative interpretation of this discrepancy: "Apparently . . . students in general are much more interested in their own freedom than they are in freedom for other people" (Rokeach, 1973, p. 237), and were informed that such hypocritical values were particularly characteristic of those unsympathetic to the civil rights movement. Students in the control condition simply completed the survey, and received no interpretation. The experimental intervention impacted not only value rankings three weeks and three months later (cf. Rokeach & Cochrane, 1972), but several unobtrusive behavioral measures as well, which were not overtly linked to the value study. Students from the experimental group were three times more likely to volunteer in response to a telephone solicitation for help from the National Association for the Advancement of Colored People, and in a separate experiment maintained significantly more eye contact during an interracial conversation. Nearly two years later, experimental group students in social sciences were twice as likely to have selected a major in ethnic studies, and eight times as many had changed their course of studies from natural sciences to social sciences or education, relative to students from the control group. Rokeach (1973) commented that "genuine lasting changes in values, attitudes, and behavior had been effected as a result of a single experimental session" (p. 313). These findings parallel the results of brief motivational intervention designed to induce change (cf. Bien et al., 1993; Miller & Rollnick, 1991).

Transcendence

Quantum change may occur through the triggering of executive self-regulation processes, via perceptual alteration, or by dissonance among values. Such changes may even occur without conscious effort or desire for change by the individual, as in unexpected and uninvited transformations. Yet many of our own subjects, and those reported by other investigators, experienced their changes as being acted on by some external agent or force. In this context, quantum change might be conceptualized more generally as a subset or possible effect of transcendent experiences (Noble, 1987). Whether one chooses to understand quantum changes as literally an "act of God" will, of course, depend on one's own beliefs and concepts regarding God. In any event, quantum changes commonly have a transcendent quality, as described by James (1902), Maslow (1970), and others (cf. Noble, 1987). The experience is usually profoundly positive, powerfully memorable, and subjectively and markedly different from ordinary experience, in ways that subjects find difficult to put into words. A transient altered state of consciousness often occurs, altering perceptions of time, meaning, identity, and reality. People who have such experiences also commonly report an ineffable but clear sense of being passive recipients, that is, of the event happening to them without (or in spite of) their own effort or intention. It is here that we encounter the fascinating and sometimes discomfiting boundary of psychology and spirituality that was such congenial terrain for William James. Although clearly believing in God, James insisted that transcendent experience need not be seen as a random miracle, but can be subjected to scientific investigation: "The God whom science recognizes must be a God of universal laws exclusively, a God who does a wholesale, not a retail business" (1902, p. 390). The call of James, and of our subjects, is to consider a still higher order primary experience of transcendence, of which changes in behavior, values, perceptions, and attitudes are merely aftereffects.

OPEN QUESTIONS

With a few exceptions, psychologists have curiously avoided exploration of what appear to be some of the most dramatic examples and types of human change. They have been mostly ignored as "noise in the system" (Edwards et al., 1992), as outliers or fabrications. Behavioral science has tended to focus instead on successive approximations, the gradual modification of responses in a linear or curvilinear fashion. Yet numerous observations suggest that relatively sudden and profound changes can and do occur, at least occasionally, in the organized and enduring patterns of behavior usually regarded as personality.

Within mathematics, various approaches have been derived for modeling discontinuous shifts in physical states. Describing the basis of Thom's (1975) catastrophe theory, Woodcock and Davis (1978) wrote,

> the theory is controversial because it proposes that the mathematics underlying three hundred years of science, though powerful and successful, have encouraged a one-sided view of change. These mathematical principles are ideally suited to analyze—because they were created to analyze—*smooth*, continuous, quantitative change: the smoothly curving paths of planets around the sun, the continuously varying pressure of a gas as it is heated and cooled, the quantitative increase of a hormone level in the bloodstream. But there is another kind of change, too, change that is less suited to mathematical analysis: the *abrupt* bursting of a bubble, the discontinuous transition from ice at its melting point to water at its freezing point, the qualitative shift in our minds when we "get" a pun or a play on words. Catastrophe theory is a mathematical language created to describe and classify this second type of change. It challenges scientists to change the way they think about processes and events in many fields. (p. 9)

To be sure, successive approximations appear easier to comprehend and predict, and are more readily arranged for scientific observation. It is tempting to ignore quantum changes as anomalous, inexplicable exceptions to the rules of behavior. Behavioral science is not alone in this; medicine has similarly ignored unconventional remissions (Weil, 1983). Yet it is precisely through the exceptions to established expectations that a science itself sometimes undergoes important transformations. If behavior is lawful, and people sometimes show massive and enduring reorganizations of behavior at a personality level, there are important phenomena still to be understood. Psychologists are just beginning to document and describe the observations. What kinds of changes occur? To what extent do such changes endure?

Science typically proceeds beyond description by hypothesizing principles for organizing and predicting observations. Who undergoes such transformation, under what conditions? Are there precursors of quantum change? Are there consistent patterns or types? Which changes endure, and why? Within understanding at this level lies the potential for comprehending and developing strategies to induce quantum change. If, as seems to be the case, these are often profoundly positive developmental events, is it possible to facilitate them? Could therapeutic strategies be designed to trigger quantum change? The reorganization of personality is, after all, an historic objective of long-term psychotherapy.

As occurred with the advent of behavior therapies, the development of effective psychological procedures capable of inducing quantum change would and should raise important ethical questions. Rokeach (1973) apparently induced unanticipated life changes in his research subjects. Under what circumstances, and in the service of what goals, would it be ethical to induce such change? Could Ebenezer Scrooge have given informed consent for his personality transformation, when its essence was a fundamental reorganization of his values and perceptions? Psychologists may be a long way from facing such issues, but it is not too early to begin the dialogue.

In any event, it seems time to recognize that personality change can and does occur, albeit with unknown frequency, in ways that do not seem to fit our current models of behavior. Not all of these changes are judged by all parties to be positive. Although quantum changes are ancient, not new phenomena, psychologists are only at the beginning of describing them, and at some distance from comprehending them. What would be new is for psychologists to develop a language for describing, and systems for studying and understanding quantum change. Therein may lie seeds of a quantum change in psychology itself.

REFERENCES

Alcoholics Anonymous. (1976). *Alcoholics Anonymous: The story of how many thousands of men and women have recovered from alcoholism* (3rd ed). New York: AA World Services.

Apter, M. J. (1982). *The experience of motivation: The theory of psychological reversals.* San Diego, CA: Academic Press.

Barlow, D. H., Abel, G. G., & Blanchard, E. G. (1977). Gender identity change in a transsexual: An exorcism. *Archives of Sexual Behavior, 6,* 387–395.

Barlow, D. H., Reynolds, E. J., & Agras, W. S. (1973). Gender identity change in a transsexual. *Archives of General Psychiatry, 28,* 569–576.

Barrett, C. L. (1989). Presidential address and introduction to special issue: SPAB comes of age. *Psychology of Addictive Behaviors, 3,* 95–106.

Bergin, A. E. (1985). Proposed values for guiding and evaluating counseling and psychotherapy. *Counseling and Values, 29,* 99–116.

Bien, T. H., Miller, W. R., & Tonigan, J. S. (1993). Brief intervention for alcohol problems: A review. *Addiction, 88,* 315–336.

Conaway, J. (1991, November 3). Quantum change: When personal transformation happens overnight. *Albuquerque Journal,* pp. C1, C3.

Dickens, C. (1984). *A Christmas carol.* New York: Penguin Books. (Original work published 1843)

Edwards, G., Oppenheimer, E., & Taylor, C. (1992). Hearing the noise in the system: Exploration of textual analysis as a method for studying change in drinking behavior. *British Journal of Addiction, 87,* 73–81.

Festinger, L. (1957). *A theory of cognitive dissonance.* Stanford, CA: Stanford University Press.

Goetzmann, J. (1975). Metanoia. In C. Brown (Ed.), *The new international dictionary of New Testament theology* (Vol. 1, pp. 357–359). Grand Rapids, MI: Zondervan.

Haley, J. (1963). *Strategies of psychotherapy.* New York: Grune & Stratton.

Hunt, W. A., & Matarazzo, J. D. (1970). Habit mechanisms in smoking. In W. A. Hunt (Ed.), *Learning mechanisms in smoking* (pp. 65–90). Chicago: Aldine.

James, W. (1902). *The varieties of religious experience.* Cambridge, MA: Harvard University Press.

Kafka, F. (1948). *The great wall of China: Stories and reflections.* New York: Schocken Books.

Kanfer, F. H., & Gaelick, L. (1986). Self-management methods. In F. H. Kanfer & A. P. Goldstein (Eds.), *Helping people change* (3rd ed., pp. 283–345). Elmsford, NY: Pergamon Press.

Karoly, P. (1977). Behavioral self-management in children: Concepts, methods, issues, and directions. In M. Hersen, R. M. Eisler, & P. M. Miller (Eds.), *Progress in behavior modification* (Vol. 5, pp. 197–262). San Diego, CA: Academic Press.

Kurtz, E. (1979). *Not-God: A history of Alcoholics Anonymous.* Center City, MN: Hazelden.

Loder, J. E. (1981). *The transforming moment: Understanding convictional experiences.* New York: Harper & Row.

Maslow, A. H. (1970). *Religions, values, and peak experiences*. New York: Viking Press.

McMullin, R. E. (1986). *Handbook of cognitive therapy techniques*. New York: Norton.

Miller, W. R., & Brown, J. M. (1991). Self-regulation as a conceptual basis for the prevention and treatment of addictive behaviours. In N. Heather, W. R. Miller, & J. Greeley (Eds.), *Self-control and the addictive behaviours* (pp. 3–79). Sydney: Maxwell Macmillan Publishing Australia.

Miller, W. R., & Rollnick, S. (1991). *Motivational interviewing: Preparing people to change addictive behavior*. New York: Guilford Press.

Myers, I. B., & McCaulley, M. H. (1985). *Manual: A guide to the development and use of the Myers-Briggs Type Indicator*. Palo Alto, CA: Consulting Psychologists Press.

Noble, K. D. (1987). Psychological health and the experience of transcendence. *The Counseling Psychologist, 15*, 601–614.

Nowicki, S., & Duke, M. P. (1974). A locus of control scale for college as well as non-college adults. *Journal of Personality Assessment, 38*, 136–137.

Orford, J. (1985). *Excessive appetites: A psychological view of addictions*. New York: Wiley.

Osgood, C. E., Suci, G. J., & Tannenbaum, P. H. (1978). *The measurement of meaning*. Urbana: University of Illinois Press.

Premack, D. (1970). Mechanisms of self-control. In W. A. Hunt (Ed.), *Learning mechanisms in smoking* (pp. 107–123). Chicago: Aldine.

Rokeach, M. (1973). *The nature of human values*. New York: Free Press.

Rokeach, M. (1983). *Rokeach Value Survey*. Palo Alto, CA: Consulting Psychologists Press.

Rokeach, M., & Cochrane, R. (1972). Self-confrontation and confrontation with another as determinants of long-term value change. *Journal of Applied Social Psychology, 2*, 283–292.

Sarason, I. G., Johnson, J. H., & Siegel, J. M. (1978). Assessing the impact of life changes: Development of the Life Experiences Survey. *Journal of Consulting and Clinical Psychology, 46*, 932–946.

Sherry, D. F., & Schacter, D. L. (1987). The evolution of multiple memory-systems. *Psychological Review, 94*, 439–454.

Spilka, B., Hood, R. W., & Gorsuch, R. L. (1985). *The psychology of religion: An empirical approach*. Englewood Cliffs, NJ: Prentice Hall.

Tellegen, A., & Atkinson, G. (1974). Openness to absorbing and self-altering experiences ("absorption"), a trait related to hypnotic susceptibility. *Journal of Abnormal Psychology, 83*, 268–277.

Thom, R. (1975). *Structural stability and morphogenesis: An outline of a general theory of models*. Reading, MA: W. A. Benjamin.

Tonigan, J. S., & Miller, W. R. (1990). *The Religious Background and Beliefs Scale (RBB)*. Unpublished instrument, University of New Mexico, Center of Alcoholism, Substance Abuse, and Addictions.

Watzlawick, P., Weakland, J. H., & Fisch, R. (1974). *Change: Principles of problem formation and problem resolution.* New York: Norton.

Weil, A. (1983). *Health and healing: Understanding conventional and alternative medicine.* Boston: Houghton Mifflin.

Woodcock, A., & Davis, M. (1978). *Catastrophe theory: A revolutionary new way of understanding how things change.* New York: Viking Penguin.

12

THE CRYSTALLIZATION OF DISCONTENT IN THE PROCESS OF MAJOR LIFE CHANGE

ROY F. BAUMEISTER

This volume is devoted to the broad questions of whether, how often, and how personality changes. This particular chapter takes a narrower focus on one centrally important step in the subjective process of change, namely the crystallization of discontent. Focusing on the subjective side of change allows me to sidestep the somewhat more recalcitrant problem of establishing personality change with objective measures, because it is clear that subjectively people do believe that they change. Although subjective and objective processes are not necessarily related, in empirical fact they often are related, and indeed subjective processes may be vital causes or mediators of personality change. People engage in considerable interpretive activity to make sense of their lives and themselves (e.g., Harvey, Orbuch, & Weber, 1992; Harvey, Weber, & Orbuch, 1990), and any major change in a person's life will most likely have to be accommodated (if not mediated) in the person's self-interpretations.

Among these subjective processes of self-interpretation is one that I have called the *crystallization of discontent* (Baumeister, 1991). It can be understood as the forming of associative links among a multitude of un-pleasant, unsatisfactory, and otherwise negative features of one's current life situation. Prior to a crystallization of discontent, a person may have many complaints and misgivings about some role, relationship, or involve-ment, but these remain separate from each other. The crystallization brings them together into a coherent body of complaints and misgivings. The totality of perceived negative features does not necessarily change through the process of crystallization, but crystallization enables them to remind the person of each other. The subjective impact can be enormous, because a large mass of negative features may be enough to undermine a person's commitment to a role, relationship, or involvement, whereas when there are many individual and seemingly unrelated complaints that arise one at a time, no one of them is sufficient to undermine that commitment.

Consider the beginnings of a divorce, for example. A couple may have a series of disagreements on many seemingly small, unrelated issues, such as who should have washed the dishes last night, or whether one spouse had the right to purchase a small item of furniture without consulting the other first. Although these may be quite upsetting at the time, they can generally be accepted without resorting to divorce, such as by ascribing them to one or another spouse having a bad day. A bad day is not sufficient cause to question or dissolve a marriage. But when the bad days coalesce into a bad year—one form of crystallization of discontent—the desirability of the marriage can begin to be affected. In the preceding example, as long as the person saw the argument over the dishes and the argument over the furniture as unrelated, there was nothing substantial enough to threaten the marriage. But when they are seen as related to each other, and pre-sumably to other arguments as well, then one may begin to perceive the relationship as afflicted by pervasive conflict or to perceive the spouse as chronically uncaring and inconsiderate, and these broader perceptions can be a crucial step toward divorce.

I argue that the crystallization of discontent reverses the patterns by which people normally interpret the events and circumstances of their lives. It therefore requires some explanation as a departure from the usual mode of self-interpretation, and yet its very unusualness helps make it a potent precursor of major change. This chapter focuses on political, religious, marital or romantic, and other forms of identity change, rather than on personality change per se, but identity change through the crystallization of discontent can be understood as one major mechanism of insight-me-diated personality change.

Indeed, my own research has focused on change in life's meaning rather than change in personality per se, but the two are closely related. There is ample reason to believe that personality change is most likely and most enduring when it is accompanied by major changes in life circum-stances. In particular, when all of one's social relationships remain constant, personality change is considerably more difficult, because people tend to assume that others' personalities will remain stable and consistent (e.g., Jones & Nisbett, 1971). As a result, people experience social pressure to remain consistent with the way others perceive them (e.g., Baumeister & Jones, 1978; also Tedeschi, Schlenker, & Bonoma, 1971), and such con-sistency pressures constitute a formidable obstacle to personality change. Presumably for that reason, research shows that significant changes in trait self-esteem level occur most commonly around the time of major life tran-sitions such as graduation and moving (Harter, 1993). By the same token, brainwashing and other efforts at making over an individual's personality are most effective when all the person's preexisting social ties are severed and repudiated (e.g., Baumeister, 1986).

Research evidence about major life change, and particularly about the subjective processes involved in it, is difficult to find. Relatively few psy-chological studies have dealt with it, perhaps partly because of the practical and methodological difficulties in tracking people over relatively extended periods of time and through substantial changes in their circumstances. To some extent, this can be compensated by drawing on the other social sciences, which in the past two decades have accumulated a variety of evidence about subjective processes in divorce, religious conversion, polit-ical conversion, and similar transitions (see Baumeister, 1991). This broad, interdisciplinary body of information constitutes the empirical basis for this chapter. Although the amount of evidence is not large, the fact that it is spread through different social sciences has at least one powerful advantage, namely that it is relatively immune from charges of methodological artifact. If different researchers in different fields using different methods with dif-ferent biases reach similar conclusions, one can have considerably more confidence in those conclusions than if the same number of researchers in the same field using the same methods reached the same conclusion.

HOW COMMITMENTS ARE MAINTAINED

In order to understand and appreciate the role of crystallization of discontent in major life change, it is necessary to consider the opposite process by which people avoid change and maintain their commitments to existing roles and relationships. Although there may be objective causes of which people are unaware, it is also necessary that some subjective processes operate to maintain commitments, because commitment is in the final analysis a subjective condition. For example, if Martin were to lose all interest in, respect for, and liking for his church, it seems doubtful that he would continue to be an active member of that church. Thus, people's interpretations of everyday outcomes and events carry the potential for fostering or hindering change, by reinforcing or undermining their subjective commitment to the roles and relationships they have.

It seems fair to assume that the majority of roles and relationships are not invariably sources of bliss and advantage. There are both costs and benefits associated with nearly every activity. Furthermore, it seems fair to assume that people will tend to prefer activities in which the benefits outweigh the costs. Analyzing exactly how to compute the trade-off may be difficult. This difficulty is further complicated by the necessity of comparing alternatives, because people may stay in a role or relationship that seems to offer more costs than benefits if it is nonetheless the best alternative they have (e.g., Johnson & Rusbult, 1989). Still, it seems a reasonably safe assumption that the roles and relationships people will most tend to preserve will be the ones that are the most attractive bargains (in the sense of having the most favorable cost–benefits ratios).

An important qualification, however, is that it is the subjective appraisal of the attractiveness of the cost–benefit ratio that is most important (as opposed to the objective or actual balance of costs and benefits). To avoid cognitive dissonance, people may minimize costs and exaggerate benefits. If people systematically distort or misperceive the costs and benefits associated with certain options, they may repeatedly make nonoptimal choices. By the same token, a person may initiate a major life change even if there is no objective change in the costs and benefits associated with his or her current circumstances, provided that the person subjectively reappraises these circumstances and subjectively arrives at a changed conclusion about the balance of costs and benefits. To put it simply, it is how things seem, rather than how they are, that influences commitment.

Stability in life will therefore be supported by any processes that help people exaggerate the benefits and downplay the costs of their current roles and relationships. Fortunately, there appear to be many processes of that sort. Taylor and Brown (1988) proposed that broad patterns of positive illusions, based on small but pervasive distortions in the way people process information about themselves, enable people to maintain their preferred views of themselves and their worlds. Similar processes appear to help people maintain commitments.

Central to many of these commitment-maintaining processes is the pattern of treating problems, costs, and disadvantages as isolated, unrelated, atypical, and temporary matters, whereas the positive aspects and outcomes are seen as strongly interrelated and as tied to the central, typical, and permanent features of the role or relationship. In this way, the bad things can be dismissed or ignored, because even if they are quite distressing or troublesome at the time, they are not seen as sufficiently important to threaten the commitment itself. People seem to realize that occasional problems are to be expected, and as long as these are isolated and occasional, there is no reason to abandon a serious commitment that is seen as bringing many positive features.

Thus, attributional patterns are central to the process of maintaining commitments. Holtzworth-Munroe and Jacobson (1985) coined the term *relationship-enhancing* attributions to refer to a particular pattern of interpreting the actions of one's spouse or intimate partner. Specifically, when the partner does something positive, good, or desirable, the person makes a dispositional attribution, which is to say the person regards that action as typical and as indicative of the (fine) kind of person one's partner is. Meanwhile, when the partner does something unpleasant or harmful, the person tends to make external and unstable attributions, such as attributing it to external stress or accident. Holtzworth-Munroe and Jacobson contrasted this pattern with what is found among distressed couples, who make stable, internal attributions for the partner's undesirable acts while dismissing the partner's positive or beneficial acts as due to external, unstable causes. It is important to realize that exactly the same mixture of the partner's good and bad actions could conceivably contribute either to marital happiness or marital distress, depending on whether the good actions or the bad ones are selected as the intentional, typical, and characteristic ones. Marital happiness and commitment is, thus, sustained by explaining away the spouse's misdeeds while focusing on the desirable acts as reflecting the spouse's true nature and intention.

One of the best guides to the subjective processes accompanying major political conversions is Richard Crossman's (1949/1987) collection of essays by Western intellectuals who converted to Communism and later repudiated that political faith. These essays also reveal some of the processes by which Communists maintained their faith in the face of disturbing, potentially threatening events. As Louis Fischer wrote, "Developments which seemed detrimental to Russia were regarded as ephemeral, dishonestly interpreted, or canceled out by more significant and countervailing developments" (1987, p. 203). The purges and murders, for example, were regarded as symptoms of revolution and change, not of the Communist system itself, and so the horror stories coming out of Russia could be safely dismissed as irrelevant to the believer's faith in Communism.

Attributional patterns are, of course, not the only cognitive patterns that support commitment. Selective attention is also helpful. If one can simply ignore the bad things, they will exert little or no influence over one's feelings. To be sure, it may be impossible to be completely unaware of certain problems or unpleasant outcomes, but one can minimize the amount of time one spends thinking about them. By not dwelling on the bad things, their impact can be minimized. Thus, political and religious groups nearly always know that there exist people who have rejected and repudiated the faith (i.e., apostates), but contact with them is kept to a minimum (see Crossman, 1949/1987, on pressure to avoid contact with ex-Communists; and Barker, 1988; Hall, 1988; or Rothbaum, 1988, on avoiding contact with ex-members of religious groups). Likewise, information that threatens important beliefs or commitments is avoided by turning attention to other things (Newman & Baumeister, 1992), by shortening the amount of time one spends listening to it (Baumeister & Cairns, 1992), or even by simply changing the channels on the television set (Sweeney & Gruber, 1984). This information is, therefore, processed less thoroughly, and its implications (that might challenge important beliefs) are not thought through.

The key point is that people participate actively in maintaining their commitments, and this participation often involves systematic ways of defusing potential threats. Whatever might threaten or undermine one's beliefs, values, or loyalties is processed in ways that minimize the threat. These ways include ignoring it, rationalizing it, downplaying it, or seeing it as temporary and atypical. In contrast, one focuses one's attention on the good things that support one's commitments.

CRYSTALLIZATION OF DISCONTENT

Thus far, I have explained how people maintain commitments. To bring about a major change in identity, role, or personality, the mechanisms that maintain stability must be reversed, turned off, or overcome. Life change begins when the processes that prevent change break down.

The crucial step in bringing about a major life change, at least in the individual's subjective perspective, is the crystallization of discontent. The interpretive processes that maintain the commitment to a role or relationship are altered in a fundamental way. Perhaps ironically, there does not have to be any change at all in the objective circumstances; what matters is the sweeping change in the way the person perceives and interprets them.

As the previous section showed, commitment is maintained by a pattern of interpreting events. Positive events are seen as typical and characteristic, and as linked to stable or permanent aspects of the relationship or role. Undesirable or threatening developments are explained away as temporary, external, or atypical.

Thus, the essence of the commitment-maintaining strategy is to prevent the recognition of any broad pattern of undesirable or bad things. The positive, desirable occurrences are seen as integral parts of the broadly positive, desirable nature of the involvement itself, but the negative, undesirable occurrences are seen as deviations that have no bearing on the permanent, essential nature of the involvement. This way, even if there are many unpleasant or undesirable things, they do not form a serious threat to the commitment, because they are seen as exceptions. Taken together, they might conceivably undermine the person's commitment, but they are not taken together.

As a result, the commitment or involvement will seem very attractive and beneficial if the person should ever pause to reassess it. The positive aspects are linked together by associations into a coherent whole. The negative aspects are kept isolated from each other. Whenever the person is asked to evaluate the role or relationship as a whole, the person will readily recall the large body of positive features and events but not any large body or pattern of negative features or events. Even when problems or unpleasant developments do occur, they do not jeopardize the fundamental commitment, because they—as individual, isolated episodes—are outweighed by the broad pattern of positive aspects.

All of this changes, however, with the crystallization of discontent. This crystallization forms associative links between the subjective perception of costs, disadvantages, problems, unpleasant outcomes, and other undesirable features of some involvement. Instead of a motley and desultory series of unrelated problems, the person sees a broad pattern of repeated, persistent problems. Instead of a variety of bad days, the person recognizes a bad year.

It is common to use metaphors of weighing to describe the process of assessing and judging important, complex matters (e.g., Gollwitzer, 1991). Assume that people evaluate their commitments by weighing (in some subjective sense) the good versus the bad features of the commitment. Assume, even, that they are particularly inclined to conduct such reassessments whenever something bad occurs that may make them wonder whether the commitment is really worth it. Before the crystallization of discontent, each act of weighing is likely to turn out favorably for maintaining the commitment. In essence, the person weighs all the positive, desirable features against only one or two of the negative, unpleasant features, because the other bad features are seen as irrelevant.

The crystallization of discontent links all these undesirable features and outcomes together, however, so that they are all placed in the scale together. Individually, they might never outweigh the positive features, but together they may well do so. After the crystallization of discontent, therefore, the next reassessment of the role or relationship may yield a conclusion that is very different from the previous conclusions.

To other people, these changes may seem confusing and even illogical. The same problems, drawbacks, or other sources of dissatisfaction seem present after the crystallization as were there before it took place. Yet the person dismissed and discounted them previously, whereas now they have suddenly, in retrospect, become reasons for change. Thus, for example,

Stephen Spender (1987) recalled how ironic and mysterious it was that people who broke with Communism suddenly found the same anti-Communist arguments more plausible than they had during their days of loyal adherence: Abruptly they would start "producing then as reasons for their change those very objections which had previously existed for them only to be disregarded or explained away" (p. 256). When these disturbing arguments were encountered individually, they could be disregarded or rationalized, but after the crystallization of discontent, they formed part of a large and strong mass of negative argument. The new context gave the old arguments new power and importance.

The crystallization of discontent is particularly important in its implications regarding the future. By definition, isolated or exceptional events will not be repeated, and so past problems do not warn of future problems as long as they are regarded as isolated or exceptional. But once the individual perceives a broad pattern of undesirable outcomes, he or she is likely to recognize that this pattern will extend into the future. Newlyweds, for example, may have a series of nasty and upsetting arguments, but the marriage may escape unscathed as long as each argument is seen as a single, isolated episode that is not likely to be repeated. Even if there are several arguments, the couple may feel that once they resolve the core disagreement, the fights will stop. But once they begin to see the arguments as part of a broad pattern of conflict, they may realize that more arguments lie ahead, and the prospects for domestic bliss and harmony are dimmed. That recognition, and that dimming, will almost inevitably reduce the perceived attractiveness of remaining in the marriage.

EVIDENCE OF CRYSTALLIZATION

At this point it is useful to consider whether empirical evidence about life change supports the hypothesis of a crystallization of discontent. For this, it is necessary to consider a variety of types of life change. Before turning to specific spheres of change, however, it is worth considering one broad-based study. Heatherton and Nichols (1992) collected a broad set of first-person accounts of life change. Half the subjects in their study were instructed to write a description of a significant life change they had undergone; the rest were instructed to describe something about themselves or their lives that they had wanted to change but had failed to change. When these stories were examined for indications of crystallization of discontent, it was found that such indications were significantly more common in the cases of successful life change than in the case where the change had not succeeded. These results support the view that the crystallization of discontent forms a significant step in major life change.

Studies of people who leave religious groups have repeatedly found that a crystallization of discontent precedes the departure. For example, women in nontraditional religious groups often find themselves cast in subordinate roles vis-a-vis the men in the group. At first, they may accept their submission as necessary or as divinely mandated, but at some point they may come to see this as highly unfair and see themselves as exploited. The duties assigned them often include cooking, cleaning, caring for the men, and even providing sexual services. At some point, many of these women achieve the realization that their membership in the group simply perpetuates the inferior status of women rather than forming part of a divinely inspired Utopian dream (Jacobs, 1984).

Other religious groups maintain Utopian dreams that are supposedly to be realized through the actions of the group under the guidance of the leader. Current dissatisfactions and imperfections can be dismissed as temporary. Eventually, however, many of these people conclude that progress is not being made (or not made fast enough) toward the perfect society, and they realize that living in such a perfect society is not in their own personally foreseeable future. When this happens, the dissatisfactions and imperfections are reconsidered as stable, enduring features of life in this group, and this prompts many of them to leave (Wright, 1984).

Similar changes in perception are found in the accounts of the ex-Communists. One of the most famous breaks with Communism was that of the French writer Andre Gide (1987). After a much-publicized visit to Soviet Russia, he repudiated his allegiance to Communism, saying that he found oppression, inequity, and other deplorable features of capitalist society being reproduced under the Communist regime. He wrote that he would have remained silent and faithful if he had been able to believe that progress was being made toward the ideals, but he concluded instead that conditions were getting worse. Thus, the same conditions would have been acceptable to him if he had been able to continue seeing them as temporary; but once he came to perceive them as permanent, they became incompatible with his Communist faith. A similar point was made by Louis Fischer (1987), who, in two visits to Soviet Russia, found rather similar conditions and problems both times; but whereas he was able to dismiss them as temporary and atypical the first time, he felt compelled to recognize them as permanent and endemic the second. The second visit was soon followed by his break with Communism.

Marital breakup seems to show a similar pattern (Vaughan, 1986). Initially, marital dissatisfaction is felt and expressed in terms of specific and often minor problems. Instead of saying "I am not satisfied with our marriage," the person criticizes the partner's actions in many individual, particular ways. Later, however, the person comes to see the problems and dissatisfactions as part of a global pattern. Indeed, Vaughan found that when she asked people when they first felt that something was wrong with their marriage, they often divided their answers into two parts. The first part consisted of many seemingly isolated complaints and moments of dissatisfaction, but without any general perception of the marriage as failing. They said they dismissed these problems, disturbing and troublesome as they may have been, as being irrelevant to the overall relationship or as being merely a feature of the standard adjustment problems that supposedly afflict all couples. Later, however, the unhappy moments and individual problems coalesced into a global perception that the relationship was not good. The second part of their answer was, thus, centered around the crystallization of discontent. It was only after the crystallization of discontent that they began actively thinking about and preparing for divorce.

THE FOCAL INCIDENT

Many stories of significant life change feature a focal incident, that is, a particular event that seemed to supply the impetus for change. Such incidents are often described as making clear the need for change and as generating the motivation necessary for the person to carry out the change. Although such incidents may be commonly reported (e.g., Ebaugh, 1988), researchers must be cautious about accepting them at face value. People may tend to overattribute the change to the focal incident, whereas in fact the change might well have occurred without that particular event. Indeed, on reflection one is skeptical that a single event (and indeed in many cases a seemingly minor or trivial one) can cause a person to break a long-standing commitment or abandon a cherished relationship or valued role.

The hypothesis of the crystallization of discontent may be useful in placing focal incidents in their proper perspective and context. Focal incidents may call attention to problems that have already existed and may facilitate the crystallization process. If the crystallization occurs around the focal incident, that event may stand out in memory and may play an exaggerated role in the person's later accounts of the change. In actuality, however, the focal incident may have served only to dramatize the person's dissatisfaction rather than being the principal source of it. That would explain the seeming triviality of some focal incidents. For example, a single argument with one's spouse, or the discovery of a spouse's inconsiderate behavior on one occasion, would seem in many cases to be an inadequate basis for breaking up an otherwise healthy and satisfying marriage. But if the argument or the inconsiderateness causes the person to confront a broad pattern of marital dissatisfaction, the subjective change may be enormous, and the person may indeed decide to seek a divorce.

Thus, people's accounts of leaving religious cults often contain focal incidents, many of which were themselves seemingly minor but that brought home to the individual that the cult was not going to fulfill its idealistic or Utopian goals (Rothbaum, 1988). Sometimes these incidents served merely to cast the religious leaders as all too human and ordinary people who could no longer then be cast in the role of exalted spiritual guide. Rothbaum noted that many ex-cult members referred to the children's tale of the emperor's new clothes in describing their focal incident and subsequent departure from the cult. That story, of course, is a vivid illustration of a crystallization process. Everyone suspected that the emperor was not wearing any clothes, but everyone doubted his or her own senses and felt compelled to go along with the apparent consensus that the emperor was surpassingly well dressed, until the child's comment caused everyone to realize the truth. The child's comment—the focal incident in that story—did not have any causal impact on what the emperor was wearing, but rather it simply crystallized everyone's doubts about what was actually going on. The reference to this story by ex-cult members seems to indicate that they had indeed suspected the truth all along but had held their doubts in check, until a focal incident made them see the broad pattern.

The ex-Communists' accounts contained similar incidents. The history of Soviet Russia in the early part of this century contained a dramatic sequence of events that could well have shaken any true believer's faith, yet many individuals managed to preserve their faith and allegiance time after time. The ex-Communists in Crossman's (1949/1987) group each seemed to select a different incident as the one that made further Communist belief intolerable. Thus, it was not the case that a single incident had a discrediting effect on everyone, but rather each person seemed to have found his or her own doubts reaching the critical point after a different event. Although they tend to write as if that particular event made further Communist allegiance impossible, further allegiance was in fact possible for others. The change was a result of the accumulation of doubt and disaffection, not of the single incident. Each individual's focal incident crystallized his or her own growing body of discontent.

AFTER THE CRYSTALLIZATION

The process of life change does not end with the crystallization of discontent and the ensuing decision to initiate a change, of course. Although this chapter has focused primarily on that crystallization, it is worth noting briefly the subsequent course of subjective accommodation to life change. A full treatment is offered elsewhere (Baumeister, 1991).

Once the person is committed to change, his or her interpretive exertions may be directed toward supporting and justifying that change. People may reshuffle their various values and priorities in order to emphasize ones that will support the change. Thus, for example, people who are preparing to leave a marriage (Vaughan, 1986) or a religious life (Ebaugh, 1988) may place new emphasis on self-oriented values such as the right and duty to pursue individual fulfillment, advancement, and happiness, whereas previously these same individuals would have subordinated these selfish values to the sanctity of marriage and family or to spiritual advancements and obligations. The previous values helped the person justify staying; the new, self-oriented values justify leaving.

In many cases, sweeping efforts of reinterpretation recast the person's recent autobiography in a radically different light. I have called this process *rewriting the story* (Baumeister, 1991) because it often takes the form of slanting the narrative account of the involvement in a new way, as opposed to merely altering abstract generalizations. For example, Vaughan (1986) noted that happily married couples will tend to tell the story of how they first met in a highly romanticized form, portraying it as a fortunate but portentous coincidence or even as an inevitable product of a seemingly benevolent fate. Later, however, when the couple is getting a divorce, they will recast the story of how they met as being a pointless accident. Instead of the mutual attraction of soul mates, the early stages of their relationship are described as a matter of mere convenience or as a concession to loneliness.

Similar shifts occur when people leave a religious group. Loyal, devout adherents to a religious faith tend to recall the story of their conversion in compelling, inspiring terms, and their entry into the religious community is described like a coming home to one's rightful place in the universe. Members who are leaving the cult, however, recast their conversion as partial, accidental, mistaken, or as a product of their own inner confusion and neediness, and their membership in the cult is described in terms of degradation and exploitation. Indeed, the lurid accounts of ex-cult members during the 1970s led to a national scandal and a broad perception of religious cults as a threat to the American way of life. It was not until the 1980s that the publication of systematic research revealed that the vast majority of cults are small, well-intentioned, and harmless, and that most people move relatively smoothly into and out of them within a couple years, often ending up with neutral or even vaguely positive memories of the experience. The discrepancy between the two views of cults is at least partly attributable to the fact that people who are in the process of leaving a cult are motivated to rewrite the story of their involvement in strongly negative, even inflammatory, terms, whereas after the break is completed they may want to look back on this phase of their lives as not being a total loss, and so they try to find at least something positive that they got out of the experience.

Obviously, the crystallization of discontent plays a central role in rewriting the story. Things that once seemed unrelated are now related, and they are likely to figure prominently in the revised story because they form the basis for the story's new end, namely the person's departure from and rejection of the whole involvement. Probably most brides and grooms have at least some twinges of doubt about whether they are doing the right thing, but when the story of the wedding is retold 15 years into a happy marriage these twinges can either be ignored or related with an indulgent smile as being minor bits of foolishness, because they are now surrounded by a broader understanding of obviously having done the right thing. In contrast, when the story of the wedding is retold by a divorcing person, those twinges of doubt will likely loom much larger.

After the story is rewritten and the break is made, many people experience a phase that may be called a *meaning-vacuum*. This pertains primarily, of course, to life changes that involve a loss or rejection of meaning; when life change involves the addition of new meaning, such as in the transition to parenthood or in joining a new religious or political group, there is often a period of rapture and widening insight and a general sense that life is newly meaningful. On leaving a group, role, relationship, or other commitment, however, some meaning is lost, and until it is replaced, the person may feel a lack of meaning. Subjectively, this may take the form of uncertainty, lack of direction, valuelessness, confusion, or fitful vacillation.

Gradually, this meaning-vacuum is filled. In many cases, the person simply reestablishes the previous meaning with new faces. Divorced people may remarry, often choosing a partner who is unfortunately similar to the discarded one. People who leave religious cults often join a new and different cult. In other cases, however, the person makes a more fundamental change and finds a very different way to make his or her life full and meaningful.

Still, in most cases there is some continuity across the life change. The meaningful links are fundamentally altered, but they are not dissolved. To be an ex-Communist or ex-Catholic is not the same as never having belonged to those groups. Likewise, ex-spouses do not revert to being total strangers or casual acquaintances, as if they had never been married. Once the self has been defined in a certain way, this identity cannot be completely undone.

LIFE CHANGE AND PERSONALITY CHANGE

This chapter has emphasized life change, but this volume is devoted to personality change, and so it seems desirable to consider the overlap briefly. They are clearly not the same thing, but it seems likely that they are often interrelated.

The crystallization of discontent is a form of insight, and so it is most relevant to personality changes that likewise occur around insights. When the person comes to perceive and understand his or her world in an entirely new fashion, the person's basis for relating to circumstances and other people is changed. Most other people will probably tend to describe this as personality change.

Miller and C'deBaca (this volume) have reported many cases as well as a systematic study of quantum personality change, that is, sudden and sweeping personality change. These experiences often appear to derive from insights that reorganized the person's perceptions of self and world. At the core of the personality change was a change in the person's basic values; once this core changed, the rest of the person's self was likewise altered. Indeed, Miller and C'deBaca emphasize how their subjects insisted that everything seemed to change for them.

The crystallization of discontent is fundamentally similar to a change in the person's core values. The person perceives his or her life situation in a radically new way, and the values the person attaches to various roles, relationships, or commitments may be drastically altered. Although my own work has not examined how such changes lead in turn to personality change, the findings of Miller and C'deBaca suggest that such change would in fact be common.

CONCLUSION

This chapter has focused on the crystallization of discontent as a centrally important step in major life change. The crystallization can be understood as the forming of associative links between problems, conflicts, costs, objections, and other negative features of one's involvement, so that a broad pattern of dissatisfaction and shortcoming is discerned.

People maintain their commitments by preventing discontent from crystallizing. The problems that arise are understood and dealt with individually, and each one seems outweighed by the broad pattern of positive features and benefits. Hardly any single problem is sufficient to break up a happy marriage, quit a good job, or cause the person to abandon an otherwise satisfying religious or political faith. Therefore, as long as the person can keep the problems isolated from each other, no major life change is warranted.

The crystallization of discontent links together these many problems or costs that previously seemed unrelated. A multitude of problems or costs can outweigh a broad pattern of positive features and benefits and can therefore provide the impetus to initiate a major change.

In principle, the crystallization of discontent could occur without any change in the total number of positive and negative features. The crystallization is based on the formation of links, on the discernment of a pattern among the many bad features, and so it does not entail the addition of new bad features. Such changes will presumably be puzzling to relationship partners and to other acquaintances and colleagues, because the person does not seem to have any reason for abruptly making a change. When it is a subjective, not an objective, change, friends or bystanders who see a sweeping life change initiated without any objective development to initiate it may have difficulty understanding why the person is doing this.

In practice, the crystallization of discontent often seems to follow from some new cost or problem or some unpleasant incident. Still, these focal events are often seemingly minor or trivial developments, and friends are often puzzled by what seems to them a disproportionate response. The life change is often a disproportionate response to the focal incident, but that is because the subjective impact of the focal incident goes far beyond its own practical and moral implications. The focal incident prompts the crystallization of discontent: It causes the person to see the broad pattern of costs and problems, and this insight radically changes the person's global appraisal of this entire aspect of his or her life.

Nearly a century ago, Freud began to suggest how sweeping insights could bring about important changes in personality. Although many of his views have been controversial, the broad faith in the power of subjective insight to transform personality is still fundamental to many forms of psychotherapy. The crystallization of discontent suggests one mechanism by which insight may indeed lead to sweeping change in the way that the person relates to his or her social world. These changes are not necessarily the same as personality change, but it seems beyond dispute that they often can be closely and multiply related. The crystallization of discontent thus promises to provide one valuable key to understanding how people may change.

REFERENCES

Barker, E. (1988). Defection from the Unification Church: Some statistics and distinctions. In D. G. Bromley (Ed.), *Falling from the faith: Causes and consequences of religious apostasy* (pp. 166–184). Newbury Park, CA: Sage.

Baumeister, R. F. (1986). *Identity: Cultural change and the struggle for self.* New York: Oxford University Press.

Baumeister, R. F. (1991). *Meanings of life.* New York: Guilford Press.

Baumeister, R. F., & Cairns, K. J. (1992). Repression and self-presentation: When audiences interfere with self-deceptive strategies. *Journal of Personality and Social Psychology, 62,* 851–862.

Baumeister, R. F., & Jones, E. E. (1978). When self-presentation is constrained by the target's knowledge: Consistency and compensation. *Journal of Personality and Social Psychology, 36,* 608–618.

Crossman, R. H. (1987). *The god that failed.* Washington, DC: Regnery Gateway. (Original work published 1949)

Ebaugh, H. R. F. (1988). *Becoming an ex: The process of role exit.* Chicago: University of Chicago Press.

Fischer, L. (1987). Untitled autobiographical chapter. In R. Crossman (Ed.), *The god that failed* (pp. 196–228). Washington, DC: Regnery Gateway.

Gide, A. (1987). Untitled autobiographical chapter. In R. Crossman (Ed.), *The god that failed* (pp. 165–195). Washington, DC: Regnery Gateway.

Gollwitzer, P. M. (1991). *Abwägen und Planen.* Göttingen, Federal Republic of Germany: Hogrefe & Huber.

Hall, J. R. (1988). The impact of apostates on the trajectory of religious movements: The case of Peoples Temple. In D. G. Bromley (Ed.), *Falling from the faith: Causes and consequences of religious apostasy* (pp. 229–250). Newbury Park, CA: Sage.

Harter, S. (1993). Causes and consequences of low self-esteem in children and adolescents. In R. Baumeister (Ed.), *Self-esteem: The puzzle of low self-regard* (pp. 87–116). New York: Plenum Press.

Harvey, J. H., Orbuch, T. L., & Weber, A. L. (Eds.). (1992). *Accounts, attributions, and close relationships.* New York: Springer-Verlag.

Harvey, J. H., Weber, A. L., & Orbuch, T. L. (1990). *Interpersonal accounts: A social psychological perspective.* Oxford, England: Basil Blackwell.

Heatherton, T. F., & Nichols, P. A. (1992). *Micronarrative accounts of successful and unsuccessful life change experiences.* Manuscript submitted for publication.

Holtzworth-Munroe, A., & Jacobson, N. S. (1985). Causal attributions of married couples: When do they search for causes? What do they conclude when they do? *Journal of Personality and Social Psychology, 48,* 1398–1412.

Jacobs, J. (1984). The economy of love in religious commitment: The deconversion of women from nontraditional religious movements. *Journal for the Scientific Study of Religion, 23,* 155–171.

Johnson, D. J., & Rusbult, C. E. (1989). Resisting temptation: Devaluation of alternative partners as a means of maintaining commitment in close relationships. *Journal of Personality and Social Psychology, 57,* 967–980.

Jones, E. E., & Nisbett, R. E. (1971). *The actor and the observer: Divergent perceptions of the causes of behavior.* Morristown, NJ: General Learning Press.

Newman, L. S., & Baumeister, R. F. (1992). *Defensive preoccupation in response to ego threat: When bad news gets a busy signal.* Manuscript submitted for publication.

Rothbaum, S. (1988). Between two worlds: Issues of separation and identity after leaving a religious community. In D. G. Bromley (Ed.), *Falling from the faith: Causes and consequences of religious apostasy* (pp. 205–228). Newbury Park, CA: Sage.

Spender, S. (1987). Untitled autobiographical chapter. In R. Crossman (Ed.), *The god that failed* (pp. 229–273). Washington, DC: Regnery Gateway.

Sweeney, P. D., & Gruber, K. L. (1984). Selective exposure: Voter information preferences and the Watergate affair. *Journal of Personality and Social Psychology, 46,* 1208–1221.

Taylor, S. E., & Brown, J. D. (1988). Illusion of well-being: A social psychological perspective on mental health. *Psychological Bulletin, 103,* 193–210.

Tedeschi, J. T., Schlenker, B. R., & Bonoma, T. V. (1971). Cognitive dissonance: Private ratiocination or public spectacle? *American Psychologist, 26,* 685–695.

Vaughan, D. (1986). *Uncoupling.* New York: Oxford University Press.

Wright, S. A. (1984). Post-involvement attitudes of voluntary defectors from controversial new religious movements. *Journal for the Scientific Study of Religion, 23,* 172–182.

13

CAN PERSONALITY CHANGE? LEVELS OF STABILITY AND GROWTH IN PERSONALITY ACROSS THE LIFE SPAN

DAN P. McADAMS

The answer to the question, Can personality change?, depends on the level at which the psychologist wishes to confront this thing, process, or whatever it is that is called personality. One does not need to be a psychoanalyst or a depth psychologist of any sort to endorse the view that the human personality should be understood in terms of multiple, identifiable levels. For example, McClelland (1951) described personality in terms of three independent levels: the levels of stylistic traits, cognitive schemas, and implicit motives or needs (see also McClelland, Koestner, & Weinberger, 1989). Hogan (1987) suggested two different levels from which to view personality: (a) personality from the standpoint of the observer, through which is constructed the individual's social reputation, and (b)

Preparation of this chapter was supported by a grant from The Spencer Foundation. I would like to thank Todd Heatherton, Joel Weinberger, and Richard Koestner for their invaluable comments on an earlier draft of this chapter.

299

personality from the standpoint of the actor, which Hogan described as "the great uncharted frontier of personality psychology . . . the region of the self concept, of social aspiration and personal despair, of public claims and private reservations, of hopes, doubts, and self-delusion" (p. 86). Cantor (1990) distinguished between the levels of having and doing in personality. Individuals have certain trait-like dispositions, but what they do is just as strongly influenced by a level of factors that appear to be more temporally and spatially contextualized and contingent.

My own view on levels borrows significantly from McClelland, Hogan, and Cantor, as well as from others, and it incorporates my own program of research and theory-construction focused on the manifestation and meaning of narrative in human lives (McAdams, 1985, 1990, 1993). I urge personality psychologists to think about personality structure and function in terms of at least three parallel levels. Each of the levels contains a wide and varied assortment of personality constructs, making it difficult to provide any level with a single name or title that adequately conveys its essential meaning. With this limitation in mind, I have chosen three rather generic tags that the reader may apply to the three respective levels: (a) *dispositional traits*, (b) *personal concerns*, and (c) *life narrative*. The answer to the question, Can personality change?, depends in part, then, on which of the three levels one wishes to consider. As one moves from traits (Level I) to concerns (Level II) to narrative (Level III), significant change in personality becomes potentially easier to see, even during the adult years, during which time, according to McCrae and Costa (1990), personality is no longer supposed to change very much.

LEVEL I: DISPOSITIONAL TRAITS

The first level is made up of those relatively nonconditional, relatively decontextualized, generally linear, and implicitly comparative dimensions of personality that typically go by the name of *traits*. Traits provide a dispositional signature for personality, estimating a person's relative position on a series of linear, bipolar scales whose definitions are a matter of consensual agreement. For some psychologists (e.g., A. H. Buss, 1989), the trait level of personality is the only level. Personality is the traits. Even the most nonreductionistic personologists on the scene today should concede that this is a very important level of personality, partly because it is at this level that the most impressive evidence for personality consistency can be garnered. One might say that, all in all, things do not change too much at the level of such general traits as extraversion, conscientiousness, and so on, especially in the adult years. In *Personality in Adulthood*, McCrae and Costa (1990) argued forcefully that individual differences in general personality traits are remarkably stable over the adult life course. They wrote, "The data suggest to us that personality change is the exception rather than the rule after age 30; somewhere in the decade between 20 and 30, individuals attain a configuration of traits that will characterize them for years to come" (p. 10). Indeed, Caspi and Moffitt (in press) showed that trait consistency prevails even in the face of monumental changes in life circumstances.

Personality psychologists should find it reassuring that research findings document this kind of stability in people's dispositional signatures. It is the stability of where people rank, when assessed by themselves or by others, relative to their perceived peers or some implicit reference group, on dimensions typically running from "low" to "high," as in "I scored high on neuroticism" or "lower than you on dominance" or "at the 50th percentile for agreeableness." There are good reasons for the longitudinal stability of many trait measures. Twin studies suggest a significant role for genetic endowment (Dunn & Plomin, 1990; Tellegen et al., 1988), and genes may drive learning, suggesting that some environmental effects are indirectly genetic, as well. For example, parents create for their children environments and learning situations commensurate with their own and, likewise, their children's own genes (Scarr & McCartney, 1983). Caspi and Moffitt (in press) and others (e.g., D. M. Buss, 1987) have discussed how traits lead people to choose certain kinds of environments that correspondingly reinforce their standing on the same trait dimensions.

Other reasons for stability may have to do with trait measurement strategies, too. Traits are usually measured through self-report items. If items are to be reliable and valid they must be simple, comparative, and only vaguely conditional. If I am to assess myself on a trait dimension, I have to adopt a comparative stance for virtually every item. To what extent am I a "careful person," I am asked on a scale assessing consciousness. Is it true that "It takes a lot to get me mad"? To answer these kinds of trait items, as a research subject or client, I have to have some sense of just how careful people tend to be in general and how easy it is to get others mad. From one testing situation to the next in, say, a longitudinal study, I may keep rating myself the same way not just because I may believe that I have not changed all that much but also because when I answer the question about, say, shyness and I say to myself, "Well I guess I'm not as shy as I used to be," I still give myself a relatively high rating because I figure I am still shyer than Kenny Bumbales, my gregarious friend from seventh grade whom I have not seen in 25 years. The central point of this brief digression into the phenomenology of answering trait items is that the conventional formats of trait assessment, with their common reliance on simple and implicitly comparative ratings, make it more likely than might be the case with other measurement strategies that psychologists will be able to show that personality does not change. In that trait scale items tend to be simple, comparative, and only vaguely conditional, they tend to implicitly encourage consistency in responding over time, which results in the conclusion that personality may not change very much.

If personality psychologists are content to assay the dispositional signature of persons, and nothing else, then an analysis of traits may be all that is needed, and the total number of levels in personality can be said to be 1. I would submit, however, that many personality psychologists, and virtually all clinicians and laypersons, find it profoundly unsatisfying to confine their descriptions and analyses of personality to the level of traits, no matter how compelling or universal a given trait scheme. An especially compelling scheme for Level I is the Big Five trait taxonomy (e.g., Digman, 1990; Goldberg, 1981; John, 1990; McCrae & Costa, 1990), which purports to specify a universal lexicon for personality descriptors. As most readers know by now, factor-analytic studies going back to Fiske (1949) and Tupes and Christal (1961) using a wide range of rating procedures and trait schemes have consistently revealed a five-factor solution for organizing trait descriptors. The most well-known version of the Big Five labels these factors as extraversion, neuroticism, agreeableness, conscientiousness, and openness to experience (McCrae, 1992). There is little doubt that the consolidation of the Big Five framework in the 1980s marked a significant empirical and conceptual advance in personality psychology. But Big Five enthusiasts have gone too far in proclaiming that the five-factor model represents personality's long-awaited integrative paradigm (e.g., Digman, 1990). Their hubris stems from an inability or unwillingness to see beyond Level I.

In a recent article, I proposed six important limitations of the five-factor model of personality traits (McAdams, 1992). The limitations apply to all conceptual models confined, as the Big Five is, to Level I. First, the five-factor model has nothing to say about what Maddi (1980) called the *core* characteristics of human nature or what D. M. Buss (1991) referred to as *species-typical* features of personality. By contrast, such personality theories as those provided by Jung, Adler, Kelly, Kohut, Rotter, Rank, Tomkins, Loevinger, and Erikson are centrally concerned with core propositions about human functioning that cannot be translated into a trait language about individual differences (Maddi, 1980). Second, traits typically do not provide enough specific information to make for the effective prediction of behavior in particular situations and for the kind of rich description of human lives that clinicians and laypersons expect. Third, with the exception of certain biologically based approaches (e.g., Eysenck, 1973; Gray, 1982), trait assessments fail to provide compelling causal explanations for human behavior. Fourth, trait assessments disregard the contextual and conditional nature of human experience, a fact that has led enthusiasts of the Big Five to celebrate (ironically, in my view) the "transcontextual" nature of personality traits (McCrae & Costa, 1984). Fifth, trait taxonomies fail to offer an attractive program for studying personality organization and integration. The whole person is reduced to a set of scores on a series of linear continua, or what Allport (1937) dismissively termed "the psychograph."

The sixth point, though, may be the most fundamental, inherent in the very nature of trait assessment. In rating one's own or another's personality on a typical paper-and-pencil trait measure, the rater/subject must adopt an observational stance in which the target of the rating becomes an object of comparison on a series of linear and only vaguely conditional dimensions. For example, a person is seen as more or less extraverted or dominant in a general sort of way, across a wide variety of situations, conditions, and contexts. There is no place in trait assessment for what Thorne (1989) called the conditional patterns of personality (see also, Wright & Mischel, 1987). Here are some simple examples of conditional patterns: "My dominance shows when my competence is threatened; I fall apart when people try to comfort me; I talk the most when I am nervous" (Thorne, 1989, p. 149). But to make traits into conditional statements is to rob them of their power as nonconditional indicators of general trends. The conundrum is intractable: Traits cannot be traits if they are made overly conditional.

Now, there is little doubt that the nonconditional trait perspective constitutes a legitimate paradigm for social observation. It is an especially efficient and comprehensive paradigm for getting an initial read on or global outline of that which is to be rated. It is a paradigm of observation that one would be most likely to use, it would seem, when encountering a new phenomenon, that is, a new person, a stranger. Trait psychology's reliance on simple, noncontingent, and implicitly comparative statements about individuals—as contained in trait rating scales—essentially provides a psychology of the stranger, nothing more, nothing less. In providing a rationale for the legitimacy of the Big Five model of personality traits as derived from the analysis of English word lists, Goldberg (1981) wrote, "They [the five factors] suggest that those who have contributed to the English lexicon as it has evolved over time wished to know the answers to at least five types of questions *about a stranger* they were soon to meet" (p. 161). The Big Five encapsules those most general and encompassing attributions—simple, comparative, and virtually nonconditional—that one might wish to make when one knows virtually nothing else about a person; that is, when confronted with a stranger. To move beyond a psychology of the stranger, personality psychologists must move beyond traits.

LEVEL II: PERSONAL CONCERNS

How does one know that one knows another person well? What does it take to know a person? Many would say that such knowledge transcends an understanding of where that person stands on dimensions of extraversion and openness to experience. To know a person well one may also seek to obtain, for example, information concerning what the person wants, how the person goes about trying to get what he or she wants, what the person is concerned with, what the person is "into," what his or her plans for the future are, how the person feels about his or her children and wife or husband and boss, the person's plans, goals, strivings, projects, tactics, strategies, defenses, and so on. This is the stuff of Level II, for which I give the rather inadequate generic label of *personal concerns.* Compared with traits, personal concerns are typically couched in motivational, developmental, or strategic terms. Personal concerns speak to what people want, often during particular periods in their lives or within particular domains of action, and what life methods people use (strategies, plans, defenses, and so on) in order to get what they want or to avoid getting what they do not want.

It is intriguing to observe that although the field of personality has moved toward an acceptance of general, decontextualized traits like the Big Five, it has also moved vigorously in recent years toward developing units of personological analysis that are explicitly contextualized. D. M. Buss and Cantor (1989; Cantor & Zirkel, 1990; Pervin, 1990) referred to these as "middle-level units" in personality inquiry, and they included such constructs as "personal projects" (Palys & Little, 1983), "personal strivings" (Emmons, 1986), and "life tasks" (Cantor, 1990; Cantor & Kihlstrom, 1987). One might also add here defense mechanisms (Cramer, 1991) and coping styles (Lazarus, 1991); current concerns (Klinger, 1977), and concerns and motivations linked to particular developmental stages or epochs (e.g., generativity; see, for example, McAdams & de St. Aubin, 1992); strategies and tactics of personality, as in the evolutionarily grounded reproductive strategies described by D. M. Buss (1991); and adult attachment styles based on internalized working models of attachment, as described in the research of Main (1991) and Hazan and Shaver (1990). The list could go on.

Level II appears to be a vast and unwieldy realm in personality, and it is not yet clear what to include in it. Despite its resistance to a neat five-factor structure, personality psychologists should recognize its importance as a realm very different from traits, and one that cannot be reduced to traits. Level II constructs are not merely circumscribed traits. They should not be viewed as potential subheads under the generic Big Five. Many Level II constructs focus explicitly on a person's conscious articulations of what he or she is trying to do during a given period of life, what goals and goal-based concerns occupy salient positions in everyday consciousness. Such constructs are embedded in and defined by the particularities of the single human life. Cantor (1990) suggested that middle-level units speak more precisely and idiographically to the question of what people actually do in life. People have their traits, but they do things, expressing themselves in the domain of Level II.

Although the data are sparse, one would expect to see considerable personality change at Level II over the life span. Contemporary views of traits seem to imply that traits emerge, reach a characteristic level, and then remain relatively stable over time. By contrast, such Level II variables as particular kinds of personal strivings, current concerns, and developmentally linked preoccupations seem to ebb and flow over the life span, in accordance with changing situational and developmental demands. Modest, though equivocal, evidence consistent with this idea comes from a recent cross-sectional study of individual differences in four manifestations of *generativity*—that is, a concern for and commitment to the next generation—among young, midlife, and older adults (McAdams, de St. Aubin, & Logan, 1993). Controlling for income and educational differences among groups, the researchers found significant age and cohort differences in the salience of generativity as a theme in personal scripts and personal strivings. In keeping with the writings of Erikson (1963) and others (Kotre, 1984; McAdams, 1985; Ryff & Heincke, 1983; Vaillant & Milofsky, 1980), midlife adults showed a greater preoccupation with generativity themes in their open-ended accounts of personally meaningful life experiences, compared with younger and older adults. With respect to personal strivings, both midlife and older subjects expressed much higher levels of generativity than did the young adults. Midlife and older individuals have made significant generativity commitments in their lives that they have translated into discrete particular goals or things they are trying to do everyday—things like "manage my business to have enough profit to send my son to college" or "make my oldest daughter, a teacher, realize she can't change all things for all people; she's an idealist" or "agitate for justice and peace in my neighborhood and in the world."

The findings on generativity suggest that the inner and outer worlds of midlife and older adults are vastly different from those of the younger adults in this sample. Of course, it is possible that some of these differences are a function of cohort. The cross-sectional study does not prove that generativity, as one aspect of personality, changes over time. It is merely suggestive, and the lead needs to be pursued in longitudinal research. In this regard, a recent 22-year longitudinal study of psychosocial development in adulthood provides evidence for considerable personality change in directions predicted by Eriksonian theory (Whitbourne, Zuschlag, Elliot, & Waterman, 1992; see also, Franz, this volume).

Operating at Level II, Thorne (1989; Thorne & Klohnen, 1993) has explored the richness and complexity of people's conditional patterns. Her research shows that when people talk about who they are, they do not speak in expressly dispositional terms. They do not use the language of

Level I. Instead, complexly contingent self-attributions appear in an inherently episodic and narrative framework. This is not because respondents lack the clarity of thought needed to dissect their lives into noncontingent dispositional units. When asked to do so, most people have little trouble in complying, as every trait psychologist knows. Rather, individuals cannot express the coherence of personality—to themselves or to others—in noncontingent, dispositional terms. Coherence emerges in the particular episodes and contingent stories that the subject presents in order to convey his or her own phenomenal experience. When one begins to consider the coherence of an individual's self-defining narratives, then one begins to move into Level III in personality, the level of identity as an integrative life story.

LEVEL III: LIFE NARRATIVE

The limitation of Level I is that dispositions are too general and noncontingent to provide anything beyond a psychology of the stranger. At Level II the stranger becomes known, as a flesh-and-blood, in-the-world doer, striving to accomplish things, expressing himself or herself in and through strategies, tactics, plans, goals, and so on. No longer a stranger, the person conceived in the language of Level II is still lacking, however, in integration, unity, coherence, overall purpose. The strivings and goals are indicative of what a person is trying to do, but they are not enough to tell the psychologist who a person is trying to be, or, even better, what person the person is trying to make. If Level I emphasizes the having aspect of personality and Level II the doing, then Level III concerns the making of the self. A growing number of psychologists are now conceptualizing the uniquely adult agenda of making an identity—that is, finding unity and purpose in life—as an evolving narrative quest (Bruner, 1986; Charme, 1984; Cohler, 1982; Gregg, 1991; Grotevant, 1992; Hermans, Kempen, & van Loon, 1992; McAdams, 1985, 1987, 1990, 1993; Sarbin, 1986; Shotter & Gergen, 1989; Tomkins, 1987).

In my own life-story model of adult identity, I conceive of identity as an internalized and evolving story that integrates a reconstructed past, perceived present, and anticipated future into a coherent and vitalizing life myth. The story cannot be understood in the languages of Levels I or II; it is not a traitlike entity or process; it is not simply a collection of plans, strategies, or goals. Instead, my life story is the internalized narrative understanding I have fashioned of who I am and how I fit into the adult world. Incorporating beginning, middle, and anticipated ending, my story tells me how I came to be, where I have been and where I may be going, and who I will become (Hankiss, 1981). The story is created and revised across the adult years as the changing person and the person's changing world negotiate niches, places, opportunities, and positions within which the person can live, and live meaningfully. Traits and concerns can never provide a satisfying identity because traits and concerns in and of themselves cannot justify a life. They cannot tell a person who he or she is. They cannot provide a life with unity, purpose, direction, and coherence.

My own research suggests that in Western society people begin to adopt a narrative perspective on their own lives in late adolescence and young adulthood. But the origins of storymaking can be traced back to the earliest years, in the development of an early attachment bond in infancy and the appropriation of emotionally charged images during the preschool years. Furthermore, storymaking extends well across the adult life course. Contrary to some readings of Erikson (1963), I argue that identity cannot be confined to a late-adolescent stage in the life cycle. Rather, once identity emerges as a central issue in late adolescence, it does not go away, at least not typically until old age. Adults fashion and refashion stories of the self, marking important personality change through the 30s, 40s, 50s, and beyond (McAdams, 1993).

Each life story contains a number of different features, some of which appear to remain relatively stable over the adult years and some of which appear to change markedly. From the most stable (and most cognitively primitive) to the most changing (and most cognitively complex), a list might contain (a) tone, (b) image, (c) theme, (d) setting, (e) scene, (f) character, and (g) ending.

The (a) *narrative tone* of a person's identity is the emotional feel of the story, which may range globally from bleak pessimism to blithe optimism. Optimism is often conveyed through comic and romantic narrative forms, pessimism through tragedy and irony (Frye, 1957; Murray, 1989). A story's unique (b) *imagery* is made up of the characteristic sights and sounds of the narrative, emotionally charged pictures, symbols, metaphors, and the like, some of which may be traced back to early fantasy play. The (c) *themes* are recurrent patterns of motivational content in stories, manifested as characters in narrative repeatedly strive to attain their goals over time (Bruner, 1986, 1990). After Bakan (1966), the two superordinate themes in life stories are *agency* (power/achievement/autonomy) and *communion* (love/intimacy/belongingness). The story's (d) *ideological setting* is the backdrop of beliefs and values that situates the plot in a particular ontological, epistemological, and moral location. As Erikson (1963) rightly suggested, ideology provides a kind of foundation—or setting—for identity.

Standing out in bold print in life stories are certain (e) *nuclear episodes*, or key scenes such as symbolic high points, low points, and turning points. The scenes symbolize perceived changes and continuities in life, providing proof in narrative nutshells for the way a person changed direction in life or the way a person remained the same through changing circumstances. People prove to themselves and to each other that they have either changed or remained consistent by invoking concrete autobiographical incidents that affirm transformation or continuity of the self, respectively. The main characters in people's life stories are (f) personal *imagoes,* or personified idealizations of the self, scripted to play major roles and enact important conflicts in the story. Identity is complex enough to require a cast of imagoes, that is, different personifications of the self as "the good father," "the loyal friend," "the violent warrior," and so on. Integrating and making peace among different imagoes in one's life story is a psychosocial challenge of the midlife years and beyond. Finally, all life stories require a satisfying (g) *ending,* through which the self is able to leave a legacy that generates new beginnings. In midlife and beyond, life stories begin to take on the quality of "giving birth to." Men and women strive to refashion their narratives in ways that assure some kind of positive continuity with the next generation and those people and things that will ultimately survive them. Therefore, endings in life narratives are often, and ideally, about generativity, about leaving legacies for the next generation (McAdams, 1993).

How does personality change at Level III? Here the data are virtually nonexistent. But it may be worthwhile to entertain some educated hunches drawn from a wide reading of the interdisciplinary literature, including that from the humanities, concerning personality development in adulthood. Such hunches, of course, need to be subjected to empirical testing.

If traits emerge and then remain relatively stable over time, and if strivings and other middle-level units ebb and flow over time as a function of changing circumstances and developmental demands, then the model for change in identity over time is a process of continual fashioning and refashioning narrative in the direction of good form. I believe that the process is both developmentally natural and strongly shaped by culture. At times, it may manifest itself in a very conscious manner, as when a young woman decides to keep a journal or a midlife man decides to rethink his career. At other times, storymaking goes on unconsciously, implicitly, between the lines of everyday social and private intercourse. The concepts of development and growth in personality are particularly apt for Level III, for there may be an inherent developmental logic in narrative that moves one to formulate more and more adequate stories about the self over time. The especially adequate story is coherent, credible, open to new possibilities, richly differentiated, reconciling of opposites, and integrated within the context of the best and most vitalizing cultural myths of the day (McAdams, 1993). For a personologist who believes that the stories are not simply interesting avenues for getting at traits and strivings but that the stories are indeed the identities themselves, internalized and evolving narratives of the self, identity development in these terms represents real and exciting change in personality. It is time for research to determine to what extent such development does indeed occur in the lives of contemporary American adults, as well as adults in other societies.

CONCLUSION

In suggesting that personality be viewed from three distinct and non-overlapping levels, my analysis leads logically to the important question of connections between and among levels. How are the levels related to each other? How are traits related to concerns? Concerns to stories? Traits to stories? Some might suggest, for example, that traits seem the most basic level of the three, and that concerns and stories may be viewed as developing out of traits in some manner. Traits may be the raw stuff of personality, and concerns and stories may represent how people fashion the raw stuff into recognizable life patterns. Although there may be some validity in this line of thinking, I believe that it is premature to speculate with much elaboration about relationships among the levels. There are at least two reasons for my caution. First, whereas the trait domain appears to be well mapped at present, Levels II and III are relatively uncharted. The kind of geography that exists at these levels is simply unknown. Assuming that it is similar to the trait terrain is completely unwarranted, in my view. As 40 years of trait psychology now attests, a given domain requires a great deal of time and considerable scrutiny before researchers can determine indigenously adequate structure. Second, the levels do not need to exist in meaningful relation to each other in order to exist as meaningful levels. There is no holy writ dictating perfect hierarchy for our conceptions of personality, that is, neat levels feeding into neat levels according to general laws of consistency.

It may, therefore, be useful to conceptualize each of the three different levels of personality as operating within its own peculiar and respective framework, grammar, language, and format. It may be a mistake to reduce one level to the next, an error of seductive but overly facile reductionism. Given our current lack of knowledge about Levels II and III in my scheme, it is probably not even advisable at this point to engage in a zealous search for connections between levels, for in doing this the researcher may end up trying to justify one level in terms of another, like interpreting stories in terms of traits. Life stories may have very little to do with personality traits. Or, there may be some interesting connections to be discovered there. But whether there are or not, the three different levels of personality each have a unique legitimacy and range of convenience, to borrow Kelly's (1955) term. Thus, I urge psychologists to think of these levels not so much in terms of a vertical hierarchy, one on top of the other, as if the upper levels were derived from the lower ones, or vice versa. It may be better to string them out horizontally; maybe "levels" is the wrong word. Think of them as three very different domains, three very different takes on personality. They may not have all that much to do with each other. People are complex and multi-arrayed. Everything does not need to fit with everything else into a neat, unified personality. There may be no single answer to the question, Does personality change? Each of the three levels of personality requires its own unique theory of stability and change over the life span.

REFERENCES

Allport, G. W. (1937). *Personality: A psychological interpretation.* New York: Holt, Rinehart & Winston.

Bakan, D. (1966). *The duality of human existence: Isolation and communion in Western man.* Boston: Beacon Press.

Bruner, J. (1986). *Actual minds, possible worlds.* Cambridge, MA: Harvard University Press.

Bruner, J. (1990). *Acts of meaning.* Cambridge, MA: Harvard University Press.

Buss, A. H. (1989). Personality as traits. *American Psychologist, 44,* 1378–1388.

Buss, D. M. (1987). Selection, evocation, and manipulation. *Journal of Personality and Social Psychology, 53,* 1214–1221.

Buss, D. M. (1991). Evolutionary personality psychology. *Annual Review of Psychology, 42,* 459–491.

Buss, D. M., & Cantor, N. (1989). Introduction. In D. M. Buss & N. Cantor (Eds.), *Personality psychology: Recent trends and emerging directions* (pp. 1–12). New York: Springer-Verlag.

Cantor, N. (1990). From thought to behavior: "Having" and "doing" in the study of personality and cognition. *American Psychologist, 45,* 735–750.

Cantor, N., & Kihlstrom, J. F. (1987). *Personality and social intelligence.* Englewood Cliffs, NJ: Prentice Hall.

Cantor, N., & Zirkel, S. (1990). Personality, cognition, and purposive behavior. In L. Pervin (Ed.), *Handbook of personality theory and research* (pp. 135–164). New York: Guilford Press.

Caspi, A., & Moffitt, T. E. (in press). When do individual differences matter? A paradoxical theory of personality coherence. *Psychological Inquiry.*

Charme, S. T. (1984). *Meaning and myth in the study of lives: A Sartrean perspective.* Philadelphia: University of Pennsylvania Press.

Cohler, B. J. (1982). Personal narrative and the life course. In P. Baltes & O. G. Brim (Eds.), *Life span development and behavior* (Vol. 4, pp. 205–241). San Diego, CA: Academic Press.

Cramer, P. (1991). *The development of defense mechanisms.* New York: Springer-Verlag.

Digman, J. M. (1990). Personality structure: Emergence of the five-factor model. *Annual Review of Psychology, 41*, 417–440.

Dunn, J., & Plomin, R. (1990). *Separate lives: Why siblings are so different.* New York: Basic Books.

Emmons, R. (1986). Personal strivings: An approach to personality and subjective well-being. *Journal of Personality and Social Psychology, 51*, 1058–1068.

Erikson, E. H. (1963). *Childhood and society* (2nd ed.). New York: Norton.

Eysenck, H. J. (1973). *Eysenck on extraversion.* New York: Wiley.

Fiske, D. W. (1949). Consistency of the factorial structures of personality ratings from different sources. *Journal of Abnormal and Social Psychology, 44*, 329–344.

Frye, N. (1957). *Anatomy of criticism.* Princeton, NJ: Princeton University Press.

Goldberg, L. R. (1981). Language and individual differences: The search for universals in personality lexicons. In L. Wheeler (Ed.), *Review of personality and social psychology* (Vol. 2, pp. 141–166). Beverly Hills, CA: Sage.

Gray, J. A. (1982). *The neuropsychology of anxiety: An enquiry into the functions of the sept-hippocampal system.* New York: Oxford University Press.

Gregg, G. (1991). *Self-representation: Life narrative studies in identity and ideology.* New York: Greenwood Press.

Grotevant, H. D. (1992). *The integrative nature of identity: Bringing the soloists to sing in the choir.* Paper presented at the Wellington Adolescent Identity Conference, Victoria University of Wellington, New Zealand.

Hankiss, A. (1981). On the mythological rearranging of one's life history. In D. Bertaux (Ed.), *Biography and society: The life-history approach in the social sciences* (pp. 203-209). Beverly Hills, CA: Sage.

Hazan, N., & Shaver, P. (1990). Love and work: An attachment–theoretical perspective. *Journal of Personality and Social Psychology, 59*, 270–280.

Hermans, H. J. M., Kempen, H. J. G., & van Loon, R. J. P. (1992). The dialogical self: Beyond individualism and rationalism. *American Psychologist, 47*, 23–33.

Hogan, R. (1987). Personality psychology: Back to basics. In J. Aronoff, A. I. Rabin, & R. A. Zucker (Eds.), *The emergence of personality* (pp. 79–104). New York: Springer.

John, O. P. (1990). The "Big Five" factor taxonomy: Dimensions of personality in the natural language and in questionnaires. In L. Pervin (Ed.), *Handbook of personality theory and research* (pp. 66–100). New York: Guilford Press.

Kelly, G. (1955). *The psychology of personal constructs.* New York: Norton.

Klinger, E. (1977). *Meaning and void: Inner experience and the incentives in people's lives.* Minneapolis: University of Minnesota Press.

Kotre, J. (1984). *Outliving the self: Generativity and the interpretation of lives.* Baltimore, MD: Johns Hopkins University Press.

Lazarus, R. S. (1991). *Emotion and adaptation.* New York: Oxford University Press.

Maddi, S. R. (1980). *Personality theories: A comparative analysis* (4th ed.). Homewood, IL: Dorsey Press.

Main, M. (1991). Metacognitive knowledge, metacognitive monitoring, and singular (coherent) vs. multiple (incoherent) model of attachment: Findings and directions for future research. In C. M. Parkes, J. Stevenson-Hinde, & P. Marris (Eds.), *Attachment across the life cycle* (pp. 127–159). London: Tavistock.

McAdams, D. P. (1985). *Power, intimacy, and the life story: Personological inquiries into identity.* New York: Guilford Press.

McAdams, D. P. (1987). A life-story model of identity. In R. Hogan & W. H. Jones (Eds.), *Perspectives in personality* (Vol. 2, pp. 15–50). Greenwich, CT: JAI Press.

McAdams, D. P. (1990). Unity and purpose in human lives: The emergence of identity as a life story. In A. I. Rabin, R. A. Zucker, R. A. Emmons, & S. Frank (Eds.), *Studying persons and lives* (pp. 148–200). New York: Springer.

McAdams, D. P. (1992). The five-factor model *in* personality: A critical appraisal. *Journal of Personality, 60,* 329–361.

McAdams, D. P. (1993). *The stories we live by: Personal myths and the making of the self.* New York: William Morrow.

McAdams, D. P., & de St. Aubin, E. (1992). A theory of generativity and its assessment through self-report, behavioral acts, and narrative themes in autobiography. *Journal of Personality and Social Psychology, 62,* 1003–1015.

McAdams, D. P., de St. Aubin, E., & Logan, R. (1993). Generativity in young, midlife, and older adults. *Psychology and Aging, 8,* 221–230.

McClelland, D. C. (1951). *Personality.* New York: Holt, Rinehart & Winston.

McClelland, D. C., Koestner, R., & Weinberger, J. (1989). How do self-attributed and implicit motives differ? *Psychological Review, 96,* 690–702.

McCrae, R. R. (1992). (Ed.). The five-factor model: Issues and applications [Special issue]. *Journal of Personality, 60*(2).

McCrae, R. R., & Costa, P. T., Jr. (1984). Personality is transcontextual: A reply to Veroff. *Personality and Social Psychology Bulletin, 10,* 175–179.

McCrae, R. R., & Costa, P. T., Jr. (1990). *Personality in adulthood.* New York: Guilford Press.

Murray, K. (1989). The construction of identity in the narratives of romance and comedy. In J. Shotter & K. J. Gergen (Eds.), *Texts of identity* (pp. 176–205). Newbury Park, CA: Sage.

Palys, T. S., & Little, B. R. (1983). Perceived life satisfaction and the organization of personal project systems. *Journal of Personality and Social Psychology, 44,* 1221–1230.

Pervin, L. (1990). Personality theory and research: Prospects for the future. In L. Pervin (Ed.), *Handbook of personality theory and research* (pp. 723–727). New York: Guilford Press.

Ryff, C. D., & Heincke, S. G. (1983). Subjective organization of personality in adulthood and aging. *Journal of Personality and Social Psychology, 44,* 807–816.

Sarbin, T. R. (1986). (Ed.). *Narrative psychology: The storied nature of human conduct.* New York: Praeger.

Scarr, S., & McCartney, K. (1983). How people make their own environments: A theory of geneotype → environment effects. *Child Development, 54,* 424–435.

Shotter, J., & Gergen, K. (1989). (Eds.). *Texts of identity.* Newbury Park, CA: Sage.

Tellegen, A., Lykken, D. J., Bouchard, T. J., Jr., Wilcox, K. J., Segal, N. L., & Rich, S. (1988). Personality similarity in twins reared apart and together. *Journal of Personality and Social Psychology, 54,* 1031–1039.

Thorne, A. (1989). Conditional patterns, transference, and the coherence of personality across time. In D. M. Buss & N. Cantor (Eds.), *Personality psychology: Recent trends and emerging directions* (pp. 149–159). New York: Springer-Verlag.

Thorne, A., & Klohnen, E. (1993). Interpersonal memories as maps for personality consistency. In D. Funder, R. Parke, C. Tomlinson-Keasey, & K. Widaman (Eds.), *Studying lives through time: Personality and development* (pp. 223–253). Washington, DC: American Psychological Association.

Tomkins, S. S. (1987). Script theory. In J. Aronoff, A. I. Rabin, and R. A. Zucker (Eds.), *The emergence of personality* (pp. 147–216). New York: Springer.

Tupes, E. C., & Christal, R. E. (1961). Recurrent personality factors based on trait ratings (Tech. Rep. Nos. 61–67). Lackland, TX: U.S. Air Force Aeronautical Division.

Vaillant, G. E., & Milofsky, E. (1980). The natural history of male psychological health: IX. Empirical evidence for Erikson's model of psychological health. *American Journal of Psychiatry, 137,* 1348–1359.

Whitbourne, S. K., Zuschlag, M. K., Elliot, L. B., & Waterman, A. S. (1992). Psychosocial development in adulthood: A 22-year sequential study. *Journal of Personality and Social Psychology, 63,* 260–271.

Wright, J. C., & Mischel, W. (1987). A conditional approach to dispositional constructs: The local predictability of social behavior. *Journal of Personality and Social Psychology, 53,* 1159–1177.

14

PERSONALITY STABILITY, PERSONALITY CHANGE, AND THE QUESTION OF PROCESS

LAWRENCE A. PERVIN

This volume addresses the question, Can personality change? In thinking about the issue, and considering all of the excellent arguments on the subject, I was struck with the extent to which differing positions have been taken concerning whether and how much personality can and does change. Are these differing views the result of reading different literature or of drawing different conclusions from the same literature? Is there a bias in the way questions are asked and conclusions drawn? For example, does the framing of the question as Can personality change? already structure our thinking along certain lines? Would discussion follow a different course if we asked, Can personality be stable? And, to what extent do such questions misdirect our attention from the central issue of processes: What are the processes leading to stability and change in personality?

What I mean to suggest in this chapter is that there is a tendency in the field to pose questions in a way that leads to useless debate, and it is necessary to make sure that this does not happen in relation to issues of personality stability and change. I am, of course, referring here to such past

315

issues as nature versus nurture and person versus situation. I am concerned lest psychologists fall into similarly unproductive debate over the issue of stability versus change. In this chapter, then, I try to do three things. First, I attempt to demonstrate the sometimes subtle ways in which general biases enter into the literature and public discussion. Next, I consider the relevant issues in three areas: (a) intelligence and temperament, (b) longitudinal studies of personality, and (c) psychotherapy. Finally, I discuss the need to attend to processes fostering stability and change in personality functioning.

TERMS USED, RELATIONSHIPS FOUND, CONCLUSIONS DRAWN

In reading the relevant literature, I am struck by the terms that are used. Often there is a great deal of ambiguity in these terms or subtle differences that can have important implications. For example, Helson (this volume) has suggested that the way personality is defined can influence the extent to which room is left for change and that often there is a bias against change as a part of personality. In addition, Caspi and Bem (1990) considered the terms continuity and change, and then discussed the types of continuity and change that may be found, concluding that the assertion that an individual's personality has changed or remained the same over time is ambiguous. They focused on the different meanings associated with terms such as absolute stability, differential stability, structural stability, ipsative stability, and coherence or what they refer to as "heterotypic continuity," that is, continuity of an inferred genotypic attribute presumed to underlie diverse phenotypic behaviors.

However, the issue can be even wider ranging. For example, Ramey, Lee, and Burchinal (1989) examined terms such as *stability, continuity, predictability,* and *plasticity.* They concluded that the terms stability, continuity, and development are antithetical and suggested instead the use of the term predictability for describing the maintenance of relative standing in a characteristic over time, and the term plasticity for describing change in general in a characteristic over time. In their research on intellectual development they have found evidence of individual predictability and between-group plasticity: "Altering the ecology of disadvantaged children through educational intervention changed the level of their cognitive performance on the average, but did not change the across time predictability of their intellectual development" (p. 231). To terms such as these, one can add those of change and malleability. In other words, does it make a difference if one asks whether personality is predictable, plastic, changing, or malleable? Do the terms used have implicit in them assumptions concerning the nature of personality and the potential for change? Is it possible to have a view of personality that allows for both stability and change, over time and across situations—that is, an overall pattern and coherence that provides room for considerable change in parts and momentary functioning?

Obviously, the extent to which evidence of stability and/or change is found will depend on factors such as the characteristic measured, the measure used, the statistic used, the age at which the characteristic is first measured, the interval between measurements, the conditions of measurement and the conditions that have prevailed during the interval between measurements, and whether individual or group data are being considered (Caspi & Bem, 1990; Caspi, Bem, & Elder, 1989; Nesselroade, this volume; West & Graziano, 1989). Consider the issue of which characteristic is measured. McAdams (this volume) suggests that results may vary according to which level or domain is being considered. Although in basic agreement with McAdams, I would frame the matter a little differently. First, generally I would consider affects to be more stable and resistant to change than are cognitions, which are more stable and resistant to change than are behaviors. Although in some ways this may be an artificial distinction because most personality functioning of import involves affective, cognitive, and behavioral components, my sense is that these components differ in how readily they change and that this is seen most clearly in the area of psychotherapy. Although I know of no studies comparing the relative ease of changing affects, cognitions, and behaviors, indirect support for this view comes from therapists of differing orientations and neuropsychological evidence of the indelibility of many emotional associations (Greenberg & Safran, 1989; LeDoux, 1989; LeDoux, Romanski, & Xagoraris, 1989; Pervin, 1984; Rachman, 1981).

Another aspect of the measurement of change in characteristics is centrality in personality functioning. It seems likely that the more central aspects of personality functioning are less readily changed than are those that are less central, that is, those that are part of the basic character structure in the psychoanalytic sense as opposed to those that are not, or those that can be described in Kelly's (1955) terms as core constructs rather than peripheral constructs. What is being emphasized here is that personality is not just made up of components but that there is structure and organization to these components with implications for readiness to change (Magnusson, 1990).

As indicated, the measures used, the age at which measurements are taken, and the interval between measurements will all affect the conclusions that are drawn. Kagan (1992) nicely pointed out how different conclusions can be drawn from both physiological recordings, as opposed to observable overt behavior, and from testing in infancy, as opposed to early childhood. Generally, change occurs more rapidly during the early years, although much research remains to be done in changes that do and may occur during the later years of life. One of the relatively few very consistent findings in the literature is that change is greater the longer the time interval between measurements, a finding that is probably not surprising to most but is often ignored in the evaluation of stability data. Turning to the issue of conditions of measurement, Kagan (1992) and Caspi and Moffitt (in press) have both suggested that features related to an earlier time may show up only under conditions of stress. This issue is of import both in terms of how personality is defined (e.g., is it that which is most characteristically true of the person, that which shows up when adaptive resources are most being stressed, or both) and when measurements are made. The low incidence of observed change in intervening conditions may be due to minimal change in environmental conditions rather than to stability or fixity of the characteristic per se (Hanson, 1975; Wachs, 1992). The stability of the environment may be due to environmental factors influenced by the individual or by environmental factors largely beyond the influence of the individual (Loehlin, 1992; Plomin, DeFries, & Loehlin, 1977). An example of the latter would be the way in which cultural norms exert an influence toward either stability or change, an influence discussed by Cattell under the concept of coercion to the biosocial mean (Caspi et al., 1989; West & Graziano, 1989). Part of the apparent greater stability of personality in adulthood may be due to the greater freedom of individuals to select their environments, to the stable perceptions and behaviors of their partners, and to the stabilization of cultural norms rather than to a stabilization of personality in the sense of greater resistance to change. In this sense, stability does not necessarily equal fixity, and such an interpretation calls attention to the issue emphasized in the introduction, that of processes and conditions of stability and change.

Turning to questions of measures and statistics, generally the literature suggests greater stability for self-ratings and observer ratings than for objective laboratory measures, including measures of behavior in experimental situations and physiological measures (Caspi & Bem, 1990). Also, different conclusions may be drawn from the analysis of means as opposed to correlations, as well as from the analysis of group data as opposed to individual data (Block, 1971; Caspi & Bem, 1990; Ozer & Gjerde, 1989). As noted by Block, impressive mean correlations may mask considerable individual variation. In addition, when considering personality as a coherent system, small changes in individual parts measured in isolation may mask significant change in the functioning of the system as a whole.

Given these complexities, caution would appear to be warranted in drawing conclusions concerning personality stability and change. Two further points are noteworthy. First, I am struck with how much subjectivity is involved in characterizing something as having substantial stability or reasonable stability, or in characterizing a correlation as very high or moderately high. One of the things that I learned some time ago is that subjects interpret questionnaire terms such as *moderate* and *frequently* very differently. It is my strong suspicion that psychologists are not much different and that their characterization of a statistical relationship as modest or impressive has a lot to do with their own position on the issue being considered. Is a correlation of .50 over 10 years very impressive, impressive, or unimpressive? Is such a correlation evidence of substantial stability, some stability, or change?

Second, often conclusions concerning personality stability that do not follow from the data are suggested or implied. Sometimes evidence of heritability of a characteristic or the biological underpinning of a characteristic is considered to be suggestive of stability, despite repeated warnings that inherited does not mean fixed and that biology is not deterministic. Thus, for example, Costa and McCrae (this volume) suggest that "If one defined personality as the genetic basis of temperament, change would be precluded." Or, to take another example, in this case from a manuscript I recently reviewed, the authors concluded, from evidence of stability of extraversion and neuroticism over a 4-year period, that adult personality is rather impervious to changing life circumstances. Such a conclusion would hardly seem warranted given the limited variables considered, the restricted period of time, and the lack of consideration of broad boundary conditions that might foster change in specific individuals. It is one thing to find that ordinarily personality, in this case defined as extraversion and neuroticism, does not change and another to conclude that personality is impervious to change. The importance of such differences is all the greater when issues of potential social and political importance are being considered, as when conclusions concerning the malleability of intelligence are drawn from heritability or stability data.

Before turning to consideration of the issue of stability and change in three areas, I would like to make reference to the work of Bloom (1964), which I hope has not been forgotten in the intervening 29 years. In preparing to write this chapter I went back and looked at Bloom's book and found that virtually every point made in this chapter, as well as others that could be made, were included in it. In particular, I would like to note the title of Bloom's book, *Stability and Change in Human Characteristics*, and three of his final conclusions: (a) The stability of a characteristic may be a function of the constancy of the environment; (b) the most powerful environments change individuals in nonuniform ways; and (c) measuring a characteristic at various time intervals "does not reveal in any detail exactly how it has been formed, the process by which the characteristic is maintained and reinforced, and the process by which the characteristic may be altered" (p. 222).

INTELLIGENCE AND TEMPERAMENT

In this section I consider issues of stability and change in relation to two areas of functioning considered to have a high degree of stability; they are intelligence and temperament. This stability generally is tied to a strong genetic contribution and a biological–constitutional underpinning. However, it should be noted that heritability estimates for intelligence and temperament have varied from time to time and investigator to investigator, with most recent estimates suggesting that perhaps 50% of the variance in each is attributable to nonstrictly genetic determinants (Carroll, 1992; Loehlin, 1992). In addition, as already noted, *genetic* need not mean fixed, and *biologically based* need not mean biologically determined. The discussion that follows may appear to be biased in the direction of change or plasticity rather than stability or fixity. This is not to deny the importance of genetic and biological factors, but to open the area for examination and to serve as a corrective force against what may have become an excessive focus on these factors (Dunn & Plomin, 1990; Plomin, Chipuer, & Loehlin, 1990). In addition, as is emphasized throughout this chapter, ultimately it is the issue of process that must be of concern to researchers.

Intelligence

In considering intelligence, I do not get into matters concerning the nature and measurement of intelligence, but restrict myself to the evidence concerning the stability and malleability of intelligence. From the inception of the study and assessment of intelligence, there have been fundamentally differing views concerning its malleability. As described by Locurto (1991), Galton believed in the genetic basis of intelligence and viewed it as unalterable, whereas Binet believed that intelligence was not fixed and that better schooling could contribute to changes in intelligence. Over time, views concerning the malleability of intelligence have varied markedly.

How Stable Is Intelligence?

Bloom (1964), in reviewing the literature, concluded that there was increased stability with age and for shorter periods of time over longer periods of time. A more recent review by Humphreys (1992) reached similar conclusions, with the note that "seemingly high stability over one year drops with surprising speed over several years" (p. 272). In an earlier article, he suggested that the genetic and environmental substrates for intelligence provide for change, not stability, and estimated the correlation between measures of intelligence at ages 8 and 18 as .28 (Humphreys & Davey, 1988).

How Fixed or Malleable Is Intelligence?

Many individuals cite evidence of the heritability of intelligence, as well as evidence of some stability and difficulties in changing intelligence, and conclude that it is relatively fixed. Bloom (1964) suggested that the effects of the environment are greatest during the early years of rapid development and estimated the effects of extreme environments at about 20 IQ points. The French adoption studies suggest that a mean increase of 14 IQ points and a reduction by a factor of 4 in the probability of repeating a grade are possible through improvements in social conditions (Schiff, Duyme, Dumaret, & Tomkiewicz, 1982). Ceci (1992) suggested that schooling can influence IQ scores but is skeptical about whether intelligence can be so influenced. Considering more generally the potential for change in cognitive abilities, Carroll (1992) reached the conclusion that

> we do not yet have adequate knowledge of what aspects of cognitive ability can be readily modified and what aspects are more resistant to such modification. Certainly there is need for such knowledge—knowledge that would help specify the limits to which particular abilities can be enhanced, and the conditions under which such enhancement could occur. (p. 269)

Do Group Data Reflect Individual Patterns?

Reviewing the literature that suggests that there is a heritable aspect of IQ and that substantial gains in IQ are possible, Turkheimer (1991) considered the nature–nurture controversy and concluded that part of the problem may revolve around the divergence of the individual- and group-differences traditions. Clearly, group differences are important, but they also may mask significant individual variation. As noted earlier, overall stability, as reflected in correlation coefficients, may mask significant gains in functioning (Ramey et al., 1989). By the same token, stable means may mask significant individual changes.

Temperament

In considering the issue of stability and change I do not get into the question of how temperament is to be defined and measured, except to note that some authors virtually equate temperament with personality and define it in terms of heritability and stability, whereas others see personality as a much broader term and leave room for environmental influences and change over the life course (Costa & McCrae, this volume; Loehlin, 1992; Strelau, 1983; Zuckerman, 1991). In either case, most discussions of temperament focus on variables such as emotionality, activity, and sociability

(Buss & Plomin, 1984). Here I focus on the two characteristics most emphasized by trait theorists; they are neuroticism and extraversion (sociability).

How Stable Is Temperament?

Once more, results concerning the stability of a characteristic are found to depend on the age at which the characteristic is measured, the interval between measurements, and how it is measured; later measures and shorter intervals show greater evidence of stability, as do self-ratings as opposed to observer ratings or laboratory-based measures (West & Graziano, 1989; Zuckerman, 1991). Correlation estimates vary according to these factors as well as whether or not they are corrected for attenuation (Block, 1971). Across the various studies, correlations range between .17 and .61 for Neuroticism and .32 to .63 for Extraversion. A third trait, Psychoticism, shows a range from .14 to .66 (Zuckerman, 1991). Even when similar age groups and measures are used, somewhat differing stability estimates show up. Reviewing the relevant literature, Zuckerman, a proponent of the trait–biological point of view, drew the following conclusions:

> Personality is generally consistent for short periods of a few years, from childhood to early adolescence and from early adolescence to late adolescence, but less consistent from adolescence to adult life: There is consistency, particularly for traits relating to sociability, but the degree of consistency is less than would be expected by those with a biological viewpoint who underestimate the influence of environment in interaction with the genotype. . . . Apparently, personality stabilizes between adolescence and young adult life and shows good consistency thereafter, with little change in consistency of traits. (pp. 68, 85)

In sum, once more there is evidence that measures taken over shorter intervals of time and later in life show greater stability than those taken over longer intervals of time and earlier in life.

How Fixed or Malleable Is Temperament?

There is less evidence concerning the malleability of temperament than for that of intelligence. However, consider the studies by Kagan for at least a clue in this area. Returning first to the issue of stability, Kagan and his co-workers (Kagan & Snidman, 1991a, 1991b) reported moderate stability in temperament (i.e., children designated as "inhibited to the unfamiliar" and "uninhibited to the unfamiliar") between the ages of four months and two years. Children in these two categories are members of extreme groups and constitute about one third of the children studied. A majority of the children in each of these groups maintained membership in that group through the eighth year of life. However, there also is evidence that many of the children (about half) changed their behavioral profile by age 8 and, in another study, about one third of the inhibited children at age 2 were not particularly shy at 3.5 years of age. Is this evidence of stability or change?

Are there any clues as to why some children change their behavioral pattern? Kagan (1992) noted that the mothers of children who changed were less protective and more likely to impose reasonable demands on the infants. Thus, evidence is presented that change can occur in a temperament behavior profile and that the change can be related to specific environmental conditions. Kagan went on to raise the interesting question of what to do with the data; that is, how should the children be classified? The suggestion is that they have retained the same constitution yet they behave differently, so how should they be classified relative to the children who have retained their constitution and behavior profile? The interesting thing about the challenge is that the assumption of constitutional stability is made in the absence, at least in terms of what is reported, of evidence. If "biology is not deterministic" (Kagan & Snidman, 1991a, p. 43) in the behavior profile sense, need it be otherwise fixed? That is, is it not conceivable that changes in biological functioning occur as a result of changes in environmental conditions? If so, what are the boundary conditions of such changes, and which conditions are most likely to produce which kinds of change?

COMMENT

In considering the literature relevant to intelligence and temperament similar conclusions are drawn: (a) Evidence of stability is greatest for later years and shorter intervals between measurements; (b) within group data there are important individual differences in degree of stability or change; (c) thus, there is evidence for both stability and change, but which evidence is more impressive lies in part in the eyes of the beholder; and (d) beyond the issue of fixity or change, there are boundary conditions within which change is possible. There are some clues as to what these boundary conditions are for intelligence, fewer for those relating to temperament, and generally little understanding of the exact conditions and processes involved in stability and change.

PERSONALITY

Turning to consideration of personality more broadly defined, the conclusions specified above for intelligence and temperament would appear to apply all the more. As Block (1971, 1977) in particular has so well demonstrated, there is evidence of considerable consistency over time, particularly once adulthood has been reached, with considerable individual variation. Does this suggest the conclusion that personality is unchanging or perhaps unchangeable, that it is set like plaster, at least once adulthood has been reached (Costa & McCrae, this volume)? Such a conclusion would hardly seem warranted for a variety of reasons. Consider these two questions: Is there longitudinal evidence that personality can change, even once adulthood has been reached? Are there factors that mitigate against change, the consideration of which leads one to conclude that personality is not necessarily like plaster once adulthood has been reached?

Evidence of Change

Even the research that reports the most stable picture of personality leaves significant room for change. First, with all of the evidence of similarity between monozygotic twins, and of passive and active forms of genetic influence on environments, it is striking that as twins grow up they grow apart (McCartney, Harris, & Bernieri, 1990). In other words, there is evidence that as twins grow older, they become increasingly different on trait measures of personality. Why is this the case, and what are the implications for the understanding of stability and change? Second, the correlations reported in longitudinal studies, even after they are corrected for attenuation, leave room for change no matter what the age or time interval considered. Third, as noted by many contributors and in the previous sections, group data mask important individual variations. Fourth, consideration of individual variables may mask significant change when the total organismic functioning of the individual is considered (Magnusson, 1990). For example, the data of Costa and McCrae (this volume) suggest that about three fifths of the variance in personality traits is stable over the full adult life span. Aside from the question of group data, suppose an individual remained absolutely stable on three of the Big Five traits (i.e., neuroticism, extraversion, openness, agreeableness, and conscientiousness) but changed (some? much?) on two of them. How different would the profile of scores look? In considering the individual as a whole, even a small shift in two scores could result in a major change in the personality profile, one that might even appear as abrupt or chaotic but that, in fact, might be quite organized and continuous.

Conditions Fostering Stability

It is interesting to find that stability often is considered to be the normal condition of personality and, thus, does not require explanation. This comes into sharp contrast with the situation in the field of psychotherapy, to be considered in the next section, in which the lack of change is considered worthy of study, particularly under the rubric of resistance. Are there factors that operate in favor of stability and against change? First, in that genetic factors contribute to individual selection of, and influence on, the environment, the groundwork for stability may be laid. Second, once a sense of self is established, the person may seek self-verification, perhaps even to the detriment of self-enhancement (Swann, 1990). Third, once patterns of relationships with others are established, friends and partners may operate in ways that confirm and maintain the established personality. It is a virtual truism in marital and family therapy, for example, that changes in one person often lead to efforts in other parts of the system to undo the change and return the system to its former state.

In sum, a number of factors within the person and outside the person may operate to foster personality stability as well as personality change. Neither stability nor change can be assumed as the normal state of the individual, whether in childhood or later in life. It is necessary to address the question of why people do and do not change, a question most clearly faced in the area of psychotherapy, as is discussed below.

STABILITY AND CHANGE IN PSYCHOTHERAPY

If there is any situation in which the question of why people do and do not change applies, it is in psychotherapy (Messer & Warren, 1990; Pervin, 1984). Dating back to Eysenck's (1952) challenge concerning the efficacy of psychotherapy, researchers in this area have tended to focus on demonstrating that therapeutic change does occur and on the relative efficacy of alternative treatments. However, more recently there has been a shift toward investigation of when and how therapeutic change occurs (Garfield, 1992; Goldfried, Greenberg, & Marmar, 1990; Lambert & Bergin, 1992). Within such research, recognition is given to the fact that group change data can mask enormous individual differences in the amount and quality of change, including the observation that some patients get worse.

A look at the questions of interest to researchers in this area makes it apparent why this literature should be of interest to personality psychologists more generally: How does one measure change? What are the factors influencing change? What are the mechanisms of change, and are they common to all forms of psychotherapy, or do they differ from approach to approach? What are the factors leading to resistance to change? How is change maintained and what causes relapse? In addition, there has been interest in how people change on their own in comparison with how they change through treatment (Heatherton & Nichols, 1992; Prochaska, DiClemente, & Norcross, 1992).

Most grand theories of personality include some explanation of why people do and do not change (Pervin, 1993). In Kelly's (1955) terms, this is more of a focus of convenience for some theories than for others. For example, it is a focus of convenience for the theories of Freud, Rogers, and Kelly but not for Big Five trait theorists. Within those theories that emphasize change, there are differing views as to the ease with which personality change occurs, the aspects of personality most central to substantive change, and the conditions that foster therapeutic change. To briefly illustrate each of these, the psychoanalytic theory of character suggests that therapeutic change can occur but that basic character change is unlikely, in contrast with Rogers's optimism concerning the potential for change. Whereas psychoanalysis focuses on emotional change (e.g., the corrective emotional experience), earlier behavioral approaches focused on overt behavior, and current cognitive approaches focus on changes in irrational and maladaptive thoughts. Finally, it is useful to note Rogers's landmark studies of the necessary and sufficient conditions of therapeutic change (Pervin, 1993).

What is the fundamental nature of therapeutic personality change? Unfortunately, from my standpoint, gone are the days when the process of psychotherapeutic change was formulated in terms of more general principles. I am speaking here in particular of the efforts of Dollard and Miller (1950) and Bandura (1961) to interpret therapeutic change within a learning framework. Despite the import of Bandura's (1986) later efforts to focus on self-efficacy as basic to a unifying theory of personality change, my own belief is that his earlier work continues to offer much insight, insight that may be lost in the face of the cognitive revolution. In his article "Psychotherapy as a Learning Process," Bandura (1961) discussed six learning mechanisms that were involved in the process of therapeutic change: counterconditioning, extinction, discrimination learning, reinforcement of desired behaviors, punishment of undesired behaviors, and imitation of the therapist or other models. At the end of the article, Bandura (1961) considered the factors that interfered with an integration of the practice of psychotherapy with other work in the area of learning and motivation. This issue remains worthy of further attention at this time. Even the current cognitive therapy approaches are only minimally grounded in basic principles of cognitive and social cognitive psychology (Brewin, 1989).

As noted, attention must be given not only to why people do change but to why people do not change. Even the most optimistic psychologists at times bemoan the difficulties of change. Consider, for example, Watson's (1928) statement: "I used to feel quite hopeful of reconditioning even adult personalities. . . . But with humans as lazy as they are about themselves . . . the zebra can as easily change his stripes as the adult his personality" (p. 138), and Ellis's (1987) suggestion that people have a biological tendency to think irrationally in ways that interfere with healthy psychological functioning.

The issue of difficulties in producing change generally is considered under the rubric of resistance (Wachtel, 1982). Although some behavior therapists attribute the lack of change in therapy to the poor application of therapeutic principles, most behavior and all psychodynamic therapists recognize forces within the individual that resist change. Fundamental to this resistance is anxiety, either in terms of the uncertainty associated with change or in terms of exposure to old dangers and risks. The former is particularly emphasized by more cognitive theorists such as Kelly (1955) and Swann (1990), the latter by more psychodynamically oriented therapists (Wachtel, 1982). Many therapists would suggest that Mowrer's (1950) "neurotic paradox" still makes good sense, that is, that in order to change patients must face previously frightening situations, but there is a lengthy past history of reinforcement for avoidance. Finally, people often find it hard to change because change represents a blow to their narcissism, as if to change is to acknowledge that they are not good enough the way they are.

In sum, research in the area recognizes both stability and change, that some kinds of change are more possible than others, that change may or may not be followed by relapse, and that group rates mask important individual differences. After a lengthy period of attempting to demonstrate that change does occur, attention has focused on how it occurs—the question of process. Within such an analysis it is recognized that neither stability nor change need be considered the natural state or path of the organism; each calls for further understanding and explanation.

SUMMARY

In this chapter I have attempted to make a number of points that I believe are relevant to a variety of areas that address the issue of personality stability and change. These can be summarized in five points: First, research in the area of personality stability and change involves issues of definition, terminology, measurement, and conclusions drawn from results that often can be read in multiple ways. Second, there is evidence both for stability and change. This is particularly the case when individual rather than group data are considered. It may also be the case when system properties rather than isolated units are considered. Third, in most aspects of personality functioning the boundary conditions within which change is possible are not yet known. Given such uncertainty, to some extent conclusions drawn concerning the potential for change lie in the eyes of the beholder. Fourth, rather than focusing on the issue of stability versus change, or how much stability and how much change occur, there is a need to focus on the issue of process. Within such a context, neither stability nor change should be considered the natural state of the organism with only the other requiring explanation. There are forces operating, internal and external to the organism, both in favor of stability and in favor of change. As many have suggested, life may be a constant balancing of these two sets of forces. Finally, it is necessary to establish common sets of processes concerning stability and change encompassing the many areas of concern to personality psychologists.

REFERENCES

Bandura, A. (1961). Psychotherapy as a learning process. *Psychological Bulletin*, 58, 143–159.

Bandura, A. (1986). *Social foundations of thought and action.* Englewood Cliffs, NJ: Prentice Hall.

Block, J. (1971). *Lives through time.* Berkeley, CA: Bancroft Books.

Block, J. (1977). Advancing the psychology of personality: Paradigmatic shift or improving the quality of research. In D. Magnusson & N. S. Endler (Eds.), *Personality at the crossroads: Current issues in interactional psychology* (pp. 37–63). Hillsdale, NJ: Erlbaum.

Bloom, B. S. (1964). *Stability and change in human characteristics.* New York: Wiley.

Brewin, C. R. (1989). Cognitive change processes in psychotherapy. *Psychological Bulletin*, 96, 379–394.

Buss, A. H., & Plomin, R. A. (1984). *Temperament: Early developing personality traits.* Hillsdale, NJ: Erlbaum.

Carroll, J. B. (1992). Cognitive abilities: The state of the art. *Psychological Science*, 3, 266–270.

Caspi, A., & Bem, D. J. (1990). Personality continuity and change across the life course. In L. A. Pervin (Ed.), *Handbook of personality: Theory and research* (pp. 549–575). Hillsdale, NJ: Erlbaum.

Caspi, A., Bem, D. J., & Elder, G. H., Jr. (1989). Continuities and consequences of interactional styles across the life course. *Journal of Personality*, 57, 3706.

Caspi, A., & Moffitt, T. (in press). When do individual differences matter? A paradoxical theory of personality coherence. *Psychological Inquiry*.

Ceci, S. J. (1992). Schooling and intelligence. *Psychological Science Agenda*, September/October, 7–9.

Dollard, J., & Miller, N. E. (1950). *Personality and psychotherapy.* New York: McGraw-Hill.

Dunn, J., & Plomin, R. (1990). *Separate lives.* New York: Basic Books.

Ellis, A. (1987). The impossibility of achieving consistently good mental health. *American Psychologist*, 42, 364–375.

Eysenck, H. J. (1952). The effects of psychotherapy: An evaluation. *Journal of Consulting Psychology*, 16, 319–324.

Garfield, S. L. (1992). Major issues in psychotherapy research. In D. K. Freedheim (Ed.), *History of psychotherapy* (pp. 335–359). Washington, DC: American Psychological Association.

Goldfried, M. R., Greenberg, L. S., & Marmar, C. (1990). Individual psychotherapy: Process and outcome. *Annual Review of Psychology, 41,* 659–688.

Greenberg, L. S., & Safran, J. D. (1989). Emotion in psychotherapy. *American Psychologist, 44,* 19–29.

Hanson, R. A. (1975). Consistency and stability of home environmental measures related to IQ. *Child Development, 46,* 470–480.

Heatherton, T. F., & Nichols, P. A. (1992). *Micronarrative accounts of successful and unsuccessful life change experiences.* Unpublished manuscript.

Humphreys, L. G. (1992). Commentary: What both critics and users of ability tests need to know. *Psychological Science, 3,* 271–274.

Humphreys, L. G., & Davey, T. C. (1988). Continuity in intellectual growth from 12 months to 9 years. *Intelligence, 12,* 183–197.

Kagan, J. (1992, August). *Personality and the processes of change.* Paper presented at the 100th Annual Convention of the American Psychological Association, Washington, DC.

Kagan, J., & Snidman, N. (1991a). Infant predictors of inhibited and uninhibited profiles. *Psychological Science, 2,* 40–44.

Kagan, J., & Snidman, N. (1991b). Temperamental factors in human development. *American Psychologist, 46,* 856–862.

Kelly, G. A. (1955). *The psychology of personal constructs.* New York: Wiley.

Lambert, M. J., & Bergin, A. E. (1992). Achievements and limitations of psychotherapy research. In D. K. Freedheim (Ed.), *History of psychotherapy* (pp. 360–390). Washington, DC: American Psychological Association.

LeDoux, J. E. (1989). Cognitive–emotional interactions in the brain. *Cognition and Emotion, 3,* 267–289.

LeDoux, J. E., Romanski, L., & Xagoraris, A. (1989). Indelibility of subcortical emotional memories. *Journal of Cognitive Neuroscience, 1,* 238–243.

Locurto, C. (1991). *Sense and nonsense about IQ.* New York: Praeger.

Loehlin, J. C. (1992). *Genes and environment in personality development.* Newbury Park, CA: Sage.

Magnusson, D. (1990). Personality development from an interactional perspective. In L. A. Pervin (Ed.), *Handbook of personality: Theory and research* (pp. 193–222). New York: Guilford Press.

McCartney, K., Harris, M. J., & Bernieri, F. (1990). Growing up and growing apart: A developmental meta-analysis of twin studies. *Psychological Bulletin, 107,* 226–237.

Messer, S. B., & Warren, S. (1990). Personality change and psychotherapy. In L. A. Pervin (Ed.), *Handbook of personality: Theory and research* (pp. 371–398). New York: Guilford Press.

Mowrer, O. H. (1950). *Learning theory and personality dynamics.* New York: Ronald Press.

Ozer, D. J., & Gjerde, P. F. (1989). Patterns of personality consistency and change from childhood through adolescence. *Journal of Personality, 57,* 483–507.

Pervin, L. A. (1984). *Current controversies and issues in personality.* New York: Wiley.

Pervin, L. A. (1993). *Personality: Theory and research* (6th ed.). New York: Wiley.

Plomin, R., Chipuer, H. M., & Loehlin, J. C. (1990). Behavioral genetics and personality. In L. A. Pervin (Ed.), *Handbook of personality: Theory and research* (pp. 225–243). New York: Guilford Press.

Plomin, R., DeFries, J. C., & Loehlin, J. C. (1977). Genotype–environment interaction and correlation in the analysis of human behavior. *Psychological Bulletin, 84,* 309–322.

Prochaska, J. O., DiClemente, C. C., & Norcross, J. C. (1992). In search of how people change. *American Psychologist, 47,* 1102–1114.

Rachman, S. (1981). The primacy of affect: Some theoretical implications. *Behaviour Research and Therapy, 19,* 279–290.

Ramey, C. T., Lee, M. W., & Burchinal, M. R. (1989). Developmental plasticity and predictability: Consequences of ecological change. In M. H. Bornstein & N. A. Krasnegor (Eds.), *Stability and continuity in mental development* (pp. 217–233). Hillsdale, NJ: Erlbaum.

Schiff, M., Duyme, M., Dumaret, A., & Tomkiewicz, S. (1982). How much *could* we boost scholastic achievement and IQ scores? A direct answer from a French adoption study. *Cognition, 12,* 165–196.

Strelau, J. (1983). *Temperament, personality, and arousal.* San Diego, CA: Academic Press.

Swann, W. B., Jr. (1990). To be adored or to be known? The interplay of self-enhancement and self-verification. In E. T. Higgins & R. M. Sorrentino (Eds.), *Handbook of motivation and cognition* (pp. 408–448). New York: Guilford Press.

Turkheimer, E. (1991). Individual and group differences in adoption studies of IQ. *Psychological Bulletin, 110,* 392–405.

Wachs, T. D. (1992). *The nature of nurture.* Newbury Park, CA: Sage.

Wachtel, P. (Ed.). (1982). *Resistance: Psychodynamic and behavioral approaches.* New York: Plenum Press.

Watson, J. B. (1928). *The ways of behaviorism.* New York: Harper.

West, S. G., & Graziano, W. G. (1989). Long-term stability and change in personality: An introduction. *Journal of Personality, 57,* 175–194.

Zuckerman, M. (1991). *Psychobiology and personality.* Cambridge, England: Cambridge University Press.

CONCLUSION

15

CAN PERSONALITY CHANGE?

JOEL L. WEINBERGER

After an introduction and 13 chapters by leading figures in the field, what can we conclude? As is often the case when questions are posed in an apparently straightforward manner, the answer turns out to be quite complex and not straightforward at all. Whether personality can change or not depends on how it is defined and measured (Costa & McCrae; Heatherton & Nichols; Helson & Stewart; McAdams; Pervin; all this volume), on how stability and change are assessed (Alder & Scher; Helson & Stewart; Nesselroade & Boker; Pervin; all this volume), and even on the worldview that informs an investigator's thinking (Davis & Millon, this volume).

So what can we conclude? I agree with Pervin (this volume) that the field of psychology has a way of polarizing issues that often leads to unproductive debate. I therefore softpedal the sometimes serious disagreements voiced by some of the authors of this volume. (The reader can find all of the nuances and disparities in the body of the chapters themselves.) Instead, I focus on what I perceive to be a number of themes that emerge from the chapters, on which all might be able to agree. Whenever I can, I make an effort to integrate these themes with one another. Additionally, I briefly discuss psychotherapy and some change agents that may be responsible for its efficacy. Psychotherapy represents the most sustained and well-documented effort to trigger psychological change. Millions of people look to psychotherapeutic treatment as a means of achieving significant change in their lives. What changes in the course of such treatment, and what accounts for that change, can afford us valuable insights into personality and the potential for personality change.

METHODOLOGICAL ISSUES

The first theme that needs to be addressed is that of method. Any conclusions drawn are necessarily bound to the adequacy of the methods used to reach them. Method therefore logically precedes other considerations. The chapters written by Alder and Scher and by Nesselroade and Boker explore these issues in some depth. These authors agree that the best way to study personality is longitudinally. DiClemente also makes this point, and no contributor says otherwise. In fact, several rely predominantly on longitudinal data to make their points (Costa & McCrae; Franz; Helson & Stewart). So there is general agreement on the value of longitudinal studies. The best way to study personality stability and change is longitudinally.

Alder and Scher, as well as Nesselroade and Boker, go beyond the mere championing of longitudinal research. They offer valuable suggestions concerning collection and analysis of such data. They recommend multiple measurement across large segments of the life span. DiClemente supports this by showing how multiple measurement could illuminate the vagaries of addictive behavior. Again, I detect no disagreement among the various authors on these points. So it can be concluded that longitudinal studies should use multiple measurement and should cover large segments of the life span.

Some authors go into even more depth regarding method. DiClemente points out that even several assessments, covering many years, could present a false picture of stability of drinking habits (and presumably personality). Periods of sobriety and shifts in a person's willingness to alter his or her drinking habits could be missed if assessments did not coincide with the occurrence of these events. Similarly, Nesselroade and Boker warn of what they term *periodicity*. If a phenomenon under investigation waxes and wanes at regular intervals and measurement coincides with those intervals, a misleading picture of stability may result. To avoid this problem, they suggest nonregular collection of data and *bursts* of measurement in which the times data are collected are spaced close together. Their simulations demonstrate the potential value of this strategy for overcoming periodicity. They have therefore provided a valuable way to capture patterns of stability and change, unconfounded by time of measurement. So the ideal personality study would be longitudinal, cover large segments of life, and involve repeated measurement that would be collected at irregular intervals and in concentrated bursts.

To analyze longitudinal data, Nesselroade and Boker call for the utilization of multivariate methods. These allow researchers to make use of combinations of variables to represent any given personality dimension. This lessens their dependence on any one necessarily imperfect measure and enables them to triangulate on the dimension of interest, thereby increasing the likelihood of capturing it. Such methods also allow investigators to identify patterns of relationships across several variables. Thus, longitudinal studies should cover long periods of time and should be characterized by bursts of multiple measures. Multivariate techniques can then be brought to bear on these data in order to tease out their meaning.

There is disagreement on the specifics of analysis, however. Nesselroade and Boker, as well as Alder and Scher, argue that nonlinear models offer the best approach to the analysis of longitudinal data. Alder and Scher suggest that analysis proceed by way of growth curves fit to the data or shaped by theoretical considerations. DiClemente seems to favor a similar approach. Costa and McCrae, on the other hand, prefer the more traditional measures of mean-level change and test–retest correlations. The simulations of Alder and Scher, as well as those of Nesselroade and Boker, seem to provide impressive support for their positions (use of nonlinear models). But their suggested techniques have not yet been widely applied to actual (and doubtless messier) longitudinal data, whereas Costa and McCrae have done extensive work with real-world data. As Davis and Millon point out, real longitudinal data sets are often characterized by relatively small samples and imprecise measures. Findings are therefore likely to be somewhat fuzzy, and any number of curves could be made to fit to them. As a consequence, I consider the issue unresolved pending application of nonlinear models to more actual data sets. The results of such analyses might then be compared with those of more traditional procedures, applied to the same data, and the coherence of the alternative findings would speak for itself.

STABILITY AND CHANGE FINDINGS

Many studies have already been completed and their results reported. Several of the chapters present these findings. What do they have to say about stability and change? There seems to be general agreement that personality can and does change through about age 30. There is less agreement on what happens past this point in the life cycle, however. Some argue that there is great stability and little change (Brody; Costa & McCrae); others argue that there may be continuing and sometimes powerful change through adulthood (Baumeister; Franz; Helson & Stewart; Miller & C'deBaca).

I believe that these apparently opposing points of view concerning stability and change can be subsumed by the conclusions drawn by Block (1971) over 20 years ago and echoed by Helson and Stewart in this volume. There is substantial evidence for both personality stability and change. In my opinion, the chapters in this book demonstrate this quite convincingly. The trick is to understand what changes and what does not, when to expect stability and when to expect change, and why stability and change occur as they do. I believe that the chapters offer some clues to understanding these issues.

What Changes and What Remains Stable?

Costa and McCrae's data support the notion that what they term *basic tendencies* remain stable after age 30. By basic tendencies they mean five factors that consistently emerge when self-report personality questionnaires are factor-analyzed. These have been termed the Big Five (see Goldberg, 1993, and John, 1990, for more extensive discussions). Costa and McCrae (also see McCrae & Costa, 1990) have labeled these factors extraversion, agreeableness, conscientiousness, neuroticism, and openness to experience (there is some debate over what to call this latter factor; see, e.g., Goldberg, 1993).

The basic tendencies, as conceptualized by Costa and McCrae, represent abstract inclinations that can be manifested in diverse ways. Thus, two people could score high on Neuroticism, but one shows it through night terrors whereas the other exhibits obsessive rituals. Similarly, the same person could consistently score high in Neuroticism across many years but have panic attacks at the first assessment and paranoid ideation at the second. Costa and McCrae term the actual form the basic tendencies take in the real world *characteristic adaptations.* They are visible in a person's habits, attitudes, ambitions, relationships, interests, and so on. These can and do change through adulthood. Openness to experience is particularly likely to show up differently in concrete behaviors and thoughts through the life cycle.

Essentially, as I understand it, Costa and McCrae argue that people's capacities and limitations undergo little change past 30, but the ways in which they manage and express these qualities can change quite a bit. Viewed in this way, Helson and Stewart are not in such radical disagreement with Costa and McCrae. Helson and Stewart argue that personality change in adulthood occurs because associations around relatively constant wishes, motives, or basic beliefs change. The associations change; the basic wishes, motives, and beliefs may not. These constants can be identified with Costa and McCrae's basic tendencies, whereas changes in associations to these dimensions (conceptualized as new scripts, life-styles, etc.) can represent their characteristic adaptations. The change data cited by Helson and Stewart can be fit into the above scheme with relative ease. Thus, mothers displayed increases in responsibility, self-control, tolerance, and femininity (Helson, Mitchell, & Moane, 1984); and family oriented women expressed increases in generativity (Stewart & Vandewater,1993), as compared with nonmothers and career-oriented women, respectively. Conversely, women in the labor force were more independent than homemakers (Helson & Picano, 1990). These are real changes and certainly represent (characteristic) adaptations to life choices.

Franz's findings can be similarly understood. She reports that preoccupations change, from 31 to 41, in the direction of decreased agency and increased communion. Such thought patterns can be construed as adaptive responses to changing life situations.

PERSONALITY MODELS AND THEIR RELATIONSHIP TO STABILITY AND CHANGE

Basic Tendencies Versus Characteristic Adaptations

As discussed in the introduction (Heatherton & Nichols), a major issue in determining whether personality changes is the definition of personality that is adopted. In Costa and McCrae's model (see chapter 2, Figure 1), basic tendencies are central and constitute the core of personality. Although characteristic adaptations are also included in the model, they are assigned secondary importance. However, there is no a priori reason that this must be so. The chapters by Helson and Stewart and by Franz are more focused on what Costa and McCrae call characteristic adaptations. These are important objects of study, and they clearly change. Franz, as well as Helson and Stewart, seems to be saying that the way people manage their resources and the way this is affected by life's exigencies constitute the central questions of personality. I see no logical reason for preferring one over the other. Nor do I see a necessary theoretical or empirical advantage to either.[1]

I believe that these two ways of looking at personality can explain the apparently disparate conclusions reached by Brody and by DiClemente. Both attempt to understand important personality issues by way of analogy to their area of expertise. Brody bases his arguments on what is known about intelligence (Brody, 1992); DiClemente makes use of his understanding of the addictions (DiClemente, 1993). Brody concludes that personality is genetically based and is relatively stable (although he concedes that the analogy to intelligence was not perfect); DiClemente concludes that al-

---

[1]As I discuss later, McAdams (this volume) offers an imaginative model that can incorporate both viewpoints.

though personality change is complex and difficult, it does occur. Brody begins with a basic, relatively built-in capacity (intelligence). He therefore concludes, as do Costa and McCrae, that personality is stable. DiClemente begins with an adaptation to the environment (or more accurately a mis-adaptation, i.e., addictive behavior) and concludes, along with Franz and with Helson and Stewart, that there is real potential for personality change.

Finally, even within the basic tendencies model proposed by Costa and McCrae, there is room for substantial change as well as stability. These authors conclude that two thirds of the variance in personality (defined as basic tendencies) is stable after age 30. This represents substantial stability. As Pervin points out, however, this also leaves room for substantial change. If two thirds of personality is stable, then one third is not.

Levels of Personality

McAdams offers an innovative model of personality capable of reconciling Costa and McCrae's with Helson and Stewart's position. McAdams does not assign primacy to the aspect of personality emphasized by either. Instead, he posits three parallel and noninteracting levels of personality. These levels are said to exhibit differential susceptibility to change.

Level I of McAdams's model corresponds to Costa and McCrae's basic tendencies, and McAdams explicitly ties it in with their work and with the Big Five. Level I is relatively stable through adulthood. It consists of qualities the person possesses, independent of environmental exigencies. It provides descriptors for one who is seeking to describe a relative stranger.

Level II seems to correspond with Costa and McCrae's characteristic adaptations. Personality at this level is dependent on contextual and motivational issues. It is best construed in terms of relatively conscious articulations of what the person is trying to accomplish during a given period of his or her life. If Level I provides descriptors for the outside observer, Level II provides moment-to-moment consistency for the person himself or herself. It represents the person as viewed from the inside. This level can subsume Franz's findings, as well as those reported by Helson and Stewart, because change as a function of altered circumstances and developmental demands is expected at this level. Thus, Franz's finding that people become more preoccupied with generativity and communion from age 31 to age 41 may be viewed as a function of the normative demands of raising children. Similarly, as Helson and Stewart report, women involved in family, compared with those more identified with careers, are on different life paths and should show differences that correspond with these life circumstances.

The final level, Level III, seems to me to represent the existential personality. Here the person is concerned with constructing a sense of meaning for his or her functioning as an evolving person. McAdams conceptualizes this level of personality functioning as a struggle to create a viable identity or life myth. Change is not only possible, it occurs continuously at this level. Life is seen as a story unfolding, and change takes the direction of efforts to improve the narrative form of this life story. McAdams has little data to support this last intriguing level, but I think that the work of Miller and C'deBaca, reviewed later, can be construed in these terms. As I discuss, the whole focus of their subjects' lives changed. The meaning of their lives was radically altered, and they reported undergoing what amounts to existential change.

Personality as a Product of Evolution

Buss's evolutionary model of personality represents the final notion of personality offered in this book. Here personality is conceptualized as consisting of specialized psychological mechanisms designed to solve various adaptive problems. These mechanisms have presumably arisen through evolutionary selection. Stability and change are understood to be attributable to these selection processes.

Stability results from a combination of causes. The first are preexisting, evolutionary-based (and so genetic), psychological mechanisms that lead to certain types of adaptive behaviors (like ducks imprinting on the first moving object they see; Lorenz, 1935). The Big Five fall under this heading because they are seen, in this context, as resources a person can draw on to solve adaptive problems. Differences in the genetic endowment of these resources explain individual differences in the Big Five. This also corresponds to Brody's position concerning the genetics of personality. Stability may also result from recurrent adaptive problems that lead to consistent solutions and to retention of successful coping strategies.

Like stability, change is also triggered by a variety of conditions. Change becomes necessary when a new adaptive problem makes an appearance. Such an event will select for an adaptive solution if survival is to be ensured. A solution could arise from genetically based capacities not yet realized. Buss offers the development of callouses as an example of such an occurrence. The potential to form callouses is always present but only becomes manifest when friction applied to the hands triggers the adaptive response of toughening of the skin. Change can also occur when strategies of coping are altered due to selection pressures. The changes described by Franz and by Helson and Stewart are presumably attributable to such events. As life circumstances change, latent coping mechanisms emerge and new mechanisms are selected.

Gazzaniga (1992) has offered an even more radical evolutionary view. In his model, all of a person's capacities are built in through evolutionary forces. The environment then selectively triggers the relevant mechanisms. More specifically, everyone has a unique set of neural nets with all of the capacities and potential responses he or she will ever possess. These capabilities are then brought out or differentially selected by the environment. People do not learn, they only make use of what is already built into their brains.

Which Model?

The range of possible models of personality has barely been sampled, let alone exhausted, by the three presented in this volume. This is an area in which psychology suffers from an embarrassment of riches. Personality theories range from Freud's psychodynamic model (see, e.g., Freud, 1937/ 1964), emphasizing unconscious personality determinants, to Kelly's (1955) model of personality constructs, emphasizing conscious cognitive bipolar personality dimensions. And there is everything in between. (The interested reader is referred to Pervin, 1993, and Brody, 1988, for cogent overviews.) There is as yet no definitive way to choose between these theories. All can account for some but not all of the experiential and empirical data. For purposes of this volume, there is no point in reviewing the various points of view. Much more needs to be learned about the origins and development of personality before an intelligent choice can be made. It is probable that an entirely new model incorporating and integrating the insights of each will be required.

PROCESSES OF STABILITY AND CHANGE

It seems clear that stability and change both occur. How can the processes underlying each be described? The chapters by Baumeister and by Miller and C'deBaca are both expressly concerned with such description. The former describes processes underlying the maintenance and severing of commitments. The latter deals with enormous, radical change affecting the very foundations of the personality. Both describe change from the perspective of the changer.

The Crystallization of Discontent

According to Baumeister, commitments are maintained (remain stable) by a combination of attributions, selective attention, and defensive operations. A person in a stable commitment sees problems as isolated, temporary, and extrinsic to the relationship. Positive aspects of the relationship are viewed as interrelated, permanent, and characteristic of the relationship. There is a tendency to selectively attend to positive aspects to the relative neglect of negative aspects of the relationship. Defensive operations can also come into play, as when a person denies or otherwise deflects a relevant negative relationship experience.

Baumeister's central process of change involves what he terms the *crystallization of discontent*. Commitments tend to change when the heretofore isolated negative aspects of the relationship begin to become connected in a person's mind. This linking of problems previously seen as unrelated constitutes the crystallization of discontent. The person eventually comes to see a broad pattern of persistent problems—whereas before he or she saw isolated, temporary glitches—and breaks off the relationship.

Often, the crystallization of discontent comes together around a specific event that seems to symbolize and call attention to the negative aspects of the relationship. Baumeister refers to this event as a *focal incident*. Subjectively, it seems to provide the person with the realization that the relationship is a negative one. It therefore serves as a catalyst for change. This strongly resembles what Alexander (1963) termed a *corrective emotional experience*. He coined this term to describe an event occurring within psychotherapy and involving the ameliorative coupling of insight with powerful affect. It is brought about when a patient faces a troubling issue he or she has been avoiding and experiences its personal and emotional significance without being overwhelmed or condemned. (I return to this therapeutic principle when I discuss change in psychotherapy.)

What is particularly impressive about Baumeister's chapter is his use of interdisciplinary sources to support his views. Data from several disciplines, with different biases and methods, all pointing to the same phenomenon makes for a compelling case. Thus, marital breakups and defections from religious groups are both apparently preceded by a crystallization of discontent.[2] And Heatherton and Nichols (1992) found that spontaneously generated stories of successful life change usually contained accounts of crystallizations of discontent, whereas failed efforts at change generally did not.

Quantum Change

Baumeister seeks to understand normative commitments. Miller and C'deBaca have bigger fish to fry. Their objective is to examine abrupt and complete transformations of personality, which they term *quantum change*. Their prototype of such change is St. Paul's conversion from Saul of Tarsus, a major persecutor of Christians, to Paul, arguably the greatest proponent of Christianity in its history. A more recent example concerns the founder of personology, Henry Murray. Murray (1967; Robinson, 1992) reported that he altered his whole approach to life and became a psychologist after reading Herman Melville's *Moby Dick*. In McAdams's terms, Miller and

---

[2]Malcolm X's withdrawal from the Nation of Islam is a dramatic and well-known example of such an occurrence (X & Haley, 1964).

C'deBaca are concerned with Level III of the personality (i.e., the meaning of life).

Early writings by James (1902) as well as the more recent work of Loder (1981) showed that sudden conversion or massive (quantum) personality change is most often preceded by conflict and despair. Miller and C'deBaca confirm this in their sample of people who have undergone quantum change. These individuals reported a high level of negative life experiences in the year prior to their change experience. Thus, a high level of stress seems to be a precondition for quantum change.

The actual change experience involves a scanning of the environment for resolution of the stress followed by a sudden and forceful insight, intuition, or vision appearing on the fringes of consciousness. This results in great relief of the previously felt tension along with a release of pent-up energy. This energy is then used to construct new behaviors and thought patterns centering on the vision or insight. Miller and C'deBaca report that individuals who have had such experiences report that they reorganize their phenomenal world in profound ways. This sounds much like the focal incident described by Baumeister or like Alexander's (1963) corrective emotional experience, but on a much grander scale. It also seems like a profound change in what McAdams calls Level III with repercussions affecting Level II as well. That is, identity or the life myth changes (Level III), and this impacts on life tasks (Level II).

The subjects in Miller and C'deBaca's study were examined after they changed so that the data were retrospective. As these authors point out, and as other chapters in this book make clear, it would have been better to have collected prospective longitudinal data, that is, to assess individuals before and after their change experiences. This turns out to be impractical, however. Miller and C'deBaca report that the number of quantum changers in the population is low, and no one knows how to identify those likely to undergo such change. I wonder, however, if anyone has ever combed through existing longitudinal data sets to determine if they contain any such individuals. They could easily have been disguised by the usual aggregated statistics and overlooked as a result.

I have constructed a simple simulated data set to show how easily this could occur (see Table 1). Hypothetically, I have measured Neuroticism (one of the Big Five), on a scale of 1–9, at two points in time. When I correlate Time 1 with Time 2, I obtain a test–retest correlation of .66. A t test shows no difference between the means at these two times, $t(49) = -0.34$; $p = .74$. These findings exactly parallel those related by Costa and McCrae, stability of personality as traditionally reported. But an investigation of the individual data shows that three individuals (Subjects 9, 19, and 46) out of the 50 (6%) underwent as much change as the scale would allow. Their personalities certainly were not stable. If even a few such powerfully altered individuals exist in actual data sets, the knowledge

TABLE 1
Simulation of Two Assessments of Neuroticism

Subject	Scores at Time 1	Scores at Time 2
1	1	2
2	3	2
3	3	4
4	4	4
5	5	4
6	5	6
7	7	7
8	8	8
9	9	1
10	2	1
11	2	2
12	3	3
13	4	4
14	5	5
15	6	6
16	7	8
17	8	7
18	9	9
19	1	9
20	2	2
21	4	3
22	4	4
23	5	7
24	6	6
25	7	7
26	8	6
27	9	9
28	1	1
29	2	2
30	3	3
31	4	4
32	5	5
33	6	6
34	7	7
35	8	8
36	9	9
37	1	1
38	2	2
39	3	3
40	4	4
41	5	2
42	6	6
43	7	7
44	8	9
45	9	9
46	1	9
47	2	2
48	3	3
49	4	4
50	5	5

gained from intensive investigation of their personalities before and after the change would more than repay the effort of combing through the data sets to find them.

There is another potential way to locate quantum changers and obtain data from before and after their change experiences. Study of psychotherapy process and outcome research might yield such individuals. Miller and C'deBaca report that 20% of their subjects were in psychotherapy; what percentage of those in psychotherapy have quantum change experiences, however, is unknown. After all, therapeutic patients come into treatment because they are experiencing conflict, distress, and even despair. And they do change (Smith, Glass, & Miller, 1980). Surely some of them have undergone quantum change. Examination of this literature might prove rewarding.

If such data could be obtained, the analytic techniques espoused in some of the chapters could be applied to explicate the nature and process of quantum change. Nesselroade and Boker, as well as Davis and Millon, recommend the use of dynamical systems and, more specifically, chaos theory. These techniques can make sense of large effects proceeding out of small changes in circumstances. Nesselroade and Boker specifically discuss the modeling and plotting of sudden jumps, which they term *bifurcations*. The tools exist; all that is needed are the data.

SYNOPSIS OF MAJOR POINTS

Let me very briefly summarize what I believe these chapters have shown. First, the best way to study personality stability and change is longitudinally. Several chapters concern themselves with how best to conduct such studies and analyze the data they yield. The next point is that the model of personality chosen dictates what the investigator looks for and therefore whether he or she is likely to find stability or change. Unfortunately, there is no universally consensual theory of personality to guide our search. This contributes mightily to the murkiness of the stability versus change issue. Finally, even given this unclear state of affairs, there is compelling evidence for both stability and change, depending on what variables are examined and what level of the personality is taken as the object of study.

PSYCHOTHERAPEUTIC CHANGE

What about purposive efforts to alter personality? As stated at the beginning of this chapter, the best documented and most common means used to effect personality change is psychotherapy. The contributors to this volume are largely concerned with naturally occurring stability and change.

For the most part, they take no position on whether personality can be altered through planned interventions such as psychotherapy. Brody and Pervin are exceptions to this generalization. Brody argues that interventions have little effect on personality; Pervin suggests that psychotherapy can affect it. I believe that a brief look at psychotherapy is in order.

The psychotherapy process and outcome literature are huge, and I do not attempt to review them here. The interested reader can obtain a comprehensive overview in the upcoming *Handbook of Psychotherapy and Behavior Change* (Bergin & Garfield, in press). I instead briefly outline some of the major conclusions, and then describe a model for making sense of them and for explaining psychotherapeutic change processes.

Since Smith et al., (1980) published their comprehensive meta-analysis of psychotherapy outcome studies, the efficacy of psychotherapy has been generally accepted.[3] In addition to showing that a person is better off in treatment than not, the data indicate that no therapy is superior to any other (Lambert, Shapiro, & Bergin, 1986; Luborsky, Singer, & Luborsky, 1975; Smith et al., 1980; Stiles, Shapiro, & Elliot, 1986). Many of these reviewers entertained the possibility that this is so because the same general factors, cutting across the different treatment modalities, account for positive change in all forms of therapy. These have been termed the *common factors* of psychotherapy (cf. Weinberger, 1993).

Common Factors of Psychotherapy

I have reviewed the history as well as the empirical literature relevant to common factors (Weinberger, 1993). On the basis of this review, I proposed a set of common factors responsible for therapeutic change in a variety of therapeutic modalities (Weinberger, 1990, 1992, 1993). The first of these is the patient–therapist relationship. This can be divided into two aspects: transference and the therapeutic alliance.

The Patient–Therapist Relationship: Transference

Transference is a uniquely psychoanalytic concept first proposed by Freud (1912/1958). It involves a patient's misconstrual of his or her relationship with the therapist because he or she treats it similarly to past (usually parental) relationships. That is, the patient misunderstands the present because he or she is stuck in early modes of relating and transfers these past interpretations to the current therapeutic situation (Fenichel, 1945). Observation of these distortions allows the therapist to understand the development and expression of the patient's difficulties. Empirical re-

---

[3]It is generally but not universally accepted. Prioleau, Murdock, and Brody (1983) and Brody (1983, 1990) offer a dissenting view.

search supports the therapeutic value of attending to and working with the transference (Luborsky, Crits-Cristoph, & Mellon, 1986; Luborsky et al., 1985; Strupp & Binder, 1984).

The Patient–Therapist Relationship: The Working Alliance

The working alliance was also first identified by Freud (1910/1957) but has since been integrated into most other forms of treatment. It involves the therapist and patient feeling well-disposed toward one another and having a sense of working together collaboratively. Empirical data solidly support the contribution of the working alliance to positive therapeutic change (Gaston, 1990).

Exposure

The second common factor is exposure of the patient to the anxiety-provoking source of his or her difficulty. In dynamically oriented treatments, this is achieved through free association, dream analysis, analysis of parapraxes, and analysis of the transference. Cognitive treatments encourage recording and exploration of negative and anxiety-provoking thoughts (Beck, 1976; Beck, Rush, Shaw, & Emery, 1979; Ellis, 1962). Behavior therapy exposes the patient to imagined or real-life examples of fearful stimuli (Emmelkamp, 1986). This factor seems closely akin to Baumeister's notion of the way crystallization of discontent takes place. Forcing a person to attend to unnoticed and/or avoided experiences may lead to connections avoided or for other reasons not previously made. This in turn can lead to crystallization and then to change. Similarly, quantum change in Miller and C'deBaca's model is preceded by facing distress.

Mastery

The manner in which exposure leads to change is the province of the next common factor, mastery. Exposure would not be beneficial if it did not result in reduced anxiety and/or new connections. When it does have these consequences, the patient experiences a sense of mastery. Together, exposure and mastery may constitute the corrective emotional experience (Alexander, 1963) discussed earlier. This experience is critical to therapeutic success. It may lock the crystallization of previously disconnected episodes, described by Baumeister, into place. The moment when mastery is felt, and the patient's experiences all click into a meaningful whole, may come to have great significance for him or her. This may explain the affective charge of the focal incident, touched on by Baumeister. It may also account for the relief and release of energy, described by Miller and C'deBaca at the moment when quantum change begins.

Therapy differs from the phenomena described by Baumeister and by Miller and C'deBaca in that the therapist does not wait for some naturally occurring focal incident or quantum trigger. He or she purposefully sets the stage for them. Different therapeutic modalities provide mastery experiences in different ways. These range from the "working through" of psychoanalysis (Rado, 1925) to the "mastery and pleasure technique" of Beck et al. (1979).

Attributions

The final common factor concerns the explanation the patient offers for his or her treatment outcome. These attributions powerfully influence the strength and stability of therapeutic success or failure. Bandura (1982, 1986, 1989) has shown that individuals who attribute therapeutic change to their own efforts or increases in their capabilities (he terms this an increase in "self-efficacy") are likely to enjoy long-lasting improvement. Conversely, patients who attribute therapeutic gains to the therapist or his or her techniques (decrease in self-efficacy) are likely to relapse. Other researchers have reported similar results (Schoeneman & Curry, 1990; Sonne & Janoff, 1979).

What Changes in Psychotherapy?

The literature shows that therapy is effective (i.e., people change for the better), and I have offered some suggestions as to how. But is it personality that changes? The evidence is inconclusive. Smith et al. (1980) found that therapy had its strongest effects on depression and single symptoms (e.g., anxiety). Personality variables, as traditionally assessed, showed far weaker effects. Kazdin (1992) has argued that personality variables like neuroticism are not altered by treatment, which instead acts on less far-reaching personality characteristics. Similarly, Luborsky et al. (1985) believed that psychotherapy does not impact on the basic personality structure. Instead, it helps the patient become more flexible in gratifying his or her needs and making use of his or her capabilities. If Kazdin and Luborsky et al. are correct, the locus of action of psychotherapy is on what Costa and McCrae term characteristic adaptations and what McAdams calls Level II. Unfortunately, there are simply not enough data specifically focused on this issue to allow for any definitive resolution.

Something changes in psychotherapy. But what is it? I opened with an abstract discussion of method, devoid of human experience. I come full circle and close with a clinical vignette, devoid of methodological rigor. I had been seeing a patient for several months. She came to me complaining of difficulty in experiencing her emotions (among other things). She later felt that she had improved somewhat. In one of our sessions she reported that several of her co-workers had begun to notice "something different" about her. They asked her if she had lost weight (she had not). They asked her if her hairstyle was different (it was not). They walked away bemused. They did not wonder whether her neuroticism had diminished. They did not inquire as to her Level II or Level III functioning. She clearly had not undergone quantum change. But something had changed. Was it her personality? I don't know.

REFERENCES

Alexander, F. (1963). The dynamics of psychotherapy in the light of learning theory. *American Journal of Psychiatry, 120,* 440–448.

Bandura, A. (1982). Self-efficacy mechanism in human agency. *American Psychologist, 37,* 122–147.

Bandura, A. (1986). *Social foundations of thought and action.* Englewood Cliffs, NJ: Prentice Hall.

Bandura, A. (1989). Human agency in social cognitive theory. *American Psychologist, 44,* 1175–1184.

Beck, A. T. (1976). *Cognitive therapy and the emotional disorders.* Madison, CT: International Universities Press.

Beck, A. T., Rush, A. J., Shaw, B. F., & Emery, G. (1979). *Cognitive therapy of depression.* New York: Guilford Press.

Bergin, A. E., & Garfield, S. L. (Eds.). (in press). *Handbook of psychotherapy and behavior change* (4th ed.). New York: Wiley.

Block, J. (1971). *Lives through time.* Berkeley, CA: Bancroft Books.

Brody, N. (1983). Where are the emperor's clothes? *Behavioral and Brain Sciences, 6,* 303–308.

Brody, N. (1988). *Personality: In search of individuality.* San Diego, CA: Academic Press.

Brody, N. (1990). Behavior therapy versus placebo: Comment on Bowers and Clum's meta-analysis. *Psychological Bulletin, 107,* 106–109.

Brody, N. (1992). *Intelligence* (2nd ed.). San Diego, CA: Academic Press.

DiClemente, C. C. (1993). Changing addictive behaviors: A process perspective. *Current Directions in Psychological Science, 2*(4), 101–106.

Ellis, A. (1962). *Reason and emotion in psychotherapy.* New York: Lyle Stuart.

Emmelkamp, P. M. G. (1986). Behavior therapy with adults. In S. L. Garfield & A. E. Bergin (Eds.), *Handbook of psychotherapy and behavior change* (3rd ed., pp. 385–442). New York: Wiley.

Fenichel, O. (1945). *The psychoanalytic theory of neurosis.* New York: Norton.

Freud, S. (1957). The future prospects of psychoanalytic therapy. In J. Strachey (Ed. and Trans.), *The standard edition of the complete psychological works of Sigmund Freud* (Vol. 11, pp. 139–151). London: Hogarth Press. (Original work published 1910)

Freud, S. (1958). Papers on technique. In J. Strachey (Ed. and Trans.), *The standard edition of the complete psychological works of Sigmund Freud* (Vol. 12, pp. 85–174). London: Hogarth Press. (Original work published 1912)

Freud, S. (1964). An outline of psychoanalysis. In J. Strachey (Ed. and Trans.), *The standard edition of the complete psychological works of Sigmund Freud* (Vol. 23, pp. 141–208). London: Hogarth Press. (Original work published 1937)

Gaston, L. (1990). The concept of the alliance and its role in psychotherapy: Theoretical and empirical considerations. *Psychotherapy, 27,* 143–153.

Gazzaniga, M. S. (1992). *Nature's mind.* New York: Basic Books.

Goldberg, L. R. (1993). The structure of phenotypic personality traits. *American Psychologist, 48,* 26–34.

Heatherton, T. F., & Nichols, P. A. (1992). *Micronarrative accounts of successful and unsuccessful life change experiences.* Manuscript submitted for publication.

Helson, R., Mitchell, V., & Moane, G. (1984). Personality and patterns of adherence and non-adherence to the social clock. *Journal of Personality and Social Psychology, 46,* 1079–1096.

Helson, R., & Picano, J. (1990). Is the traditional role bad for women? *Journal of Personality and Social Psychology, 59,* 311–320.

James, W. (1902). *The varieties of religious experience.* Cambridge, MA: Harvard University Press.

John, O. P. (1990). The "big five" factors taxonomy: Dimensions of personality in the natural language and in questionnaires. In L. A. Pervin (Ed.), *Handbook of personality: Theory and research* (pp. 66–100). New York: Guilford Press.

Kazdin, A. (1992, August). *Does psychotherapy change personality?* Paper presented at the 100th Annual Convention of the American Psychological Association, Washington, DC.

Kelly, G. A. (1955). *A theory of personality.* New York: Norton.

Lambert, M. J., Shapiro, D. A., & Bergin, A. E. (1986). Evaluation of therapeutic outcomes. In S. L. Garfield & A. E. Bergin (Eds.), *Handbook of psychotherapy and behavior change* (3rd ed., pp. 157–212). New York: Wiley.

Loder, J. E. (1981). *The transforming moment: Understanding convictional experiences.* New York: Harper & Row.

Lorenz, K. Z. (1935). Der kumpan in der umwelt des vogels. *Journal fur Ornithologie, 83*(2), 137–215, 289–413.

Luborsky, L., Crits-Cristoph, P., & Mellon, J. (1986). Advent of objective measures of the transference concept. *Journal of Consulting and Clinical Psychology, 54,* 39–47.

Luborsky, L., Mellon, J., Ravensway, P., Childress, A. R., Cohen, K. D., Hole, A., Ming, S., Crits-Cristoph, P., Levine, F. J., & Alexander, K. (1985). A verification of Freud's grandest clinical hypothesis: The transference. *Clinical Psychology Review, 5,* 231–246.

Luborsky, L., Singer, B., & Luborsky, L. (1975). Comparative studies of psychotherapies: Is it true that "Everyone had won and all must have prizes?" *Archives of General Psychiatry, 32,* 995–1008.

McCrae, R. R., & Costa, P. T., Jr. (1990). Personality in adulthood. New York: Guilford Press.

Murray, H. A. (1967). The case of Murr. In E. G. Boring & G. Lindzey (Eds.), A history of psychology in autobiography (Vol. V, pp. 285–300). New York: Appleton-Century-Crofts.

Pervin, L. A. (1993). Personality: Theory and research (6th ed.). New York: Wiley.

Prioleau, L., Murduck, M., & Brody, N. (1983). An analysis of psychotherapy versus placebo studies. Behavioral and Brain Sciences, 6, 275–285.

Rado, S. (1925). The economic principle in psychoanalytic technique. International Journal of Psychoanalysis, 6, 35–44.

Robinson, F. G. (1992). Love's story told: A life of Henry A. Murray. Cambridge, MA: Harvard University Press.

Schoeneman, T. J., & Curry, S. (1990). Attributions for successful and unsuccessful health behavior change. Basic and Applied Social Psychology, 11, 421–431.

Smith, M. L., Glass, G. V., & Miller, F. I. (1980). The benefits of psychotherapy. Baltimore, MD: Johns Hopkins University Press.

Sonne, J. L., & Janoff, D. S. (1979). The effect of treatment attributions on the maintenance of weight reduction: A replication and extension. Cognitive Therapy and Research, 3, 389–397.

Stewart, A. J., & Vandewater, E. A. (1993). Career and family clocks in a transitional cohort: The Radcliffe class of 1964. In K. Hulbert & D. Schuster (Eds.), Women's lives through time: Educated American women of the twentieth century (pp. 235–258). San Francisco: Jossey-Bass.

Stiles, W. B., Shapiro, D. A., & Elliot, R. (1986). Are all psychotherapies equivalent? American Psychologist, 41, 165–180.

Strupp, H. A., & Binder, J. L. (1984). Psychotherapy in a new key: A guide to time-limited dynamic psychotherapy. New York: Basic Books.

Weinberger, J. (1990, April). The REMA common factor model of psychotherapy. Paper presented at the meeting of the Society for the Exploration of Psychotherapy Integration, Philadelphia, PA.

Weinberger, J. (1992). The REMA (relationship, exposure, mastery, attribution) common factor model of psychotherapy. Unpublished manuscript, Adelphi University, Derner Institute, Garden City, New York.

Weinberger, J. (1993). Common factors in psychotherapy. In J. Gold & G. Stricker (Eds.), Handbook of psychotherapy integration (pp. 43–56). New York: Plenum Press.

X, M., & Haley, A. (1964). The autobiography of Malcolm X. New York: Grove Press.

AUTHOR INDEX

Smith, M. L., 74, 344, 345, 347
Snidman, N., 322, 323
Söbrom, D., 152, 153, 163
Sonne, J. L., 10, 13, 347
Sotsky, S. M., 74
Spearman, C., 61
Spender, S., 288
Spielberger, C. D., 113, 125, 128
Spilka, B., 257
Spiro, A., 75
Spranger, E., 205
Stambul, H., 176
Stankov, L., 71
Steinberg, L., 54
Steinglass, P., 184, 185
Sternio, J. F., 160
Steubing, K. K., 193
Stewart, A. J., 206, 207, 208, 209, 215,
    216, 230, 232, 233, 235, 242, 337
Stewart, H. B., 140
Stigler, I. C., 154
Stiles, W. B., 345
Stillwell, A., 10, 11
Strauss, M. E., 33
Strelau, J., 321
Strenger, V. E., 176
Strupp, H. H., 114
Stuebing, K. K., 8
Suci, G. J., 258, 264
Sugihara, G., 141
Sutker, P. B., 176, 181
Swan, G. E., 189
Swann, W. B., 204, 325, 327
Sweeney, P. D., 286
Symons, D., 44, 49

Takens, F., 140
Tan, S. Y., 5
Tannenbaum, P. H., 258, 264
Tanner, J. M., 155
Tarter, R. E., 176, 185
Tatsuoka, M. M., 28
Taylor, C., 271
Taylor, E. B., 111
Taylor, P. A., 47
Taylor, S. E., 284
Teasdale, T. W., 73
Tedeschi, J. T., 283
Tellegen, A., 63, 210, 259, 260, 301
Thom, R., 276
Thompson, J. M. T., 140
Thompson, N. M., 8, 193

Thorndike, R. L., 158
Thorne, A., 205, 303, 305
Thornton, C. C., 189
Tomkiewicz, S., 321
Tomkins, S. S., 306
Tomlinson-Keasey, C., 218
Tonigan, J. S., 258, 273
Tooby, J., 41, 42, 43, 47, 48
Tooke, W., 44
Tubman, J. G., 110, 181, 186
Tucker, L. R., 159
Tupes, E. C., 302
Turkheimer, E., 73, 321

U. S. Department of Health and Human
    Services, 176, 177, 184, 185

Vaillant, G. E., 3, 7, 9, 26, 176, 185, 189,
    205, 213, 228, 229, 305
van Loon, R. J. P., 306
Vandewater, E. A., 215, 216, 337
Vaughan, D., 11, 289, 292
Velasquez, M. M., 193
Velicer, W. F., 11, 184
Vernon, P. E., 205
Veroff, J., 230, 231, 233, 234, 237, 239
Vicary, J. R., 181
von Eye, A., 181

Wachs, T. D., 318
Wachtel, P., 327
Walder, L. O., 67
Warren, H. C., 22
Warren, S., 325
Waterman, A. S., 210, 305
Watkins, J. T., 74
Watson, J. B., 326
Watzlawick, P., 274
Weakland, J. H., 274
Weber, A. L., 11, 281
Weghorst, S. J., 49
Weil, A., 277
Weinberger, J., 233, 234, 235, 299, 345
Weiner, B., 10, 13
Weinstock, C. S., 206
Weisberg, H. I., 154, 160
Werner, H., 206
Werts, C. E., 163
Wessler, K., 26
West, B. H., 130, 317, 318, 322
Westen, D., 44
Whitbourne, S. K., 205, 206, 210, 305

White, G. L., 49
White, R. W., 206, 207, 228, 229, 231, 242
Widiger, T. A., 94
Wilerman, L., 62
Wilkie, F., 154
Willerman, L., 66, 68
Willett, J. B., 153, 154, 155, 157, 158, 160, 165
Williams, H. L., 187
Williams, R. H., 157, 159
Willis, S. L., 72
Wills, T. A., 184
Wilson, G. T., 189
Wilson, M., 49, 53
Wilson, R. S., 62, 66
Wilson, T. D., 11
Wink, P., 210, 213, 229, 243
Winter, D. G., 230
Wittgenstein, L., 94
Wolin, S. J., 184
Wood, V., 210

Woodcock, A., 276
Wotman, S. R., 10
Wright, S. A., 289, 303
Wylie, C. R., 130, 140

Xagoraris, A., 317

Zedeck, S., 151
Zeiss, A. M., 75
Zeldin, S., 63
Zeldow, P. B., 231
Zimmerman, D. W., 157, 159
Zimowski, M., 154
Zinberg, N. E., 185
Zirkel, S., 100, 304
Zonderman, A. B., 26
Zucker, R. A., 25, 185, 186
Zuckerman, M., 128, 321
Zung, W. K., 233, 237, 243
Zuschlag, M. K., 305
Zweben, A., 184
Zyzanski, S. J., 5

SUBJECT INDEX

Behavioral psychology, 27
Big Five trait model. *See* Five-factor model
Biological factors, in change in adulthood, 210–211
Birth-order, 46

Chance, 102–103
Chaos theory, 9, 140
Character, 22
Characteristic adaptations
    basic tendencies vs., 337–338
    definition, 23
    in psychology theories, 27
    source of, 23–24
    stability in adulthood, 35–36
Cognitive–experiential self-theory, 206
Cognitive processes. *See also* Intelligence
    after crystallization of discontent, 291–294
    changes in adult thought content, 230
    in commitment-maintaining process, 283–286
    crystallization of discontent in, 286–288
    in evolutionary psychology, 43
    in organicism world hypothesis, 98
    as quantum change catalysts, 272–276
    recognition of similarities, 92–93
    root metaphor theory, 88–89
    selective attention, 285–286
Comorbidity, 76–77
Conscientiousness, 29
    in mate-retention strategies, 45–46
Constancy
    as psychology subject, 121–122
    research designs for studying, 123–129
    role of research on, 143–144
    social value of, 122
    in variability, 127–128
Contextualism
    in developmental theory, 108–112
    in four-world hypothesis, 103–106
    in units of personological analysis, 304
Coping style, 26, 113
Cross-sectional studies, 29–30
Crystallization of discontent. *See* Discontent, crystallization of

Defense systems, in metatheoretical model, 24

Depression
    genetic predisposition for, 76–77
    therapeutic outcomes study, 74–75
Descriptions of change
    in quantum change, 266–271
    self-reported, 10–14
Developmental contextualism, 107–112
Diagnosis, philosophical formism in, 94
Discontent, crystallization of
    in change process, 286–288, 294–295, 340–341
    evidence of, 288–290
    focal incident in, 290–291, 295
    identity change through, 282–283
    life-course after, 291–294
    meaning of, 281
Dynamic processes
    continuous vs. discrete, 154–155, 327–328
    in metatheoretical model, 23–25
Dynamical systems theory, 140–141

Evolutionary psychology
    adaptive problem-solving in, 43–44
    model for assessing personality change, 41–42
Expectancies, of addicts, 184
Extraversion, 29, 64, 75

Families
    change in addicts and, 184–185
Five-factor model of traits
    in adaptive problem-solving, 48
    change over life span, 68–70
    development of, 28–29, 94–95
    heritability, 64
    NEO Personality Inventory studies, 29–34
    as one level of personality analysis, 302–303
Focal events, 12–13, 290–291, 295

Gender differences
    in change in adulthood, 213–215, 229–230, 231
    in evolutionary psychology, 44
    in jealousy, 49–50
    in thought-content in adulthood, 239, 242
Genetic factors
    in change in adulthood, 210–211
    in dispositional traits, 301

heritability of intelligence, 61–63, 321

heritability of personality, 64–65

in individual adaptive problems, 47

in intelligence change over life span, 66–67

in latent traits, 60

in psychological comorbidity, 76–77

species-typical mechanisms and, 47

in stability of intelligence, 320

in trait change over life span, 68–70

Growth curve analysis

process, 155–156

role of, 155, 157, 169–170

simulated data for analytic comparison, 160–168

stability in, 156–157

of stability in longitudinal data, 164–168

statistical estimation in, 160

use of difference scores in, 157–158

vs. autoregressive models, 168–169

Guilford–Zimmerman Temperament Survey, 31, 33

Habit, 22

Idealizations, 232–233, 239, 242–243

Individual differences

in adaptive problem-solving, 45–48

in addiction, 186, 190

in change, assessment of, 157–160

in evolutionary psychological model, 42–44, 339

measurement of, vs. intraindividual variability, 127–128

in organicism, 100

in personality change, 208–210, 231

in stability, exposure to adaptive problems in, 53–54

stability studies, 31–33

Induced change, 59–60, 70–73

Intelligence

adoption studies of change in, 72–73

attempts to change, 70–73

evidence of change over life span, 65–67

genetic factors in change, 66–67

heritability of, 61–63, 321

latent trait of, 61

levels of analysis in measuring, 60, 61–63

phenotype–genotype congruence, 63

stability of, 320–321

vs. traits, as evidencing change, 59–60

Interpersonal relationships. See also Married couples

crystallization of discontent in, 286–288

as developmental factor, 208

as factor in change in addiction, 184–185

maintaining commitments in, 283–286

in model of intentional change, 183

personality change and, 4–5

in theories of adult development, 228–229

IQ scores, 60

adoption/twin studies, 62–63

environment as factor in, 321

interventions to change, 70–71

Learned behaviors, 27

Life span analysis, 15

biography as personality, 25–26

change in intelligence, 65–67, 72–73

genetic factors in trait change in, 68–70

heritability of intelligence, 61–63

heritability of traits, 63–65

hierarchies of stability in, 205–206

measuring change in, bias in, 203–204

neuroticism assessment, 75–77

personality trait continuity in, 67–68

Longitudinal studies, 29, 30–31, 334–335

of adaptive problems in married couples, 50–53

advantages of growth curve analysis in, 168–169

AT&T, 211–213

of change in adulthood, 211–217

evidence of quantum change in, 342–344

growth curve analysis of stability in, 164–168

in life span heritability of intelligence, 61–62

limitations of, 142

Mills College, 213–215

Longitudinal studies (*continued*)
    need for, 7, 218, 244
    personality research designs, 123–124
    predictors of addictive behavior, 181
    Radcliffe, 215–217
    of relative stability, 151–152
    role of, 334
    traditional analyses of stability in, 161–164, 167–168

Married couples
    adaptive mate-retention strategies, 45, 46–48
    adaptive problem-solving in, 42
    adaptive problems in, 50–53
    commitment-maintaining process, 284–285
    jealousy as factor in mate retention, 48–50
    perception of discontent by, 289–290
Measurement, 6–7, 121–123. *See also* Growth curve analysis; Longitudinal studies; Research designs
    of absolute stability, 150–151
    bias in techniques of, 7–8, 317–318
    of change as continuous, vs. discrete, process, 154–155, 169, 327–328
    equal lag intervals in, 139–140
    in five-factor model, 28–29
    frequency of, 334–335
    instrument selection, 126–127
    of intelligence, 60, 61–63
    intercorrelation of motives, 237–239
    intraindividual variability, 127–128
    of latent traits, 60, 63–64
    limitations, 142, 319
    for longitudinal analysis, 334
    multivariate methods, 124–125, 126–127, 335
    of personal dispositions, levels of analysis for, 60
    of phenotypes, 60, 63–64
    of quantum change, 257–259
    random lag intervals in, 138–139
    rank-order vs. mean level change, 203
    rate of change in, 153–155
    of relative stability, 151
    test–retest correlations, 32–33, 125, 151–152
    in Thematic Apperception Test, 227–228

therapeutic outcome, 74–76
of thought-content in adulthood, 232, 234–236
of traits, bias toward stability in, 301–302
use of difference scores in correlation research, 157–160
Mechanism
    in evolutionary psychology, 42–44
    in four-world hypothesis, 101–103
Memory, 7
Micronarrative interview, 10–14
Minnesota Multiphasic Personality Inventory, 34
Models of personality, 340. *See also* Five-factor model of traits
    in addiction research, need for, 193
    addictive behavior in process perspective, 177–179
    autoregressive analysis, 168
    basic tendencies vs. characteristic adaptations, 337–338
    bias against change in, 202–204
    biases in metatheoretical conceptions, 106
    Big Five as one level in, 302–303
    change as continuous, vs. discrete, process, 154–155
    contextualism in conceptions of, 103–106, 304
    dynamical systems theory in, 140–141
    in evolutionary psychology, 41–42, 53–55, 339–340
    formism in, 94–96
    growth curve analysis for, 155–157
    hierarchies of stability in, 205–206
    levels in, 181–183, 299–300
    life narrative in, 300, 306–310
    mechanism in, in four-world hypothesis, 101–103
    metatheoretical, 22–25, 86–88
    models of change in physical sciences and, 15
    nonlinear, 9, 335
    organicism world hypothesis in, 96–101
    personal concerns as element of, 303–306
    quantum change in, 276–277
    relevance of world hypotheses to, 91–92

in systems theory, 112–115
three-level model, 300–303, 309–310, 338–339
volitional change in, 10
Motivation. *See also* Attributions for change
  in acting on crystallization of discontent, 290–291
  in adulthood, 230–231, 242
  for change, 12–13
  instability as, 242
  interrelations of motives, 237–239
  intimacy, in adulthood, 241
  in Thematic Apperception Test, 234
Multivariate research methods, 124–125, 126–127, 335
Murray, H. A., 25

Narcissistic personality, 210
Negative change, 9
NEO Personality Inventory, 29–34
Neuroticism, 29, 64
  as comorbid condition, 76–77
  life span continuity, 75–77
  in therapeutic goals, 74
  in twin studies of change, 68–79

Openness, 29, 35
Organicism, 96–101
  in theory of development, 108–110

Paradigms, role of, 92
Pepper, Stephen C., 88–92, 115–116
Personality. *See also* Traits
  addiction and, 176, 178
  as biography, 25–26
  classification systems for theories of, 87–88
  in contextualism world hypothesis, 105–106
  in creating adaptive problems, 48, 51–52
  defining, 5–6, 22–25, 86–87, 217–218, 316
  defining change in, 8–9
  evidence of change in, 324
  heritability of, 64–65
  mechanistic view, 101–103
  metatheoretical, 22–25, 86–88
  normative state, 324–325

in organicism world hypothesis, 98–100
phenotype–genotype congruence, 63–65
research designs for, 123–129
in solving adaptive problems, 48, 52–53
as system, 112–115
Personality development
  in adulthood, research in, 149–150
  age 21 to 30, 33–34
  bias against change in theories of, 202–204
  change as continuous, vs. discrete, process in, 154–155, 169, 327–328
  conceptions of stability in, 122–123
  contextualism in theoretical synthesis of, 107–112
  dynamic processes in, 26
  of highly creative individuals, 204
  James on, 21
  longitudinal studies, 30–31, 123–124
  in metatheoretical model, 23–24
  modeled as growth curve, 155–157
  narrative construction in, 307
  normative adult change, 228–231
  personal concerns in, 305
  personality change and, 100
  research designs for assessing, 143–144
  self-concept in, 26–27
  social factors in, 207–208
  theoretical eclecticism in, 108
Phase space embedding, 141
Physical sciences
  conceptions of chance in, 102–103, 103
  psychological sciences and, 86
Political conversions, 285, 289, 291, 292
Processes of personality change
  addiction, 177–179, 186–190
Psychopathology
  comorbidities in, 76–77
  cultural determinants in, 112
  developmental etiology, 100
  incongruities in self-concept as, 27
  in organicism four-world hypothesis, 100
  personal invariance as, 114–115
  therapeutic outcome studies, 74–76

ABOUT THE EDITORS

Todd F. Heatherton received a PhD from the University of Toronto for his research on the effects of emotional distress on eating behavior. In 1990, following postdoctoral work in social and personality psychology at Case Western Reserve University, he joined the Department of Psychology at Harvard University. His primary research interests lie in examining the development, prediction, measurement, and behavioral consequences of chronic dieting (restrained eating). Current research interests also include understanding fluctuations in self-esteem, self-regulatory capacities, and narrative accounts of life change attempts. He is on the editorial board of *Psychology of Addictive Behaviors* and the *Journal of Research in Personality*.

Joel L. Weinberger is a practicing clinical psychologist and assistant professor at the Derner Institute of Advanced Psychological Studies at Adelphi University. He received a PhD in clinical psychology at the Graduate Faculty of the New School for Social Research and conducted postdoctoral work in human motivation at Harvard University. His areas of specialization include human motivation, unconscious processes, longitudinal personality research, and psychoanalytic and integrative psychotherapy. He has been published in all of these areas and is currently writing a book on unconscious processes.